U STATES 1898-1928

Progressivism and a Society in Transition

THE UNITED STATES 1898-1928

Progressivism and a Society in Transition

J. Leonard Bates

University of Illinois
at Urbana-Champaign

McGraw-Hill Book Company

New York   St. Louis   San Francisco   Auckland   Düsseldorf
Johannesburg   Kuala Lumpur   London   Mexico
Montreal   New Delhi   Panama   Paris   São Paulo
Singapore   Sydney   Tokyo   Toronto

To Dan
and Alan

THE
UNITED STATES
1898–1928
Progressivism and a
Society in Transition

1 2 3 4 5 6 7 8 9 0 D O D O 7 9 8 7 6 5

This book was set in Times Roman by Black Dot, Inc. The editors
were Robert P. Rainier and Joseph F. Murphy; the designer was
Joseph Gillians; the production supervisor was Dennis J. Conroy.
R. R. Donnelley & Sons Company was printer and binder.

Library of Congress Cataloging in Publication Data

Bates, James Leonard.
    The United States, 1898–1928

    ([The Modern America series])
    Bibliography: p.
    Includes index.
    1. United States—History—1865–1921. 2. United
States—History—1919–1933. 3. Progressivism (United
States politics) I. Title. II. Series.
E756.B37   973.91   75-17794
ISBN 0-07-004050-8

CONTENTS

PREFACE

Though intended primarily for college students in advanced courses dealing with twentieth-century United States history, this book should be of use to anyone who has an interest in the period under consideration—which was clearly one of the most fateful in the history of the United States and the world. Problems then were not so different from those today. Leaders in public life were trying to make their governments function efficiently and to rise to the challenges of a new age. The country was changing swiftly and inexorably. Science and technology made possible the automobile, the tractor, the radio, the motion picture, and all the other things that overwhelmed the village and the horse and buggy. Immigration, long a powerful force, was now bringing to America millions of Catholics and Jews from Southern and Eastern Europe who often looked "different." At the same time, black people of the South began to head northward, responding to the apparent need for factory workers. Divisions in society were wider than today, and discrimination was often flagrant. Meanwhile, the United States became inextricably involved in world affairs, first through the Spanish-American War and newly won islands in the Caribbean Sea and distant waters of the Pacific Ocean. Then came intervention in the Great War of 1914–1918. Nothing was quite the same after that holocaust, which killed many millions, disrupted empires, brought the Communists into power in Russia, and helped to prepare the way for a series of social disasters.

There is drama in the life of a people; this book has tried to capture some of it. I have organized the chapters essentially as essays with a major theme indicated by the subtitle, "Progressivism and a Society in Transition." It seems to me that the urge to progress was a powerful one throughout this period and that Americans generally were optimistic concerning the future. Obviously the various groups entertained different conceptions of progress, but virtually everyone wanted freedom and opportunity in the evolving society; and they expected the role of government to be a larger and more positive one than it had been in the past. If they could get control of that government, they would try to harness it to the purposes they favored.

My emphasis has been derived partly from the courses I teach, including research seminars that have focused on the progressive era, World War I, and the 1920s. We learned from each other in these classes, and the students probably taught me more than they could ever realize. In a different category as teacher is Dewey W. Grantham, professor of history at Vanderbilt University, who really made this book possible and helped to determine my approach. It was he who proposed a series of three volumes on the twentieth century with each volume giving an emphasis to politics and to what is sometimes called the "social analysis of politics." Each of the three authors readily agreed to pursue his interest in social groups and to do so, insofar as possible, in a systematic way, relating to the formation of public policy.

It is a pleasure to express my thanks to everyone who made a contribution to this enterprise. With grants from the Graduate College of the University of Illinois, I was able to have research assistants for a number of years; and each of the four, Gerald S. Grinde, John P. Kyriazis, Louis Christian Smith, and John P. Wolgamot, served well indeed, sometimes going beyond the call of duty. Former students, as indicated above, have added immeasurably with their papers, articles, books, and ideas. I think especially of Daniel W. Barthell, Margery H. Bennett, James A. Brooks, Dominic L. Candeloro, George Cullom Davis, Charles L. De Benedetti, William B. Glidden, John E. Hodge, William P. Koscher, Larry H. Powell, Stephen C. Shafer, Ralph A. Stone, Arvarh E. Strickland, Richard A. Swanson, and Robert A. Waller. Richard Swanson also helped with a critical reading of some early chapters, and Ralph Stone did the same, to my great benefit, by reading the chapters on foreign policy.

A number of others have read at least portions of the manuscript, taking time from busy schedules. They have saved me from errors and contributed greatly both to style and content. James J. Farrell, William R. Keagle, Roy C. Turnbaugh, Jr., and Philip R. Vander Meer—all of the University of Illinois—gave sound advice on points of importance. My colleagues in the history department, Robert L. Harris, Jr., Frederic C. Jaher, Thomas A. Krueger, and Winton U. Solberg, came to my rescue at one time or another; and Professor Solberg was almost "on call" since his study in the library happens to be close to mine. J. Harvey Young of Emory University kindly read the first chapter for me. Richard S. Kirkendall of Indiana University and Richard Lowitt of the University of Kentucky each went through the first seven chapters, and I am grateful for their lengthy and perceptive comments. My wife, Dorothy Pettit Bates, served as listener-adviser whenever the need arose and also volunteered to help make the index. Now I come back again to Dewey W. Grantham, who read the entire manuscript, some of it twice, and who contributed advice that was indispensable together with warm encouragement when necessary.

I have tried to acknowledge in the bibliographical statements following each chapter how heavily I am indebted to other writers on this period. Frequently in the text, too, allusions will be found to this rich and often controversial literature. Of course, the books had to be accessible in order for me to use them, and I have been fortunate indeed to do most of my writing and final checking in the University of Illinois Library with its splendid resources and able librarians. On countless occasions, they have helped to provide me with the books or the advice I needed.

Finally the time has come to say that I am responsible for errors of detail and interpretation that may be found, since I have enjoyed the last word concerning the manuscript.

J. Leonard Bates

THE UNITED STATES 1898-1928

Progressivism and a Society in Transition

Chapter 1

The Idea of Progress: An American Heritage

In the nineteenth century and for some years after 1900 almost all Americans were believers in "progress," though they differed widely at times as to what the word meant. They believed somehow in the special mission of America and its people. Examples of faith and optimism are easy to find in the statements of editors, ministers, businessmen, political leaders, and others. This idea of progress, which has affected the United States so powerfully in both its thought and its action, seems to have originated long ago in the Reformation of the sixteenth and seventeenth centuries, when Christian men and women by the thousands obtained a new basis for their faith. Evil would be overcome; tyranny and hardship could be battled against successfully with divine help. The Renaissance and later the Enlightenment gave a new emphasis to achievement of a secular and humanistic type.

By the eighteenth century, as colonization proceeded in America and people crossed the ocean in growing numbers, progress seemed to find its greatest opportunity. There was land to be found and a freedom almost unparalleled. There was a lift to man's spirit. The New World was different, and its people would be different. Undoubtedly the years that followed brought some remarkable achievements, adding to the belief in America as a land of promise. The wealth of the country was developed and exploited chiefly by individual effort, notwithstanding the attempts by the British and others to regulate and control the colonial economy. This policy of mercantilism came under attack and was swept away finally in the American Revolution. As the Americans were assailing the economic "tyranny" of George III, so they also attacked his political tyranny and other unnatural restraints placed upon a free people. From Britain itself came supporting arguments. Adam Smith, for example, published his *Wealth of Nations* in 1776. This classic attack on mercantilism argued powerfully that economic progress would come through free competition and the removal of impediments to trade. The economic man, by his endeavors, would benefit also the society at large. Almost miraculously, as the Americans gained their independence and looked across vast territories to the interior, they had the ideas with which to occupy—and conquer—that land.

They had the government as well. In the 1780s and the decades following, American statesmen created a republic, formulated a Western policy for the admission of new states, and managed to survive another war with Britain. The patriotism of Americans soared to new heights. In the Monroe Doctrine, the young government announced itself as the champion of the entire hemisphere and a foe of alien systems threatening the New World.

By a succession of purchases, treaties, wars, and threats of war, the United States rounded out its continental borders from Maine to California, from Biscayne Bay to the Puget Sound. In the process, it routed the red men, the "savages," who stood in the way. These Indians were heathen, in the view of most whites, and they did not work. Wasting their time in hunting and fishing and in tribal ceremonies, they were little better than animals of the forest. The land they occupied belonged, rightfully, to those who could take it and use it, who could make the "desert to bloom," who could build in the wilderness a civilization of Christian people.

With the westward movement, and partly because of it, came a process of democratization, often associated with the name of Andrew Jackson. The states were moving toward universal suffrage (for men who were white) and a variety of reforms, including the right of women to own property in their own name; public education; temperance; prison reform; and the abolition of slavery. Inexorably, it seemed, the opportunity that existed in America was enlarging the rights of individuals and reducing the sway of privilege. Ideas of the "perfectibility of man" were seriously advanced. The spark of divinity in every human breast could lead on to endless achievement and the amelioration of social ills. A spreading romantic movement contributed to this democratic optimism which found spokesmen in Ralph Waldo Emerson, Walt Whitman, and a host of popular writers.

Not everyone was so hopeful. In midcentury came a setback, the crisis of the Union, the struggle between North and South. In the march of America, however, this was but a temporary interruption. The Union prevailed. The slaves were freed. Democracy and opportunity were extended. A greater nation was now free to develop.

White people of the Southern states could not accept so readily this interpretation of a war that devastated their countryside, impoverished their people, and subjected them for some years to military control. But they were the minority. In the North and West, generally, the Civil War was a triumph for democratic government. In countless towns and villages, year after year, on the Fourth of July and other appropriate occasions, the success of America was celebrated. The Grand Army of the Republic and the martyred President, Abraham Lincoln, had saved the Union. Even Ulysses S. Grant, with his reputation as President somewhat blemished, remained a hero. The South, meanwhile, had its own heroes and its "Lost Cause." It remained for generations a backwater of national life, making economic gains but scarred psychologically; and it did not recover its political power. As C. Vann Woodward has eloquently shown, the South thus lay outside the American tradition of success.

In the Civil War, and in other events, God's favor seemed apparent. Americans in the nineteenth century were a religious people, belonging in the main to great churches of an evangelical faith—Baptist, Methodist, Presbyterian. A belief in God and in Jesus Christ as a personal savior affected strongly the lives of millions. This was a passionate faith, and a failure to conform religiously in the church, the grade school, or even in college could lead to reprimands and social pressure. The purpose of an education was to improve the character, perhaps even more than the mind. While progress must occur, it should be chaste and proper. Not only did the faithful accept the necessity of church attendance, prayer, Bible reading, and the surrender to Christ as savior, they believed in divine guidance for themselves and their nation. They believed that the beneficent rule of an Almighty God was clearly demonstrable. The famed historian George Bancroft, sharing this popular confidence, portrayed the history of America as the unfolding of a divine plan, not without pain and suffering but, nevertheless, one blessed from on high.

According to popular mythology, success did not, and should not, come easily. A life of struggle was good for the soul. Even writers with the stature of James Russell Lowell enlarged upon the theme:

What doth the poor man's son inherit?
A patience learned of being poor,
Courage, if sorrow come, to bear it,
A fellow-feeling that is sure
To make the outcast bless his door;
A heritage, it seems to me,
A king might wish to hold in fee.

Hard work made the "soul to shine." The poor, with their strong hands and hardy spirit, could proceed to prove their worth. Pity the rich man's son, wrote Lowell, with soft hands, a taste for "dainty fare," and a "sated heart." He was not really happy, and his character suffered from such a life. The literature of self-improvement, with its sentimentality and stereotypes, was inescapable. It filled page after page in the McGuffey Readers and similar sources of edification. Sometimes this was a rags-to-riches theme, exploited most notably in the Horatio Alger stories. The young hero made his way to fame and fortune, as in the story *Helping Himself,* while he retained his personal integrity; he thwarted villains and managed the rescue of those who deserved it.

Not everyone could succeed. The country also had its misfits and dreamers, the sick and the poor. Americans were not without sympathy for those less fortunate and they did give aid; but they believed, in essence, that such people deserved to be poor. They lacked character, brains, fortitude. They could have done better if they tried. To be a failure in a land of success was a heavy burden, psychologically. Few were so bitter as to become radical; they tended, rather, to blame themselves for their own misfortunes. There was still a chance for success, perhaps, in another shop, on some other farm or a distant frontier. If personal failure had to be admitted, one could still place faith in the future when another generation would have its chance.

In the years after the Civil War came a significant transition. First occurred a fantastic acceleration of economic growth. It was the era of "robber barons," of a friendly federal government with favors to give, of new corporations, railroad building, state making, and the rise of great cities. Floods of immigrants contributed mightily to the work that was done and to the national achievements.

Indispensable to the economic growth of the period was a new age of science in which the leading name was that of an Englishman, Charles Darwin. His *Origin of Species* appeared in 1859, and few writers throughout history have had a greater effect. Darwin was by no means the first to think of evolution, but he brought new evidence to bear and advanced his theory of natural selection. A host of admirers soon were fascinated with the subject and through their own writing and speaking added to the popular knowledge. Notable thinkers such as Herbert Spencer and William Graham Sumner developed their theories of "social Darwinism"; that is, of a struggle for survival in human society similar to that among lower forms of life.

The theory of evolution made people think about old ideas in a new way. Had living things actually evolved, from simple forms to the complex, over millions of years? Had human beings themselves evolved in this way and would they continue to do so and to improve, with the "fittest" surviving and propagating their kind? Darwinism seemed to affect almost every department of knowledge. It was a source of disruption but, also, a new integrating principle. Excitement swept the colleges and universities.

Andrew Carnegie read the works of Darwin and Spencer and stated later in his *Autobiography* that light had come to him "as in a flood"; everything was made clear; he had "found the truth of evolution." He continued: " 'All is well since all grows better' became my motto, my true source of comfort. Man was not created with an instinct for his own degradation, but from the lower he had risen to the higher forms. Nor is there any conceivable end to his march to perfection. His face is turned to the light; he stands in the sun and looks upward."

To Carnegie, then, evolution meant progress. Already he had believed in the greatness of America and the vast gains that were possible through the leadership and enterprise of men and women like himself. In his "Wealth," an article published in the *North American Review,* and in *Triumphant Democracy* (1886) he established himself as a spokesman for the business point of view, with ideas based considerably on Spencerian theory. Not everything was sweetness and light; the nation had problems in its industrial order and in features of human behavior. Carnegie was optimistic, nevertheless, that the fit would lead the unfit and that through long periods of time America would steadily improve—not only in its wealth and production—but in the education and character of its people.

There was an endless variety of reform thought. Socialists and anarchists, for example, obviously did not agree with Andrew Carnegie. Yet the Marxian socialists did accept a "linear" theory of progress, leading inevitably in their dialectic to the final socialist state. Carnegie, in his own way, also relied upon natural laws and "determinism" in the evolutionary order to assure a capitalist state. Some thinkers, heavily influenced by religion in many instances, were adherents to "conservative natural law." They saw a divine plan in the American Constitution, in the balanced system of government, and in the law as it had evolved. Essentially they were believers in a laissez faire society, with its liberties and opportunities; but to assure further progress, the protection of property seemed imperative.

In these same years also appeared the "reform Darwinists," as they later came to be named. Essentially these thinkers by the 1880s were sensitive to the problems in American society, and they rejected both on moral and intellectual grounds a complacent view of the past, or of "natural law." They turned social Darwinism around, in effect. They, too, accepted evolution but proceeded to show that it meant an open universe, not a closed one; that ideas and institutions were in a state of flux; that capitalism, for example, or Christianity, might not be able to last in its existing form. Whatever the past history of evolution, they avowed, man could now use his intelligence to improve society. It was ridiculous not to do so. Henry George, Lester Frank Ward, Charles Peirce, William James, John Dewey, Oliver Wendell Holmes, Jr., and many others contributed to this new way of thought.

Henry George was a transitional figure whose ideas powerfully affected a generation of public men and women. In 1879 he published *Progress and Poverty,* a classic volume which sold almost 2 million copies in the next twenty years. What George contributed, above all, was a critical analysis of the American economy. He could not accept a system which produced so much poverty along with its cities, factories, and usual forms of "improvement." Theoretically, competition in economic pursuits was fine; but each man should have his own land and the right to liberty and opportunity. In fact, George believed, opportunity was declining. During a visit to New York he was impressed with the contrast between "monstrous wealth and debasing want." In the Western states and territories he studied the evils of land monopoly. George called for a government program of action that would tax the "unearned increments," or speculative profits on land. Wealth, he argued, was *socially* produced by the labor of all and government had a responsibility to act concerning the problems that existed.

Lester Ward, a pioneering sociologist, struck mighty blows against a "natural law" that had produced so many millionaires and such appalling inequities in the distribution of wealth. This had happened not because some were "fitter" than others but because of accidents in birth, business chicanery, and low strokes of cunning. In modern times, at least, natural law was not working and was indeed a cloak for the perpetuation of injustices. Government action was therefore required. No longer should government be feared and deplored, as it had been in the days of kings and despots. Now the people could vote and hold office, they could make the changes they wanted, and good leadership was possible.

Charles Peirce and William James provided a philosophy for the new age. Rejecting absolutes, they based their thought on change, and its inevitability. Philosophy must evolve, must be relative to time and social needs. It was a method of study and experimentation rather than a static

PROGRESS AND POVERTY

AN INQUIRY INTO THE CAUSE OF INDUSTRIAL DE-
PRESSIONS AND OF INCREASE OF WANT
WITH INCREASE OF WEALTH

THE REMEDY

BY

HENRY GEORGE

TO THOSE WHO,

SEEING THE VICE AND MISERY THAT SPRING FROM

THE UNEQUAL DISTRIBUTION

OF WEALTH AND PRIVILEGE,

FEEL THE POSSIBILITY OF A HIGHER SOCIAL STATE

AND WOULD STRIVE FOR ITS ATTAINMENT.

SAN FRANCISCO, *March*, 1879.

Figure 1 From the Title Page and Dedication of an American Classic. Rejected at first by publishers, the book had to be printed privately.

system. The validity of a philosophy depended ultimately on whether or not it worked. John Dewey, having similar ideas, plunged into the task of reforming education and society. His method, in essence, was a scientific one, based also upon a faith in the human potential. These men did not discard what they considered the ethical values of society.

Extremely important, also, were the "new economists" of the 1880s and 1890s. They were located mostly in the universities, and many had formerly studied in Germany. In 1885 a small number inaugurated the American Economic Association. These economists, including Richard Ely, Simon Patten, E. R. A. Seligman, and Edmund J. James, were reacting against the weakness and inefficiency of the federal government and generally against the doctrine of laissez faire. They believed that the concepts of limited government might have been all right for the past times of Thomas Jefferson and Andrew Jackson but were entirely inadequate for a nation of some 70 million, with growing numbers concentrated in the cities, with a great labor force, and with many problems crying out for solution. These writers clearly anticipated, on important points, the thinking of intellectuals like Herbert Croly of the progressive era and Rexford Guy Tugwell of the New Deal. Direct connections can often be traced, as between Simon Patten, a professor at the University of Pennsylvania, and young Tugwell, his student and protégé who went on eventually to be an adviser to Franklin D. Roosevelt in the campaign of 1932 and after.

The extent to which these scholars talked in a twentieth-century idiom is rather amazing. Thus Edmund James (later president of the University of Illinois) called for a recognition of the interests of the consumer, which had been too long ignored. The increased productivity of America, resulting from mechanization, should lead to a new theory of economics to replace what was merely a "system of production" often identified with Adam Smith. Americans should have the benefit of a wide distribution of goods, of protection from carelessly produced and danger-ous products, and they should have a friendly government that would intervene in their behalf. James believed in pure food and drug laws, in the preservation of forest lands and other action to protect the natural resources, including a great campaign of nationwide publicity better to inform the people of their God-given heritage. Education was so impor-tant that the national government must give aid on a large and continuing scale. Labor unions were indispensable to a modern economy. Workers, in his view, would not abuse the powers gained through organization; but, in any case, they simply could not negotiate in the old way, that is, individually with their employers. Freedom of contract, under modern circumstances, was a myth.

Richard Ely, Patten, and the others of this group rejected emphatically the doctrines of a negative state. As Ely expressed the idea, "Christian morality is the only basis for a state professedly Christian." Extreme individualism to him was "social anarchy." Government was a tool, and an extremely valuable one, in the attempt to create a better social order. Edmund James, agreeing, once referred to the institution of government as a precious thing, among the "divinest gifts of God to men."

Many economists, along with others, tested out their ideas in the city, in the movement for municipal reform, which gained prominence by the 1890s. Edward W. Bemis, Edmund James, Ely, and others believed in "gas and water socialism," as it was often called, or the assumption of municipal control over essential public services and natural resources. A monopoly was not necessarily bad, but it should, in the interest of the consumers, be under public control. Actual ownership of the prime necessities of life, like water, gas, and electricity, seemed crucial to some of these leaders. They hoped, too, that people of the cities would become deeply involved in civic affairs, that the level of citizenship would be greatly enhanced. Clearly, the efforts of this sort had a mixed success, at best. Yet ideas from the municipal scene went on to have much broader scope in decades to come, as for example in the control of resources on a nationwide basis and in national reform movements generally.

Some of these economists were lay leaders in the "Social Gospel" movement, although it was led predominantly by Christian ministers, deeply concerned men aiming to mitigate the ills of a capitalist society. A few were socialists who regarded a planned and cooperative society as far more in keeping with Christian precepts than the junglelike struggle for survival so common in the nineteenth century. The socialist novel *Looking Backward,* by Edward Bellamy, can suggest the views of this group. For the most part, however, Social Gospel leaders were moderate men and good Christians, seeking in a fair-minded way to improve life on earth for greater numbers of people. The "brotherhood of man and the Fatherhood of God" was a noble cause indeed and it did not seem an impossible one.

American literature in the late nineteenth century faithfully reflected the optimism and moralism of Americans, although an underlying concern with serious problems was often to be found. A few "realistic" writers, led by William Dean Howells, dared to explore questions of life and morality in a business civilization. A growing interest in psychology was best exemplified in the novels of Henry James, whose brother was the philosopher and psychologist William James. Emerging in the 1890s were the "naturalists," most notably Frank Norris, Theodore Dreiser, and Jack London, who sometimes went beyond realism, portraying their subjects as victims of the environment and of their own heredity. Whatever their motives or social philosophy, the naturalists contributed to a growing literature of revelation and criticism. So, too, at times did Mark Twain, Ellen Glasgow, Hamlin Garland, and others. In the main, however, American fiction continued to be a polite and genteel literature that the public seemed to expect.

In his book *The American Mind*, Henry Steele Commager has described the 1890s as "the watershed of American history." Though the topography is somewhat blurred, he says, the "grand outlines" can be seen:

> On the one side lies an America predominantly agricultural; . . . conscious of its unique character and of a unique destiny. On the other side lies the modern America, predominantly urban and industrial; inextricably involved in world economy and politics; . . . experiencing profound changes in population, social institutions, economy, and technology; and trying to accommodate its traditional institutions and habits of thought to conditions new and in part alien.

This final decade of the nineteenth century was indeed a significant one, a turning point, a time of culmination for many problems that had been visible since the Civil War. Ideas of progress were now severely tested. The depression of the 1870s had made apparent the possibility of class warfare. For a frightening moment in 1877 the great railroad strike of that year took on the proportions of a social upheaval. Recurrent depression, in a new economy of industrialized cities and masses of workers, was something different than the economic cycles in an agrarian economy. The 1880s brought further difficulties, and the Haymarket riot in Chicago badly scared the middle class. Meanwhile, the farmers were agitated over a downward trend in the price of farm commodities and the declining status of agriculture generally. Westward expansion, proceeding at a rapid rate, often into areas where rainfall was scant, created a precarious living for hundreds of thousands. A vast influx of immigrants added to the existing problems. The country was growing at a fearful rate, stretching and distending itself. It was a "society without a core," Robert Wiebe has argued in his *Search for Order* (1967).

The problems, then, were partly cultural. In many localities of the North and West, Catholics felt severely threatened by Protestant majorities, identified usually with the Republican party. One issue alone, the possibility of discrimination against parochial schools, caused much agitation among the Catholics, who looked to the Democrats primarily for help.

In the last years of the century, the situation worsened economically. Alarm over the growth of monopoly brought the passage of the Sherman Antitrust Act in 1890, without really alleviating the problem. Dissatisfaction with the high tariff and other policies of the Republicans, both locally and nationally, resulted in a Democratic sweep of Congress in 1890. Two years later Grover Cleveland defeated Benjamin Harrison for the presidency. The great Homestead strike, at the plant of Andrew Carnegie, had national repercussions. The farmers, meanwhile, were persuaded in sizable numbers that neither of the major parties would listen to their complaints or take the necessary action, and they turned to a third-party movement, that of the Populists. Then, shockingly, in 1893, came another full-blown depression. Thousands of businesses failed, "armies" of unemployed workers roamed the country, and the Pullman strike convulsed Chicago. Meanwhile, the Populist party gained in strength, while some Democratic leaders turned toward the left. There was a genuine fear among conservatives that radicals might seize control of the United States.

Nothing so dramatic actually happened, but the results of the depression were indeed momentous. Studies have shown conclusively that the off-year elections of 1894 assumed the proportions of a political earthquake. Democrats were defeated everywhere as their party was blamed for the depression that had started in the preceding year. Nor did the Populists succeed at the polls in 1894 or in 1896. The real beneficiary was the Republican party, which gained new adherents notably in the cities and went on to a great era of national supremacy under William McKinley and Theodore Roosevelt.

Although the radicals were defeated, fears and tensions remained. John Higham has shown, for example, that the depression of the 1890s stimulated the "nativist" tendencies of Americans, leading in this instance to attacks on the Catholic minority and a strong movement for immigration restriction. Among the economic conservatives something of a crisis psychology developed, as reflected in decisions of the federal courts. The due process clause of the Fourteenth Amendment provided a new legal "device" by which private property was protected, even more effectively than in the past. In the Pullman strike of 1894 the Sherman Antitrust law was diverted from its original purposes and was used, instead, to defeat a troublemaking labor union. By the *Pollock* decision of the same year, the federal income tax was held unconstitutional, thus delaying a necessary tax reform. The Supreme Court, and many members of the judiciary, were clearly in a reactionary phase.

Businessmen were notably affected by another concern of the depression period. This was the surplus of products (or the difficulty of sales) and the belief that foreign markets must be found. This idea was by no means novel, but it did gain strength in the 1890s. In one way or another, Americans were wondering about their hard times and failures. Was it possible that fundamental changes were occurring in the very nature of national development? The federal census of 1890 revealed that the United States no longer possessed a true frontier; and soon thereafter the historian Frederick Jackson Turner implied that a turning point had indeed arrived. The advantage, so long enjoyed, of open land and expansion and a society in which many would move upward, improving their status, might soon be a thing of the past. Was this possible?

In a recent sophisticated analysis, Walter LaFeber has argued that American foreign policy was profoundly altered in the nineteenth century as the result of the economic crisis at home; that is, of domestic surpluses and apparent stagnation. Many intellectuals, businessmen, and leaders in the government believed that the nation had to look abroad, especially to Latin America and the Pacific. President McKinley and his advisers did not stumble absentmindedly into the war of 1898 and thus acquire new colonies and bases for the United States. Rather, that war and its results were a logical outcome of problems on the domestic scene. The need for new markets, says LaFeber, was the dynamic factor in a developing American imperialism.

Had the United States, then, lost confidence in its own people and resources? Had the idea of progress gone into eclipse, or the sense of a special mission, with its religious overtones? There can be no doubt that the late nineteenth century was a time of difficult adjustment and confusion, as suggested by the titles of historical works covering the period, or aspects of it: *The Response to Industrialism,* by Samuel P. Hays; *The Search for Order,* by Robert Wièbe; *The Quest for Social Justice,* by Harold U. Faulkner; *The End of American Innocence,* by Henry F. May. Yet the vast majority of Americans believed that answers could be found, that problems would be solved. Few indeed wished to destroy the American system or to overturn the government. They would, in fact, give the benefits of that system to other parts of the world.

Out of the depression came a new surge of confidence. Writing recently on Chicago and its problems a scholar has noted that the "turmoil of 1893–94 ushered in a decade of feverish concern over social reform." The city of Chicago wanted to be a great city, the "Capital of Civilization," and its leaders had now learned that changes must be made. The corruption, the poor sanitation, the lack of adequate housing, the poverty, the hostility between capital and labor—these and other problems demanded attention. The Civic Federation, a middle-class organization composed mostly of businessmen, undertook some noteworthy reforms. Increasingly, it seemed, the "better people" were recognizing that their fate was bound up with that of the less fortunate and that ways must be found to extend the benefits of the American economic system, without industrial warfare. David P. Thelen in a study of Wisconsin entitled *The New Citizenship* (1972) has arrived at a similar conclusion. The people of the state were profoundly disturbed by the depression, and they were determined to explore the various possibilities for correcting social and economic conditions. Far more than they had been, they were ready to cross class lines, to transcend "social barriers," to contribute to a new "civic consciousness." Thelen continues: "The new citizenship thus brought forward the 'New Woman,' the 'New Religion,' and the 'New Education,'" and led to an "emerging social progressivism." With the return of prosperity in 1896–1897, such ideas of change and progress did

Figure 2 Cover Illustration of *Collier's Weekly* for June 1, 1901. Old soldiers in the center photograph, with their American flags, are identified as Confederate veterans in Nashville, Tennessee.

not disappear but, rather, spread through the country with an increased influence.

In a sense, Americans had reason to be optimistic more than ever before in their national history. During the war with Spain in 1898 Northern boys and Southern boys fought together against a common enemy, and former officers of the Confederacy even commanded troops of the United States. Such occurrences were important to the American people psychologically, for the nation seemed to achieve a unity that had been absent in the previous fifty years. Virtually all whites now accepted black racial inferiority. Meanwhile, the United States was rapidly emerging as the greatest industrial power on earth, with a science and technology that commanded respect, if not awe. It also took its place in international affairs and was poised, quite possibly, to supplant the older, "decadent" nations of Europe. In a thousand ways the nation was preparing itself for a better future; or so it seemed. The future presented opportunities, indeed, but also difficulties that the people of 1898 could hardly anticipate.

SUGGESTIONS FOR ADDITIONAL READING

The theme of this chapter may be explored through a wide variety of books. A good place to begin is with Ernest Lee Tuveson, *Redeemer Nation: The Idea of America's Millennial Role,* Univ. of Chicago Press, Chicago, 1968, and Arthur A. Ekirch, Jr., *The Idea of Progress in America, 1815–1860,* Columbia, New York, 1944. Merle Curti, *The Growth of American Thought,* Harper, New York, 1943, is an intellectual history of high quality. Frederick Merk, *Manifest Destiny and Mission in American History: A Reinterpretation,* Knopf, New York, 1963, undertakes to explain the faith and moralism of Americans as expressed in foreign policy. Paul C. Nagel, *This Sacred Trust: American Nationality, 1798–1898,* Oxford, New York, 1971, is a study of the "national purpose" and the sometimes wavering faith in progress.

Interpretations of the American character are so numerous that only a few examples may be mentioned. Most penetrating of all is an analysis by the Frenchman Alexis de Toqueville in his *Democracy in America,* published originally in the 1830s. Some sixty years later Frederick Jackson Turner wrote his famous essay, ascribing basic American traits to the continuous influence of the frontier. This may be read conveniently in Turner's *The Frontier in American History,* Holt, New York, 1920. Reacting in part to Turner's hypothesis, which he considered inadequate, especially for modern America, David M. Potter wrote the insightful *People of Plenty: Economic Abundance and the American Character,* Univ. of Chicago Press, Chicago, 1954. A large part of the consciousness of a people is legend or myth, and this has been brilliantly examined in Henry Nash Smith, *Virgin Land: The American West as Symbol and Myth,* Harvard, Cambridge, Mass., 1950.

Several books on the Southern United States will suggest the complexity of that region's history from the viewpoint of both blacks and whites. See Charles G. Sellers, Jr. (ed.), *The Southerner as American,* Univ. of North Carolina Press, Chapel Hill, 1960; Wilbur J. Cash, *The Mind of the South,* Knopf, New York, 1941; and C. Vann Woodward, *The Burden of Southern History,* Louisiana State Univ. Press, Baton Rouge, 1960.

Two books are well-nigh indispensable for the economic ideas and the conflict of ideas relating to national development. See Richard Hofstadter, *Social Darwinism in American Thought, 1860–1915,* Univ. of Pennsylvania Press, Philadelphia, 1944, and Sidney Fine, *Laissez Faire and the General-Welfare State: A Study of Conflict in American Thought, 1865–1901,* Univ. of Michigan Press, Ann Arbor, 1956. James Willard Hurst, *Law and the Conditions of Freedom in the Nineteenth-Century United States,* Univ. of Wisconsin Press, Madison, 1956, is a significant effort to show the "interplay of law and other social institutions." See also Arnold M. Paul, *Conservative Crisis and the Rule of Law: Attitudes of Bar and Bench, 1887–1895,* Cornell, Ithaca, N.Y., 1960. The march of industry can be examined in Thomas C. Cochran and William Miller, *The Age of Enterprise: A Social History of Industrial America,* Macmillan, New York, 1942; Edward C. Kirkland, *Industry Comes of Age: Business, Labor and Public Policy, 1860–1897,* Holt, New York, 1961; and Joseph F. Wall, *Andrew Carnegie,* Oxford, New York, 1970. A pioneering study by Arthur M. Schlesinger, *The Rise of the City, 1878–1898,* Macmillan, New York, 1933, is still valuable, but it might be compared with later works, for example, Blake McKelvey, *The Urbanization of America [1860–1915],* Rutgers, New Brunswick, N.J., 1963, and Charles N. Glaab and A. Theodore Brown, *A History of Urban America,* Macmillan, New York, 1967. On the success tradition and those who failed to succeed, see Irvin G. Wyllie, *The Self-made Man in America: The Myth of Rags to Riches,* Rutgers, New Brunswick, N.J., 1954, and Robert H. Bremner, *From the Depths: The Discovery of Poverty in the United States,* New York Univ. Press, New York, 1956.

An interesting comparison may be found in Van Wyck Brooks, *The Confident Years: 1885–1915,* Dutton, New York, 1952; Henry Steele Commager, *The American Mind: An Interpretation of American Thought and Character since the 1880's,* Yale, New Haven, Conn., 1950; and Henry F. May, *The End of American Innocence: A Study of the First Years of Our Own Time, 1912–1917,* Knopf, New York, 1959. Notwithstanding the dates in his title, May takes a long look back into the nineteenth century.

An introduction to American politics, rather broadly considered, may be obtained from the following books. Eric F. Goldman, *Rendezvous with Destiny: A History of Modern American Reform,* Knopf, New York, 1952, is a stimulating account. A brief but path-breaking effort is Samuel P. Hays, *The Response to Industrialism, 1885–1914,* Univ. of Chicago Press, Chicago, 1957. Rather similar in its viewpoint and sociologically oriented is Robert H. Wiebe, *The Search for Order, 1877–1920,* Hill and Wang, New York, 1967. Leonard D. White, *The Republican Era: A Study in Administrative History, 1869–1901,* Macmillan, New York, 1958, shows how interesting and revealing such a study can be. John D. Hicks, *The Populist Revolt,* Univ. of Minnesota Press, Minneapolis, 1931, is a classic account. David P. Thelen, *The New Citizenship: Origins of Progressivism in*

Wisconsin, 1885–1900, Univ. of Missouri Press, Columbia, 1972, illustrates the importance of carefully researched and imaginative state studies. Important, too, are some works that have employed sophisticated methods of quantification. See Richard Jensen, *The Winning of the Midwest: Social and Political Conflict, 1888–1896,* Univ. of Chicago Press, Chicago, 1971, and Samuel T. McSeveney, *The Politics of Depression: Political Behavior in the Northeast, 1893–1896,* Oxford, New York, 1972.

No one interested in this period should fail to read some contemporary classics such as Henry George, *Progress and Poverty,* Appleton, New York, 1880 [1879]; Edward Bellamy, *Looking Backward,* Ticknor and Company, Boston, 1888; Josiah Strong, *Our Country,* Baker & Taylor, New York, 1891; and Frederic C. Howe, *The City: The Hope of Democracy,* Scribner, New York, 1905.

Chapter 2

Beginning
a New Century

The United States moved buoyantly into the twentieth century as if literally on a sea of prosperity. Writing in 1909, the financial historian Alexander D. Noyes noted a striking fact. The country's condition was reversed from that of 1894, when it had been "crippled" industrially and financially. Now, fifteen years later, it exhibited a prosperity that was "the wonder of the outside world." A "complete revolution" had occurred in the nation's position, not only in comparison to its earlier, internal troubles but "in its relation to other industrial states." The one thing needed for good times was an expanding market, and this the country was able to find, partly through luck. Failure of the crops in India and in Europe during 1896–1897 afforded a wonderful opportunity, since American farmers had bumper crops in those same years. By 1897, references to an "American invasion" were often heard in Europe. Rather startling was a rapid rise in the export of manufactured articles; such shipments actually doubled between 1893 and 1899. At the same time, the United States led the world in steel production, with 37 percent of the total output. The Spanish-American War served as a further stimulus, and for the first time citizens of the United States began to lend heavily in Europe, strongly suggesting the approach of a new financial status. Soon, perhaps, New York would replace London as banker to the world.

By various signs the nation had arrived at an advanced stage of economic development. The basis was its industrial plants, thousands of them, concentrated primarily in the Northeast and Middle West, along with the necessary transportation facilities. Numerous factors, however, were important. The United States did not lack for labor, either native or foreign-born, and it was abundantly blessed in natural resources. Science and technology were indispensable, providing countless inventions and improved techniques in the factory, and in work situations generally. An increasing sophistication was suggested by the high value of products from the foundries and the machine shops, which in 1890 totaled almost as much as that for iron and steel production. The improvement of business management, the growth of "finance capitalism," a process of integration and combination occurring in the corporate system, and the rise in membership of the trade unions—all were evidence of a vast change since the 1870s.

A phenomenal growth of cities had occurred by 1900, especially in the industrial areas of the East and Middle West. The railroads and good transportation by water had much to do with this. New York increased its population from a little over 2 million in 1880 to almost $3^1/_2$ million by 1900. Chicago, which passed the million mark in 1890 and continued to grow rapidly, became the second largest city, while Philadelphia dropped to third place. Boston, Baltimore, St. Louis, New Orleans, San Francisco, Minneapolis-St. Paul, Cleveland, Cincinnati, and dozens of other cities had become bustling centers of commerce and industry. By 1910 fifty cities had a population of 100,000 or more. If towns a little smaller were included, every region of the country now boasted a significant urban development.

Conditions of prosperity deeply affected the tone of American life. The hope and buoyancy were extraordinary. Indeed, the attitudes of Americans on many subjects can hardly be appreciated apart from the facts of prosperity and the promise of more to come.

There was, of course, another side to this that should not be neglected. There was racial injustice, poverty, and a wide range of problems. Organized protest inevitably occurred, particularly in the labor movement, but the most remarkable thing was a lack of radicalism and a willingness to work within the system.

The vast majority did their best in an often-difficult situation and enjoyed the pleasures that were available. The size and variety of the United States help to explain the limited appeal of radicalism. Freedom of movement was important. To move to the nearest town or city, or the county next door, was always conceivable, even if New York, San Francisco, or the gold fields of Alaska seemed too remote. Seldom in history had a country experienced so much activity, so many diversions and (apparent) opportunities. The vast network of railways, the interurban and city systems, and the newly invented automobile were important for economic reasons but also for their recreational value and possibilities of "escape."

Americans had never looked to the outside, to the rest of the world, as they did at the turn of the century following the Spanish-American War. Their primary concern continued to be internal and local as it had been for most of the nation's history. But there were new things to think about and, occasionally, to worry about. Recently acquired interests in Puerto Rico, Cuba, Hawaii, Guam, and—above all—the Philippine Islands occupied much space in newspapers and popular magazines. National involvements beyond the continental boundaries were seen in close relation to the earlier creation of territories and states and to the worldwide "mission of America," whatever exactly that was. Like Great Britain and France, and Germany more recently, the United States had become an imperial power and seemed unable to escape its "destiny."

The end of a century is an exciting time to be alive, and this was particularly true around 1900, for much was happening at home and abroad, and people's imaginations ran wild with thoughts of the future and what it might bring. No one could doubt that the center of world power still lay in Europe, that intellectually, militarily, and otherwise Western Europe was still dominant—but not necessarily for long.

One stirring event was the death of Queen Victoria on January 22, 1901, after a reign of some sixty years. Crowned heads and leaders from all over the Continent, many of them relatives of Victoria, attended her funeral. Among them was her nephew, Kaiser William II of Germany, who had been devoted to the British queen. With the death of this grand old lady, one symbol of European interdependence was gone.

Many Americans paid deference to European leadership and cultural attainments. Others were disdainful of the trappings of royalty, the obsolete customs of the Old World. Suspicion of England was traditional, while partiality toward one nation or another was to be expected in a country of many immigrant stocks. "The joke of the century" was a newspaper's description of inaugural ceremonies for Edward VII, who acceded to the British throne. He was "a short fat man, with a protruding abdomen, waddling beneath enormous royal robes, . . . covered with jewels," and surrounded by "tall thin men in petticoats, short fat men in bathgowns" and a generally "amusing medley" of people involved in something like a "cheap masquerade." Actually Edward VII was an urbane man of much ability who was to help improve relations with the United States.

The end of Queen Victoria's reign had been marred by the Boer War, which continued under her successor and aroused keen interest in the United States; it also gave a hint of the nature of warfare to come. For three years the British were unable to defeat the Boers, or Dutch farmers, of South Africa. *Collier's* noted in 1901 that British officers there had finally been ordered to substitute carbines for the swords they had been carrying in the field. "Demands of self-preservation," in fact, already had led many to abandon their swords and hide their insignia of rank; otherwise they were conspicuous targets for Boer marksmen. So went this process in the "degradation of war from a highly poetic pursuit to a mere butcher's business."

In its own imperialistic ventures, the United States was having problems and some second thoughts. The Philippine campaign to pacify the natives—recently "freed" from Spain—was a long and bitter one. One American casualty was Major General Henry W. Lawton, a big, powerful, handsome man, noted for a long and distinguished career and for his capture of Chief Geronimo back in 1886. On December 10, 1899, leading his troops in the Philippines, he was killed.

No event was more shocking to Americans at the turn of the century than the assassination of their President, William McKinley. Reelected in 1900, with Theodore Roosevelt on his ticket, he opened his second term in a time of prosperity and high hopes. Many were critical of him for overseas adventures and for policies of economic conservatism at home, including sound money and high tariffs. Few indeed had anything against him personally; he was a kindly, thoughtful Christian gentleman. But at least one person had a different conception of the President. On September 6, 1901, McKinley attended the Pan-American Exposition in Buffalo, New York, and was patiently shaking hands with a line of well-wishers in the Temple of Music. A young man, with a handkerchief over his right arm, suddenly reached out and fired two shots, knocking the President backward. After lingering a week, McKinley died of complications. The assassin, it developed, was an anarchist from Cleveland named Leon Czolgosz. His action did little to help the cause of anarchism or radicalism in the United States; just the opposite, in fact.

The age that includes the events just described is not one that fits any labels precisely. The Gay Nineties were not very gay, and the Age of Innocence was not very innocent. There was, however, a distinctive way of life and a spirit in the air unlike that of any other epoch. To capture these "times" is not easy, for America was a land of contrasts and of constant change. Nevertheless, the general tone may be sensed merely by scanning newspapers or popular magazines from the years in question. That the Gay Nineties had some basis in fact is readily apparent from these publications.

Well before 1900, photographs, large illustrations, and bright colors were in frequent usage. They contributed to a feeling of gaiety and expansiveness. By this date, also, outdoor activities and organized sports had become extremely popular for millions living both in the country and in urban areas. One scholar has recently described an "arcadian myth," a back-to-nature movement, which strongly affected the lives of millions, as seen in organizations like the Boy Scouts and the Campfire Girls. The manifestations were many. There was a new interest in nature study, wilderness, and the preservation of rural values. For some the movement meant an occasional outing or perhaps a house in the suburbs, providing new opportunities. Baseball, football, tennis, golf, yachting, polo, fishing, camping, bicycling, and swimming—these perhaps received most attention in the newspapers and journals. In illustrations that were vividly detailed readers could enjoy vicariously a hunting scene in the Rocky Mountains, a man and woman in sports attire fishing in the Adirondacks, or a crowd in New York City attending an outdoor band concert.

According to Thorstein Veblen in his *Theory of the Leisure Class* (1899), an interest in sports was an excellent way to prove oneself a member of the upper class, or to take on some airs of the idle rich. Another theory has stressed the "virility impulse," alleging that the American male of this era was driven to prove his masculinity. What better way to do so, if wars were temporarily scarce, than through athletic feats? The description of football games, for example, was in the language of valorous combat. Brave warriors out on the field waged heroic battle, while up in the stands or on the sidelines their ladies cheered them on. Whatever the exact reason, this generation could heartily admire, rather than make fun of, the likes of Theodore Roosevelt and his strenuous endeavors.

Ladies' dresses in 1900 were down at the ankles, or near the ground, but their bathing suits were up near the knees! One drawing in a magazine depicted an "Idyll of the Beach," a handsome young man in bathing suit with his eyes fixed on an equally attractive young woman, jauntily attired for fun in the surf. Romance, it appeared, might find a way.

This was an adventurous age. For the well-to-do, motorcar racing was a new and mildly dangerous sport. Balloons were launched, and dirigibles maneuvered about. Submarines went down the ways. Expeditions to discover the North Pole were among the most exciting events, comparable to the space flights of sixty or seventy years later. Technological developments, wars, and imperialistic schemes afforded countless opportunities for dramatic news reporting.

The vast possibilities of electricity were becoming apparent. Thus an article in *Popular Science Monthly* for 1900 considered some of the latest developments in x-rays, including their use in dentistry. The wonders of magnets, coils, armatures, and other equipment for trolley cars were the subject of another article. And the "Palace of Electricity" at the Paris Exposition, a brilliantly lighted structure, created excitement. In the cities of America some people now had homes lighted by electricity.

In journalism of the day, the seamier side of life was not neglected. In fact, some publications exploited the pseudoscientific, the bizarre, the freakish. This was, after all, the heyday of the yellow press. But popular fiction was sentimental, if not mawkish. Life was romanticized and glamorized, and the same tendency often carried over into nonfiction writing.

Idealism and moralism permeated the age, or at least its rhetoric. This was most apparent in numerous articles on religious subjects. Polygamous Mormons were a source of much concern, even after Utah was admitted as a state in 1896 and its people apparently had abandoned their heathenish practices. Brigham Henry Roberts, described as a "polygamist from Utah," was refused a seat in Congress early in 1900. *Outlook* magazine applauded and offered this observation about the problem presented by a man like Roberts: "A clearly recognized attack on the home, as based on the marriage of one man to one woman, arouses . . . [the national] conscience as perhaps nothing else could do." Titles alone reflected the times and indicated not a little alarm over the threats to religious orthodoxy. Following are examples: "Is the Christian Religion Declining?"; "What Jesus Would Do"; "Are Scientific Studies Dangerous to Religion?"; "Immortality: Its Place in the Thought of Today"; "The Non-Existence of the Devil"; "The Religion of Democracy." One of the more curious of such articles was entitled "Sex after Death." It argued earnestly that male and female souls would exist together in a life hereafter making possible renewed companionship and the "fulfilment of our dearest hopes."

Sex was of much interest (as usual), especially anything categorized as sexual misconduct. While the United States was changing remarkably in some areas of life and thought, it remained Victorian in its attitudes toward male and female. Journal articles frankly considered some questions, and subtle indications of sexual mores are to be found in fiction and nonfiction, in advertising, in drawings of the female figure, and in accounts of daily news events, including criminal assaults, murder, divorce proceedings, and the like. Many notions of the time are truly amazing and suggest dark recesses of the Victorian mind. There was also a quality of simplicity that could be touching.

American innocence, a frequent theme in literature, is illustrated by a girl who had studied art in Paris and believed she must write a magazine article warning her contemporaries of that city: "I say openly that I know the majority of the leading studios for men in Paris to be hotbeds of immorality." If young artists must study in Paris, she said, they should keep in themselves "the purity which I pray it may be America's province to further for the world."

In the 1890s *Arena,* an important reform publication, ran a number of articles relating to sexual problems. Its founder and long-time editor, Benjamin O. Flower, wrote several of these himself, including a series on the subject "Well-Springs and Feeders of Immorality." Flower had a deep concern over poverty, prostitution, and various social evils. "The lust for gold and the lust of the flesh," he said, "are the two well-springs of present day misery, degradation and crime. . . ." He deplored the double standard of the time, which permitted a philandering man, the "betrayer" of a maiden, even though his "crime" was known, to be welcomed into respectable society. Such a standard accepted the necessity of red-light districts, where young men of the best families could go and "sow their wild oats," as the expression went. Every city of any consequence had such districts, operating wide open, some with small cubicles or cribs, from which women openly solicited. Highly fashionable bordellos were also common. One mayor of a Western town is said to have lived in the local bordello while his family was away on a European tour.

Flower wanted to root out the causes of prostitution, including ignorance, wage slavery, and laws of "consent" that placed girls and young women at a severe disadvantage. But some of his ideas seem curious indeed to a later generation. He believed that children inherited the lust of the father, whether that father was married or not. Many children were "cursed" before they were ever born "with the lecherous appetites of a morally depraved man." He estimated there were "100,000 impure men" in New York City who would soon become the fathers of babies infected "with the virus of triumphant animalism." A child should be the "blossom of love" rather than the "offspring of lust."

Warming up to his subject, Flower wrote an article called "Prostitution within the Marriage Bond." He argued: "So long as girls will wed fallen men and condone the sowing of wild oats, the double standard of morals, with its race-debauching influence, will prevail." Men should control their lust, for children begot of lasciviousness were cursed with their father's sexual drives. The common prostitute was a much freer person, he asserted, than "the wife who is nightly the victim of the unholy passion of her master, who frequently further inflames his brain by imbibing stimulants." Education in sexual matters would be a long step toward reform, Flower believed. The United States needed a moral reformation so that the heredity of its people would be improved.

Here was a strange combination of the new belief in improving the environment along with an assertion of hereditary influences. Carried to its worst extremes this hereditary emphasis became an attack on blacks, "new immigrants," and others of allegedly inferior quality who polluted the American stock. A proposed remedy was the sterilization of social defectives.

Modesty and decorum in the Victorian era were hardly what they seemed. Behind the pictures of grace and elegance, and the "pure" men and "pure" women, were attitudes of social or moral superiority that could have tragic consequences. Also, the double standard of sexual behavior gave encouragement to masculine promiscuity, while the women of "good name" were effectively repressed. One bold study in 1900, conducted by a gynecologist, maintained that Victorian repression had led to a high incidence of homosexuality among women of the upper class.

If American attitudes on sex were misguided, mischievous, or even reactionary, the same can be said for the race question—except with greater emphasis. This question, too, can be examined in newspapers and journals of opinion, as well as in numerous scholarly works.

Racism was rampant at the turn of the century. C. Vann Woodward and others have shown that during the 1890s especially a pattern of "Jim Crow," or racial segregation, was fastened on this country. The system was created predominantly south of the Mason and Dixon line where some 90 percent of all blacks lived. But segregation was nationwide. "Separate but equal" was the law of the land, as interpreted by the United States Supreme Court, while the real emphasis of the law lay on separation—not equality. Frightful injustices occurred. The number of lynchings in the first year of the new century was more than 100, and from 1889 to 1930 the total was 3,714. Hardly less alarming were race riots that flared up early in the 1900s, both in Northern and Southern states. Afro-Americans seldom fought back in those days. They were hunted down, riddled with bullets, tortured, castrated, burned at the stake, and made to die in the most brutal ways that could be devised.

All of this did not happen without protests. There were the well-known, impassioned outcries of black leaders like W. E. B. Du Bois. Blacks who were not so prominent, and whose lives perhaps were in greater danger, made similar objections. In the South Carolina constitutional convention of 1895 several blacks boldly defended their race and, in effect, dared the white majority to allow the same rights to one race as to another. Simply permit them, they said, in accordance with American shibboleths, to get ahead if they were able to. One educator, an ex-slave, writing in a national journal, denied there was a race problem except as it

THE CRISIS

RECORD OF THE DARKER RACES

Volume One   NOVEMBER, 1910   Number One

Edited by W. E. BURGHARDT DU BOIS, with the co-operation of Oswald Garrison Villard, J. Max Barber, Charles Edward Russell, Kelly Miller, W. S. Braithwaite and M. D. Maclean.

CONTENTS

PUBLISHED MONTHLY BY THE

National Association for the Advancement of Colored People

AT TWENTY VESEY STREET   NEW YORK CITY

ONE DOLLAR A YEAR   TEN CENTS A COPY

Figure 3 First Issue of a Noted Publication.

had been created by whites: The Afro-American's enemies attempted to prove that he had deteriorated in a condition of freedom, but this was a conclusion from prejudice and juggled statistics. The black, in fact, had done well, considering his handicaps; what he needed was a chance.

A small minority of whites, North and South, also opposed the dominant trend of thought and action. An investigator from the University of Chicago, for example, believed that environment was of major importance in explaining failures among the blacks, including a high incidence of criminality; at least, there was no conclusive evidence to the contrary. Many whites occupied a middle ground. For example, Professor Nathaniel S. Shaler of Harvard University considered Negroes a "wonderful folk" who had adapted to a new climate after their forcible move from Africa, as no other people had ever been able to do. They should receive aid from whites in their upward social struggle. He did not believe, however, in giving them political rights like those of the more experienced white majority.

How was it possible, a later generation would ask, that one-tenth of the citizens in this country were largely disfranchised and that thousands of this minority were brutalized, lynched, and otherwise persecuted? How could such things occur at the dawn of the twentieth century, in a time of developing science and industry, and when Populists, progressives, and other reformers sought an enlargement of democracy? Any explanation must take into account a number of things that were happening and the relative importance assigned to them by white people of that day. Most Americans were absorbed in their business, their private affairs, their amusements such as those described previously. Furthermore, they and their fathers and forefathers had always had a blind spot on the question of racial justice—except when the issue was forced upon them in some way, as in the Civil War. Most important of all, perhaps, was an idea that the race question would never be solved except over a long period of time. Industrial progress and the education of both races would eventually bring about a great enlargement of opportunities and a lessening of tensions.

The fact was that the racism of the late nineteenth and early twentieth centuries was supported by the latest scientific and scholarly work. Americans of that generation were enamored of science. They heard from men with scholarly credentials that the black race was clearly of a lower order in the long evolutionary process. According to some commentators, it was thousands or even millions of years behind the more favored Europeans of the temperate zones and their American descendants. Charles Darwin had not attempted directly to apply his concept of natural selection to the racial situation. But others did so. It was easy to say that the African was an inferior in the struggle for survival and to use scientific verbiage in justifying some of the things that happened to him. The English philosopher and evolutionary thinker Herbert Spencer addressed himself to problems of society, and by his interpretations he contributed to anti-Negro thought. About the same time, a French count, Arthur de Gobineau, wrote *The Inequality of Human Races.* His study of the civilizations of antiquity led him to conclude that "all civilizations derive from the white race, that none can exist without its help, and that a society is great and brilliant only so far as it preserves the blood of the noble group that created it." The admixture of other blood would cause degeneration, he said. Sir Francis Galton was another race theorist and a pioneer in the study of heredity. He concluded that the black was a primitive hereditary type, "childish" and stupid, far below the intellectual level of whites.

Men of all nationalities in the Western world were writing in this vein. Darwinism, Anglo-Saxonism, anti-Semitism, the "white man's burden," the "Yellow Peril"—these and similar concepts convey the mood of the day. The Harvard psychologist William McDougall, the paleontologist Henry Fairfield Osborn, the geographer Ellen Churchill Semple, and many other scholars contributed to nativist and racist thought. Often they were pursuing their studies and had no real intention of providing ammunition for the extreme racists. But indirectly that was precisely what they were doing.

The country was flooded for a time with racist literature of the most incredible sort, such as a book entitled *The Negro a Beast* and another book in reply trying to prove in 238 pages that the Negro was *not* a beast. The most spectacular example of all this writing was a novel called *The Clansman,* published in 1905 and made into a movie under the title *The Birth of a Nation* in 1915. Thomas Dixon, the author, was a Baptist minister from North Carolina who served for many years as a pastor in New York City. This popular novel revealed American romanticism, sentimentalism, and pseudoscience as well as attitudes on race. Essentially the author justified and glorified the practice of lynching in defense of white civilization. White Klansmen (of the Civil War era) were shown as heroes, defending the honor of Southern womanhood and meting out to the black man, Gus in this instance, exactly the treatment that a rapist deserved. Such ideas contributed to the organization and growth of the modern Ku Klux Klan.

Sometime around 1915, perhaps as late as 1919, the tide of racial thought began to move in a different direction. In the period of World War I, however, the vast majority of psychologists and other scholars were still assuming the fact of black inferiority and were conducting their studies and writing books largely elaborating on what they already believed. The IQ tests of the United States Army, for example, helped to "prove" that Americans generally were not very bright but that black men were the least intelligent of all. Then, rather abruptly it seemed, new and better studies began to shake the foundations of this racist scholarship. By 1930 it was hardly respectable in the academic world to hold the views that were so common a decade earlier.

Some prominent individuals renounced their previous interpretations. Howard W. Odum, a sociologist at the University of North Carolina, was one of these. At least an important minority had never accepted the extreme racist doctrines. Franz Boas, the anthropologist, was far ahead of his time in saying essentially that each racial or cultural group had to be studied on its own merits, that each had value for its own members, if not for others. An easy assumption of superiority, such as that in the Christian nations of the Western world, was totally unwarranted.

Boas was a remarkable man, whose ideas had a wide effect, partly through the influence of his students. After a period of pioneering work, he taught at Clark University in Worcester, Massachusetts, was associated in Chicago with what became the Natural History Museum, and finally went to Columbia University as its first professor of anthropology (1899). His students and associates included Margaret Mead, Ruth Benedict, Robert Lowie, Clark Wissler, Elsie Clews Parsons, and others who had a tremendous impact in changing people's minds about race, color, and culture. Like so many who affected American thinking in this period, Boas was European. Born and educated in Germany, he took an epochal voyage in 1883 to East Greenland, in the Arctic, where he lived with Eskimos. On the basis of long experience, he made up his own mind about what these North people were like: "I had seen that they enjoyed life, and a hard life, as we do; that nature is also beautiful to them; that feelings of friendship also root in the Eskimo heart; that, although the character of their life is so rude as compared to civilized life, the Eskimo is a man as we are; that his feelings, his virtues and his shortcomings are based in human nature, like ours."

Later studies of American Indians led him to the same conclusions. He took an interest, as well, in Afro-Americans and rejected the idea that they had no culture, that they were innately inferior in mentality and creative capacity. Rather, their African past gave proof of cultural ability and sophistication. So far as they had failed in America it was largely a matter of environment, or the lack of opportunity. Boas gave continuing emphasis to the worth and dignity of all individuals and of each human culture.

Franz Boas was in a very small minority in 1900. Nevertheless, when all phases of American thought are taken into consideration, it is clear that developments slowly were providing additional support for view-

Figure 4 Family from Hungary on Arrival at Ellis Island. (*Photograph by the Bureau of Immigration, published in* National Geographic Magazine *for May 1907.*)

points like his. The fundamental bases of change were science, technology, and urbanization, with the growth of problems that demanded new methods and new answers.

Few questions were more important in the America of 1900 than the so-called melting pot, or the "salad bowl," as Carl Degler has named it. The ethnic groups did not really mix. Many countries admitted immigrants in the nineteenth century, but the United States received a far greater variety of national types than did other nations such as Australia and Argentina. In the period 1860 to 1900 about 14 million immigrants arrived. Every year from the turn of the century to 1914 added approximately a million new arrivals. While Germans, Irish, and British had predominated in the nineteenth-century migrations, the later decades brought Italians, Slavs, Jews from Eastern Europe, and others referred to as the "new immigrants." They congregated mostly in cities of the East and Middle West, forming a great labor force, unorganized and poorly paid.

Figure 5   Scottish Family. (*Photograph by the Bureau of Immigration, published in* National Geographic Magazine *for May 1907.*)

Figure 6   Jewish Family from Russia. (*Photograph by the Bureau of Immigration, published in* National Geographic Magazine *for May 1907.*)

Figure 7 Italian Family Seeking Lost Luggage, Ellis Island, 1905. (*Photograph by Lewis W. Hine in the International Museum of Photography at George Eastman House.*)

Immigrants were almost always at the bottom in the job scale, while natives supervised the work. Those who started low, like the Irish, might make their way up, while replacements filled the lower vacancies. Immigrants who went into agriculture often bought out native farmers and contributed to a horizontal mobility comparable to that on a vertical scale in the industrial system.

Immigrants moved to almost every part of the country, except the South, where the race question and availability of cheap labor discouraged settlement. The great concentrations numerically were in states like Massachusetts, New York, Pennsylvania, and Illinois. Germans were to be found primarily in the Middle West; the Irish more often in the East. Yet the Irish were in fact widely scattered, from Boston and New York, to Chicago, to the farm lands of Wisconsin and Nebraska, the copper mines of Butte, Montana, and the streets of San Francisco. Italians as well were widely distributed, with concentrations in the Northeast, in Chicago, and in California. Scandinavians found their homes mostly in the upper Middle West but lived as well in New England and the far

Northwest. Particular patterns of the immigrant settlements, sometimes temporary, were striking and significant. North Dakota, for example, in 1910 had 27 percent foreign-born, and another 40 percent of its people were second-generation American; thus almost 70 percent were of recent foreign extraction. Entire new towns were occasionally formed by mass immigration. Hungary Hollow, Illinois, a steel town, had 15,000 Bulgarians in 1910.

One of the momentous changes resulting from immigration was the new religious makeup of the population. By the early twentieth century the United States had three great churches, or religious communities, of Protestant, Catholic, and Jew. Church attendance was on the rise; and Americans, according to some assessments, were more religious than before, in spite of powerful secular forces simultaneously at work. In a process of puritanization, many immigrant groups, like some from Scandinavia described by Marcus Lee Hansen, became more sedate and restrained in their social customs. They tended increasingly, for example, to conform to American standards of Sunday observance and temperance. This may have been a reaction to native criticism, or it may have been an attempt by the group to keep closer control over their own people. Some immigrant additions added particular vitality to religion. This was true of Lutherans, who gave a new intellectuality to a Protestantism in America, which had become much watered down in its theology.

Immigration, on the whole, added to American conservatism. This was in spite of the occasional radicals who got into the country or those who became radicalized after arriving because of misfortune and suffering in the economic struggle for survival. In politics, one way for immigrants to "prove" themselves and become more acceptable was to stay out of anything tinged with radicalism, like the Populist movement or the Industrial Workers of the World. The vast majority were cautious in this respect.

A very important group with strongly emerging influence by the late nineteenth century were the Irish. They had come by the millions and had the advantage, as did the English and some others, of knowing the language and of looking basically like native Americans. Still, the reception accorded the Irish in America bred in them a kind of anxiety, one scholar has noted. The English, on the other hand, felt their own superiority and usually showed it.

The Irish were mostly an urban group in America, though having a peasant background. They had large families and tended to help each other as a people. They slowly made gains up the economic ladder and in politics and religion. Something in their background of religious and political struggle in the old country made them adept in the same areas of

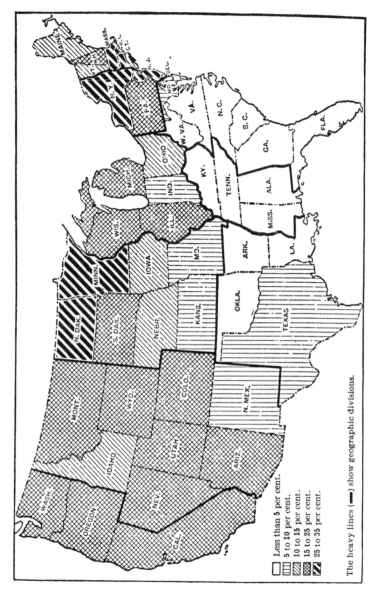

Figure 8 Percentage of Foreign-born Whites in Total Population, 1910. (*From The Survey, March 1, 1913.*)

The heavy lines (▬) show geographic divisions.

Less than **5** per cent.
5 to **10** per cent.
10 to **15** per cent.
15 to **25** per cent.
25 to **35** per cent.

action in the United States. Certainly they knew the importance of political power, a matter of life and death, and the church to them often meant no less. In spite of their image as a vigorous, hard-drinking, brawling people, many were total abstainers, adding some strength to the native American temperance movement. In politics, Irish emerged as mayors and councilmen in the 1860s and thereafter. Often they provided leadership for the polyglot people of the cities, including Catholics in great numbers. The mere fact, however, of a similar faith did not mean the existence of sweetness and harmony. Thus Irish and Germans in Wisconsin were keen rivals for power, as in the control of churches and parochial schools.

Several features distinguished this essentially new, and potentially powerful, church on the American scene. The different ethnic groups vied for control, as noted above, and the older, native Catholics were overshadowed. The church occupied itself with large problems of molding the different national groups into stable elements of the American population. Schools had to be established, newspapers printed, charitable organizations activated to care for orphans, the sick, the weak. Meanwhile, Catholics came under nativist attacks. At times these were particularly virulent, as in the 1890s under the stress of depression conditions. The American Protective Association was a notable hate group. Catholics under such attack drew in "upon themselves." They had feelings of inferiority, perhaps, and of enhanced sensitivity. They had new reasons to establish their own schools and to fight periodic attempts to eliminate parochial schools, or to strike back at those who attacked them.

Meanwhile, however, the increasing power of Catholics in politics and their conservatism on economic questions gave them hope of public acceptance. Their total numbers had risen from a mere $1^{1}/_{2}$ million in 1850 to 12 million by 1900. In addition to politics, a source of great potential strength was the working class. The Catholic Church never lost that class. Some of its religious leaders in America were notably sympathetic with workers in their struggles with the forces of capital. James Cardinal Gibbons of Baltimore, for example, helped to persuade Pope Leo XIII to take a liberal or moderate course. In the famous encyclical *Rerum novarum* of 1891 he recognized the rights of private property but, more important, the rights of workers and labor unions. Catholics were antisocialist at this time and later anticommunist but with a strong penchant for welfare work and efforts to attain social justice. Father John A. Ryan, a prolific writer and social activist, became the greatest name in this sphere.

Catholics did not really gain an importance commensurate with their total numbers in the country. Struggles with religious and secular problems provide part of the answer. Also, as Father John Tracy Ellis has observed, they were often anti-intellectual, disinclined to seize the opportunities for advancement. And the prejudices of native Americans kept Catholics out of many places they might otherwise occupy.

There can be no doubt that class divisions existed in America. Thoughtful people were deeply concerned, in fact, at the gap between rich and poor and the inordinate influence upon the entire society of a few with swollen fortunes. Everywhere Americans had a good awareness of the place they occupied in the social scheme of things, and few could rest comfortably if they had failed by the age of forty to "make it," whether in business, agriculture, or the professions.

Always in America, the rise of an aristocracy was preceded by money, by the profits of landed estates, or of trade and industry. This was true although theoretically, "gentlemen were born, not made," as the patriciate liked to think. In cities like Boston, Philadelphia, and Charleston a relatively stable upper class did indeed develop. At its best, such an aristocracy offered culture, intelligence, and creativity along with its wealth and show. Recognizing an obligation to the community or nation, it sent dedicated individuals into public service. It was able to stay in power by a network of marriages and by perceptive adjustments to the economic realities, by wise investment and business innovation. Yet eventually the aristocracy was overwhelmed by immigration and the dynamics of twentieth-century America.

True members of the American patriciate sought to avoid publicity and the crasser aspects of life. They had little use for big spenders and high livers. According to one theory, the famous watering places of this era went through a cycle that began when writers and other creative people were attracted by the scenery. Then came "solid" visitors and residents including ministers, professors, and some millionaires who were looking for a good, simple environment for their children. Finally came the "bad" millionaires who proceeded to build lavish residences, parade their wealth, and destroy the old pleasant aspects of the place. Cleveland Amory concludes that "this theory, which amounts to a sort of Gresham's Law of Resorts—i.e., that bad millionaires drive good millionaires out of circulation—holds up remarkably well." At Newport, Rhode Island, for example, there was an "intellectual period" when Bancroft, Longfellow, the Jameses, and others gave the resort a high reputation. But soon came the "naughty millionaires" from New York, striving to outdo each other with "cottages" such as that of Mrs. W. K. Vanderbilt, costing $11 million.

New York's Four Hundred, led for many years by Mrs. William Astor, helped to give notoriety to the nouveau riche of the late nineteenth century. Acting as her social arbiter was Ward McAllister, who once declared that he could not include more than 400 people in fashionable society of the great city. "If you go outside that number you strike people who are either not at ease in a ball room or make others not at ease." A recent scholar has concluded: "An infamous image of wasteful expenditure tarnished the reputation of the Four Hundred. Breakdown of family life, however, endangered its very existence. Relatively rapid upward mobility, leisure and luxury corrupted the wealthy New Yorkers in a manner and degree impossible for older elites disciplined by a more modest, settled and busier way of life."

While the gay rich kicked up their heels, flaunted their wealth, or quietly dissipated, millions of Americans lived in poverty. Such a condition was especially hard to justify as the nation began its recovery from the depression of the 1890s, inaugurated its career as a new, "great" world power in 1898–1899, and moved into a new and "better" century. "Progress and Poverty," as Henry George had labeled it earlier, was *not* a satisfactory program for the future.

The poor you have "always with you," according to the Bible, but to estimate their number has always been difficult. In 1904 Robert Hunter undertook this task, that of doing the most systematic study of the poor ever attempted in America. His effort was noteworthy for two reasons. First, he was a reformer (and sometime Socialist) who exemplified an introspective trend in the country, a growing alarm over big business and special privilege: something had to be done. Second, Hunter's book is a minor classic and an excellent source of information.

By his definitions, the United States had two large groups of deprived people, the first of which was a most serious problem. These were the working poor, barely eking out an existence. A group of less importance were the loafers and drifters, people beaten by life and surviving only by some kind of aid. Every city had them: "Negroes, Whites, Chinese, Mexicans, Half-breeds, Americans, Irish, and others [he said] are indiscriminately housed together in the same tenements and even in the same rooms. The blind, the crippled, the consumptive, the aged,—the ragged ends of life; the babies, the children, the half-starved, underclad beginnings in life, all huddled together, waiting, drifting. This is pauperism." The great problem, as Hunter saw it, was to prevent others from dropping into this "lowest level of humanity."

Members of the working class meanwhile strove mightily, even desperately, to avoid a loss of wages, a drop into the abyss. For thousands upon thousands of them the "dread of public pauperism" was the "agony of their lives." They hated the thought of failure, or of any charity. Hunter saw this group sympathetically: "There are great districts of people who are up before dawn, who wash, dress, and eat breakfast, kiss wives and children, and hurry away to work or to seek work. The world rests upon their shoulders; it moves by their muscle; everything would stop if, for any reason, they should decide not to go into the fields and factories and mines."

Even the more fortunate, the skilled ones, could last perhaps three weeks without employment. It was much worse for the unskilled. As soon as they stopped work, suffering stared them in the face. "They are the millions who possess no tools and can work only by permission of another." Turning for help to English scholars, who had antedated Americans in population studies, Hunter showed that a working man, living by hard manual labor, absolutely required good shelter, clothing, and food. His livelihood depended upon his own health and that of his family. One of the greatest hazards was the industrial accident which, in a moment, could destroy him and thus the support of his loved ones.

Hunter decided that no less than 10 million Americans were in a condition of poverty. This meant that their total family income was about $500 a year or less, and often far below that figure, as in the South. He deplored a condition of affairs in which so many were below the poverty line and so many millions of others not far above it. "I am at a loss to understand," Hunter wrote, "why well-known and generally recognized poverty-breeding conditions, which are both unjust and unnecessary, are tolerated for an instant among a humane, not to say a professedly Christian people." He was concerned over the concentration of wealth and the widespread refusal to recognize, in places of authority, that social problems were socially created.

Thus, as Robert Hunter helped to reveal, the United States had no reason for complacency about its steel production, its success in the export markets, or the general conditions of prosperity noted earlier. The disparities in wealth, and in the opportunities to obtain wealth, were enormous. Even the middle class seemed to be threatened by great corporations and "malefactors" who had no regard for democratic traditions or the finer things of life. In actuality the nation had a myriad of problems. It also had a proven capacity for self-criticism and reform, and the outlines of a reform movement had begun to appear even before 1900.

SUGGESTIONS FOR ADDITIONAL READING

A number of books from Chapter 1 are recommended for this chapter too, especially Woodward, Hofstadter, Fine, Cochran and Miller, Bremner, Van Wyck Brooks, Commager, May, Hays, and Wiebe. For a systematic treatment of economic history see Harold U. Faulkner, *The Decline of Laissez Faire, 1897–1917*, Rinehart, New York, 1951, which is vol. 7 in The Economic History of the United States. George E. Mowry, *The Era of Theodore Roosevelt, 1900–1912*, Harper, New York, 1958, begins with chapters that skillfully analyze the United

States in its material, intellectual, and political aspects around 1900. Mark Sullivan's *The Turn of the Century,* Scribner, New York, 1926, is the first of six volumes in a journalistic and entertaining account, *Our Times: The United States, 1900–1925.* A later attempt to understand America through its journalism is Maxwell H. Bloomfield, *Alarms and Diversions, The American Mind through American Magazines, 1900–1914,* Mouton, The Hague, 1967. The following books are interesting new approaches to the period: Peter J. Schmitt, *Back to Nature: The Arcadian Myth in Urban America,* Oxford Univ. Press, New York, 1969; Donald K. Pickens, *Eugenics and the Progressives,* Vanderbilt, Nashville, Tenn., 1968; and William L. O'Neill, *Divorce in the Progressive Era,* Yale, New Haven, Conn., 1967. Cleveland Amory, *The Last Resorts,* Harper, New York, 1948, is a fascinating look at high society. A recent analysis is "Style and Status: High Society in Late Nineteenth-Century New York," by Frederic Cople Jaher, in Jaher (ed.) *The Rich, the Well Born, and the Powerful: Elites and Upper Classes in History,* Univ. of Illinois Press, Urbana, 1973.

On immigration and social problems generally the list of books is long indeed. Maldwyn Allen Jones, *American Immigration,* Univ. of Chicago Press, Chicago, 1960, gives a good introduction to its subject. Marcus Lee Hansen, *The Immigrant in American History,* Harvard, Cambridge, Mass., 1940, is a classic treatment of major themes. Oscar Handlin's *The Uprooted: The Epic Story of the Great Migrations That Made the American People,* Little, Brown, Boston, 1951, is an impressionistic book that should be read in conjunction with others, such as John Higham, *Strangers in the Land: Patterns of American Nativism, 1860–1925,* Rutgers, New Brunswick, N.J., 1955, and Edward M. Levine, *The Irish and Irish Politicians: A Study of Cultural and Social Alienation,* Notre Dame Univ. Press, South Bend, Ind., 1966. Two general works on religion are John Tracy Ellis, *American Catholicism,* Univ. of Chicago Press, Chicago, 1956, and Winthrop S. Hudson, *American Protestantism,* Univ. of Chicago Press, Chicago, 1961. See also Will Herberg, *Protestant, Catholic, Jew: An Essay in American Religious Sociology,* Doubleday, Garden City, N.Y., 1955. Indispensable for their subjects are Henry F. May, *Protestant Churches and Industrial America,* Harper, New York, 1949, and Robert D. Cross, *The Emergence of Liberal Catholicism in America,* Harvard, Cambridge, Mass., 1958. A careful study with broad implications is Stephan Thernstrom, *Poverty and Progress: Social Mobility in a Nineteenth Century City,* Harvard, Cambridge, Mass., 1964.

For a good general introduction to Afro-American history see John Hope Franklin, *From Slavery to Freedom: A History of Negro Americans,* 4th ed., Knopf, New York, 1974. George B. Tindall, *South Carolina Negroes, 1877–1900,* Univ. of South Carolina Press, 1952, is a model study. Aspects of racial thought and of the caste system may be examined in C. Vann Woodward, *The Strange Career of Jim Crow,* 3d rev. ed., Oxford, New York, 1974; Rayford W. Logan, *The Negro in American Life and Thought: The Nadir, 1877–1901,* Dial, New York, 1954; and I. A. Newby, *Jim Crow's Defense: Anti-Negro Thought in America, 1900–1930,* Louisiana State Univ. Press, Baton Rouge, 1965. For Franz Boas one may read his own numerous works, but see also Melvin J. Herskovits, *Franz Boas: The Science of Man in the Making,* Scribner, New York, 1953.

Chapter 3

Progressivism: Its Growth and Diversity

Three periods of reform are justly famous in American history: the Age of Jackson, the era of progressivism, and the New Deal. Each of these was broadly concerned with problems and grievances of its time. In the instance of progressivism, the central issue seemed to be "irresponsible wealth" and selfish control of government, although much of the difficulty was actually rapid growth—including that of the corporations—and a cultural lag. Those who led in the progressive movement, such as Theodore Roosevelt, were born near the middle of the nineteenth century and, as they came to maturity, caught the vision of a great and growing country which must not fail. With the blessings of its natural wealth, commerce, and industry, America also had the benefits of constitutional government. Its people had proved before and would prove again that they could adjust to the challenges of a new age. The modern city, for example, was a problem that no one could blink away, but it was also an opportunity, the "Hope of Democracy," as some saw it, where life could be splendid indeed.

Strong and determined leadership was a characteristic of progressivism as exemplified by Roosevelt, Woodrow Wilson, William Jennings Bryan, Robert M. La Follette, Eugene V. Debs, George W. Norris, Charles Evans Hughes, William E. Borah, Hiram W. Johnson, Gifford Pinchot, William G. McAdoo, and Jane Addams. Scores of men and women, not quite so prominent perhaps, had these same characteristics of vigor and determination. Often they fought each other. The battles were of epic proportions.

Progressivism was not a single movement but, rather, exhibited an endless variety and much that was contradictory, occurring in a period of relative prosperity. Moralism and idealism were mixed with realism, pragmatism, and "efficiency." Individualism jostled with nationalism; ideas of justice with racism and nativism. There was the woman's rights movement, the single-tax movement, the labor movement, the social justice movement, the antimonopoly movement, the conservation movement, and so on. The city was growing, and the farm was changing. Much of life seemed to be changing. Somehow the old and new struggled to reach a new synthesis.

The existence of sectional and regional variations was apparent. A populist influence continued long after 1900 and was by no means lacking in importance, especially in the South and West, where "Bryanites" and agrarians continued to be numerous. It has been argued that the Southern states of this period should not, by any stretch of the imagination, be considered progressive. How could they be, when racism was rampant, when lynchings occurred every week of the year; when black men below the Mason and Dixon line were almost completely disfranchised and generally were made the victims of a segregated society? Nevertheless, the South experienced a reform movement—"for whites only"—that differed but little from efforts occurring in other parts of the United States. A "blind spot" on race really existed all over the country, and little reason for pride could be found. The Jim Crow system for blacks was a national one, though worst in the South; while Orientals and American Indians faced their greatest difficulties in the Western states, where they principally lived.

If the South was impeded by its strong traditions, other sections also suffered constraints. In much of the West, people lived in sparsely populated, semiarid areas where they had to scramble for a living. All too frequently large corporations, insufficiently checked by other interests, exercised an inordinate influence. The Anaconda Copper Company in Montana and the Fuel and Iron Company of Colorado may serve as examples. Even in the coastal states of California, Oregon, and Washington such troubles existed. Something approaching a popular democracy was extremely difficult to obtain. The West, indeed, with its hallowed traditions of individualism, its heroes of the frontier, was slow in assuming a regulatory responsibility that the situation had long warranted. The region often sought help from Washington, but not bureaucratic interference. Land and resources were highly important.

Populous states east of the Mississippi and north of the Potomac were potentially the most enlightened and progressive of all. They had been compelled to adjust, even if painfully, to some problems of a new age. New York, for example, was long accustomed to the existence of labor unions, and politicians there necessarily cultivated the labor vote. "Bossism" reached a kind of maturity, with many tangible benefits. Diverse economic interests, a degree of prosperity, a growing profession- al class, colleges, universities, public libraries, hospitals, and the like contributed to the superior status of the East. At the same time, the states there had their own form of failure and parochialism. Millions lived in poverty in their cities and industrial towns. The economic power of the United States was concentrated in this area; and the bankers of Wall Street, the textile manufacturers of Fall River, and the steel men of Pittsburgh or vicinity would not willingly relinquish it. Leadership of the United States Senate at the turn of the century reflected the economic situation. Nelson Aldrich of Rhode Island, Orville Platt of Connecticut, and their political allies were closely associated with large business interests of North Atlantic states.

No area counted more heavily in the progressive movement than cities and states of the Middle West. Why this was so is not entirely certain, but much depended upon the local situation, the stage of industrialism, and the determination of critics and crusaders who were living there.

Progressivism, it seems clear, had two main emphases that often led eventually to the same course of action. One of these was a belief in freedom, or the restoration of freedom. The goals of the progressives, Richard Hofstadter once decided, were "profoundly individualistic." But a second emphasis was perhaps even more important. Most leaders of the movement believed in the creation of a positive state—a government that gave services to its people. Some came to believe in the sort of factory and social legislation, utility regulation, and limited government owner- ship that is associated with the New Deal. A few wanted to go farther than the New Deal ever went. It was not uncommon to talk of individualism or freedom but to learn in practice that the government had to be used as a principal agency for doing necessary work. Only the government, for example, could regulate the great interstate corporations or lead the way in conservation of natural resources. Only through governmental or cooperative action could innumerable problems be solved. A social awareness and willingness to act were far more apparent by 1910 than a generation earlier.

While the causes of this great reform movement are obvious in a sense, they are also elusive. Facile generalizations are not persuasive. Responding essentially to the new industrial era, cities and states became laboratories for experimentation and possible solution of their problems. People in one state looked to other states, particularly to those regarded as most advanced or innovative, and had no hesitation about appropriating their ideas or specific reforms. Sometimes, of course, they rivaled each other. The federal government also was in a process of adjustment. Well before 1900 there was a considerable body of progressive theory and of practical experience as well.

Massachusetts had probably come to be "the most highly organized of all the states," asserted Raymond L. Bridgman in 1900 in the *New England Magazine,* and he saw it as a model of progressivism. His article was entitled "The Natural History of a State." Using analogies from natural science, he showed his optimism about the evolution of the Massachusetts body politic. This "political person" was developing "new organs" to add to those from decades past, intended to "be in the service of the people . . . to secure for them progress in the struggle of life and justice at the hands of their fellows." The state board of education had started in 1837, the board of agriculture in 1852, and eventually over thirty such executive organs were developed, many to meet the rising problems of business, labor, and industrial monopoly. As a historian of the state, Bridgman was well informed and he raised questions which had some implications for the nation generally. Thoughtful men, he said, looked at Massachusetts and what it had achieved and wondered if this was not the logical pattern for other parts of the country, too, including the national government. Massachusetts' railroad commission, for example, had forced the roads to be servants to the people, not their masters, while allowing stockholders a reasonable profit. "Why should we not extend this system to all monopolies which exist by virtue of law, and make the body politic, as a living organism, the master of all the activities which it creates and protects?" He recognized the danger that commissions might be manipulated by the interests they were supposed to control; that monopolies might "fool the people for a while." But education, discussion, and agitation would enable the people, at last, to "come into the full possession of their own powers."

Bridgman was writing like a true progressive, though addicted to scientific jargon more than some were. Certainly, too, he did not recognize sufficiently the obstacles to reform. These were serious enough in his own state, of which he had written so fondly. Leaders of Massachusetts became fearful in this period of the economic rivalry from other regions, especially the South. Too much regulation of business at home could place the old commonwealth at a competitive disadvantage.

Another state endowed significantly with a progressive heritage was Illinois. The legendary Abraham Lincoln was a continuing source of inspiration to those who believed in government "of, by, and for the people." In 1892 the state gained another hero—or villain, as the case might be—when John Peter Altgeld was elected governor on the Democratic ticket and proceeded to serve a single, tumultuous term. A German immigrant, largely self-educated, a lawyer, millionaire, author, and humanitarian, Altgeld was sympathetic toward the poor and extremely critical of capitalistic injustice. He avidly supported public education through larger appropriations for teachers colleges and the University at Urbana. Fearless in his public positions, he pardoned the surviving anarchists imprisoned after the Haymarket bombing. He was a much-loved and much-hated man, so much so that when he died (in 1902) there was some difficulty in finding a clergyman who would conduct the funeral services. Therefore the social worker Jane Addams spoke. And the famous trial lawyer Clarence Darrow, who almost worshipped Altgeld, also paid his final respects.

"Altgeld's America," as Ray Ginger has called it, included some remarkable people who lived in the city of Chicago, or nearby, and whose influence was more national than local. Jane Addams opened Hull House on the south side of Chicago in 1889. Patterned after Toynbee Hall in the slums of London, it was intended to serve the poor, but also to provide a means for understanding them. It was a haven for the newly arrived immigrants and other poor people, as well as a training ground—or mecca—for humanitarians and social workers. Florence Kelley, for example, came to Hull House in 1891 and stayed for eight years, serving for a time also as Chief Inspector of Factories for the state of Illinois. She finally went on to her important work as secretary of the National Consumers' League. These women were not merely interested, as do-gooders and Christian sentimentalists, in the plight of the poor. They conducted scientific studies and called for practical, remedial action. Julia Lathrop, Alice Hamilton, and many others associated with Hull House had an influence that is incalculable.

Merely to list some of the socially concerned intellectuals in Chicago is to get a good idea of the excitement there around the turn of the century. Henry Demarest Lloyd, a close friend of Jane Addams, wrote his *Wealth against Commonwealth* in 1894 and was active in public affairs until his death in 1903. Thorstein Veblen, teaching at the University of Chicago and editing the *Journal of Political Economy,* published his iconoclastic *Theory of the Leisure Class* in 1899. John Dewey, also teaching at the University and doing some of his most important work in educational experimentation, published *School and Society* in 1899. Louis Sullivan, becoming the "Whitman of American Architecture," pioneered in functional design and expressed his philosophy verbally as well. "In a democracy," he said, "there can be but one fundamental test of citizenship, namely: Are you using such gifts as you possess for or against the people?" Finley Peter Dunne ("Mr. Dooley") was an editor of the *Chicago Journal* while also publishing classic works of humor and social commentary. Louis F. Post was editing the *Public*, a journal of liberal if not radical opinion. Clarence Darrow, much like Louis D. Brandeis in Boston, was turning his enormous talents and energies to the defense of laboring people, or the underdogs of society, and he allied himself with Altgeld, Mayor Edward F. Dunne of Chicago, and others in the fight for political reform.

In Michigan, meanwhile, the Republican party supplied a rather unlikely crusader. He was Hazen S. Pingree, a wealthy shoe manufacturer, who was elected mayor of Detroit in 1889. A New Englander by birth, Pingree worked in a shoe factory as a young man before enlisting to serve in the Union army. Following the war he moved to Detroit, worked briefly again as a laborer, and then began his rise to the top of Detroit's economic and political elite. Pingree was an honest man who showed a fair-minded attitude toward the employees in his factory. Nevertheless, on becoming mayor, he surprised almost everyone by his battles against the special interests.

Pingree started off slowly as a "good government" leader who would do little except run the city with greater efficiency and try to root out corruption. Detroit was a manufacturing center of 200,000 with a population predominantly of foreign origin: Germans, Irish, and Poles especially. Like other cities rapidly growing in this period, it was infested with "men on the make," who exploited the populace deliberately or by force of circumstance. The new mayor reacted as a servant of all the people. He battled the lighting company, the city railway, the ferry company, and the toll roads that demanded tribute for access into the city. Taking a close look at taxes, he decided they were inequitable and must be reformed. In 1893, when the depression struck, he was sensitive to the human misery now so widespread. He saw a responsibility to help the poor, and boldly stated his position on the subject: "I believe that our wealthy citizens, many of whom have accumulated the fortunes which they now enjoy through the sweat and toil of the laboring classes, owe a duty to those who have created their wealth." His old friends and associates did not respond favorably; in fact, they read him out of Detroit's "Four Hundred." Undeterred, Pingree went ahead as the acknowledged champion of the city's working classes. In 1896 he became the governor of Michigan.

As the Democrats had the example of Altgeld to look to, so the Republicans had Hazen Pingree. In both the parties, long before 1900, men of ability and integrity had demonstrated a type of leadership similar to that later made famous by the two Roosevelts and Woodrow Wilson. However, some of these leaders who emerged in the 1890s were tainted by the depression and the bitterness that surrounded it. They often were regarded as traitors to their class as Franklin D. Roosevelt would be later in the 1930s.

La Follette of Wisconsin bore some of this stigma. He rose in the nineties protesting against the Republican machine, trying to talk issues and to make fundamental changes in state government. After an early career as state's attorney in Dane County (Madison) and three terms in Congress as a Republican, he began his agitation for reform aiming to win the governor's mansion. Finally he succeeded and from 1901 to 1906 put into motion what is termed the "Wisconsin Idea." He then went on to the United States Senate. Unquestionably La Follette was dynamic, determined, and capable. He was also formidable. Vilification could not stop him. Nor was he concerned about his social position, or winning the esteem of fellow senators and politicians. One of his habits in Washington was to "call the roll" on his opponents, showing how they had voted, or whether they had voted at all. This could be effective in forcing action.

The Wisconsin Idea did not differ markedly from what was occurring in other areas of the country except in the degree of success achieved. La Follette once commented that the movement in his state would be a successful one if it could be shown "that Wisconsin is a happier state to live in, that its institutions are more democratic, that the opportunities of all its people are more equal, that social justice more nearly prevails, [and] that human life is safer and sweeter." Such idealism did not hide the fact that La Follette was a practical-minded leader, seeking tangible reforms. He and his successors in the gubernatorial chair soon had a proud record of achievement, including one of the best civil service systems in the United States and the first state income tax. Wisconsin benefited enormously from the development of its state university which was occurring simultaneously with the rising reform movement. La Follette and his heirs were able to draw heavily upon the intellectual resources of the teachers and scholars who were gathered at Madison. The German heritage of the state also facilitated reform. Efficiency and the use of expert knowledge were very much a part of the Wisconsin program.

Wisconsin would never be the same again after "Battling Bob" La Follette. But others had an influence too; and, in fact, over a period of years this state produced a galaxy of reformers, many of whom went on to careers of distinction in the national capital. One of those doing his work essentially in Wisconsin was a public servant named Charles

McCarthy, who made an original and lasting contribution that went far beyond the borders of his adopted state. McCarthy earned a Ph.D. degree in history at the University of Wisconsin and went on to become a "legislation expert for the Wisconsin legislature." He developed the system for a legislative reference library which other states and the Library of Congress in Washington soon began to emulate. Though an efficiency expert of sorts, McCarthy was also a fighting reformer, proud of the achievements in his state. In 1912 he published a book on the Wisconsin Idea, while he and his assistants in the same period were advisers to the reformers nationally, helping with their problems of research.

No state demonstrated the possibilities of leadership in the cities more dramatically than did Ohio. Toledo's Samuel M. Jones and Cleveland's Tom Johnson were remarkable men who, like so many others, were deeply disturbed by the callousness or stupidity of contemporary institutions. Each was a businessman, turned idealist. Each was blessed with an instinctive political sense, though inexperienced at first in political affairs. Not only did they enjoy success as politicians, they made converts and sent them out into a broader world of reform. Most important of this group eventually was Newton D. Baker of Cleveland and Washington, D.C. Brand Whitlock, who was associated with Jones, and Frederic C. Howe, one of the Cleveland galaxy, proved to be faithful lieutenants and distinguished writers as well; they enhanced their own reputations while describing vividly the struggle for reform that had occurred in their respective cities.

Samuel "Golden Rule" Jones, an immigrant from Wales, was compelled to work long hours from childhood because of his parents' poverty. He had little formal education. In 1864 he went to Titusville, Pennsylvania, in the oil fields, becoming first a worker and then a producer. Having invented an oil-well appliance, he went to the industrial city of Toledo and started what was called the Acme Sucker Rod Factory. There he gained a local reputation for his attempts to apply Christian principles of brotherhood in his factory. Largely by accident, he received the Republican nomination for mayor in 1897. Two years later when the Republicans had had enough of him, he ran as an independent and was reelected; he repeated this performance in 1901 and 1903.

Without question, Jones was a bit eccentric, and he became the butt of many jokes. A man of passionate enthusiasms, he was just discovering in his fifties the excitement of great literature. He was "full of Tolstoy" when Brand Whitlock first met him, so they proceeded to discuss the great Russian and other writers. He also discovered Oscar Wilde's *Ballad of Reading Gaol* and liked to quote from memory or to apply these and other lines for inspirational purposes. The works of Emerson expressed his own philosophy, but most of all he loved Walt Whitman.

Jones was also developing his own literary style and discovering that he could write and speak with facility. Not surprisingly, he tried his ideas on the employees in his factory, enclosing letters to them in the pay envelopes. *Letters of Labor and Love* they were entitled when eventually published. In his factory Jones had a large room, serving as an auditorium, which was called Golden Rule Hall, and next to the factory for use in good weather was Golden Rule Park, devoted to the use of the people. Here came radicals, reformers, speakers of all persuasions.

Whitlock wrote of his friend Jones:

> He was like an evangelist, in a way, and his meetings were in the broad sense religious, though he had long since left his church, not because its ministers were always condemning him, but for the same reasons that Tolstoy left his church. His evangel was that of liberty. He had written a number of little songs. One of them, set to the tune of an old hymn he had heard in Wales as a boy, had a noble effect when the crowd sang it:
>
> Ever growing, swiftly flowing,
> Like a mighty river
> Sweeping on from shore to shore,
> Love will rule this wide world o'er.

Jones's achievements in Toledo were mostly those of education and inspiration. He wanted municipal control of utilities but failed to achieve it; he did succeed, however, in preventing the city streetcar company from obtaining a twenty-five-year franchise. He favored the eight-hour day for workers and introduced it in city departments and on jobs done under contract for the city. He added such municipal services as kindergartens for the schools, playgrounds, golf courses, and band concerts. Seeing the necessity for state or national action to alleviate local conditions, he worked for home rule for cities so that they could escape legislative interference, and he was an active member of the League of American Municipalities. He called for direct participation of citizens in their government and nonpartisan action for the public good (in which he showed the way). In 1899 Jones even ran for governor of Ohio but was forced to do so on an independent ticket, and lost.

This warmhearted man made enemies among the church element and "do-gooders" because he wanted people to enjoy themselves and refused especially to close down the saloons. His major emphases were on those things that he believed would fundamentally alter the human condition—economic reforms, opportunity, and justice before the law. Like Altgeld of Illinois, Brand Whitlock, and many others of the time, Jones was appalled by injustices in the courtroom and brutalities inflicted by the police. He personally took a hand and improved these conditions, for example, by giving his own money to provide legal aid. With Jones's death in 1904, Whitlock and others continued to fight for aspects of his program. They bucked the Republican machine, and were successful in making Whitlock the new mayor.

Meanwhile, in nearby Cleveland, Tom Johnson had been following a course much like that of Jones. There was, in fact, considerable interchange between these two friends, though Johnson ultimately had a greater impact both in the state and nation. The Cleveland man was a practical-minded leader, experienced, gifted, and personable. He proposed to fight the forces of *privilege* in all their forms and manifestations. He would make Cleveland, Ohio, "A City on a Hill" for all to see and emulate. His effort was clearly a splendid one, although in the end he believed that he had failed. One of his admirers was Edward W. Bemis, economist and public-utility expert, who declared that Johnson was "the greatest administrator, [and] the most efficient executive, greater than Jefferson, Jackson, Altgeld, Pingree or Jones." Testifying to his personal appeal was Frederic Howe: "I had greater affection for Tom Johnson than for any man I have ever known. He was as dependent upon those he loved as he was indifferent to the hostility of his enemies. He had as much time for affection as he had for work, and he was greedy for both."

Tom Johnson was effective because he knew what the obstacles were and what he was fighting. Originally a Southerner, he became a businessman at an early age, an inventor, a financial success, a manager of streetcar companies. He entered the competition for control of the lines in Cleveland, and one of his competitors there was Mark Hanna. Beyond his managerial skill, he acquired a technical knowledge of mechanical problems involved in the street railways; also of the new source of energy, electricity. He went to Detroit and Brooklyn as an expert to manage their streetcar systems for a time. All of this was not enough, for he turned to politics and was elected to Congress twice in the early nineties before he ran for the mayor's job in Cleveland.

A turning point in Johnson's life had come one day when, riding the train, he read *Social Problems,* by Henry George. Soon he read *Progress and Poverty,* by the same author. Not long after that he met George in person and they became fast friends. From being an aggressive businessman, well trained in the methods of aggrandizement and monopoly power, he became a "single taxer," following George's ideas. Johnson now believed in the social creation of wealth and the rights of the people to share equitably in that wealth. Demonstrating his new attitudes, he began to give away or spend for public purposes his own fortune of perhaps $3 million, even though his family objected.

Like so many other city reformers, Johnson was a "gas and water socialist," not because he had truly socialist views but because he believed that natural monopolies should be brought under public control. Individual enterprise was fine, but not under conditions of special advantage given by a city council, state legislature, or other public agency. Most immediately, in Cleveland, he was concerned with franchise grants to street railway companies and to gas, water, and electric companies under which they were permitted the utilization of public roads and properties without adequate return to the people. Rates charged were high, while corporate taxes were ridiculously low. To maintain their special privileges these companies had corrupted the city. Johnson hoped to bring them under municipal control and to force them to pay their share of the tax burden. For nine years he and his followers fought a continuing battle on these issues and with a considerable degree of success, waging, in part, an educational campaign. Shortly after Johnson left office in 1910, fare reductions on the streetcars and a sliding scale of profit taking gave the city essentially what he had wanted.

The Johnson group also inaugurated a program of tax studies, almost from the day he became mayor, and contributed to longtime agitation and reform, both on the local and state level. In fact, the legislature's control over municipal powers of taxation gave Johnson no choice but to enter state politics. He did so and became a powerful figure in affairs of the Democratic party. Tax bills of some importance were passed, and finally in 1910 the legislature enacted a comprehensive tax reform that placed Ohio among the most advanced of all the states.

Johnson had a remarkably efficient and talented city administration. Of greatest importance to the mayor was Newton D. Baker, a cultivated young lawyer who bore the burden of the administration's legal battles. Edward Bemis, the utility expert, became manager of the city waterworks department. William Springborn, administering the department of public works, brought new efficiency to care of the streets, city lighting, and garbage collection and disposal. Public health, building inspection (under a new code), and other city services were similarly improved. Johnson was showing by example the advantages of municipal control and leadership, going far beyond mere routine services. Expansion of the park and recreational facilities, for example, was on a par with that in the most progressive cities of the day. As the historian Hoyt L. Warner describes Johnson's efforts: "The city contributed as never before to the joy and health of the community."

In cities all over the United States, urban reform was popular, if not irresistible. Here was the principal source of leadership for the progressive movement. City affairs were related intimately to those of the state, and state affairs to those of the nation. Almost inevitably, therefore, men and women advanced, if possible, to a broader field of endeavor. The movement for reform evolved and expanded, gaining publicity all the while.

National prosperity was fundamentally important to the growth of progressivism. By 1900 one could argue for reform and be "respectable"; this had not been possible for Pingree, Altgeld, or William Jennings Bryan in the depression atmosphere of the 1890s. Without a doubt, the depression placed its stamp psychologically on the decade that followed. Reformers wanted to avoid the taint of radicalism or demagoguery. The ills of American society, they believed, could be eliminated or ameliorated without aligning class against class and without taking drastic action that might precipitate another deflationary cycle. This approach encouraged steady efforts to improve the country in a variety of ways. It also left room to attack "swollen plutocrats," the "idle rich," "wild-eyed radicals," and others who were considered to be antisocial or benighted in their activities.

The course of moderation found support in a rising middle class. Increasingly visible on the American scene was a mélange of city intellectuals and organized professionals, a manifestation of the maturing society. These people believed in change, and through their work and writing often pointed the way. Merely to list the professional organizations would require several pages. Some broke off from the parent groups, as specialized interests could no longer be satisfactorily accommodated, or as sharp differences developed. Among the older organizations were the American Medical Association (1846), the American Statistical Association (1839), the American Social Science Association (1865), and the American Society of Mechanical Engineers (1880).

Then came new developments at the turn of the century. The number of professionals grew rapidly, and their urge to organize and to "join" was apparent. In the realm of social science there were, for example, the following new groups: the American Historical Association (1884), the American Economic Association (1885), the American Academy of Political and Social Science (1889), the American Psychological Association (1892), the American Anthropological Association (1902), the American Political Science Association (1903), and the American Sociological Society (1903). Among the engineering groups were the American Society of Naval Engineers (1888), the American Society for Engineering Education (1893), the Society of Automotive Engineers (1905), and the American Society of Sanitary Engineers (1906). The American Federation of Labor began in 1886, the National Association of Manufacturers in 1895, the National Municipal League in 1894, the National Tuberculosis Association in 1904. It is hardly too much to say that the members of these various organizations ushered in a modern America.

An emphasis on efficiency was one aspect of the new middle class. In this field the great name was that of an engineer, Frederick W. Taylor, who rose to prominence in the 1890s. As a result of his "time and motion" studies, Taylor argued that a tremendous increase in work efficiency was possible. Others took up the idea, and America became almost crazy on the subject of efficiency—in business, in industrial management, in education, in the management of natural resources, and in government service generally. Church leaders, socialist leaders, and almost all Americans were affected.

But the idea of efficiency did not necessarily mean what it seemed to mean. It acquired connotations of progress, morality, and patriotism that went far beyond a mere scientific definition. A rising young writer of this period, Carl Sandburg, became a proponent of efficiency, doing articles on the subject. At the same time, he was a poet and a passionate believer in human rights. He believed that the movement for efficiency could be reconciled with traditional virtues of justice and democracy. Sandburg would probably have agreed with the young lawyer and historian Benjamin Parke De Witt, who wrote in 1915 that the aim of efficiency was "to sharpen the instrument of democracy." De Witt continued:

> The efficiency movement is concerned merely with improving government, the tool of democracy; it has no part in directing its use. If government is controlled by the people, the efficiency movement becomes an asset. If government is controlled by interests inimical to the people, it is no reason for discarding the efficiency movement. It is an added reason why the people should capture the improved government which the efficiency movement has created.

The political successes of progressivism could never have occurred without public support. And public support came, in considerable part, from the effects of "muckraking." The muckrakers might be regarded, rather strictly, as those who wrote articles of criticism and "exposure" for popular consumption, and who published books intended for the same audience. More broadly speaking, they were doctors, economists, historians, and writers of every kind who addressed themselves to the evils of America—or the alleged evils—and who seemed to be calling for reform. Henry George, for example, was a self-taught economist whose *Progress and Poverty* (1879) continued to have an impact in the twentieth century, some twenty years after he published it. Other books, such as *How the Other Half Lives* (1890), by Jacob A. Riis, and *Wealth against Commonwealth* (1894), by Henry Demarest Lloyd, added to the upsurge of anger over social injustice and monopoly power. *Arena Magazine,* in the nineties, was a pioneering journal of the muckraking type.

Most of the muckrakers were able people who got their facts straight and wrote without undue sensationalism. The facts often were sensational enough. Lincoln Steffens, Ida Tarbell, Ray Stannard Baker, Burton J. Hendrick, Charles Edward Russell, John Spargo, Marie Van Vorst, Upton Sinclair, Frank Norris, Christopher Connolly, George Kibbe Turner, Mark Sullivan, Herbert Croly, Walter Lippmann, and Walter Weyl— these have been respected names in the history of journalism or popular fiction. A few, like Croly and Lippmann, rank with the ablest of American commentators on public affairs. Overwhelmingly, the muckrakers were concerned about the "promise of American life," as Croly named it, and with finding ways to realize that promise. The mere fact of study and description was a start, but some went another step with works that were perceptively interpretive and philosophic.

The muckraking journals attained great success in sales. Older, genteel magazines had been fortunate to gain a circulation of 100,000; but *McClure's,* leading the way in muckraking by 1904, pushed its circulation up to 750,000. *Hampton's* magazine went from 13,000 to 440,000; *Everybody's* to 735,000; and *Collier's* to 1 million by 1912. *Cosmopolitan* and *The American Magazine* also had large sales.

As Robert Cantwell has observed, this writing succeeded not because it was sensational but because it was new and down-to-earth. Few had read anything to equal the articles by Lincoln Steffens on politics and corruption in various American cities or by other writers on insurance scandals, labor trouble, race riots, exploitation of children, prostitution in Chicago, corporate domination of Montana, and the like. Not surprisingly, some who read this literature over a period of years were moved to take action, especially when they found vigorous leaders locally or on the national scene.

All the political parties were affected by the ferment of progressivism. Reform elements had a voice in party affairs and usually a powerful voice for the first two decades of the century. In his pioneering work, *The Progressive Movement* (1915), Benjamin De Witt chose a graphic way to show this political influence. He devoted, successively, a chapter each to the progressive movement in the Democratic party, in the Republican party, in the Progressive party of 1912, in the Socialist party, and in the Prohibition party. De Witt saw the beginnings of a powerful national movement as occurring in the Democratic party, with William Jennings Bryan as leader, in the 1890s. Although beaten in the campaign of 1896, Bryan had fought for the idea that "government is to be used, not for the few, but for the many"; the idea was not forgotten. William Allen White, a Republican journalist who opposed Bryan at the time, later praised him fulsomely as the first man in a generation "large enough to lead a national party" and as one who had "boldly and unashamedly made his cause that of the poor and the oppressed."

Bryan led a national party, but his popularity was limited chiefly to Democrats of the South and West. He illustrated a strong, continuing current of agrarianism and sectionalism in the country's politics. From the beginning, Bryan was a controversial figure; to some a demagogue or a fraud, to others a hero. There was no doubt, however, of his influence in the Democratic party for thirty years, notwithstanding his defeats for the presidency in the campaigns of 1896, 1900 and 1908. He supported Woodrow Wilson in 1912 and then contributed significantly to his reelection in 1916. Bryan thrilled and inspired countless audiences over the years with his oratory, thus adding to the fires of progressivism. On the basis of new, convincing studies, it is clear that Bryan was a warm and sincere man, who never abandoned his crusade for a more just society, although his values were those primarily of rural America. He was a democrat with a small "d" who believed in the Declaration of Independence, and he was a Christian who wanted to apply principles of brotherhood on earth. This pioneering progressive often sounded radical as he talked of government ownership of the railroads, the telegraph, and telephone; of the eradication of monopoly and corruption; of the need to extend popular government in countless ways. His faith in the popular will was so great that it sometimes led him to act as if the voice of the people was "the voice of God." That could be alarming, and it could be a mistake.

Bryan never gained political power, except in a subordinate role. It was the Republican party that controlled the country from 1897 to 1911 and which, therefore, had the responsibility to guide the nation in a time of great change. The GOP enjoyed many advantages. Its tradition of nationalism, dating from the Civil War period, made the use of government power something that could be understood and justified. Such power might be used for the benefit of all the people, in a twentieth-century setting. But the Republicans had a problem—the strength of business interests and of great corporations which often made the party little more than a tool of the special interests. The rise of state leaders, like La Follette in Wisconsin and Albert B. Cummins in Iowa (as well as Pingree in Michigan) showed the possibilities. Regulation of business had become a reality; moreover, the people seemed to like it.

Many Republicans now visualized a new approach to government, similar to that later advocated by Herbert Croly, in his *Promise of American Life* (1909). This notable figure in American journalism called for a blending of the Hamiltonian tradition of strong government with Jeffersonian ideals of humanitarianism. Laissez faire would no longer suffice. Political leaders should accept the necessity of a purposeful direction and guidance in government. They must infuse new vigor into the system, and to do this they must convince the American people that they had a fair chance to get ahead economically. Business must be regulated, and taxation made more equitable. Whether these goals could be achieved through the Republican party rested largely in the hands of Theodore Roosevelt, after McKinley's death in 1901.

The Socialist party of the early twentieth-century was truly a political party. Its members agreed on little, except that capitalism had not succeeded very well and that it must be reformed, eventually to be replaced by a system stressing public control of the major means of production and distribution. Very few American Socialists believed in violent revolution. Perhaps nothing proves this better than the career of Eugene Debs of Terre Haute, Indiana, the Socialists' perennial candidate for the presidency. James Whitcomb Riley wrote of his fellow Hoosier, "God was feeling mighty good when he created 'Gene' Debs, and He didn't have anything else to do all day." Debs had "As warm a heart as ever beat betwixt here and the Judgment Seat." From the first to last Debs was a humanitarian, a man who loved his fellow men, who was impelled at much personal sacrifice to be a radical labor leader, a Socialist, and a pacifist. His rhetoric could be passionate, but he aimed to defeat capitalism at the polls by using the powers of persuasion and the ballot. He was an "evolutionary Socialist," as were Victor Berger of Milwaukee, Morris Hillquit of New York, and other leaders who had the greatest influence in the party. The state, incidentally, with the most Socialists in 1910 was Oklahoma. Much of the national membership was in agricultural regions, although the party was essentially labor-oriented.

Benjamin De Witt noted in his contemporary history of progressivism that the Socialists had become moderate. They had moved so far from an extreme left position that many of them differed but little from advanced progressives in the other parties. They could "almost meet on common ground." Whether in the Socialist party or outside there was a growing belief in the "socialization of certain activities." The progressive movement was going in that direction.

Two other parties had a distinctive influence in the history of progressivism, particularly in its later phases. First, there was the Progressive party of 1912, consisting predominantly of Theodore Roosevelt and his thousands of admirers, who broke away from the GOP with momentous effects. This third-party movement became an integral part of political history from 1909 to 1916. Second, there was the Prohibition party, which had been a national organization since 1872. Its candidates garnered few votes, but the party symbolized an upsurge of sentiment in the country to outlaw the sale of alcoholic beverages. The Prohibitionists also supported a long list of reforms, including woman suffrage, the direct election of Senators, the income tax, protection for the rights of labor, prohibitions on child labor, and action to suppress prostitution. Women were especially active in the prohibition fight, and this was a training ground for many in public affairs. State by state, in the Southern and Western parts of the country, the idea of prohibition had success. Here was a movement within the broader progressive movement that eventually proved irresistible. Such "wheels within wheels" were frequently to be found in the period.

Obviously progressivism was a highly complex phenomenon. People of reform sentiments in the several parties could not really cooperate. Party loyalty still counted for much, and to get the Democrats and Republicans together was particularly difficult. Then, as now, men talked of reorganizing the parties so that all the liberals could be in one organization while the conservatives were in another—but to no avail.

Who were the progressive leaders? What was their motivation? Where did they find support? Such questions are interpretive and the motivational query is particularly difficult to answer. The foregoing pages have perhaps established the fact that many persons around 1900 were deeply concerned over poverty, corruption, business monopolies, injustice, and special privilege. There was a solid core of idealism, of genuine concern, in this movement. Yet some of the progressives, it seems safe to say, had motives little different from those of others ambitiously finding their way in this world. To understand the progressives, they should be scrutinized no less closely than hard-bitten conservatives. The fact is that they had mixed motives, much as people always have had.

Richard Hofstadter, in his *Age of Reform* (1955), advanced an interpretation drawn from social psychology. According to this theory of a "status revolution," members of well-established families and of professions like law, teaching, and the ministry, had been superseded by the nouveau riche in the late nineteenth-century; or, if their own status had been rising, they were still dissatisfied with it in relation to the power of others. Increasingly, then, they entered politics with a determination to give to the "best people" the kind of influence in government that they ought to have. Such a view, when accepted, tends to take the gloss off the picture of heroic and self-denying reformers.

Another interpretation, associated especially with George E. Mowry, has stressed the middle-class origins of the progressive leaders. There can really be no doubt of these origins, but a number of scholars in recent years have shown that the conservatives, as well, came from the middle class and were quite similar in religion, education, and the like. The middle-class explanation is helpful in describing the progressives, but it does not adequately explain why particular people went to the left of the political road and others to the right of the road in their philosophy and affiliations. Heredity, environment, and special circumstances all contributed, rather obviously, to the makeup of any individual.

What of the upper class? It is perfectly apparent that many of this group went into government with a fine intention of public service. Samuel P. Hays, however, has made the point that in some places businessmen or members of a professional elite were aiming to make government function more efficiently. This often meant a kind of class government rather than turning governmental powers over to the people generally or sponsoring actions to enhance democracy. The role of businessmen in the period is much better understood as a result, particularly, of the work done by Robert H. Wiebe. There was no monolithic bloc of businessmen either for or against progressivism. They differed greatly among themselves, often on the basis of regional location or perhaps the size of their firm. Many in the business community were well educated and, on some subjects, fair and enlightened. Those most likely to give strong and continuing support to the progressive movement were businessmen of an independent type, who could afford to speak and act freely.

What of the working class, including those of recent foreign extraction? The wage earners, like the farmers and businessmen, were affected not a little by what they conceived to be in the interest of their own group. Since they were primarily city dwellers, and poor, they wanted help in the form of better working and living conditions, better pay, and a friendly attitude from city hall. They were not concerned as much with "good government" as were the middle-class Protestant reformers. If a boss seemed to be on their side, they were likely to give him support in spite of his notoriety. They opposed prohibition for its interference with personal liberty. They saw nothing wrong with a drink of whiskey or beer. They opposed "blue laws" and woman suffrage. Nevertheless, there was much in the broad spectrum of progressive reform to which workers gave their approval. J. Joseph Huthmacher and John D. Buenker are among those who have demonstrated that in states like Massachusetts, New York, and Illinois the contribution of workers and people of immigrant stock was great indeed.

Catholic leaders were emerging in this period, and many of them added their weight to the progressive cause. It was far from negligible. There was, for example, Mark Fagan of New Jersey, whose parents were Irish and very poor. Fagan went on to become, in 1901, the mayor of Jersey City on the Republican ticket. Skeptical-minded Lincoln Steffens, after studying Fagan and his administration in 1909, finally decided that he understood the mayor. He was "a Christian, a literal Christian, . . . a giver of kindness, sympathy, love." This "gentle man" had proven that he could grapple with modern problems and govern both effectively and honestly. James D. Phelan of San Francisco, Thomas J. Walsh of Montana, Charles McCarthy of Wisconsin, Edward F. Dunne of Illinois, and Alfred E. Smith of New York were some others of the Irish Catholic group.

The progressive movement, then, was broad and encompassing. Very little about it could be explained simply. The great impetus came from the city (although agrarian influences were important, too, especially in the South and West). From the city it moved to the states and from the states to the federal government; but a certain give and take could be found at all times, as might be expected in the American federal system. Without any question, the whole movement picked up in excitement when a new President moved into the White House in September 1901. For this leader from New York, still in his early forties, was known for dash and vigor, and as governor of his state had made a record that could be termed progressive.

SUGGESTIONS FOR ADDITIONAL READING

Major interpretive works on the phenomenon of progressivism include a variety of assessments, old and new, sympathetic and critical; most are quite readable: See Benjamin P. De Witt, *The Progressive Movement*, Macmillan, New York, 1915; Harold U. Faulkner, *The Quest for Social Justice, 1898–1914*, Macmillan, New York, 1931; John Chamberlain, *Farewell to Reform*, Liveright, New York, 1932; Richard Hofstadter, *The Age of Reform, From Bryan to F.D.R.*, Knopf, New York, 1955; Russel B. Nye, *Midwestern Progressive Politics, 1870–1958*, Michigan State Univ. Press, East Lansing, 1959; David W. Noble, *The Progressive Mind, 1890–1917*, Rand McNally, Chicago, 1970; and Gabriel Kolko, *The Triumph of Conservatism: A Reinterpretation of American History, 1900–1916*, Free Press, New York, 1963. See also the following books, mentioned previously: Henry May, *Protestant Churches and Industrial America* (1949), Eric Goldman, *Rendez-vous with Destiny* (1952), Samuel P. Hays, *The Response to Industrialism* (1957), Robert Wiebe, *The Search for Order* (1967), and George Mowry, *The Era of Theodore Roosevelt* (1958). Mowry's *Theodore Roosevelt and the Progressive Movement*, Univ. of Wisconsin Press, Madison, 1947, and *The California Progressives*, Univ. of California Press, Berkeley, 1951, helped to place him in the forefront among scholars of modern reform. His later writing along with that of Richard Hofstadter, did much to establish the "middle-class interpretation" of progressivism, although in recent years that interpretation has been seriously challenged. A "lower-class interpretation" has been delineated by J. Joseph Huthmacher, for example, in *Senator Robert F. Wagner and the Rise of Urban Liberalism*, Atheneum, New York, 1968, and in his articles published earlier; also by John D. Buenker, *Urban Liberalism and Progressive Reform*, Scribner, New York, 1973. See also the various articles on progressivism published during the 1960s in *Mid-America* (Chicago).

Turning to the specialized and thematic works, Samuel P. Hays, *Conserva-tion and the Gospel of Efficiency: The Progressive Conservation Movement, 1890–1920,* Harvard, Cambridge, Mass., 1959, is indispensable for its subject, though didactic in tone. Samuel Haber, *Efficiency and Uplift: Scientific Manage-ment in the Progressive Era, 1890–1920,* Univ. of Chicago Press, 1964, traces the development of a fascinating movement. Robert H. Wiebe, *Businessmen and Reform: A Study of the Progressive Movement,* Harvard, Cambridge, Mass., 1962, is excellent. No comparable monograph for labor is available, but Irwin Yellowitz, *Labor and the Progressive Movement in New York State, 1897–1916,* Cornell, Ithaca, N.Y., 1965, has broad implications. Roy Lubove, *The Progressives and the Slums: Tenement House Reform in New York City, 1890–1917,* Univ. of Pittsburgh Press, Pittsburgh, 1962, is an able study of the leading attempt to achieve housing reform. Similarly valuable is Allen F. Davis, *Spearheads for Reform: The Social Settlements and the Progressive Movement,* 1890–1914, Oxford Univ. Press, New York, 1967, and his *American Heroine: The Life and Legend of Jane Addams,* Oxford, 1973. James H. Timberlake, *Prohibition and the Progressive Movement, 1900–1920,* Harvard, Cambridge, Mass., 1966, treats the prohibition movement as an integral part of progressivism, with its urge toward human betterment. Louis Filler, *Crusaders for American Liberalism,* Antioch Press, Yellow Springs, Ohio, 1939, is a readable and far-ranging account of the muckrakers. An interesting analysis of the leading muckraker is Justin Kaplan, *Lincoln Steffens: A Biography,* Simon and Schuster, New York, 1974. Suggestive of the many valuable books dealing with progressivism, at least in part, are the following: Eleanor Flexner, *Century of Struggle: The Woman's Rights Movement in the United States,* Harvard, Cambridge, Mass., 1959; Aileen S. Kraditor, *The Ideas of the Woman Suffrage Movement, 1890–1920,* Columbia, New York, 1965; Lawrence A. Cremin, *The Transformation of the School: Progressivism in American Education, 1876–1957,* Knopf, New York, 1961; and David A. Shannon, *The Socialist Party of America: A History,* Macmillan, New York, 1955.

State and regional studies, often biographical, are numerous. For the South, the student might begin with C. Vann Woodward, *Origins of the New South, 1877–1913,* Louisiana State Univ. Press, Baton Rouge, 1951; Jack Temple Kirby, *Darkness at the Dawning: Race and Reform in the Progressive South,* Lippincott, Philadelphia, 1972, and Dewey W. Grantham, *Hoke Smith and the Politics of the New South,* Louisiana State Univ. Press, Baton Rouge, 1958. Earl S. Pomeroy, *The Pacific Slope,* Knopf, New York, 1965, is particularly valuable on California, Oregon, and Washington. For the states generally the number of scholarly books has been increasing, although many states are still not covered. See Richard M. Abrams, *Conservatism in a Progressive Era: Massachusetts Politics, 1900–1912,* Harvard, Cambridge, Mass., 1964; Robert F. Wesser, *Charles Evans Hughes: Politics and Reform in New York, 1905–1910,* Cornell, Ithaca, N.Y., 1967; Hoyt L. Warner, *Progressivism in Ohio, 1897–1917,* Ohio State Univ. Press, Columbus, 1964; and Robert S. Maxwell, *La Follette and the Rise of the Progressives in Wisconsin,* State Historical Society of Wisconsin, Madison, 1956. Aspects of bossism and urban reform can be found in Melvin G. Holli, *Reform in Detroit: Hazen S. Pingree and Urban Politics,* Oxford Univ. Press, New York, 1969; Jack Tager, *The Intellectual as Urban Reformer: Brand Whitlock and the Progressive*

Movement, Press of Case Western Reserve, Cleveland, 1968; Walton E. Bean, *Boss Ruef's San Francisco,* Univ. of California Press, Berkeley, 1952; Joel A. Tarr, *A Study in Boss Politics: William Lorimer of Chicago,* Univ. of Illinois Press, Urbana, 1971; and Harold Zink, *City Bosses in the United States,* Duke, Durham, North Carolina, 1930. The last is a fascinating look at the leadership in many cities.

Herbert Croly, *The Promise of American Life* (1909), previously mentioned, is one of the best contemporary works, noted for its theoretical and philosophical quality. Walter Weyl, *The New Democracy,* Macmillan, New York, 1912, and Walter Lippmann, *Drift and Mastery,* Kennerley, New York, 1914, are similar attempts to understand the new American society and to help give it direction. Another classic of a different type is Ray Stannard Baker, *Following the Color Line: An Account of Negro Citizenship in the American Democracy,* Doubleday, New York, 1908.

Chapter 4

Theodore Roosevelt and American Society

In December 1907, the President of the United States sounded a familiar note on the need for decency and morality among his fellow citizens. He wrote to a friend: "One of the chief things I have tried to preach to the American politician, and the American businessman, is not to grasp at money, place, power, or enjoyment in any form, simply because he can probably get it, without regard to considerations of morality and national interest—which means the interest of the neighbor, for the nation is simply all of our neighbors combined." Such ideas of Theodore Roosevelt might seem conventional, but they were passionately held and frequently were acted upon with a great sense of the dramatic.

Roosevelt had in mind the sober purpose of welding his people together, of enhancing social cohesion and social responsibility. His morality was not simply a matter of old-fashioned religion or ethical behavior. One of his many admirers, the Emporia, Kansas, newsman William Allen White, stated rather extravagantly in 1910: "Perhaps Mr. Roosevelt is wrong in some of his tenets. But, right or wrong, he has inspired more men to righteousness in public life than a millionaire could call forth with all the millions of Wall Street. And all the King's horses can't pull Americans back to the lower idea of the last century. The gain is permanent."

The inspirational impact of this twenty-fifth President was a very real thing. Ideas were weapons with Theodore Roosevelt. Preeminently he was a man of *action,* determined to get results with the Congress, with businessmen, labor leaders, and others. At the same time, he knew the art of compromise; he was one of the greatest politicians in American history during his eight years in the presidency. The same cannot be said of his post-Presidential years when his faulty judgment led him to commit horrendous blunders. Few have done so much in one lifetime to build up a political party and then to break it down again; or to give Americans a sense of such pride and unity only to help destroy it.

Born in New York City in 1858, Roosevelt inherited both wealth and a tradition of public service. The family had enjoyed good fortune for generations, on both his mother's and father's side, and eventually TR received some $200,000 from his father's estate. Hardly less important was the heritage of a distinguished ancestry, including merchants, bankers, planters, manufacturers, physicians, lawyers, clergymen, two members of the United States Senate, a governor of Georgia, and many others. Long before Roosevelt's birth his ancestors had acquired the habit of gracious and comfortable living. They believed in public service and conscientiously performed many tasks for the towns, colonies, and states of America (and for the Southern Confederacy on his mother's side). As a bright young man and a budding author, Roosevelt knew and was proud of the traditions mentioned. Noblesse oblige was a part of his inheritance.

Roosevelt's struggle for health in his early years is a familiar story. Not so well known is the encouragement he had from loving and doting parents who gave him every advantage, including the desire to develop his talents. The most important schooling he received was in the family, from his father, from private tutors, and from the experience of wide travel in the United States and abroad. In a book on Woodrow Wilson's early years, Harry W. Bragdon has strikingly compared Wilson's boyhood with that of Theodore Roosevelt, noting that each had indulgent parents; each had a strong father; and each came to some sort of crisis about the age of twelve because of their sheltered lives. Both were dreamers of great dreams, and somehow both found the capacity to move into a world of competition outside the home and to make their dreams a reality. At the age of ten TR toured in Europe, and several years later he spent many months on the Continent, living for a time in Dresden and learning some German and French. Such privileges did not have the effect of turning Roosevelt against his own country but helped to convince him, rather, of how great America was and could yet become. Of no small importance was the young man's passion for nature study. This awakened his interest in the flora and fauna of many lands and in every part of the United States.

Roosevelt left home for Harvard College in 1876 with the idea that he would continue his study of natural history and become a scientist. But other interests quickly developed, both in his studies and outside the classroom. Most impressive of all, he started a book in his senior year while carrying his regular work with honors, and he published the volume some two years after graduation. A naval history of the War of 1812, this project reflected a lifelong interest in the Navy and things military. One more step in his formal education remained. He studied law for a time at Columbia College in his home city of New York. Meanwhile, TR got married. While a student at Harvard, he met Alice Hathaway Lee, a Boston girl whom he considered the "sweetest, prettiest sunniest little darling that ever lived." Family doubts had to be overcome, but this was not too difficult, and at the age of twenty-two Roosevelt entered a short but blissful marriage.

To marry young was not unusual among the well-to-do, but to enter politics, at the bottom of the ladder, was unusual. TR joined the Republican club in his New York City district, mingled with the politicians, and in 1881 was nominated and elected to the State Assembly. Thus his political career was launched. He would run for mayor of New York in 1886 (unsuccessfully), serve in the Civil Service Commission under Benjamin Harrison and Grover Cleveland, become a police commissioner in New York City, join the McKinley administration as Assistant Secretary of the Navy, and go on to be Governor of New York, Vice President of the United States, and President—all by the age of forty-three.

His rapid rise was interrupted by personal tragedy and a temporary departure from public life. Almost incredibly, his young wife died of Bright's disease, following childbirth, on the same day that his mother died of typhoid fever, on February 14, 1884. The shock was severe, but Roosevelt's devotion to duty and powers of discipline are apparent in his early return to work at Albany. TR commented: "It was a grim and evil fate, but I have never believed it did any good to flinch or yield for any blow, nor does it lighten the blow to cease from working."

In the summer of 1884 Roosevelt went to Dakota Territory and stayed for two years. When he lived the life of a cattleman and adventurer, riding, roping, and fighting, sharing in the joys and dangers of the Great West, he truly captured the national imagination. Every American was, vicariously, a "Westerner." Now Roosevelt would be known through his books on the West and perhaps the newspaper stories of his exploits. Never again could he be thought of as merely an Eastern dude or a New Yorker.

Roosevelt was not a shrewdly calculating man, making all the necessary moves to reach the Presidency. For the most part, he was living his own life, as he wanted to live it. He was also lucky. Yet somehow the "damn cowboy," as Mark Hanna later called him, was beginning to understand what the times required in America. They called for higher standards in public office, for honesty and devoted service. But idealism was not enough. The leader must be practical, too, and brave. No better way could have been found to prove one's courage and practical virtues than to live on the frontier for a time, to plunge into local politics with men of the "roughneck" variety, and to lead a charge in the Spanish-American War. On a jungle trail in Cuba, in 1898, a Spanish bullet missed TR's head, hitting a tree nearby and filling his "eyes and ears with tiny splinters." Such adventures made him a hero. When he returned to New York from Cuba, the situation in the GOP politically favored his selection for the gubernatorial race. Just as the politicians needed him inside the state in 1898, they wanted him out of the state two years later. This desire helped to give him the vice-presidential nomination with McKinley. "Teddy's luck" was demonstrated most clearly in 1901, when the President died of an assassin's bullet. Roosevelt now had his great opportunity.

A recent book on Roosevelt's gubernatorial career, by G. Wallace Chessman, has emphasized the continuity of his ideas. It seems apparent that TR did not, as has often been stated in the past, undergo drastic changes after reaching the White House. His basic beliefs about character, duty, and service were formed early in his life. His political techniques came largely from experiences of the 1880s, when he served in the legislature, ran for mayor of New York, and thought seriously about politics and qualities of leadership. Significantly, he decided in 1884 to support James G. Blaine for President, in spite of previous doubts about his character. He refused to join the Mugwumps when they bolted the ticket, and he continued thereafter to be "regular" in his state and national career until he formed the Progressive party in 1912. Roosevelt was clearly a reform governor when he reached that high office in 1898. Chessman writes: "Broadly conceived in the interests of the people, the Roosevelt program rested firmly upon the concept of the square deal by a neutral state. Neither political machines, nor great corporations, nor any group or individual with a special objective endangering the general good should dictate policy."

How did Roosevelt come to such a view? Undoubtedly he did so in considerable part because he lived in the state of New York, where a heterogeneity of interests virtually compelled politicians to avoid a nar-

Figure 9   The New President. (*From a photograph in* Collier's Weekly, *September 21, 1901.*)

row or parochial policy. Still, Roosevelt had his own ideas. They help, very considerably, to explain his public policies as governor, President, and ex-President.

In his penetrating book *The Republican Roosevelt,* John M. Blum has stated: "If Roosevelt had any supreme belief it was in character, individual character and national character." A later generation may conclude that some of the Rooseveltian preachments were strange indeed, if not ridiculous, but essentially he was calling for a greater people and a greater country. He was also doing his best to arouse his fellow citizens by personal example. Roosevelt once wrote to Augustus Saint-Gaudens, the sculptor: "I am very proud of America and very jealous of American achievement." He did not mean, he emphasized, "mere material achievement," if "taken purely by itself." That was hardly worthwhile. Roosevelt reacted strongly against the "money-grubbers" of his day, those businessmen who could not see beyond the dollar sign. Also New York's Four Hundred, or the idle rich of the time, were degenerates of a sort. The rich, whose power was based almost entirely on wealth, had little attraction for him. Roosevelt wrote: "I do not see very much of the big-moneyed men in New York, simply because very few of them possess the traits which would make them companionable to me, or would make me feel that it was worthwhile dealing with them. To spend the day with them at Newport, or on one of their yachts, or even to dine with them save under exceptional circumstances, fills me with frank horror."

In his discussion of women and their place in American society, Roosevelt did not appear at his most convincing. Yet these ideas help to reveal his basic beliefs and his "strenuosity" on the subject of improving American society. TR believed fervently that woman's place was in the home, that she had a duty to bear children and to raise them with love and wisdom. The husband's responsibility, also, was primarily to his family, though he must act in a somewhat different capacity as provider and protector. He must play a specific role, according to the requirements of honor and duty, as his wife must also. Roosevelt was not so old-fashioned, or anti-intellectual, as to say that women should not be allowed to develop their abilities and tastes. But, first of all, they had a duty to the nation and to the "race." TR worried greatly that the birth rate was diminishing at the turn of the century. Nothing could be more disastrous than to commit racial suicide.

As he perceived the women of his day (1902), they evinced far too frequently an "easy, good-natured kindliness, and a desire to be independent." This was in no sense an adequate substitute for the "fundamental virtues." Writing to Hamlin Garland, in 1903, he elaborated on the subject: "The pangs of childbirth make all men the debtors of all women. . . . A race whose men will not work and will not fight ought to die out, and unless it will either work or fight it generally does die out. And of course if the women flinch from breeding the deserved death of the race takes place even quicker." He had only contempt for those who failed in their duty, assuming they lacked a reasonable excuse. By the same token, he honored "beyond measure" those who were willing to do their "full duty" in life.

The duty to work and achieve, in TR's view, applied equally to palefaces of the East and redskins of the West. In his *Hunting Trips of a Ranchman* (1885), Roosevelt asserted that the Western Indians had no real claim to the land, for they were nomads and had themselves butchered previous occupants. Neither red men nor white men had the right to retain the land and resources, unless they used them productively. Those who failed to work would "perish from the face of the earth." Cruel though it seemed, this doctrine was "just and rational." Mercy "to a few" at "the cost of justice to the many" was totally unwarranted. The Indians could find little comfort in that philosophy.

Roosevelt was intrigued with the subject of "race" and with ethnic or national characteristics. Often his ideas were fascinating. He was a variety of the Darwinist type, believing in superior and inferior peoples and a struggle for survival. Such thinking could easily degenerate into the rankest kind of prejudice, discrimination, and brutality. With Roosevelt it did not. To him the "Anglo-Saxons" were a superior people, but this was a matter of environment or opportunity, rather than heredity. Color did not matter greatly to him, or religion, or customs that were somewhat strange. He greatly admired the Japanese, for example, as a vigorous, efficient, and talented people. He valued an individual, of any kind, who had the courage and ability to prove himself. Once he declared: "I cannot consent to take the position that the door of hope—the door of opportunity—is to be shut upon any man, no matter how unworthy, purely upon the grounds of race or color." Again, rejecting the test of color, he pointed out that the people of Northern Europe, fair-skinned, blond, or red-haired, had been the barbarians in Roman times. They had changed and other people, too, could change and progress.

Anti-Semitism was widespread at the turn of the century, and Roosevelt was accused of sharing in this prejudice. He denied it, claiming that he treated the Jews "precisely and exactly as I treat other Americans." By implication, he was somewhat patronizing, although his purpose seems to have been that of recognizing the Jews and giving them the rewards they ought to have. Obviously, political benefits would also be forthcoming for Roosevelt and his party. He once wrote that it would be "a particularly good thing for men of the Jewish race to develop that side of them which I might call the Maccabee or fighting Jewish type." They had obviously been successful in business, and their "high-minded" philanthropy was well known. "Unreasoning prejudice" against them would be reduced, however, if they also participated more conspicuously in "rough and manly" work that must be done. Partly for that reason, while police commissioner in New York City, he had encouraged Jews to enter the force. Roosevelt got considerable pleasure from the way he had handled one speaker in the city who was notoriously anti-Semitic. TR assigned forty Jewish policemen to protect the man during his visit.

A question that plagued Roosevelt throughout his Presidency was that of blacks in the South. The New Yorker was a product of the Civil War generation and of a Republican party that took, rather seriously, the problems of the black people, recently freed from slavery. More than most, Roosevelt remained loyal to idealistic slogans of his party, and to principles of the thirteenth, fourteenth, and fifteenth amendments. On becoming President, he was immediately confronted with the necessity to make decisions that did not always square with his noble professions. Like others of his time, Roosevelt considered the race problem primarily a Southern affair, although national leaders like himself must share occasionally in the agony of decision making.

Roosevelt puzzled over the questions involved. Some things that happened were shameful. They damaged the image of America that he sincerely cherished. He simply could not understand the extremes of racial prejudice that made even a moderately liberal action on his part intolerable to the racial bigots and would-be lynchers. In a Memorial Day address of 1902 Roosevelt declared: "From time to time there occur in our country, to the deep and lasting shame of our people, lynchings carried out under circumstances of inhuman cruelty and barbarity."

In a long letter to Lyman Abbott of *Outlook,* the President gave a discerning analysis of the racial problem, in its several dimensions. There was in the South a large group determined to keep the blacks subservient and, in fact, to reintroduce a "form of serfage or slavery." They hated and despised the blacks but, at the same time, were determined to exploit their labor. To drive the blacks out of the trades was a part of their effort, and they were determined to keep the black people from rising "in any way." Unfortunately, the "absence of protest from the north" had gone a long way toward encouraging this white element in the Southern states. Roosevelt saw little to do immediately except to try and alleviate the problem through specific actions; and he praised highly, for example, a federal judge in the South, whom he had appointed, and whose decisions against the evils of peonage were gratifying.

Looking back, it is easy to find fault with Roosevelt on the race question. For example, he invited Booker T. Washington to the White House in 1901 and never had him back again, after being lashed by criticism from Southern whites. He was always torn between his desire to win friends among the white Southerners and his hope to do something for the Afro-American, whom he knew had been treated most unjustly. Roosevelt did, in fact, form a political alliance with Booker Washington, calling upon him for advice concerning federal appointments in the South. A few blacks actually won appointments. The race, as a whole, however, did not have cause to be happy with Roosevelt or his administration.

Roosevelt's worst mistake occurred in dealing with the so-called Brownsville riot in the summer and fall of 1906. Members of a black regiment stationed at Fort Brown in Texas on the Rio Grande River had been involved in several disputes with local residents, who were bitterly opposed to the presence of black soldiers. On the night of August 13, shortly after midnight, someone started firing guns outside the fort. Apparently all the soldiers were inside the walls and were not responsible, but on the basis of evidence presented by the mayor of Brownsville and a few local citizens, a group of black soldiers were said to have shot up the town, killing one man and injuring a police officer. The white commanding officer decided that some of his men were indeed responsible. No soldiers could be found, however, who seemed to know anything about the affair.

Without a trial and on the basis of facts that were disputed, Roosevelt decided to discharge the entire regiment, about 160 men. If they had been white, he said, he would have taken the same action. To him it was unthinkable that anyone wearing the uniform of the United States Army should refuse to reveal what he knew about such an incident. Since none would speak, they must all be punished, receiving a dishonorable discharge. Meanwhile the soldiers found champions, not only in the black community but in the United States Senate and elsewhere. Roosevelt was forced on the defensive. He eventually retreated somewhat and permitted his discharge order to be rescinded in particular instances.

Whatever the President's failures regarding racial matters, it would have been difficult to find any white person at the time who could have given more enlightened leadership. In theory at least—and often in practice—Roosevelt was a defender of an open society, based on individual ability.

Even more important than the racial problem, in Roosevelt's mind, was that of capital and labor. Like many public men and women of his generation, the New Yorker had a "horror of anarchy and disorder and pandering to the mob"; but he deplored, no less, economic injustice, the repression of workers, and the fact that the "most cultivated and refined men," with some exceptions, were not interested in the "masses" of the great cities or their problems. Roosevelt, in other words, was wise enough to choose the middle way. He denounced the "dull, purblind folly of the very rich men"; those who were greedy and arrogant and who protected themselves carefully by hiring the ablest lawyers. On the other hand, doctrines of socialism seemed to him extremely pernicious. The reformation of society must come primarily from the development of qualities in the heart and mind, from individual initiative and achievement. A socialist society, in his view, would make this impossible. To Philander Knox, formerly his Attorney General, Roosevelt wrote on November 10, 1904: "It would be a dreadful calamity if we saw this country divided into two parties, one containing the bulk of the property owners and conservative people, the other the bulk of the wageworkers and the less prosperous people generally; each party insisting upon demanding much that was wrong, and each party sullen and angered by real and fancied grievances." To avoid such a catastrophe the friends of established government must pursue a policy that was just and farsighted. Obviously Roosevelt thought he was doing precisely that.

In his attitude toward "bigness," toward corporations and labor unions notably, TR was ahead of his time. He recognized the impossibility and the futility of breaking up the industrial or commercial corporations. To regulate them, however, and to chastise an occasional lawbreaker was quite another matter. The actions he brought against the Northern Securities Company and a few other combinations were sufficiently successful—and well publicized—to give him the reputation of "trustbuster," even though it was not deserved.

William H. Harbaugh has convincingly described Roosevelt's developing liberalism on the question of organized labor. He was far more sympathetic to workers in the period of his Presidency than he had been earlier. The White House was easily accessible to union leaders such as Samuel Gompers of the American Federation of Labor and John Mitchell of the United Mine Workers. TR came to believe that large unions were necessary and that working conditions must be improved through employers' liability laws, eight-hour laws, and the like. Collective bargaining had his support, although he never really accepted the idea of a closed shop or union shop. He believed that the individual worker or "hold-out" should also be protected in his right *not* to join a union. Court injunctions used against labor were important in this period and damaging in their consequences. Roosevelt objected strongly to the injunctions, if employed by judges against the legitimate and peaceful activities of employees. But what was legitimate? Roosevelt's position remained ambiguous, particularly since he had no hesitancy in attacking Eugene Debs or others whom he considered radical and dangerous. Most workers had a different conception of a dangerous radical.

Roosevelt could not please everyone. But he had all the qualities necessary to be successful as a President in the first years of the twentieth century. Even his weaknesses, by later standards, were such as to increase his popularity in his own time. He was eminently human. He was vigorous, patriotic, nationalistic. He was well informed, with excellent skills as a writer and speaker. He tried sincerely to solve national problems and to serve as an arbiter among conflicting groups. The people of America yearned for a leader to match their own aspirations, and in Theodore Roosevelt they found him.

SUGGESTIONS FOR ADDITIONAL READING

For two contemporary views of an "organic" society, with which Roosevelt agreed, see Edward A. Ross, *Sin and Society: An Analysis of Latter-Day Iniquity*, Houghton Mifflin, Boston, 1907, and Herbert Croly, *The Promise of American Life* (1909), previously mentioned. E. Digby Baltzell, *The Protestant Establishment: Aristocracy & Caste in America*, Knopf, New York, 1964, develops the thesis that Roosevelt, a member of the aristocracy, believed in the necessity of opportunity for all groups in the society, as did Franklin D. Roosevelt and many others.

Leonard D. White, *The Republican Era*, mentioned earlier, gives a good treatment of growth and change in the federal government and therefore of the situation that Roosevelt found on becoming President. Howard K. Beale, *Theodore Roosevelt and the Rise of America to World Power*, Johns Hopkins, Baltimore, 1956, contains a cogent discussion of TR's personal qualities and attitudes on race.

Roosevelt has been fortunate in his biographers, although the brilliant Henry F. Pringle treated him with some amusement and sarcasm in *Theodore Roosevelt: A Biography*, Harcourt, Brace, New York, 1931. Later scholars have taken TR seriously and rated him as a "great" or "very good" President. See G. Wallace Chessman, *Governor Theodore Roosevelt: The Albany Apprenticeship, 1898–1900*, Harvard, Cambridge, Mass., 1965; the works of George E. Mowry, mentioned earlier; John M. Blum, *The Republican Roosevelt*, Harvard, Cambridge, Mass., 1954; and William Henry Harbaugh, *Power and Responsibility: The Life and Times of Theodore Roosevelt*, Farrar, Straus & Cudahy, New York, 1961. Blum's book is a notable, succinct interpretation of Roosevelt, concentrating on the Presidency, by one who helped edit the Roosevelt papers. That editing project also led to a gold mine of information in Elting E. Morison (ed.), *The Letters of Theodore Roosevelt*, 8 vols., Harvard, Cambridge, Mass., 1951–1954. A critical essay on Roosevelt may be found in Richard Hofstadter, *The American Political Tradition and the Men Who Made It*, Knopf, New York, 1948. Dewey W. Grantham, "Theodore Roosevelt in American Historical Writing, 1945–1960," *Mid-America*, vol. 43, pp. 3–35, January 1961, is a thoughtful review of the literature.

Roosevelt's difficulties with the race question have recently been examined in Ann J. Lane, *The Brownsville Affair: National Crisis and Black Reaction*, Kennikat Press, Port Washington, N.Y., 1971. But see also Richard B. Sherman, *The Republican Party and Black America: From McKinley to Hoover, 1896–1933*, Univ. Press of Virginia, Charlottesville, 1973. A warm and informative family history is Hermann Hagedorn, *The Roosevelt Family of Sagamore Hill*, Macmillan, New York, 1954.

Chapter 5

Roosevelt and Executive Power

Theodore Roosevelt is famous, most of all, as a powerful, free-wheeling Chief Executive. Undoubtedly he influenced directly such successors as Woodrow Wilson and Franklin D. Roosevelt; and, in a general sense, he has contributed immensely to modern conceptions of the presidency. In particular spheres of activity, including the conservation of natural resources, he was highly influential, and that subject will receive attention in this chapter, while his attitudes on foreign policy and major actions in that field will be treated in a later section. One method of gaining insights into the Roosevelt years is to look at Congress during his two terms. To what extent did TR manage to dominate that body, and to what extent was he compelled to issue executive orders, to talk, and to "preach," because of his actual inability to control the Congress or its formidable leaders, of both parties? Without question, Roosevelt was inhibited, impeded, and occasionally tomahawked by the legislative leaders of government.

From 1897 to 1911 both houses of Congress were under the control of Republicans, while the Presidents (McKinley, Roosevelt, and Taft) were also of the Republican party. Horace Samuel and Marion Merrill in a recent book, *The Republican Command,* have emphasized strongly the significance of congressional leaders. Such men as Nelson Aldrich and Joseph Cannon could not be dominated by Roosevelt, although they found, as he did, that compromise was often desirable. On questions of foreign policy, notably, the President had advantages. In questions of appointment, at the policy levels, he also had much in his favor. When things could be done by executive action, as they often could, Roosevelt made the maximum use of his authority. When he needed money, however, he had to look to Congress. The creation of new agencies, appropriations for the Army and Navy, and many other matters required that the President work with and cultivate the members of Congress. He was more than willing to do this, on most occasions.

Four men were acknowledged leaders of the Senate in the early 1900s. They and their colleagues exercised considerably more power than did the House of Representatives until the year 1903, when Joe Cannon of Danville, Illinois, assumed the position of Speaker. Cannon declared that the House had been slighted too long, and he did this to the resounding cheers of his fellow representatives. A changed relationship was soon apparent between the two houses of Congress, while Roosevelt had no illusions about the sources of legislative power.

The real leader of the Senate group was Nelson Aldrich of Rhode Island. Aldrich was a man of superior ability, as were others of his inner circle—William B. Allison of Iowa, Orville H. Platt of Connecticut, and John C. Spooner of Wisconsin. They worked well together, complementing each other's abilities. They dominated the major committees, and little could be done without them. Most of these were old men near the end of their careers. Only Aldrich would continue on into the Taft administration. But they had lieutenants whose views were similar and who would carry on, or try to do so, against a rising opposition. One lesser member of the Senate Old Guard, Thomas C. Platt of New York, wrote to Senator Allison: "I consider the interests of the government as embodied in you and Senator Aldrich. What you say goes. Kindly keep me posted as to what you do, so that I may not go astray."

Nelson Aldrich served in the Senate from 1881 to 1911, and he represented preeminently the business interests of the Northeast. He had been a businessman in a Rhode Island mill town before leaving to serve briefly in the Union army. Back on the job, he soon married well and his business activities expanded. Most of his wealth accumulated after he entered the Senate. Aldrich formed close associations with Wall Street interests and was a good friend of J. P. Morgan. The two were, in fact, much alike—intelligent, arrogant, and formidable. Both enjoyed travel and were collectors of art objects. Senator Aldrich, like most politicians, had a charming manner when he wished to use it; he was a handsome and graceful man. Another characteristic was that he did not make speeches often on the Senate floor. Rather, he moved about, talking, persuading, arranging things. He had the capacity to yield a bit, to compromise to avoid defeat. Like the man in the White House (Roosevelt), he tended to be a political realist; he loved power and had no desire to lose everything over a minor point.

Aldrich had his weaknesses too. He knew little about the Middle West or West, and tended to be disdainful toward the American public. The people were noisy, excitable, and fickle. He avoided public appearances, hardly bothered to read the paper, and ignored most appeals and complaints that came in his mail. Some were bitter over the knowledge that this political chieftain, most powerful in Congress, came from the smallest state and that he and others were elected partly by controlling thinly populated rural districts, the "rotten boroughs."

By contrast with Aldrich, Platt of Connecticut was representative of industrial New England, rather than the financial districts. He was an expert on the tariff and business matters and occupied positions on key committees. A much-admired man, he died in 1905. William B. Allison of Iowa had the greatest influence of any Senator from the Middle West. He understood his state and region and advised Aldrich capably. Senator Allison was closely associated with railroad interests of the Western United States but somehow managed to avoid unfavorable publicity. Even so, by the time he died in 1908 his influence had lessened because of the rising progressive movement, in which his own state played a significant role. The fourth member of this powerful Senate group was John C. Spooner of Wisconsin, a product of the Republican machine against whom Robert M. La Follette had rebelled. Spooner had talent in abundance. He was a lawyer of outstanding ability and an adviser to Aldrich, who knew very little about legal matters. Spooner also was quick-witted, logical, and a very able debater—some thought the ablest in the Senate. Gradually, however, Spooner lost influence because of the La Follette movement in Wisconsin. In 1907, two years before his term was to expire, he resigned his Senate seat and went to New York, where he was a corporation lawyer for many years.

By the end of Roosevelt's two terms, only Aldrich remained of the four senatorial leaders mentioned. But new lieutenants joined him. There were, for example, Winthrop Murray Crane of Massachusetts, Stephen B. Elkins of West Virginia, and Eugene Hale of Maine. Thomas H. Carter of Montana and others like him, less well known, gave loyal support. Aldrich continued to be a formidable influence.

"Uncle Joe" Cannon has been described as a curious combination of a "city slicker" and a "rube." Alice Roosevelt Longworth once was scheduled to play poker with the Speaker, along with a group of friends. When she reported this to William Howard Taft, he warned her not to get "between Uncle Joe Cannon and a spittoon." This was not a joke, she discovered; the Speaker demanded a spittoon and used it frequently during the evening. Cannon was a likable man with a sense of humor but with very definite ideas on a number of subjects. He knew that the House of Representatives ought to function with him as a virtual dictator, and he knew what was good for the United States, no less than Theodore Roosevelt did. Born in 1836, Cannon had been a lawyer since 1858; the basis for his Old Guard Republicanism thus went back into the Civil War era. His experience in Illinois and his legal and business connections made him a spokesman for conservative interests typically found in towns and small cities. Where Aldrich represented Wall Street, Cannon represented Main Street. The tariff to him was almost sacred, and tampering with the American business structure was dangerous indeed.

If Theodore Roosevelt is judged by his relationship with the Big Four in the Senate and, to a lesser extent, with Cannon, his political caution and conservatism are apparent. His moralism was generously tempered with pragmatism. Soon after becoming President, he wrote Aldrich that he hated "to be a nuisance," but wanted very much to have him look over and criticize his message to Congress, then being prepared. Two years later, in a letter to Taft, the President defended Aldrich and the other Republican leaders in Congress: "You are unjust to Senator Aldrich. My experience for the last year and a half . . . has made me feel respect and regard for Aldrich as one of that group of Senators, including Allison, Hanna, Spooner, Platt, of Connecticut, Lodge and one or two others, who, together with men like the next Speaker of the House, Joe Cannon, are the most powerful factors in Congress." He went on to say that he sometimes disagreed with them, and he knew that some were closely associated with special interests. Nevertheless, "taken as a body, they are broad-minded and patriotic, as well as sagacious, skillful and resolute." It was necessary to fight with them at times, but they were men of honor, and could be induced to compromise. Working with them was easier than with the so-called reformers in Congress and the radicals.

In this opinion of 1903, Roosevelt was possibly influenced by the approaching presidential election and the necessity of holding the Republican ranks firm. But three years later he expressed a similar view, to the effect that he had been able to "get on very well" with Speaker Cannon over the past four years. He had experienced more difficulty with members of the Senate, a "less coherent body." In another letter of 1906 Roosevelt asserted that the House, under Cannon's leadership, had accomplished a "phenomenal amount of good work." And in a letter to Cannon himself he gave clear evidence of their relationship:

> Now, Uncle Joe, stand by me if you can [on a bank bill]. After you told me that the Appalachian forest reserve upon which I had set my heart simply was not to be considered, I acquiesced and took my medicine. For the last two years I have accepted your view as to just what we should say on the tariff—or rather as to what we should not say—and I am satisfied that it was wiser than the course I had intended to follow. Do help us out on this.

Toward weaker members of Congress, or those in a minority, Roosevelt was not so courteous and charitable. For example, he could hardly find the words to express his contempt for Senator Hale of Maine, who opposed an expansionist foreign policy. The President wrote: "No financier and mighty few mob leaders can be worse than a man like Senator Hale. He is of course an arrant physical coward, and this accounts for part of his gibbering fear of seeing the army or the navy efficient. . . . Down in his shriveled soul he would far rather see the nation kicked than see it fight to avoid being kicked; so there isn't any argument we can make that will appeal to him." Roosevelt explained that he had most of his trouble with the "puzzle-minded obstructionist," the "rancorous partisan," and the "unlicked demagogue." The conservatives on Capitol Hill, those "improperly insensitive to the influence of great corporations," were comparatively less difficult. Of course, he had to fight them too.

Roosevelt was contemptuous toward the Senate Democrats and especially those from the South. Benjamin R. Tillman of South Carolina, Joseph W. Bailey and Charles A. Culberson of Texas, John T. Morgan of Alabama, Augustus O. Bacon of Georgia, and Edward W. Carmack of Tennessee—these were singled out in one of his letters. They did "more harm to the country as a whole," he declared, than any Northern Senator who might be lacking in ability or distinctly corrupt. Southerners of the type mentioned played "the meanest and pettiest kind of personal partisan politics." They also "dragooned" other Democrats by charging them with being subservient to the Republicans. Roosevelt's strictures came partly from his inability to understand the South, to alter its racial patterns, or to win the votes of the region. Clearly he was himself a strong partisan.

In one outburst Roosevelt referred to Robert M. La Follette, then conducting a filibuster (1908), as "an entirely worthless Senator." In a more sober judgment, written to the English historian George Otto Trevelyan, the President said that he simply had to do the best he could with Congress. There were some avowed enemies of his in the Senate, like Arthur Pue Gorman of Maryland (a Democratic leader); and there was a whole "tribe of fat-witted" ones, headed by Bacon of Georgia. It was impossible, in the circumstances, to get more than one-third or half of what was desirable from these lawmakers. Still, his administration had accomplished a great deal.

On the last point, Roosevelt was quite correct. He maneuvered through the two houses some bills that helped considerably to modernize the United States government. In February 1903, a bill was passed establishing the Department of Commerce and Labor. Roosevelt used a trick, indicating that the Rockefellers were opposed to the bill, to get it through. Here in this department was a recognition of the new, complex problems of business and labor and of the need for better, more ethical business. Established within the department was the Bureau of Corporations, which concerned itself primarily with the abuses of big business. It received the authority to investigate problems relating to interstate business and proceeded to conduct studies and write reports of importance. From this source, for example, the President obtained some of his information on the railroad problem, contributing to an important measure of 1906. In somewhat the same way, the new Bureau studied the depletion of timber resources and found that approximately four-fifths of the standing timber had passed into the hands of private owners. Water power, too, and the growing concentration of control were the subject of an investigation.

Roosevelt asked for but did not obtain a major revision of the Sherman Antitrust law. Congress was willing to cooperate to the extent of adding staff and money for the prosecution of antitrust suits. Meanwhile, Roosevelt continued to spread his views about the necessity of government regulation. The great combinations were not necessarily "bad," but they must be brought under control. There should be a new commission, much more powerful than the Bureau of Corporations, which would exercise surveillance over business conducted across state lines.

The subject of railroads and their alleged malpractices demanded attention. Public concern had steadily mounted over a period of years. The Interstate Commerce Commission, dating from 1887, failed to solve the problem of high rates or of discriminatory rates as between particular shippers. The free pass (often handed out by railroad officials as a form of bribe) was another abuse. The high incidence of injuries, or deaths, among railroad employees was a further indication of the search for profit, even at the cost of human life. Figures from the ICC on railroad workers in 1901 showed that 1 of every 399 was killed and 1 in 26 was injured. Among those in the more dangerous jobs, such as firemen and brakemen, 1 of every 137 was killed and 1 of every 11 was injured. The interstate character of the railroads seemed to make the safety factor a matter for federal action.

But high rates and abuses in rate making attracted the most attention. Leaders in many states called upon the Congress to take action. Senator Jonathan P. Dolliver of Iowa, a major figure in the movement, commented that the Republicans would "lose nothing by standing for what the public wants and what the head of the Republican administration is urging." The House of Representatives also felt the public pressure, as indicated by the fact that seventeen rate bills were introduced in 1905–1906. Previously, in 1903, the Roosevelt administration had won a victory that satisfied almost no one. The Elkins Act of that year prohibited the railroads from giving rebates to favored shippers. But the law was difficult to enforce, and railroad officials were willing, in any event, not to give such rebates. An agitation soon followed that eventuated in the Hepburn Act of 1906, a measure of major importance. For the first time, the ICC gained genuine authority to regulate the rates. The Commission was enlarged from five to seven members. Its jurisdiction now included express companies, ferries, bridges, and pipelines—the last having become important in the developing petroleum industry. A uniform bookkeeping system was required of all interstate carriers. The issuance of free passes was forbidden. The Commission now enjoyed a significantly enlarged authority to reduce those rates found to be unreasonable. Formerly the burden of proof had rested upon the ICC, that is, to show that its orders were reasonable. Now, under the Hepburn Act, the burden was shifted to the railroads, should they take a ruling to court. The ICC ordered many reductions and was able to make them stick. A remaining source of contention was the "physical evaluation" of railroad properties. The President decided not to press for this provision, but without it—according to La Follette and some others in Congress—no government agency would possess the knowledge or the authority necessary to fix the rates where they truly ought to be.

Notwithstanding some criticism, Roosevelt performed admirably in obtaining the Hepburn Act of 1906. As he frequently did, he practiced the "art of the possible." He won the support of Old Guard leaders partly by offering to drop the idea of tariff reductions, which were not very important on his personal agenda. Cleverly, however, he used the possibility of tariff reform as a threat, over a period of many months, while other difficulties with Congress were being discussed. The President's maneuverings are analyzed in detail in John Blum's *Republican Roosevelt*, where Blum concludes that, by his "mastery of political devices, in contest with another master" (Aldrich), the President had reached his goal.

In this same period occurred the fight for another piece of

"consumer" legislation—the Pure Food and Drugs Act. A related provi-sion for federal inspection of meat products also passed in 1906 and the furor concerning it contributed to the success of the general legislation. Harvey W. Wiley, who led in this agitation over a period of years, was a chemist in the Department of Agriculture and had formerly been a state chemist in Indiana. He represented a growing group of specialists, including doctors, scientists, and public officials who believed that the time had come when protection must be provided for the buying public, through federal leadership. Many business groups, including the National Board of Trade, were advocates of higher standards and federal regula-tion. The quality of foods and drugs was by no means a new problem but industrialization had led to vastly increased production, shipment of commodities over long distances, and the use of new additives and preservatives—as well as entirely new products—that often created a health hazard. Patent medicines alone, which were consumed in enor-mous quantities, constituted a difficult question. The "medicine men" fought valiantly to protect their nostrums. Some liquor interests, too, who produced "rectified" products, were alarmed at the idea of federal inspection. Not a few business interests, for philosophical reasons in part, could not accept the notion of governmental interference in a sphere such as this. "Let the buyer beware" was a slogan long accepted in certain quarters of the business world.

Nevertheless, the advocates of regulation grew stronger. By 1905 several muckraking articles had helped to create popular support. Edward Bok, for example, published an article attacking patent medicines in *Ladies' Home Journal;* and Samuel Hopkins Adams entered the battle with articles in *Collier's.* Most important was the publication in 1906 of Upton Sinclair's *The Jungle,* which described an appallingly unsanitary situation in the packing houses of Chicago. Finally, Theodore Roosevelt brought his influence to bear. Ordering his own investigation of the packing industry, he decided that *The Jungle* was essentially correct; conditions were deplorable. Already a pure food bill had passed the Senate. Roosevelt, with his usual skills, helped to force a better measure through the House. More difficult was the effort to attain a meat inspection act, against strong opposition from the meat packers and their friends in the House. Continuing pressure from the President and threats to publish a new government exposé led to gratifying results. The measure of 1906 provided for a staff of inspectors under civil service rules. Any packing houses that refused to cooperate would fail to receive the government's stamp of approval. Given the public mood, and the decline of sales in meat products, the packers had to conform.

The basic legislation was the Pure Food and Drugs Act, which emphasized the branding of products and the listing of certain harmful ingredients. With Harvey Wiley as chief, the Bureau of Chemistry became the enforcement agency, and it developed an esprit de corps that was remarkable. The Bureau succeeded in improving the quality of foods, banning injurious preservatives, and checking some of the worst abuses in patent medicines. The deficiencies, however, were numerous. Cosmetics were not covered at all in the original act, and problems of administration and enforcement soon developed. Still, this was a significant beginning that led to periodic amendments and improvements and eventually to a new basic law of 1938 and the Food and Drug Administration.

Roosevelt's lack of success in obtaining some types of legislation may be attributed to the persistence of powerful opposition in Congress. As noted, he did not even try to reduce the tariff, for reasons that were partly political. There was "dynamite" in it, he once wrote. Such a question could tear his party apart and destroy any chance for constructive gains in connection with railroad reform or other matters. For similar reasons, he did not support a child-labor bill, strongly advocated by Senator Albert J. Beveridge of Indiana. Beveridge, in a passionate address of early 1907, exposed in graphic detail the atrocities of child labor in textile mills, coal mines, and elsewhere, affecting hundreds of thousands of children, many less than ten years old. A strong movement was beginning to develop for national action concerning the evil. But the opposition was much stronger. Roosevelt's friend Henry Cabot Lodge, for example, representing a textile state, was adamantly opposed to a meaningful law as were many other senators. The President chose not to fight, or even argue, on this question, announcing that action should be left to the states.

The man in the White House was not lacking in humanity, and one may imagine that he had pangs of conscience over the plight of children, just described. Certainly he showed sensitivity and a perception far beyond that of most contemporaries concerning the difficulties of working people generally. In the fall of 1907 he spoke caustically of those citizens who were "singularly callous to the needs, sufferings, and feelings of the great mass of the people who work with their hands." What he had in mind specifically were the advantages of an employer's liability bill, then before Congress, affecting the railroads operating in interstate commerce. Roosevelt showed his awareness of the catastrophic effects upon a man's family when he was killed or injured on the job and of the need for a plan of compensation benefiting railroad employees. He and his supporters in Congress pressed for the passage of this bill, and they were successful.

Theodore Roosevelt is remembered not for his mastery over Congress, but for a boldness and virtuosity that enabled him to take advantage of the presidential office, in the situation of his own time. His ability to preach from his high office, to dazzle the news reporters, to dramatize a problem, and to carry out many policies on his executive authority really had no parallel in American history. He was an able administrator who surrounded himself with able men. His capacity for disciplined effort, and the systematic production, for example, of major addresses, state papers, and extensive correspondence gained him the admiration of subordinates such as Taft and Gifford Pinchot. He had benefited from his career as a literary man and a publicist of sorts. Throughout his life Roosevelt was an insatiable reader, carrying books with him and seizing every chance to bury himself in their pages. It was not an accident that he seemed to have the word or literary allusion for every occasion, whether used as a compliment or a epithet.

Almost from the moment he assumed the presidential office, Roosevelt revealed a determination to use his new authority, in many spheres of activity. Scholars have examined carefully, for example, the manner in which he moved inexorably to wrest control of the Republican party from Mark Hanna, now a Senator and recently a close friend and adviser of William McKinley. In the same period the new President acted boldly to settle the anthracite coal strike of 1902. His handling of this affair was crucial, in fact, in the rivalry with Hanna. Robert H. Wiebe has concluded that the issues were extremely complicated, a "confusion of ironies"; but Roosevelt was at least willing to take his chances on forcing a settlement—against the wishes of the coal mine operators. To a public concerned over alleged shortages of coal and familiar with the arrogance of Big Business, Roosevelt emerged as a hero. He also helped the miners to receive a 10 percent increase in pay. The biggest winner in this controversy, however, was Roosevelt himself.

With the possible exception of foreign affairs, no subject illustrates the Rooseveltian leadership more clearly than the conservation of natural resources. The "first conservation crusade" could not have occurred without him, and even his political critics, such as Senator La Follette, testified to his valuable contributions in this field. It was not strange that Roosevelt should have had an enlightened attitude on the question of natural resources. From his youth he had been intensely interested in the study of birds and other wildlife; and he was an amateur taxidermist. When he first enrolled at Harvard he intended, with his father's approval, to become a scientist, but he was discouraged by what he termed the narrow approach then taken toward natural history. As Roosevelt grew older the hunter in him conflicted with the pure scientist, but he understood the necessity of preserving wildlife and continued to study and enjoy nature. He appreciated the importance of wilderness, or wild country; some of these areas so important to the American past should not be allowed to disappear completely. Yet Roosevelt was, in general, a "utilitarian," a believer in development of resources and sustained yield, as in the case of forests. His residence in the West and his travels gave him an understanding of public lands and of irrigation questions, for example, that many Easterners did not have. While Governor of New York Roosevelt listened to the advice of Gifford Pinchot, the forester, and was much impressed. Frederick H. Newell, an engineer and water expert, was another who influenced him. Great naturalists like John Burroughs sang the praises of the President for his undoubted knowledge of the outdoors and his genuine concern to achieve the best policies that were possible.

The word "conservation" was used first in its modern sense in the time of Roosevelt, and the origins of this movement are noteworthy. The beginnings lay far in the past. Wherever there was careful use of resources, including scientific agriculture, or the protection of the "king's forest," or of his game preserve, there was something similar to later, modern policies. Europe was far ahead of the United States in this experience, at least until the late nineteenth century. When settlers came to America, they "came as conquerors," one writer has noted. Forests were enemies to be burned or eliminated, so that crops could be grown. Such forests were also the hiding places of wild animals, or of "dangerous savages." From the very beginning, therefore, Americans were accustomed to fighting the alien wilderness and using up recklessly the wealth of wildlife. Since the country seemed so large and bounteously blessed with land and resources, there was no need to be careful. Men were accustomed to farming extensively—mining the soil, in effect—and moving on to other places where the soil was still rich. By the late nineteenth century, railroads, lumber companies, mining companies, cattle companies, and others were playing a considerable part in this process of exploitation.

From mistakes of the past, and from new influences as well, came the reforms ultimately known as conservation. One impulse was a new appreciation of nature that developed in the nineteenth century and that may be described as an aspect of romanticism. James Fenimore Cooper, Washington Irving, and other writers of the period, along with artists such as Thomas Cole, helped to bridge the gap between man and nature, to inculcate a love of nature rather than a medieval fear. The Transcendental movement helped to provide "new eyes," as one scholar describes it. Ralph Waldo Emerson did much, for example, to lay the philosophical foundation for a new spiritual relationship with nature. John Burroughs and John Muir were notable among those who carried these ideas on into the twentieth century. The direct influence of this group was aesthetic and spiritual, contributing to the national park movement and the wilderness cult. Theodore Roosevelt, outdoorsman and nature lover, had much in common with these thinkers. He wrote of his visit to a great Sequoia grove in company with John Muir: "The majestic trunks, beautiful in color and in symmetry, rose round us like the pillars of a mightier cathedral than ever was conceived even by the fervor of the Middle Ages."

The heritage was a rich one. George Perkins Marsh in 1865 had written *Man and Nature,* an influential analysis of the human environment. Frederick Law Olmstead was a landscape architect, a pioneering figure, coplanner of Central Park in New York City and a leader in calling for the establishment of the great Yosemite Park in California—"for the benefit," Olmstead said, "and free use of the people." The idea of democracy was important in the developing movement. Theodore Roosevelt, in his *Autobiography,* paid tribute to a number of men, including John Wesley Powell, a one-armed veteran of the Union army, later famous for his exploration of the Colorado River and for his role of leadership in the United States Geological Survey. Powell, along with F. H. Newell, Charles D. Walcott, and Senator Francis G. Newlands of Nevada, did much to establish the nation's irrigation system.

W J McGee was another scientist with the Geological Survey, often described as the "brains" of the conservation movement. But the man singled out by Roosevelt for highest praise was the forester Gifford Pinchot. Of him TR wrote: "He was the foremost leader in the great struggle to coordinate all our social and governmental forces in the effort to secure the adoption of a rational and farseeing policy for securing the conservation of all our national resources." Roosevelt said that he ranked Pinchot first among all the public officials of his administration.

Since scientists were so prominent in the conservation movement, it is tempting to give an overweening importance to "science," or "efficiency." Samuel P. Hays has emphasized this interpretation. But men like Roosevelt and Pinchot were idealists and do-gooders as well as scientists. Conservation to them was a moral movement and a matter of justice to their own generation and generations to come. The word "efficiency," which they often used, might better be described as "social efficiency," for it was imbued with connotations of religion, democracy, and service. Also, as time passed, leaders in the movement were caught up in the progressive cause and turned leftward in their thinking. Some conservationists were radicals, believing in the social ownership of great natural resources and therefore the inherent right of everyone to a share. Such ideas were fine theoretically but difficult indeed to put into practice in a capitalistic America.

Almost one-fourth of Roosevelt's first annual message to Congress on December 3, 1901, was devoted to the conservation of natural resources. It was a remarkable treatment of the subject. He thus revealed his concern over existing problems and his plans for the future, which—to a surprising extent—were soon made a part of national policy. Doubtless he had the advice of Pinchot and other specialists, but his personal knowledge on many subjects was clearly apparent. He took care to emphasize that he was not a visionary; these were practical questions that must be acted upon realistically. "The forest and water problems," he said, were perhaps "the most vital internal questions of the United States." Protection of the nation's forests would not, as some believed, prevent them from being used but would, in fact, give the assurance of "larger and more certain supplies." The development of the nation's water resources and the protection of its forests, in his judgment, must go on concurrently. The President saw many possibilities and sounded, at points, like a good preservationist:

> Some at least of the forest reserves should afford perpetual protection to the native fauna and flora, safe havens of refuge to our rapidly diminishing wild animals of the larger kinds, and free camping grounds for the ever-increasing numbers of men and women who have learned to find rest, health, and recreation in the splendid forests and flower-clad meadows of our mountains. The forest reserves should be set apart forever for the use and benefit of our people as a whole and not sacrificed to the short-sighted greed of a few.

Roosevelt's program was an admirably balanced one for his time. Almost inevitably, however, the greatest questions were "utilitarian" ones that demanded attention, along with related problems of business and industrial development. The forests, waterways, coal lands, petroleum lands, and grazing lands were notably important. Some argued that such resources, when on public lands, should be sold to private interests or made available for quick development. Others feared monopoly. Roosevelt and his supporters wished to call a halt to private acquisition, to withdraw the public lands from private entry or sale, and to study the entire question. Some of these lands, like the national forests, might be permanently withheld and supervised by rangers. The trend under Roosevelt and succeeding Presidents was in this direction, that is, toward the retention of the public domain and access to resources on a temporary or leasing basis. But the difficulties were considerable. First, the nation's resources had not, for the most part, been studied carefully and classified, and until this classification occurred there could be no intelligent management of what were really multiple resources in any particular area; second, the public lands at that time were almost entirely in the Western states, and federal control, or the threat of it, produced a hostile Western reaction. This "economic sectionalism" affected both political parties. It made necessary the establishment of a forest policy, for example, or a water policy, that did not interfere too seriously with economic growth in the relatively undeveloped Western states.

The first major step in Roosevelt's administration helped to alleviate Western opposition. Dating from his annual message described above, the President called for the establishment of a reclamation policy, with the *national* government (as he termed it) using its resources and interstate powers to construct dams, reservoirs, and irrigation facilities. The government would bear the initial burden of financing and leadership with the expectation of repayment by the water users over a period of years. In 1901–1902 such proposals received serious consideration in Congress, and a further concession was made to Western opinion. Money received by the government from Western land sales would now be placed in a special reclamation fund, with which irrigation projects could be started. Obviously additional money could also be appropriated, and eventually it was, in large amounts.

While passage of this bill was still in doubt, Roosevelt sent an appeal to "Joe" Cannon in the House of Representatives:

> I do not believe that I have ever before written to an individual legislator in favor of an individual bill, but I break through my rule to ask you as earnestly as I can not to oppose the Irrigation measure. Believe me this is something of which I have made a careful study, and great and real though my deference is for your knowledge of legislation, and for your attitude in stopping expense, I yet feel from my acquaintance with the far West that it would be a genuine and rankling injustice for the Republican party to kill this measure.

The party did not kill this measure, and the Reclamation Act of 1902 soon had the President's signature. Ironically, however, the leader who received most praise, other than the President himself, perhaps, and whose name was attached to the bill, was a Democratic Senator from Nevada, Francis G. Newlands. Roosevelt fumed over what he considered this undeserved credit, but he could do nothing about it.

In several other instances Roosevelt accomplished the passage of significant measures. In 1905 he achieved what he had long advocated, the transfer of forest reserves from the jurisdiction of the Interior Department to the Forestry Bureau of the Agriculture Department, where Gifford Pinchot was eagerly waiting to take charge. (Curiously, the forests and the foresters had been in different departments.) Pinchot, now becoming chief of the newly organized Forest Service, enjoyed a greatly enhanced authority. In 1906 the President and his supporters in Congress succeeded in passing another type of measure, the Antiquities Act, which facilitated the protection of historic spots, landmarks, Indian ruins, and similar places by Presidential proclamation. A short time thereafter

Roosevelt proclaimed the Grand Canyon as a national monument. Thus it received protection until, in 1918, it became a national park.

It is no exaggeration to say that Roosevelt initiated a great conservation system and that he did it primarily on his executive authority. So much was done, in fact, that only a brief summary is possible in the remaining space. Through the Forest Service, with Pinchot as the dominating influence, the nation embarked upon a program of experimentation in land use, for the national forests (as they were renamed) actually contained much more than trees. Inevitably there were grazing lands interspersed with timbered areas and streams or rivers flowing through. Some areas were suitable for agriculture, and no one knew just where precious minerals might be found. Pinchot boasted of his willingness to permit multiple use such as homesteading on agricultural lands, the grazing of livestock under supervision of rangers, and even the construction of dams under conditions suitable to the government. Obviously the forests must be protected, meanwhile, against every kind of foe, including fires. Trails and fire towers had to be constructed, trees planted, studies conducted, and all the programs inaugurated that meant "sustained yield" to the professional foresters. Under appropriate supervision, logging of mature timber was permitted. Pinchot acted as an adviser to Roosevelt on numerous matters and as a conservation propagandist to the nation. The Secretary of Agriculture, James Wilson, gave a free hand to the Forester, and Pinchot organized an able staff, with an esprit de corps hardly to be matched. The Roosevelt "system" demanded collaboration between officials in the two departments primarily concerned, Agriculture and Interior, and an acceptance of the necessity for bold action concerning the public lands.

Step by step, the program gained momentum, while the opposition raged. One Westerner lamented, some years later, about the great harm that had been done: "We had a wild, crazy era of conservation sweep across this country." Most aggravating to many critics was the continuing policy of land withdrawals by action of the Chief Executive. Such lands, they argued—with considerable exaggeration—were held out of use and seriously handicapped economic development in the West. In Roosevelt's two terms, a total of 234 million acres were withdrawn, including almost 150 million acres of forest lands. In one notable instance the President used his authority to withdraw forest areas in the Pacific Northwest just before the House of Representatives passed a bill denying him the very power to make such withdrawals. This conflict (in 1907) suggested the growing difficulties between Congress and the White House.

But Roosevelt proceeded. A Public Lands Commission, appointed by the President, investigated the operation of land laws and made suggestions for improvements. In 1907 the famous Inland Waterways Commission undertook its study of the nation's streams and their relation with other natural resources. From this work, in which the President himself joined the touring members, came the invitation to a White House conference on May 13, 1908. This was a great and unprecedented occasion, lasting several days, with the President, the Vice President, seven Cabinet members, thirty-four governors, nine justices of the Supreme Court, the members of some seventy national societies, business leaders, and others participating. It was precisely the kind of affair in which Roosevelt could convey his enthusiasm and exercise a powerful personal influence. He gave the opening address, and many others followed with an enthusiasm that was contagious.

As a result of this White House conference, the crusade for conservation continued on new fronts, for governors, scientists, and others returned to their home states with new ideas and determination. Roosevelt also appointed a National Conservation Commission, headed by Pinchot, whose assignment it was to take an inventory of the national resources, the first genuine attempt to tackle such a task. About six months later the members reported, and Roosevelt called their study "one of the most fundamentally important documents ever laid before the American people." It was, indeed, quite an advance over previous guesses. Capping the various meetings was a North American conference on conservation, held at the White House in 1909, shortly before Roosevelt left office. He advocated as well the holding of a world conference, but his successor, Taft, did not follow through on this idea.

Perhaps the best example of Roosevelt's interest in "human" conservation was his Country Life Commission, appointed in 1908. The President commented in making his appointments that much attention had been given by government agencies to the problems of agriculture, so far as crops and production were concerned. It was time, now, to think more constructively of the people involved. "The great rural interests," he wrote, "are human interests, and good crops are of little value to the farmer unless they open the door to a good kind of life on the farm." Liberty Hyde Bailey of Cornell University headed this Commission, with Gifford Pinchot, Henry C. Wallace, and Walter Hines Page among the best-known members. They sought to learn about farmers and their problems, both by soliciting mail and by discussions held in the agricultural regions all over the country. Many of the recommendations finally adopted were excellent and were acted upon in the presidential administrations that followed. One dramatic result was a campaign to eradicate hookworm in the Southern states, after members of the Commission became aware of the prevalence of this disease and of the steps necessary to combat it.

As suggested previously, there were weaknesses in the Roosevelt program. Most of his effort had bypassed the Congress, and had depended on the personal leadership and cooperation of a small group of men in the executive departments. According to Samuel P. Hays, this was a movement of elitists, who intended to direct the nation's resource policy on the basis of scientific principles. While they employed the rhetoric of "democracy," their real purpose was centralized direction and "efficiency." However that may be, Roosevelt, Pinchot, and their friends believed that the national interest would be served by policies they were pursuing. They rejected any shortsighted program that seemed to favor a few. Practically speaking, they had a difficult problem of persuasion and of reconciling the conflicting economic interests. Roosevelt offered concessions to his Western critics and strove to work with the politicians, but he had a mixed success. When his administration ended, the new policy for natural resources, for the most part, had not been translated into statutory law. It rested on a shaky foundation.

On election night in 1904 Theodore Roosevelt had made a decision that hampered him for the remaining years of his Presidency and that drastically affected his future; William Harbaugh has called it the "worst political blunder" of his career. The President declared in unequivocal language that he would not seek a third term. Soon he would be a political "has-been" and, knowing this well, congressmen and others did not defer to him as they might otherwise have done. Roosevelt soon realized his mistake and privately expressed his frustration. He and his family loved the White House and did not want to give it up. There were critics who believed that Roosevelt was engaged in devious politics and would, at last, "reluctantly" accept renomination from his party in 1908. Instead he went his way in the last Presidential years, doing the best he could and aiming to choose a successor who would carry forward his policies.

Notwithstanding Roosevelt's leadership, the Republican party was in some disarray by the off-year elections of 1906. Generally speaking, GOP candidates did well, actually increasing their margin over the Democrats in the Senate, while losing twenty-eight seats in the House of Representatives. Discontent was apparent, however. Organized labor, disgruntled with its status, following a fight with Speaker Cannon and the House Republicans, turned toward the Democrats. In some portions of the West and Middle West the progressive movement surged onward, while the Democrats as a party looked stronger. The tariff was a continuing source of concern to Roosevelt, for many Republicans believed emphatically that the duties must be reduced. Most serious was the panic of 1907–1908 which revealed serious weaknesses in the banking system. Speaker Cannon apparently blamed the trouble on Roosevelt, as did many businessmen, for his radical statements and strictures on the business community which had allegedly undermined public confidence in the nation's economic system. The President countered with a charge that "malefactors of great wealth" had stimulated the panic in an effort to discredit his administration. Meanwhile, Roosevelt's time was running out, and he recognized that his opponents were pleased if not gleeful at the thought. His hope now was twofold: first, to clarify his program of reform through messages to the Congress, through White House conferences, and through urging further action; second, to seek the best possible man for his replacement.

William Howard Taft was Roosevelt's choice for the nomination, after other possibilities such as Elihu Root and Charles Evans Hughes had been eliminated; both were New Yorkers, like TR, and Root had too many business connections. Secretary of War since 1904, Taft formerly had been a judge in Ohio, a Solicitor General of the United States, and Commissioner General of the Philippine Islands. The President denied that he was trying to "dictate" Taft's nomination, but that was precisely what he did in June 1908. To most Republicans, however, Taft seemed an excellent choice, and he had little difficulty defeating William Jennings Bryan in the fall campaign. Roosevelt, meanwhile, prepared for a hunting trip to Africa, to last an entire year; his "main reason," he said, was to prevent anyone from making the accusation that he was still running the government or that Taft was letting him run it. If Roosevelt could be believed, in November 1908 he had complete faith in the man soon to succeed him: "Taft will carry on the work substantially as I have carried it on. His policies, principles, purposes and ideals are the same as mine and he is a strong, forceful, efficient man, absolutely upright, absolutely disinterested and fearless."

Roosevelt had made a fine record, on the whole. He proved himself a twentieth-century man responsive to the needs of the country and bold enough to act. His flair for leadership eventually placed him near the top of some presidential rankings, along with greats of the past. But a question of some importance still remained as the Roosevelt administration came to an end. Had the departing president made a mistake in his choice of William Howard Taft? Roosevelt could not be sure on this point, nor could the country, until Taft, assuming office, began to establish his own record.

SUGGESTIONS FOR ADDITIONAL READING

Many of the works mentioned earlier will be applicable to this chapter. See especially those by Blum, Mowry, Harbaugh, Hays on conservation policy, Wiebe on businessmen, and also the volumes of Roosevelt letters. Horace Samuel and Marion G. Merrill, *The Republican Command, 1897–1913,* Univ. of Kentucky Press, Lexington, 1971, is a good general study of the powerful leaders in

Congress and of TR's concessions to them. Two sources from the first family are well worth reading: Theodore Roosevelt, *An Autobiography,* Scribner, New York, 1913, and Alice Roosevelt Longworth, *Crowded Hours: Reminiscences,* Scribner, New York, 1933. For a recent analysis see Richard Lowitt, "Theodore Roosevelt," in Morton Borden (ed.), *America's Eleven Greatest Presidents,* 2d ed., Rand McNally, Chicago, 1971. Biographical studies of congressional leaders are numerous, though uneven in quality. Among the best are John A. Garraty, *Henry Cabot Lodge: A Biography,* Knopf, New York, 1953; John Braeman, *Albert J. Beveridge: American Nationalist,* Univ. of Chicago Press, 1971; Leland L. Sage, *William B. Allison: A Study in Practical Politics,* State Historical Society, Iowa City, Iowa, 1956; and Thomas R. Ross, *Jonathan Prentiss Dolliver, A Study in Political Integrity and Independence,* State Historical Society, Iowa City, Iowa, 1958. Belle Case and Fola La Follette, *Robert M. La Follette,* 2 vols., Macmillan, New York, 1953, is an important work though partial to the Senator; while Nathaniel Wright Stephenson, *Nelson W. Aldrich: A Leader in American Politics,* Scribner, New York, 1930, is favorable to its subject. Two studies of Democratic Senators are Francis B. Simkins, *Pitchfork Ben Tillman, South Carolinian,* Louisiana State Univ. Press, Baton Rouge, 1944, and John R. Lambert, *Albert Pue Gorman,* Louisiana State Univ. Press, Baton Rouge, 1953; while J. Rogers Hollingsworth, *The Whirligig of Politics: The Democracy of Cleveland and Bryan,* Univ. of Chicago Press, Chicago, 1963, examines the party and its problems. Blair Bolles, *Tyrant from Illinois: Uncle Joe Cannon's Experiment with Personal Power,* Norton, New York, 1951, is a readable account. One look at a business leader, interested in politics, is Frederick L. Allen, *The Great Pierpont Morgan,* Harper, New York, 1948.

Following are a number of books that relate especially to domestic issues of the Roosevelt Presidency: Elsie Glück, *John Mitchell, Miner: Labor's Bargain with the Gilded Age,* John Day, New York, 1929; Arthur M. Johnson, *The Development of American Petroleum Pipelines: A Study in Private Enterprise and Public Policy, 1862–1906,* Cornell, Ithaca, N.Y., 1956; Gabriel Kolko, *Railroads and Regulation, 1877–1916,* Princeton Univ. Press, Princeton, N.J., 1965; J. Harvey Young, *Toadstool Millionaires: A Social History of Patent Medicines in America before Federal Regulation,* Princeton Univ. Press, Princeton, N.J., 1961; Oscar E. Anderson, Jr., *The Health of a Nation: Harvey W. Wiley and the Fight for Pure Food,* Univ. of Chicago Press, Chicago, 1958; Robert J. Cornell, *The Anthracite Coal Strike of 1902,* Catholic Univ. Press, Washington, D.C., 1957; A. Hunter Dupree, *Science in the Federal Government: A History of Policies and Activities to 1940,* Harvard, Cambridge, Mass., 1957; Paul R. Cutright, *Theodore Roosevelt, the Naturalist,* Harper, New York, 1956; Hans Huth, *Nature and the American: Three Centuries of Changing Attitudes,* Univ. of California Press, Berkeley, 1957; Roderick Nash, *Wilderness and the American Mind,* Yale, New Haven, Conn., 1967; M. Nelson McGeary, *Gifford Pinchot: Forester-Politician,* Princeton Univ. Press, Princeton, N.J., 1960; Harold T. Pinkett, *Gifford Pinchot: Private and Public Forester,* Univ. of Illinois Press, Urbana, 1970; Gordon B. Dodds, *Hiram Martin Chittenden: His Public Career,* Univ. of Kentucky Press, Lexington, 1973; and Elmo R. Richardson, *The Politics of Conservation: Crusades and Controversies, 1897–1913,* Univ. of California Press, Berkeley, 1962.

Chapter 6

Taft and His Circle

The "Era of Theodore Roosevelt," as George E. Mowry demonstrates in his book of that title, did not end in 1909 but extended on to 1912, when the former President ran again, this time on the Bull Moose ticket. His erstwhile friend and opponent in the election, William Howard Taft, might have admitted the appropriateness of the Rooseveltian label. He knew painfully well that he lived and governed, or tried to govern, in the shadow of Roosevelt. Soon after Taft was inaugurated in March 1909, he wrote a remarkable letter indicating the extent to which he had relied upon his predecessor and still looked to him as mentor. The occasion was Roosevelt's departure for Africa. Taft said to him in part:

> If I followed my impulse I should still say 'My dear Mr. President,' I cannot overcome the habit. When I am addressed as 'Mr. President' I turn to see whether you are not at my elbow. When I read in the newspaper of a conference between the Speaker and the President, or between Senator Aldrich and the President, I wonder what the subject of the conference was, and can hardly identify the report with the fact that I had a talk with the two gentlemen. . . .

I want you to know that I do nothing in the Executive Office without considering what you would do under the same circumstances and without having in a sense a mental talk with you over the pros and cons of the situation. . . . I can never forget that power that I now exercise was a voluntary transfer from you to me, and that I am under obligation to you to see to it that your judgment in selecting me as your successor and bringing about the succession shall be vindicated according to the standards which you and I in conversation have always formulated.

Thus Taft recognized, as everyone else did, the peculiar nature of his Presidency. To understand the Taft administration it is necessary to know the attitudes of Taft and his advisers on a given question and, also, the current relationship between the President and ex-President. Almost from the start, in 1909, their cordiality was strained, and a little more than a year later they were actually involved in a fight. It was a strange and confused turn of events that pitted these old friends against each other.

The new President was an able man who might have succeeded at some other time, but the years in which he served were not opportune for his particular gifts. It is probable that any Republican leader, including the ebullient Roosevelt, would have suffered severe difficulties in the period 1909 to 1913. The party was divided, with the progressives steadily increasing in strength. Difficult decisions had to be made on whether to work with Aldrich and Cannon, as Roosevelt had previously done, or to look elsewhere for support. Progressives in the Senate now included La Follette of Wisconsin, Albert B. Cummins and Jonathan P. Dolliver of Iowa, William E. Borah of Idaho, Joseph L. Bristow of Kansas, Albert J. Beveridge of Indiana, and Joseph M. Dixon of Montana. In the House there were George W. Norris of Nebraska, Victor Murdock of Kansas, Charles A. Lindbergh of Minnesota, Augustus P. Gardner of Massachusetts, and others. These men represented a changing spirit in the country and a growing determination to institute democratic reforms. To keep the peace between the Old Guard Republicans on one hand and the militant progressives on the other, a leader of political skill was required. William Howard Taft was not that man.

The Ohioan had never held an elective office and was interested in politics only sporadically. He did not really want the presidential nomination in 1908 and had to be persuaded to take it by his wife (who was politically and socially ambitious) and by Roosevelt. His fondest dream was to preside as Chief Justice over the United States Supreme Court. Though an unpolitical man, the impression that Taft conveyed was often one of great affability. He was a large and rotund person, 6 feet 3 inches tall, weighing over 300 pounds and frequently close to 350, depending on his adherence to a diet. He sometimes shook with laughter, and his big smile was familiar to those who read the daily newspaper or journals of opinion.

"Will" Taft was frequently the butt of "fat man" jokes, and he had other susceptibilities that could make him seem amusing. His faithful aide, Archibald Butt, was surprised to discover that the new President easily dropped off to sleep on public occasions. "He has the faculty of sleeping sitting up," Butt wrote, "and while this may indicate some trouble somewhere in his great bulk, I am inclined to think it indicative rather of a phlegmatic temperament." Butt decided that he should station himself close to the President during speeches or performances, ready to give him a poke if necessary to avoid public embarrassment. By comparison with Roosevelt, Taft seemed to be sorely lacking in energy. He tended to procrastinate, for example, in the preparation of speeches and sometimes performed poorly as a result. Recognizing his own difficulty in this regard, he once blurted out: "I would give anything in the world if I had the ability to clear away work as Roosevelt did. I have never known anyone to keep ahead of his work as he did. It was a passion with him."

By comparison with officeholders in general, the President (and future Chief Justice) had a highly productive career. He was also a proud and sensitive man. While serving under Roosevelt, he was so impressed by him and so much a part of the governing circle that his views seemed almost identical. Basically, however, he was tough-minded and had strong ideas, which became much more apparent in 1909 and thereafter.

The question must inevitably arise as to whether Taft was a progressive in his leadership, and, if so, by what criteria? Certainly he considered himself, in the beginning, a good progressive, carrying forward the policies of his predecessor. There can be no question that the legislative record of his administration was a creditable one, in the progressive tradition, and that on railroad regulation and "trust-busting," for example, he went well beyond Roosevelt. But Taft's ideas and methods were different, and in some respects he was significantly more conservative than Roosevelt. Moreover, he began to react vigorously against the extremes of progressivism, as he understood them; and by 1912 he regarded himself as a battler for the hallowed principles of constitutional government. He stood proudly with conservative men, who were trying to save America from the likes of Roosevelt, La Follette, Bryan, and Debs.

Richard W. Leopold, Norman M. Wilensky, and others have shown that ideology was highly important in this period, and Wilensky has argued convincingly that Republican leaders were divided primarily on the basis of ideas rather than differences in family background, economic position, education, or "status." One distinction, however, was that the conservatives tended to be older men, in their fifties and above, who had enjoyed a long association with the Grand Old Party. Wilensky's analysis is extremely useful as a group study of various leaders associated with Taft and exercising a strong influence during his administration.

A significant point in understanding these men was their willingness to accept some changes in the economic sphere. Taft, Elihu Root, Winthrop Murray Crane, Nicholas Murray Butler, and others were prepared to support a degree of federal regulation and of governmental service when private enterprise seemed unable to do the job. The problem of monopoly was one which they regarded as a serious threat to society, and they accepted the necessity of some federal action. They were not, therefore, merely an appendage to powerful business interests of the day, although often they seemed to be.

Old Guard or conservative leaders in the party were not so optimistic about human nature as were the progressives, and they were far less willing to invite "the people" into governmental affairs. This political difference was extremely important. Their ideas were similar, in tone, to those expressed generations earlier by the founding fathers, who had created a balanced government, with a separation of powers, an appointive judiciary, and a number of features to protect individual rights and private property. Another influence was the Populist revolt of the 1890s. Republicans generally had verged on panic at the idea of a Populist government and they had not forgotten the "demagogic" appeals of William Jennings Bryan. Conservatives in the party were still determined, fifteen years later, to oppose relentlessly the extremes of popular democracy. A final influence, of considerable importance, may be termed the "survival of the fittest" idea, or social Darwinism. These conservatives were elitists of a sort who believed that the best people ought to rule. They did not necessarily equate the best with the richest, as business leaders and publicists had often done in the late nineteenth century, but wealth and success counted heavily with them.

Taft had studied at Yale with William Graham Sumner, who preached the natural *in*equality of man, and the conservatives agreed with Sumner that men were indeed unequal; some were fit to lead and others to follow. Taft wrote in his *Popular Government* (1913): "We are not in favor of the rule of all the people as an end desirable in itself. . . . We are in favor of a rule by as many of the people in a democracy as will secure a good government and no more. The result will be good because it secures the happiness of the individual." Nicholas Murray Butler, president of Columbia University, stated in a similar way, "True democracy will carry on an insistent search for these wisest and best [men], and will elevate them to posts of leadership and command." Senator George Sutherland of Utah, a social Darwinist heavily influenced by Herbert Spencer, rejected the notion that "some mysterious virtue" was to be found in "mere numbers" of people. The great work of leadership in government demanded an ability and a specialized knowledge that few could give.

An emphasis on morality, duty, and efficiency was very much a part of the conservative philosophy. Taft once referred to the "fixedness of moral principles which we learned at our mother's knee." Virtue was not only admirable, it was practical. Men of character, succeeding in their private endeavors, should become, eventually, leaders of the community and the nation, as their parents had been before them.

Although sharing to a considerable extent the hopes and ideals of progressive leaders, the conservatives thought of themselves as practical-minded, hardheaded, and unsentimental. They were realists who saw through the phoniness of the latest popular crusade or demagogic appeal. They were not to be deterred or seduced by the plaudits of the crowd and promises of personal preferment. They were suspicious, therefore, of some things that the reformers campaigned for enthusiastically. Taft commented that "a constant contemplation of the suffering and misfortune in the world" had led many to lose their sense of proportion and to forget the "real progress" that had already been made, improving the lives of millions. "We live in an age of reform," Taft declared, "I hope of real reform." But he regretted the "sham reformers" and "crank reformers," who had no "practical sense" of what reform actually was.

Taft and the conservatives, as a group, gave obeisance at the shrine of the Constitution and the law. They thus differed both intellectually and emotionally from a growing number of doubters on this subject. They were little affected by a new jurisprudence often associated with the name of Oliver Wendell Holmes, Jr., who had written in his *Common Law* (1881): "The life of the law has not been logic: it has been experience. The felt necessities of the time, the prevalent moral and political theories, institutions of public policy, avowed or unconscious, even the prejudices which judges share with their fellow-men, have had a good deal more to do than the syllogism in determining the rules by which men should be governed." In contrast to Holmes, Taft believed that "judicial exactness" could be attained, and he depended rather too much upon precedents. Archie Butt, perhaps with some exaggeration, made a striking statement: "President Taft will do anything if he has the law on which to base his act. The law to President Taft is the same support as some religious zealots get from great religious faith. And the fact that the law is unpopular would not cause him to hesitate a minute."

Paradoxically, to an extent, conservatives like Taft deplored a tendency to pass too many laws. "The lesson must be learned," he said, even though it was a difficult one, "that there is only a limited zone within which legislation and governments can accomplish good." He continued: "We can, by passing laws which cannot be enforced, destroy that respect for laws and habituated obedience to law which has been the strength of people of English descent everywhere." It was argued by some at the time that laws and institutions long accepted by society were, in fact, faulty and unjust ones that ought to be overturned or repealed. Taft and his group could not accept such a view. Fundamentally they were pleased with America, with the leadership of those like themselves, with economic growth, industrial expansion, and the mission of America in world affairs.

Along with the majority of Americans, Taft was not very sympathetic toward new immigrants of the North and West or blacks of the South, the latter suffering under newly imposed laws and diverse forms of "Jim Crow." Archie Butt, himself a Georgian, observed the new President during a Southern tour and delivered a judgment on his attitude that was indeed harsh: "The Negroes have greeted him coldly everywhere, and he in turn has done nothing to placate them. In no place has he pandered to them, and he has seemed to avoid them everywhere. He dislikes the Negro, and his highest ambition is to eliminate them in politics." Butt added that, partly in consequence, Taft was marvelously popular with Southern whites. One can speculate that the President's years in Cincinnati, across the river from Kentucky, had contributed to a racist viewpoint and that the Darwinian influence had further convinced him that the blacks were, unquestionably, an inferior people. As Taft viewed the Italians, Poles, Russian Jews, and others of the new immigration, they, too, seemed inferior. Millions could not speak English and great numbers did not want to. Others were anarchists, or the "instrument of demagogues" and corruptionists. The "nucleus of the socialist party," he asserted, was the foreign-born. Nevertheless, Taft looked to the future with hope. As the immigrants and their children became educated and acquired property, the process of "Americanization" would be accelerated. Breathing the "spirit" of American institutions, they would be assimilated, with time, much as the earlier immigrants had been.

The treatment of Taft's administration below will illustrate further the conservative tendencies of his thought and, to a lesser extent, of his specific policies. He and his advisers were aware of the necessity for change. They knew that it had to come and that, without it, there might be a revolution. But, again, they were determined to govern in an orderly way and with due respect for the Constitution and past experience. They believed in the depravity of human beings generally and their inequality, so far as ability was concerned; in the existence of natural laws that limited the possibilities for progress, and the great importance of high, moral leadership. They had a genuine fear of the excesses of democracy. This was especially evident in the period 1910 to 1912 as Old Guard leaders battled against the rising tide of insurgency.

Soon after Taft defeated Bryan in November 1908, he began the task of selecting his Cabinet. For those who followed these choices with some attention, there were strong indications that the jurist from Ohio was different indeed from his predecessor. "I shall be attacked," Taft wrote to Roosevelt, "for having more lawyers in my Cabinet than I ought to have." Taft was quite right on this point; he had an overabundance of legal-minded men who could be expected to think much as he did. Philander C. Knox of Pennsylvania was Secretary of State, George W. Wickersham of New York was Attorney General, and Richard A. Ballinger of Seattle was Secretary of the Interior. All were lawyers, as were Jacob M. Dickinson of Tennessee, the Secretary of War; Frank H. Hitchcock of Massachusetts, the Postmaster General; and Charles Nagel of Missouri, Secretary of Commerce and Labor. Not a single member of Taft's Cabinet could be characterized as progressive.

The new President started off badly, and, even worse, he seemed to repudiate his promise to retain Roosevelt's personal friend James R. Garfield as head of the Interior Department. Garfield had been an architect of the Roosevelt conservation policy, along with Gifford Pinchot, while Taft's appointee was clearly less sympathetic to that program. At the least, this was a serious misunderstanding, for which Taft was primarily responsible, and it prepared the way for the famous Ballinger-Pinchot controversy of 1910.

The custom of President-watching is an old and honorable one in the United States, but seldom have the American people had "two for the price of one," as they had in this developing Taft administration. Archie Butt, for example, had an ideal opportunity to follow the course of events. Kindly and gracious, he was a great favorite with the Tafts and their friends, as he had been with the Roosevelts. A tragedy in the Taft household helped to make him a confidant of the President. Helen Herron Taft ("Nellie") was the real politician of the family, according to her husband; and she was, in fact, a talented and knowledgeable woman to whom he often looked for advice. But soon after the inaugural ceremonies she suffered a severe stroke, affecting her speech and walk. She could not accompany her husband as she had in the past and preferred to remain out of the public view. Her illness and isolation undoubtedly handicapped the President in his decision making, while also contributing greatly to the worries of his months in the White House. Archie Butt, meanwhile, seemed to be with the President everywhere, and, writing to his sister-in-law, Clara, he left an invaluable record of this period.

Time and again, Butt compared his new boss with his old boss, mostly to Taft's disadvantage, so far as personal qualities were concerned. A few weeks after the inaugural, during a trip to New York, Butt wrote:

From the minute we left Washington I began to miss excitement, which always attended President Roosevelt on these trips. Even before we left Washington, President Taft took no notice of the crowd . . . which had assembled at the depot. He entered his car and never came out to wave a good-by. . . . There was a large crowd at Baltimore, and the President never went even to the platform to wave his hand—and so it was all the way to New York.

Butt exchanged comments with Jimmie Sloan of the Secret Service staff, an able man, wise in the ways of politics. "What an opportunity he is missing," Sloan said. Butt in essence agreed, although he referred to Sloan as being "too much under the magic of TR."

Butt gave many examples in his correspondence of Taft's "indifference to people in general." This was a perplexing thing, since the President was personally a friendly man. Soon the news reporters began to complain that he was not giving them information as he should, and when Butt reported this to his boss he blurted out that the people had elected him and, "damn it," they were going to have to take him as he was. In the back of his mind he was doubtless thinking that he absolutely would not behave as his predecessor had done, feeding news to the press every hour or two. Butt further observed how deliberate the President was and how he would sit and listen for hours to a congressman but would not promise anything; rather he would "take it under advisement." This, too, was very different from TR.

Taft's manner, or his style as President, seemed to be a calculated thing, based on his experience as a judge, his political philosophy, and a certain determination to act differently from Roosevelt. If people thought the new President was "soft," Butt observed, they were quite wrong: "He never permits his heart to govern his mind." He seemed very complacent, but in actuality he could fire people from their jobs and refuse to give favors "with an indifference which is impossible to most men of his apparent type." Once he told Butt that he wanted to avoid those "intimacies" which had caused Roosevelt to be heavily criticized. Taft, in effect, was a tough-minded administrator whose conservative philosophy was reflected in the way he functioned. "Demagogic" possibilities of the presidential office were appalling to him. He would do his duty, without fanfare, relying heavily upon experts such as the lawyers he had brought into his Cabinet. These methods were anachronistic and dangerous in the sense that they could be compared by observers with those of Old Guard leaders in the Congress, whose disdain for "the people" was well known. Aldrich and Cannon had developed almost to a science the private, or furtive, control of the public business, and it was against this, in large part, that the progressives were protesting.

The Taft administration and its policies could not be equated with those of the business community. Businessmen, it was true, identified themselves with the Republican party, and they looked hopefully upon Taft. They knew that he had a "reserve" of character and principles that could serve the country well. If only, said the *Commercial and Financial Chronicle,* he would not attempt to "masquerade as a poor copy of another man whose policies have proved a dead failure"; that is, TR. Taft's reform attitudes on the tariff, the trusts, and a few other questions made him suspect. By early 1910 the *Chronicle* let out a wail concerning one of the President's ideas: "We venture to assert that no such rule-or-ruin proposal has ever before emanated from the executive head in modern times."

Actually the business world had good reason to feel safe. Time and again, for example, in his inaugural message, the new leader expressed his concern for economic stability and the expansion of international trade, while he virtually adopted the business position on labor injunctions and the secondary boycott.[1] Though calling for tariff reductions, the conservation of natural resources, and other reforms, he intended to guard against "unwise or excessive paternalism." Most reassuring to business were his Cabinet appointees, as described previously, and the type of individuals who served as personal and private advisers. Of these, perhaps none was more important than Winthrop Murray Crane, the junior Senator from Massachusetts. Senator Crane had assumed his position in 1904 after serving previously for three terms as Governor of Massachusetts. He was widely admired as a businessman of great wealth who had also demonstrated ability and integrity in governmental affairs. Almost immediately, as one writer observes, Crane joined the oligarchs of the Senate. His wealth and social position may be suggested by the announcement of his son's marriage in 1905, when almost 2,000 invitations were sent out to some of the most distinguished families in America. As a political leader, Crane functioned efficiently, behind the scenes, speaking to men privately and confidentially. It was a mark of distinction with him that in all the years of his Senate career he never felt the necessity to deliver an address on the floor.

A second adviser of similar type was Elihu Root, formerly the Secretary of War under TR and later his Secretary of State. In 1909 he became a Senator from New York. Famed as a lawyer, Root never lived down his years of service to large corporations, devising for them, in Richard Leopold's phrase, the means by which they could "organize,

[1]The injunction, as used against labor, was based on the principle that courts had a right to forbid particular actions that might cause injury. The secondary boycott was one organized against employers not directly involved in the dispute to bring additional pressure against employers who were involved.

consolidate, and operate without fear of litigation or state interference." In his later career, Root was cherished as a friend for his knowledge of public affairs, keen sense of humor, and fine qualities generally. He was also a conservative in his political philosophy. Leopold, in fact, judges him to have been "the ablest, most constructive conservative in American public life since 1900." This distinguished leader believed, as others of his group did, in the depravity of human nature. He feared especially the potential for harm from an unchecked majority of Americans who might vault into power. The rights of the minority must be protected, and this could best be done by upholding the Constitution and the laws. Root was an excellent counselor on many problems, but President Taft needed badly to turn to others, more closely in touch with ordinary people of America, for some of his advice. Seemingly, he lacked the capacity to do this.

From Taft's standpoint, however, there was nothing wrong. He had found excellent advisers. They would do their duty conscientiously and well, and they would even fight, if necessary, for "correct principles of government." This, in fact, was what they had to do, as the GOP moved from one crisis to another, starting soon after Taft took office.

SUGGESTIONS FOR ADDITIONAL READING

Surprisingly few books have been written about William Howard Taft, although those on Theodore Roosevelt will customarily have much to say about his friend from Ohio, as well. For background on the Taft family and Ohio politics see the following: Ishbel Ross, *An American Family: The Tafts, 1678 to 1964,* World Publishing, Cleveland, 1964; Zane L. Miller, *Boss Cox's Cincinnati: Urban Politics in the Progressive Era,* Oxford, New York, 1968; and Warner, *Progressivism in Ohio,* mentioned previously. Henry F. Pringle, *The Life and Times of William Howard Taft: A Biography,* 2 vols., Farrar & Rinehart, New York, 1939, is readable and informative. Less voluminous but highly useful are Paolo E. Coletta, *The Presidency of William Howard Taft,* Univ. Press of Kansas, Lawrence, 1973; Walter V. Scholes and Marie Scholes, *The Foreign Policies of the Taft Administration,* Univ. of Missouri Press, Columbia, 1970; and Norman M. Wilensky, *Conservatives in the Progressive Era: The Taft Republicans of 1912,* Univ. of Florida Press, Gainesville, 1965. Richard W. Leopold, *Elihu Root and the Conservative Tradition,* Little, Brown, Boston, 1954, is highly recommended, as is the more comprehensive treatment, Philip C. Jessup, *Elihu Root,* 2 vols., Dodd, Mead, New York, 1938. Other books will help delineate the "Republican Command," especially that by Samuel and Marion Merrill, mentioned previously. See also Carolyn W. Johnson, *Winthrop Murray Crane: A Study in Republican Leadership, 1892–1920,* Smith College, Northampton, Mass., 1967; Dorothy Ganfield Fowler, *John Coit Spooner: Defender of Presidents,* University Publishers, New York, 1961; Forrest Crissey, *Theodore E. Burton: American Statesman,* World Publishing, 1956; Everett Walters, *Joseph Benson Foraker: An Uncompro-*

mising Republican, Ohio History Press, Columbus, 1948; and Irwin Hood (Ike) Hoover, *Forty-two Years in the White House,* Houghton Mifflin, Boston, 1934.

Archibald W. Butt, *Taft and Roosevelt: The Intimate Letters of Archie Butt, Military Aide,* Doubleday, New York, 1930, is a fine source for the period up to 1912, when Butt died on the *Titanic.* Taft's own writing, though not so lively, is often revealing, for example, *Popular Government: Its Essence, Its Permanence and Its Perils,* Yale, New Haven, Conn., 1913.

Chapter 7

Taft: A Crisis
of the Conservatives

In March 1909, William Howard Taft launched into the first great fight of his administration. He called a special session of Congress to consider the question of tariff revision. Showing more courage than Roosevelt had, and less political sense, he sought a tariff that would reduce the Dingley rates of 1897 but still give protection to American producers, as they needed it. Taft's emphasis on the tariff may be traced back to his days at Yale and his study with William Graham Sumner. He had thought for years that the tariff was too high and ought to be reduced, differing with Roosevelt, for example, who had usually discounted it as an issue. Taft realized that the tariff was "dynamite," that it touched the pocket nerve of millions and the interests of highly privileged Republicans, and that it could divide and even destroy his party. Still he continued toward tariff reform, though he did not exercise a strong personal leadership that might conceivably have brought success.

The President and the Congress now clashed. Taft did not have, by any means, the assurances from the Republican leaders that he needed to have, and the difficulties of his position were quickly revealed. The House of Representatives, rather surprisingly, passed a bill with some reductions (the Payne bill, named after Sereno E. Payne of New York); but the House sent it on to the upper chamber with knowledge that it would be drastically revised. That quickly happened under the leadership of Nelson Aldrich, chairman of the Finance Committee and the dominating figure in the upper house. The bill that came out of his committee contained some 600 raises. Furthermore, the ad valorem, or percentage method, of fixing rates was not used in every schedule, and often it was difficult to know exactly what changes had been made. It was an extremely complicated and deceptive tariff measure.

With some signs of encouragement from the President, a small band of Republican progressives in the Senate decided to fight. La Follette was the leader, along with Jonathan Dolliver of Iowa. Beveridge of Indiana, Joseph E. Bristow of Kansas, and Moses E. Clapp of Minnesota were most active in assisting, while half a dozen other Senators—mostly from the Middle West—got in their licks. They studied the bill night after night for weeks, trying to master every detail. They analyzed the duties on hides, cotton, wool, iron, and all the other items, each trying to be an expert on a selected schedule. Some worked almost to exhaustion. When debate opened, they took their turn in critical examination of the details, and they indicted the managers of this cynical measure. In a stunning performance, they humiliated Aldrich, showing a greater knowledge of many provisions than he had; they defied his leadership. For months they kept it up, through April, May, and June. Finally, they had to give up. Aldrich retained his control of the Senate majority, and the bill passed easily. Still it had to go to the conference committee and to the President for his signature.

Through this long fight, the President followed a vacillating course. He exerted some pressure on Aldrich and even threatened a veto, though few took him seriously. In the end Taft won on some points, the most important relating to the tax provisions. Federal tax policy was moving at this time toward an epochal change, under which the tariff would decline precipitously from its historic role of filling the federal coffers, and the income tax would emerge. Increasingly Americans believed that taxes should be based, in large part, on ability to pay. Roosevelt and Taft were among those affected by this thinking, and Taft seemed to grasp the fact that an income tax was inevitable. He did not, however, simply want the passage of a provision which might be held unconstitutional, as had happened previously in 1895; he preferred the more cautious method of constitutional amendment. A bloc of progressive Republicans and Democrats opposed any delay, however, and insisted on the inclusion of an income tax provision in the Payne-Aldrich bill. Taft used his influence, working with Aldrich, to effect a compromise. A corporation tax was included in the bill and also a provision for an amendment, which had to be submitted to the states, assuring the constitutionality of the income tax.

As George Mowry has shown, the progressive bloc could not defeat this plan, but they believed that Taft had betrayed them. While the President basked in the glory of his "victory," progressives were confident, as most of the country was, that Taft had suffered an ignominious defeat; that he had failed to assert his leadership; that he had been taken in by Aldrich and company. *Collier's* quoted Senator Dolliver to the effect that Taft was a "large and well meaning good man closely surrounded by persons who know exactly what they want." To be sure, the President was not so weak as this statement made him seem to be. Rather, he had acted in accordance with his principles and political instincts, which placed him closer to the party leadership, with its apparent stability and orthodoxy, than to the "insurgents" of the Congress (as he sometimes called them), who often seemed a wild-eyed bunch.

Taft now proceeded to make a difficult situation worse. In a speech of September 17, 1909, at Winona, Minnesota, he reviewed the new law at length, citing its reductions and constructive features. His tone was in part defensive, and his critics must have laughed at one piece of tomfoolery: "Now, the revision downward of the tariff that I have favored will not, I hope, destroy the industries of the country. Certainly it is not intended to." Most damaging politically was an idea that he expressed toward the end and then repeated for emphasis: the Payne bill, he asserted, was "the best tariff bill that the Republican party ever passed." Noting the fact of opposition among the progressives, he gave them a little lecture on representative government, the rule of the majority, and the necessity for responsible party organization. According to some Republicans, he tried to read them out of the party. Without being aware of the fact, Taft offered some good prophecy to the American public: those who were disgruntled over this bill, and wanted to work for a drastic revision of duties, might try the alternative of the Democratic party—if they believed the Democrats would actually live up to their promises.

The damage done by this tariff fight, and Taft's role in it, was enormous. It did much to set the tone of his first two years, to destroy his reputation with the progressive Republicans, and to stimulate the growth of politically independent thinking. One long-time Republican, a Montana editor distinguished in his guild, wrote in the following manner to Thomas H. Carter, the senior Senator from Montana and an Old Guard reliable:

The tariff business was a bad job. I heard the first echoes of the general discontent in casual interviews with Americans, while I was in Europe; I got more of it on the steamer, coming home, where there were many Americans and time to talk and I have heard scarcely anything else from anyone since. Even in this highly protected wool region there is no one who raises his voice in praise or even defense of that "best of tariff laws." The administration is thoroughly discredited. . . . There never was in my recollection such absence of partisan feeling and such unanimity of silent but earnest rebellion against the things that are.

He urged Carter, an old acquaintance, to "cut loose from the Aldrich leash."

Amid these repercussions from the tariff, another great controversy was raging. The Ballinger-Pinchot affair must be traced back into the Roosevelt administration when Gifford Pinchot as Forester (in the Agriculture Department) and James R. Garfield as Secretary of the Interior were able to collaborate closely on a number of matters affecting their departments. They were personal friends and generally in agreement on a vigorous, coordinated program for conservation of water power, forests, and other resources. Secretary of War Taft sometimes resented their activities. When Taft as President-elect decided to appoint Richard Ballinger as his Secretary of the Interior, rather than to keep Garfield on in the position, it was not merely a routine matter. It could be interpreted as a symbolical act. The excessively zealous, if not illegal, methods of Pinchot were to be brought under restraint.

Samuel P. Hays has emphasized, in an excellent discussion, that the source of disagreement was largely administrative. That implied, also, a clash of ideas. Both Taft and Ballinger were legalistic in comparison with the Pinchot group, and both were concerned that Congress should not be bypassed in the shaping of conservation policies. Ballinger also favored local (private) development in many instances where his predecessors had not, and he favored the loosening of federal controls. Almost immediately, in the spring of 1909, he initiated policies that conflicted with those of the recent past, and the sparks began to fly. Ballinger was determined, but the U.S. Forester was a formidable man with many resources, including his skills at publicity and his many friends among the newspaper fraternity. Never to be forgotten was another friend of his, off hunting big game in Africa.

Extremely important in the developing dispute was the problem of water power in the Western states. Still relatively undeveloped, the great rivers and the streams that fed them were now recognized to have a marvelous potential. Yet complex questions remained of governmental jurisdiction and the extent to which private development could occur without the interference or surveillance of federal authorities. Quickly Ballinger clashed with F. H. Newell and George Woodruff in the Reclamation Service of his own department. They were holdovers from the previous administration and were fully committed to a coordinated policy, with "federal reclamation for the common good," as Elmo R. Richardson had described it. Ballinger, by contrast, had a much more restricted view, believing that the government could not "dictate to a State how non-navigable waters shall be used or whether they shall be used at all." He objected specifically to the executive withdrawal of some areas in the Pacific Northwest (public lands), thought to have potential as power sites. The Secretary decided that many such withdrawals were not justified, and he restored them to the public domain, thus making them available for private access and development. Pinchot and his group protested. Taking his case to the White House, the Forester was successful. In April 1909, the Secretary decided to re-withdraw the water-power sites in question.

Next, and most important, came a dispute over certain lands in Alaska. For more than a decade the territory in Alaska had been a subject of dramatic interest to Americans. The gold rush to the Klondike had fired the popular imagination, and it was not surprising that a dispute over coal lands, some ten years later, would gain special notoriety. The problem of Alaskan development, generally speaking, was a difficult one. How should this latest frontier, and a vast one at that, be handled? How should the resources be developed? How closely should the federal government, as administrator of the territory for the American people, supervise its economic development? In a time when the fear of trusts and monopolies was rampant, it was only natural that precautions should be taken concerning the relatively untouched riches of Alaska. With reference to coal land, single claimants might obtain title to a tract no larger than 160 acres. This was not enough for those anticipating costly development, and the law invited subterfuge. With this problem in mind, Roosevelt had withdrawn the Alaskan coal lands, hoping to achieve a leasing system that would permit equitable development. Meanwhile, the claimants to the land had the right to proceed with their work and to apply for title. Assuming there had been no fraud and no collusion, the claimants should get their land.

But charges of fraud soon filled the air. Louis Glavis, a field agent for the Interior Department, decided that collusion had occurred in the so-called Cunningham claims, consisting of thirty-three tracts, and that the Morgan-Guggenheim syndicate in Alaska was soon to take over. He feared that the Interior Department, under Ballinger, was preparing to accept the validity of the claims and to grant title. Getting nowhere in his own department, Glavis turned to Pinchot and poured out his suspicions. The latter then talked with the President, and Glavis did too. After brief consideration of the charges, Taft denied any wrongdoing in the case; he had young Glavis fired for insubordination. Yet for some months to come,

Taft had to endure Gifford Pinchot's criticisms and unwanted advice. *Collier's* also published an article by Glavis, and the controversy went on relentlessly. According to Archie Butt, writing in September 1909, "The President says Pinchot is a fanatic and has no knowledge of discipline or interdepartmental etiquette, and he will not stand for such insubordination as he has been guilty of." Butt added: "He got very angry and raised his voice several times, so that we could easily hear all he was saying in the House."

Three months later Pinchot was still the U.S. Forester, though the pressure increased to fire him. Pinchot, in fact, was virtually asking to be fired, and the President, sensing this, did his best to avoid the final break. The Forester had now decided that the best thing for conservation policy was to dramatize the differences between the Roosevelt policies and the Taft policies—as he saw them; to defeat Taft on this matter and, perhaps, to bring Roosevelt "back from Elba," as the expression went. Increasing numbers of Republicans, disillusioned with the administration, were looking to Roosevelt as the possible savior of the party.

Finally Taft could delay no longer. Pinchot gave him the last excuse necessary when he wrote a letter to Senator Dolliver stating his views on the controversy and thus directly violated a Presidential order to avoid such public discussion. Dolliver read the letter to the Senate, as Pinchot expected. Soon thereafter, on January 7, 1910, Taft wrote a letter of dismissal, concluding with the statement: "By your own conduct you have destroyed your usefulness as a helpful subordinate of the Government, and it therefore becomes my duty to direct the Secretary of Agriculture to remove you from your office as the Forester." Pinchot had expected this. He was, in fact, exultant and gave a party at his Washington home to celebrate, with hundreds of well-wishers. Soon he spoke to his admiring subordinates in the Forest Service, delivering a farewell address. They sent him off with thunderous applause.

"Pinchot's Gambit," as one scholar has called it, led to a congressional investigation, to words of approval and friendship from Theodore Roosevelt, and to public vindication of a sort. The long-range results are not so clear. Without a doubt, however, this affair damaged further the reputation of Taft and Ballinger. Whatever might be said of the Forester—and his motives were not always the purest—he was a fighter with a masterly knowledge of the public lands. He was also sincerely concerned with the need for a strong federal program and executive leadership, as described previously. His testimony in the congressional hearing was forceful and effective, although it was less than generous to Secretary Ballinger, against whom he made a personal attack. Glavis, when his turn came to testify, did extremely well. Representing Glavis was Louis D. Brandeis, who brilliantly helped to expose the weaknesses in the administration's policies and procedures.

The net result of all this was that Taft showed up as a bungler and a President in whose hands the public interest was not entirely safe. Ballinger, in testifying, did not improve his image either. This was partly because he had chosen as his legal adviser a lawyer from Tennessee who lacked experience in public land matters and whose views were antediluvian. Also, Ballinger was incensed at the charges against him, and he lacked the temperament to defend himself calmly and with the necessary skill. The vulnerability of public men has seldom been demonstrated more graphically than in this Ballinger-Pinchot affair. *Collier's,* which had led in the muckraking attacks, had the following to say about Taft in March 1910:

> He thinks he has a judicial temperament, and in conversation frequently appeals to this possession, as evidence that he is likely to be right. Alone in his library, with law books and an abstract case, he may be fully as judicial as he imagines. In the world of man, he is the toy of the politicians, lawyers, and money-makers with whom he plays golf, walks, and eats—the most gullible President, in regard to his associates, since Grant left the Battlefield for the White House.

One story about Taft went like this, in essence: If he went into a woods at night, and there was a bear trap there, and later you wanted to find Taft, all you would have to do would be to look in the bear trap.

Officially Taft's administration was cleared of blame as a result of the congressional inquiry. Yet even the majority report (Republican) emphasized that the great coal fields should not be monopolized. And the Cunningham claims were canceled. The Democrats, in a minority report, castigated both the President and his Secretary of the Interior, while eulogizing the great public servant Gifford Pinchot, who had "dared to be insubordinate, if such he was, in the interest of his country." A third report came from Edmond Madison, a Representative from Kansas, a longtime judge in Dodge City, and an insurgent Republican. Apparently he tried, very conscientiously, to assess the evidence in this case. He concluded that Pinchot and Glavis had been essentially right, and that Ballinger was not the kind of man who ought to preside over the public lands of the United States.

Meanwhile, Ballinger held on to his office, while the recriminations continued. When he finally did resign, in March 1911, his successor was Walter L. Fisher of Chicago, usually identified with the Pinchot group of conservationists and highly satisfactory to them as a replacement. More than anything else, the force of public opinion and the worsening crisis in the Republican party had brought the downfall of Richard Ballinger. He was, for the rest of his life, a bitter man, convinced that he was the victim of cruelly unjustified attacks. That Taft kept Ballinger on for so many months is understandable, but from a political standpoint he should have let the man go, long before, about the same time he fired Pinchot.

In another great dispute of the Taft administration the President was not directly involved. Yet his attitude, once again, subjected him to harsh criticism from the progressive wing of his party. This was the attempt in the House of Representatives to strip the Speaker of his powers to appoint the members of committees, and especially to appoint the Rules Committee. Speaker Cannon was a master of parliamentary tactics, but he met in this engagement someone as determined and resourceful as he was. George W. Norris of Nebraska had been in the House since 1903. He became a reformer, an insurgent, for whom politics was nearly a religion in the opportunity it offered for service. When he discovered that Speaker Cannon reigned in the House almost without restraint, Norris was indignant, as so many others were. The Payne-Aldrich tariff and the arbitrary fixing of rates under pressure from the tariff lobby did much to open his eyes. By 1910 Norris was a prominent insurgent, and he waited for an opportune moment to challenge the Speaker. He depended upon the element of surprise, and he believed that in the ultimate vote a combination of the Democrats and insurgents would destroy the Speaker's authority.

Norris knew that the Speaker would not even recognize him, or let him offer a resolution, under normal procedures. So he waited for a time when he could claim precedence for his resolution under the Constitution and virtually compel its consideration. He waited patiently for months. Finally he saw his opportunity, jumped to his feet, and the battle was on. After a day and a night of parliamentary maneuvers, Cannon made a ruling against Norris. This ruling, however, had to be put to a vote of the members and—as Norris had planned—the Democrats and insurgents together were able to beat the regulars. Thus the "long dynasty of the all-powerful Speaker came to an end," as Norris wrote later.

With good reason, the insurgents believed that Taft had opposed them in their fight. He had done so, at least mildly, from the beginning of his administration. By 1910 the President frankly considered the insurgents disloyal to the Republican party, and for that reason, as he admitted, he was denying them the patronage privileges that could be expected by faithful Republicans.

The so-called insurgents argued that they, in fact, had supported the President more often than had the Old Guard, and that they were better Republicans. The charge that they were disloyal to the GOP was infuriating to these longtime members of the Republican party. They cited their support of the administration on innumerable matters, in contrast to Aldrich and Cannon and their legislative troops who used the party machinery to work for privileged interests. All the talk of majority rule and responsible party government was meaningless, so long as GOP leaders cynically disregarded the popular will.

If one looks at Taft's record generally, and at his legislative achievements, he was not a crashing failure, as the tariff fight, the Ballinger-Pinchot affair, and other controversies seemed to make him. His record, for example, on the conservation of natural resources was a good one. As noted before, he stressed the necessity of cooperation between the executive and legislative branches and was glad to support, therefore, a gesture in this direction—a provision of the Pickett Act (1910) that gave congressional permission for withdrawals of land by the President. (Roosevelt, Pinchot, and many others thought that such congressional permission was wholly unnecessary.) In the fall of 1909, acting on the advice of the Geological Survey and Secretary Ballinger, the Taft administration withdrew for protective purposes some 3 million acres of petroleum land located in California and Wyoming. Taking another step, Taft created in 1912 two naval petroleum reserves in the San Joaquin Valley of California. If this policy succeeded, public petroleum supplies would be saved in a natural "reservoir" for the eventual use of the Navy. The expansion of national parks was another matter that interested both Taft and Ballinger. The President, in his annual message of December 1910, called for the establishment of a bureau that would provide for the care and control of parks. He also recommended that the "greatest natural wonder" of the United States, the Grand Canyon, should be given protection by placing it in a new national park, and a few years later this was done. Recommendations for soil conservation, the enlargement of national forests, reforestation, the prosecution of land frauds, and many other conservation measures could not leave much doubt that Taft was seriously concerned and well-intentioned on this great subject.

The President also carried forward the movement for effective regulation of the nation's railroads. With the Mann-Elkins Act of 1910 the federal government considerably enlarged its power to regulate interstate commerce. Under the Hepburn Act of 1906 carriers had been able to retain their original rates (usually raises), if they went to court. But this new legislation empowered the ICC to suspend such rates and to take the initiative in rate revisions. The ICC also gained authority over the telephone, wireless and telegraph. In 1913, shortly before the administration ended, the Physical Evaluation Act was passed, providing for a study of railroad properties, much as La Follette had earlier demanded. Presumably, with a thorough knowledge of railroad assets and the condition of their equipment, rates could be fixed more efficiently and equitably.

On trust policy Taft seemed to show up well. He and his Attorney General, George W. Wickersham, believed in a competitive economic system, and they acted vigorously to achieve it. In Taft's four years of Presidency, his Justice Department brought seventy-eight court actions against trusts, more than during all the presidential administrations that preceded him. Obviously he benefited from the momentum that had developed under Roosevelt, but his trust-busting record was a far better one. A notable victory was that in the Standard Oil case of 1911. The great company was broken into thirty-three component parts. Nothing, however, could prevent a continuing cooperation among them, and some argued that the dissolution had, in fact, made very little difference in the company's influence. In this decision the Supreme Court announced its "rule of reason," which further weakened the effect of the decision. The Court said, in effect, that a restraint of trade, prohibited under the Sherman Antitrust law of 1890, was not illegal unless it was an *unreasonable* restraint. Successful action against trusts became more difficult since they all claimed to be "reasonable," or socially useful.

If Taft had been able, he would have placed on the statute books a plan for federal incorporation of companies operating in interstate commerce, thus permitting tighter control. In a lengthy message to Congress, he argued the merits of such a plan. Sounding like his predecessor in the White House, Taft said that he accepted the fact of bigness in modern America. But he declared: "We must insist that the suppression of competition, the controlling of prices, and the monopoly or attempt to monopolize in interstate commerce and business, are not only unlawful, but contrary to the public good, and that they must be restrained and punished until ended."

Other achievements of the Taft administration included the creation of postal savings banks, the establishment of the Bureau of Mines, the division of the Department of Commerce and Labor into two departments of Cabinet level, and the admission of two new states, Arizona and New Mexico. The Sixteenth Amendment, assuring the constitutionality of the federal income tax, was proclaimed shortly before Taft left office. The Seventeenth Amendment, providing for the direct election of senators, went to the states in May 1912 and was ratified about a year later. In many fields of action, such as the establishment of a Children's Bureau in the Department of Commerce and Labor (1912) and requirements for safety appliances on the railroads, the administration could claim a progressive record and a humane one, in the tradition of Roosevelt.

According to Taft and his supporters, this record should be viewed in perspective as another chapter in the proud history of the GOP, dating from Abraham Lincoln and the 1850s. Generally speaking, Republicans of the post-Civil War era were contemptuous of Democrats, and they held almost in reverence the great achievements of their leaders. Admittedly, the GOP was now in trouble; quite possibly the Democrats would come into office as a result. Such an eventuality would be painful to the Republicans and many who were deserving would be lost to the public service. But there might be benefits as well. For the Democratic party, it was widely believed, did not really have the competence or integrity necessary to govern the United States. Nor did the insurgent Republicans. A short period of power would demonstrate the incapacity of these charlatans, and a chastened electorate would turn back, gratefully, to the GOP.

By the early months of 1910 it was quite apparent that insurgent agitation might open the gates to the enemy. Old Guard leaders simply could not understand the malcontents, or admit their sincerity, or listen to them with anything approaching objectivity. Senator Tom Carter of Montana, a standpatter, faithfully reflected the views of conservatives in the party hierarchy and the methods, as well, by which they had exercised power for so long. Shortly before Roosevelt returned to the United States and began to identify himself with progressives in the party, Senator Carter let loose a blast against these men: "As for Insurgency little need be said. It is an article manufactured by self-seeking politicians who find gratification in the notoriety of it and the hope of faring well if ruin comes to the party. My opinion is that the next elections will give some of these Insurgent gentlemen a violent awakening." As if to outdo Carter, one of his friends with the *Chicago Daily Journal* wrote: "A good many crimes are being plotted these days in the name of insurgency. It is fast degenerating into something like the old Populist party, a camp for the soreheads and discards of both parties."

Having pride in their party and their contributions to the national weal, Republican leaders found the public attacks being made upon them exceedingly difficult to bear. In the House, in the Senate, and in the muckraking press, they were often portrayed as allies of special privilege and enemies of the people. Carter burst out, "Every man in public life seems to be a chosen target for all kinds of villification [sic] and misrepresentation, and do what he may the storm seems to be unavoidable." He feared that these attacks against anyone who had "a dollar invested in business" might soon bring on a condition of extreme economic instability. Carter used the fear of depression to discourage criticism of business or tampering with the economic system. Robert Wiebe, in his study of businessmen in the progressive era, has referred to this as "panic-crying."

Sometimes the Republicans waxed philosophical. James S. Clarkson, writing to Carter, commented that these were strange times indeed when almost everyone believed that the "old order" was passing but no one knew just what was to come. To one friend, then aligning himself with the insurgents, Carter made a strong appeal. But finally he admitted, sadly, that the party might fail, the insurgents might have the strength to turn the country over to the Democratic party. He quoted President Harrison concerning his defeat in 1892: "Old experience is not instructive; each generation must have its own."

Carter was himself involved in a fight for reelection in 1910, as were his friends and fellow Republicans all over the country. This was a decisive year in American politics. The fights inside the Republican party, state by state, were bitter, and they made the later division of 1912 very nearly unavoidable. No longer could a common pride and a mutual distaste for Democrats hold the GOP together. Disagreements had gone too far. Roosevelt, by entering the campaign in the summer of 1910, and by announcing his program for the "New Nationalism," revealed dramatically the differences between himself and Taft. At Osawatomie, Kansas, on August 31, the former President began his address by referring to the "long struggle for the rights of man." And he went on: "Our country—this great republic—means nothing unless it means the triumph of a real democracy, the triumph of popular government, and, in the long run, of an economic system under which each man shall be guaranteed the opportunity to show the best that there is in him." Quoting Lincoln, he said that labor was the "superior of capital," and deserved "much the higher consideration." Property, he declared, must "be the servant and not the master of the commonwealth." Special privilege must be driven out of government, both local and national. He called for a graduated income tax on the wealthy and an inheritance tax hitting the "big fortunes." On and on Roosevelt went in a statement of extreme progressivism that was almost incredible to President Taft and the Old Guard leaders. He even attacked the judiciary by saying the times demanded courts that were interested in "human welfare rather than in property." Roosevelt attempted in other speeches and appearances to serve as a conciliator for the party, but he failed almost completely.

The political tendencies of 1910 can be illustrated by a number of states. One of the best for this purpose is Montana, where the principal contenders were a Democrat and a Republican, running for the U.S. Senate. However, they did not run directly against each other but rather sought to gain control of the legislature—which would actually do the electing under the system then required by the Constitution. The next senator would be chosen in the new session of the legislature, by joint balloting of the two houses, when the members chosen in November took their seats. The balloting might continue for weeks. Opportunities for manipulation of the legislators and outright purchase of votes were very great indeed.

Tom Carter was the incumbent Senator, whose seat was at stake. Already described as an Old Guard type, Carter had been in the Senate since 1905 and earlier served in the same body from 1895 to 1901. He started his career as a delegate from Montana Territory and became Montana's first Representative in 1889. From 1892 to 1896 he was chairman of the Republican National Committee; in that office he was intimate with national leaders of the party. Through his long period of public service, and through his oratorical and other abilities, Carter had built a loyal following.

Unfortunately for him, however, he was identified with business interests and with standpat politics in this period of rampant progressivism. His Montana colleague in the Senate, Joseph M. Dixon, a Republican progressive, did not assist in the campaign, and two years later Dixon actually managed the national Progressive campaign for Theodore Roosevelt. Carter was bitter over the situation because, he said, Dixon and other insurgents in the state were doing all they could to undermine the Republican party and to belittle the policies of President Taft, that "great, strong, whole-souled man." By his own defense of Taft, Cannon, and Aldrich and his close friendship with people like Winthrop Crane of Massachusetts, Carter revealed his Old Guard affinities. Carter also opposed the direct primary and the popular election of senators. He ran a campaign in 1910 that strongly resembled the methods used by the Republicans against Bryan in 1896, in spite of warnings that the times had changed; that a campaign of chicanery and manipulation would no longer work. Apparently Carter was too stubborn and too steeped in methods of the past to pay much attention.

Carter's opponent was Thomas J. Walsh, a lawyer and a progressive Democrat who had considerable support among progressive Republicans in the state. Walsh was noted as a friend of labor and an advocate of popular democracy, including the primary and popular election of senators. Like many in his state, he deplored the excessive influence of the Anaconda Copper Company and its allies in political affairs of Montana. Both Walsh and Carter lived in Helena, the state capital, and even attended the same church. Both were Catholics of Irish extraction.

Campaign methods used by the two men differed significantly. Walsh traveled the state and talked essentially about the issues. As an "out" he needed to make himself better known and to get able men, who were friendly toward him, to make a run for seats in the legislature. Bluntly and not incorrectly, Walsh argued that Carter was an Old Guard Republican whose views were out of date. Walsh campaigned as a citizen of conscience and a progressive, seeking the support of like-minded people, whatever their political affiliation. Carter, meanwhile, lived up to his reputation as a puller of strings. Alarmed over opposition to him in the U.S. Forest Service, allegedly by friends of Pinchot, he wrote to the White House, asking that action be taken to keep the foresters out of politics. To Charles G. Dawes of the Central Trust Company in Chicago (later Vice President of the United States), he wrote concerning a "large ditch contract" in Ravalli County in western Montana. The vote in the county would be close, he believed, and he was "extremely anxious to have the good will and cooperation of the representatives of the Company on the ground." Obviously Carter wanted the workers to be pressured into voting his way. Similarly, he wrote to Alexander McKenzie in St. Paul, Minnesota, concerning a "large sewer contract" in Missoula, Montana; perhaps the vote there could be influenced.

Carter made other appeals to men high in the financial world and the United States government, the most important of which related to the transcontinental railroad companies in Montana and the Anaconda Copper Company. He was puzzled to find that the leaders of the Northern Pacific Railway were trying to get out of politics; they would not throw their support his way. In contrast, the executives of the Great Northern Railway and the Milwaukee Road were doing all they could. Carter was particularly anxious that the Anaconda Copper Company should give its full support. He communicated with Senator Crane of Massachusetts and Senator Boies Penrose of Pennsylvania to use their influence at the company's main office in New York City, and he sent his personal business representative for conferences in the East. Soon assurances of support were forthcoming. Ironically, about this time Carter felt compelled to deny that he owed anything much to the great financial interests of his state. Those forces, he said, were Democratic in their politics. His own reliance had always been placed in an "appeal to the plain, common sense of the average citizen."

All of Senator Carter's efforts were in vain. So many Republicans were disenchanted in the eastern counties of Montana, largely in the farming and ranching regions, that the legislature went Democratic. Carter could not win his reelection. Nor could Walsh win, because of opposition from the copper interests during the legislative balloting. But another Democrat gained the Senate seat. Two years later Walsh captured the second seat that had belonged to Joseph M. Dixon. Thus in two years the Republican civil war in Montana cost the party both its seats in the United States Senate.

Throughout the country the same thing was happening. The GOP lost the House of Representatives in the elections of 1910 by a margin of sixty-seven seats. The Republicans managed to hold on in the Senate but lost ten places in that body. As noted earlier, Roosevelt's speeches proved ineffectual in this campaign. Even his good friend Henry L. Stimson failed in a bid to become Governor of New York. Taft could do little.

The plight of the Republicans was pathetic in some respects. Aldrich

Figure 10 Standpatters and Insurgents, as Drawn by John T. McCutcheon, September 25, 1910. (*Rare Book Room, University of Illinois Library.*)

gave up his Senate career in 1911, a year before his party lost control in that body. The Old Guard was passing, it seemed to some, into oblivion. Senator Carter wrote in January 1911 that he had just returned from a funeral in West Virginia, where "we laid our old friend [Senator] Elkins at rest on the western slope of a wind-swept hill." A few months later Senator William O. Bradley of Kentucky wrote to Carter: "The Senate is indeed a desolate place. When I look around and miss so many cherished friends I feel that I would willingly resign could a Republican succeed me." In the same year Senator Carter suffered a fatal illness. And three years later Bradley was himself dead, to be replaced by a Democrat. The times were indeed changing.

In 1911 and 1912 President Taft launched a "counterattack," as one scholar has termed it, against the insurgents threatening to seize control of the party. Taft was no longer the timorous leader of his first two years in the White House, or a fumbling, vacillating politician. While the insurgents were perfecting a new organization called the National Progressive Republican League, Taft assumed a vigorous course of action, using his position of strength as the President and titular leader of his party. Such a course placed him in alignment with Old Guard leaders throughout the nation. Inevitably he moved to the right in his political thinking, although the actual policies of his administration reflected the ambivalence that has been noted before.

Early in 1911 a significant change occurred in the White House staff. The Presidential secretary had gained notoriety for his attempts to influence policy and for his hostility toward Theodore Roosevelt. Finally, Taft let the man go. In his next choice he was more fortunate but, again, he chose an aide whose political views were decidedly conservative. Charles D. Hilles had been for a time an Assistant Secretary in the Treasury Department. He now became a trusted political adviser and the manager of Taft's developing campaign to win renomination. What this meant, as well, was a struggle against the insurgents and, eventually, against Theodore Roosevelt.

In mid-September 1911, the President set forth on a tour of the West that lasted for seven weeks. Norman Wilensky has shown that this visit to some twenty states was vastly more important politically than either contemporaries or scholars have realized. The Presidential secretary, Hilles, carefully prepared the groundwork for his chief's appearances, and they seized every opportunity to confer with "hundreds of politicians, officeholders, and civic leaders." In San Francisco, Hilles even worked out plans with the Democratic boss of that city by which he would help destroy the local insurgent Republicans. The President delivered over 300 speeches, insisting that he was doing his best to be fair and to achieve a constructive administration. Taft and his aide found room for much encouragement. They concluded that even in the states most hostile to the administration they could harvest a substantial number of delegates.

Through the fall and winter, Hilles continued his political work. It was necessary to give assistance to the local Republicans who could be counted upon, to gain control of the state committees, to control the organization of conventions—which would select the delegates—and to schedule conventions to meet early before the opposition could effectively organize. In some states delegates were chosen by primary elections, and in other states as well this method might be adopted. Taft and Hilles, knowing the difficulty that primary elections presented to them, did all they could to oppose the movement to this system. In a number of states, including delegate-rich New York, the regular Republicans were blessed with powerful leaders and organizations. Hilles gave the necessary support, and in other, more troubled states he threw his weight to those factions that would stay with the President. He aimed to obtain, by convention time in June, no less than 540 delegates, the majority needed for nomination.

In the meantime, both Taft and Roosevelt were going their separate ways, still hoping to avoid a final irrevocable break. Both men, however, were convinced that they must speak out on matters of principle, and both made mistakes of judgment. George E. Mowry has argued persuasively that Taft made an error of momentous importance when, in 1911, he decided to prosecute the United States Steel Corporation for violation of the Sherman Antitrust law. His timing could not have been worse. The basis of this suit was that the steel company, during the panic of 1907, had absorbed the Tennessee Iron and Coal Company, ostensibly to prevent its imminent collapse but actually for the profit there was in it. Politically this case was dynamite. Roosevelt as President had talked with the leaders of U.S. Steel, had decided their action was justifiable, and had promised they would not be prosecuted. The Taft administration, in effect, was trying the former President, along with the steel company. TR was furious. In the first place, the case was an insult to him and his administration. In the second, according to Roosevelt's view, Taft was pursuing an outmoded economic policy with his attacks on business; he seemed incapable of understanding the inevitability of bigness and the necessity of regulation by the government rather than a futile policy of economic disruption. Roosevelt was so agitated that he published a defense of his trust policy in *Outlook* magazine. He also became more susceptible to the idea that he should enter the fight for the Republican presidential nomination.

A second issue affected the two men in a similar way. As shown before, Taft was enamored of the courts while Roosevelt felt no great respect for the judiciary and believed its members had assumed too large a function in the federal system. By 1911 many progressives were denouncing the obstructionist role of the judges and their excessive concern for the rights of property. Roosevelt believed that the judiciary had handed down decisions of such a nature as "almost to bar the path to industrial, economic, and social reform." One proposal for placing a check upon the state courts was the recall of judges, or the recall of judicial decisions. Judges, like other public officials, should be subjected more closely to the will of the people. This question boiled up conspicuously in a dispute over the admission of Arizona to the Union. The people of that territory went through the process of framing a constitution which, according to traditional procedure, had to be approved by the people of the territory, the Congress, and the President.

Arizonians, however, included a provision for the recall of their state and county judges, with safeguards that seemed to Taft completely inadequate. He therefore wrote a veto message of some seven pages, lecturing the citizens of Arizona and the nation on the nature of popular government: "This provision of the Arizona constitution . . . seems to me so pernicious in its effect, so destructive of independence in the judiciary, so likely to subject the rights of the individual to the possible tyranny of a popular majority, and, therefore, to be so injurious to the cause of free government, that I must disapprove a constitution containing it." The intensity of Taft's feeling was quite apparent. He admitted that the people of an area, like Arizona, ought to know best what to put into their own constitution. But this matter was so important that he had to speak out and give warning of the dangers. Only infrequently, Taft believed, were judges' decisions affected by personal biases of a political, social, or economic nature.

In the Senate, meanwhile, two of Taft's conservative supporters showed their dismay over the recall idea. Elihu Root, an opponent of the direct election of senators, woman suffrage, and popular democracy generally, was among those who attacked the Arizona recall. Outstanding as a critic was George Sutherland of Utah, later a Justice of the Supreme Court. He delivered what his biographer has termed "the most noteworthy address, perhaps, of his entire senatorial career." Taft and his supporters had a temporary success on the Arizona matter. Leaders in the territory were forced to delete the provision for judicial recall. On attaining statehood, however, they promptly readopted it, and Taft could do nothing.

By early 1912 Taft arrived at the conclusion that he and Roosevelt were separated by veritable chasms on the subject of the judiciary and that his old friend and mentor had really gone over to the radicals. For Roosevelt, in addressing the Ohio constitutional convention in Columbus, announced that he was in favor of the recall of judicial decisions. Even Roosevelt's friends, like William Allen White, were greatly alarmed, while Taft and some of the conservatives almost had apoplexy. To those who believed that the courts had been the cornerstone of a "gloriously free government," almost a "divine institution" in America, this latest mouthing from the former President was simply intolerable. Not a few of his critics suggested that he had gone crazy.

Finally the parting of the ways had come. Roosevelt tossed his hat into the political ring. Bitterly he and Taft fought for the Republican nomination, while La Follette—who had led the progressive forces for many months—dropped into third place in the race. In some states Taft and TR met almost head to head as they campaigned, and the President's state of Ohio best illustrated the divisions in the GOP and the personal acrimony that had developed. Roosevelt was an imaginative speaker, and Taft on occasion did as well, so that words like "fathead," "puzzlehead," "Guinea-pig brain," "egotist," and "apostate" enlivened the debate. A rumor circulated that the Rough Rider was a drunkard. One of the many deeply involved emotionally in this incredible situation was Alice Roosevelt Longworth—Roosevelt's daughter, a favorite of Taft's, and the wife of Nicholas Longworth, who was supporting Taft. The latter, a conservative Congressman from Cincinnati, had a family that was now passionately anti-Roosevelt; so Alice found it necessary to avoid her in-laws for a time. The strain was such that she suffered from "a chronic cold and cough, indigestion, colitis, anemia and low blood pressure—and quite marked schizophrenia." (But her basic robustness is suggested by the fact that she is very much alive some sixty-five years later.) The election returns in Ohio were embarrassing to Taft. His vote was 118,362; Roosevelt received 165,809 and captured forty-two of the forty-eight GOP delegates.

Leaders in the Republican party rallied their forces during the spring and summer of 1912. Obviously many had divided loyalties and could decide only with difficulty whether to follow Roosevelt or Taft. A notable example was Elihu Root, personally a favorite with both the leading contenders but finally compelled by the situation and his sense of duty to choose sides. Root's support was to mean a great deal in the crisis. He was a statesman with the necessary influence and personal force to throw the decision of his party one way or the other. The national convention scheduled for June 18 in Chicago promised to be a closely contested battle for the nomination, with the President having the lead in delegates, while Roosevelt enjoyed much the greater personal popularity. In the thirteen states that held primary elections TR obtained 278 delegates while losing just 82. It was by no means impossible for the former President to capture the nomination. He stood about 90 votes short of the 540 necessary to win. Over 250 seats were contested, including a number that might be assigned to the Rough Rider, enabling him to reduce Taft's lead and create a deadlock. Everything depended, therefore, upon who organized the convention and made the crucial decisions concerning the rival delegates and their credentials.

In a hotly contested vote, Root was selected as temporary chairman. His sympathies by now lay with Taft and the regulars, and his actions in the chair may have been decisive in the final outcome. With assistance from Root, the credentials committee repudiated the challenges mounted by Roosevelt delegates. Senator Crane, William Barnes of New York, James E. Watson of Indiana, and others of the regular group—along with

Root in the chair—were highly successful in keeping the convention under tight control. In spite of bitter debate and charges of fraud and "steamroller" tactics, the pro-Taft delegates retained their seats. Soon thereafter the President was placed in nomination by Warren G. Harding, and he won easily on the first ballot.

Shortly before his victory at the convention, Taft wrote of the "chaos" there and the possible consequences. "If I win the nomination," he said, "and Roosevelt bolts, it means a long, hard fight with probable defeat. But I can stand defeat if we retain the regular Republican party as a nucleus for future conservative action." Later in the summer, after Roosevelt had held his Bull Moose convention and organized the third party, Taft commented again: "I have no part to play but that of a conservative, and that I am going to play." According to Taft, both Roosevelt, the renegade Republican, and Woodrow Wilson, the Democrat, were radical candidates against whom he must uphold the principles of sound government. He was determined to do so.

This crisis in the GOP was far more serious than Taft realized. He could not know how long the wounds would take to heal or how greatly the Democrats would benefit, under Wilson's leadership. The Republican party would never be the same again, or occupy the same place of distinction in American history.

SUGGESTIONS FOR ADDITIONAL READING

The division in the Republican party and the falling out between Roosevelt and Taft has been a subject of considerable fascination. Books by George Mowry, mentioned previously, are especially recommended as the standard scholarly works; they are also good reading. A recent treatment, aimed at the general public, is entertaining and useful, partly for its stress on the personalities, both major and minor. See William Manners, *TR and Will: A Friendship That Split the Republican Party,* Harcourt, Brace, New York, 1969. Several works will help to explain the Taft administration and its dilemmas, more or less sympathetically. Donald F. Anderson, *William Howard Taft: A Conservative's Conception of the Presidency,* Cornell, Ithaca, N.Y., 1973, attributes Taft's failures to a lack of political skill, primarily, rather than to philosophical conservatism. Joel Francis Paschal, *Mr. Justice Sutherland: A Man against the State,* Princeton Univ., Princeton, N.J., 1951, skillfully portrays a Representative and Senator from Utah who went on in the 1920s to join Taft on the Supreme Court. William T. Hutchinson, *Lowden of Illinois,* 2 vols., Univ. of Chicago Press, Chicago, 1957, devotes considerable attention to Lowden's congressional career and his sometimes reluctant support of Taft and the Old Guard. Randolph C. Downes, *The Rise of Warren Gamaliel Harding, 1865–1920,* Ohio State Univ. Press, Columbus, 1970, contains a chapter on the "War of 1912 in Ohio." Claudius O. Johnson, *Borah of Idaho,* Longmans, Green, New York, 1936, describes an independent Republican who would neither bolt with Roosevelt in 1912 nor give his support to Taft. For Taft's foes and critics in Congress, see Kenneth W. Hechler, *Insurgency: Personalities and Politics of the Taft Era,* Columbia, New York, 1940; Laurence James Holt, *Congressional Insurgents and the Party System, 1900–1916,* Harvard, Cambridge, Mass., 1967; Richard Lowitt, *George W. Norris: The Making of a Progressive, 1861–1912,* Syracuse Univ. Press, Syracuse, New York, 1963; Claude G. Bowers, *Beveridge and the Progressive Era,* Riverside Press, Cambridge, Mass., 1932; and A. Bower Sageser, *Joseph L. Bristow: Kansas Progressive,* Univ. Press of Kansas, Lawrence, 1968. See also studies of other leaders mentioned previously.

On the disputes over conservation policy, the books by Hays and Richardson, noted before, should be supplemented with James Penick, Jr., *Progressive Politics and Conservation: The Ballinger-Pinchot Affair,* Univ. of Chicago Press, Chicago, 1968, and Alpheus T. Mason, *Bureaucracy Convicts Itself: The Ballinger-Pinchot Controversy of 1910,* Viking, New York, 1941. Autobiographical accounts are important for the conflicts of this period. See Robert M. La Follette, *Autobiography: A Personal Narrative of Political Experiences,* La Follette Company, Madison, Wis., 1911; George W. Norris, *Fighting Liberal,* Macmillan, New York, 1946; Amos R. E. Pinchot, *History of the Progressive Party,* Helene M. Hooker (ed.), New York Univ. Press, New York, 1958; Samuel Gompers, *Seventy Years of Life and Labor: An Autobiography,* vol. 2, Dutton, New York, 1925; and Theodore Roosevelt's autobiography. The letters of Archie Butt will also be valuable.

Chapter 8

Woodrow Wilson: The Urge to Service

Many of the progressive leaders were "preachers" of one sort or another, trying to carry their gospel into public affairs and even world affairs. Often they had acquired essentially a religion of humanity. George Norris, for example, once wrote: "The truth is that my religion and my politics are one and the same. . . . A government in its truest sense, is only a method of bringing to humanity the greatest amount of happiness and is founded, after all, upon the love of man for man." Even those progressives who seemed to be fundamentalist in their religion, such as William Jennings Bryan, were likely to be propagandists for the Social Gospel, aiming to clean up political and economic institutions and to improve life on earth in every way possible. By general agreement, the foremost leader of a ministerial type was Woodrow Wilson. The best and worst possibilities of such leadership in high office have been attributed to Wilson.

There is really no simple explanation of this minister's son and scholar in politics—as may be suggested by all the controversy that still surrounds him. Wilson has been castigated for his moralism and for allegedly acting as if he thought he were Jesus Christ. He has also been praised lavishly, for example, by the historian William L. Langer, as a leader who went from "the wisdom of today to the wisdom of tomorrow, to the wisdom which is for all time." The truth actually lies somewhere in between. This much is certain: Wilson was not a narrow-minded Presbyterian whose God was the God of the Old Testament. As president of Princeton University he did not hesitate to employ a professor of philosophy named Frank Thilly, when Thilly let it be known that he was not a member of any church and for that reason could prove an embarrassment at Princeton; Wilson thought otherwise. In an address of 1904 the University president asserted his strong belief in a "gospel of love" and his opposition to a religion based on fear. He went on: "It is a noteworthy thing that we reserve the beautiful adjective 'noble' for the men who think less of themselves than of some cause or of some person whom they serve. We elevate to the only nobility we have, the nobility of moral greatness, only those men who are governed by love." Constantly while at Princeton, Wilson spoke in the inspirational language of "service." His inaugural address there was entitled "Princeton for the Nation's Service."

This leader in academe seems to have become, by 1906, a "Christian realist." That is, while a good Christian of the Presbyterian Church, he did not believe in a rigid or legalistic system of ethics. The philosophy of humanity counted for much with him, and decisions of a moral nature were to be made in a contextual sense, in relation to the particular circumstances of a problem. He was not, then, as dogmatic religiously as is often alleged. On the other hand, Wilson was a strong personality, charged with electricity, to use his own phrase; there was no doubt that he could be self-righteous in the assertion of his views or in his determination to act.

The evidence with which to settle some points of controversy about Wilson has recently been made available. In the 1960s Arthur S. Link and his editorial associates gained access to Wilson's letters and papers from the first forty years of his life, including the extremely important correspondence with his father and mother. No one previously had used this material. For the first time it became possible to study carefully the Wilson family relationships and to determine with some reliability the influences that affected young Thomas Woodrow. These sources are extremely rich and detailed, and they explode any simplistic interpretation of psychological problems in the family. They leave no doubt that Wilson was eminently successful as a student, teacher, scholar, and college administrator to the year 1906. They give added importance to a recurrent health problem that hit with devastating force in 1906, when

Wilson had been president of Princeton for four years. In the 1890s he had suffered a minor stroke, but the latest occurrence permanently impaired the vision in his left eye and threatened to end his career, as the discussion below will evidence.

Any attempt to explain Wilson should take into account the matter of his health, along with his personal drive and ambition, and the academic career which was to become a springboard into politics. The present chapter will examine him along this "road to the White House," from 1856 to 1913.

Woodrow Wilson's career was a remarkable one in several respects. He was the first man of Southern birth and origin to hold the presidency since the Reconstruction period. He was and is the only product of the American university system and recipient of a Ph.D. degree to make his way to the White House. Few if any presidents have mastered the art of writing as Wilson did. Few have had a life of the mind that was so interesting. His intellectual activity, mostly at a high level, is attested to by the collected letters and papers and by his published works. The explanation of this outpouring is, in part, that he mastered a difficult shorthand system when a young man, learned the use of a typewriter, and wrote innumerable letters and papers on his own machine.

The future president had a fine heritage intellectually. His father, Joseph R. Wilson, was a Presbyterian minister who held appointments in Staunton, Virginia (where Thomas Woodrow was born), and in other Southern cities. The Reverend Wilson had an ability far above the ordinary, serving now and then as a college professor and as a writer on religious subjects, in addition to his ministerial duties. His wife also had outstanding ability.

Young Wilson's education began in the home with family prayers, instruction by his parents, recitations, and literary readings. He also attended local schools and went for his college work to Davidson in North Carolina for one year, to Princeton for his degree, and to the University of Virginia for a year of law school. He tried the practice of law briefly, then made up his mind to attend Johns Hopkins University in Baltimore as a graduate student in history and political science.

In these college years Wilson was interested not only in his academic work but in the literary societies and various activities, including sports, oratorical contests, debating, and writing. He began to win prizes for essays on subjects like William Pitt, Earl of Chatham, and "Prince Bismarck." He had the thrill, moreover, of getting some work into print. His writing in the seminars at Johns Hopkins formed the basis of a book published under the title *Congressional Government: A Study in American Politics* (1885).

The young scholar argued, in essence, that America's political system lacked leadership, that the executive branch was much too weak, while the real power resided in standing committees of Congress. What he really favored was the adoption of a Cabinet system, similar to that in England. There would be "ministerial responsibility," with a fusing of legislative and executive powers, subject to the popular will. At this time, Wilson had not received the Ph.D. degree. Yet his book was widely reviewed and was eventually reprinted many times. He had struck just the right note of controversy on a timely subject, and his literary style, as usual, commanded attention.

Of Wilson's intellectual talent there could be no doubt. He did, however, reveal some traits that might cause trouble in a political career. While at Johns Hopkins, he wrote to his fiancée, Ellen Axson, concerning the literary society and his activities in it: "I have a sense of power in dealing with men collectively which I do not feel always in dealing with them singly. . . . One feels no sacrifice of pride necessary in courting the favour of an assembly of men such as he would have to make in seeking to please one man." Wilson felt a sense of shyness and reserve in dealing with most people outside his family circle. He also seemed to need love and affection in larger quantities than he was able to give in return. Thus he wrote to his future wife in 1883: "There never was a man more dependent than I on love and sympathy . . . "; and later in 1885, in similar vein: "There surely never lived a man with whom love was a more critical matter than it is with me."

In June 1885, Wilson was married to Ellen Axson, the daughter of a Presbyterian minister in Rome, Georgia. He was exceedingly lucky in this marriage, for his bride was intelligent, beautiful, and wise beyond her years. Not only did she become a loving and devoted homemaker, she also understood Wilson and encouraged him in his career and his friendships, even occasionally with other women.

Wilson did his teaching at Bryn Mawr, Wesleyan (in Connecticut), and at Princeton, continuing as a professor at his alma mater from 1890 to 1902, when he became president. As a lecturer he was brilliant. Someone remembered that he always entered the classroom smiling. He was informed and persuasive, and he knew how to entertain. He could "talk about potatoes," someone quipped, "and make it sound like Holy Writ." Meanwhile, his publications rolled from the presses, helping to make him widely known and in considerable demand as a speaker off campus.

Wilson's performance as president of Princeton was, at first, eminently successful. He initiated reforms such as the preceptorial system of directed study and improvements in curriculum. He brought to an end the practice of hiring Princeton men primarily for positions on the staff, and many of his new appointments were distinguished. Generally he put a new life and intelligence into the school. In some efforts at change and reform, however, he failed, as in his attempt to eliminate the undergraduate eating clubs, which were socially exclusive and seemed detrimental to the ideals of a modern university. Wilson was trying, also, to make the Graduate School the focal point in Princeton's growth and improve its standards both socially and intellectually. After a long struggle, he suffered defeat at the hands of the trustees and Dean Andrew West of the Graduate School. Various scholars, including Arthur S. Link, have found close parallels between the difficulties experienced by the president of Princeton University from 1906 to 1910 and those experienced by the President of the United States from 1918 to 1921. In both instances disagreements over policy became, for Wilson, fundamental conflicts involving the essence of his life's work.

These troubles now merit a reevaluation on the basis of Wilson's stroke, suffered in May 1906, a matter of months before the squabble at Princeton. On the morning of May 28, Wilson had awakened to find himself completely blind in his left eye, while his right arm was partly paralyzed. In all probability the main artery to his brain had experienced a blockage, creating a condition that might have proved fatal or extremely serious. The doctors' reports were alarming, at best, since the diagnoses indicated high blood pressure and arterial problems that could not really be cured. The patient was told, however, to manage his life much more carefully, with the necessary rest, relaxation, and mild exercise. Wilson took these instructions seriously, and the result was a changed pattern of behavior, partly deliberate, but to some extent probably unintentional. He had less time now for social contacts, for chitchat, and theoretical discussions. He was more demanding of the facts and of quick results. He seemed more impulsive and aggressive; also, at times, inconsistent. To Dr. Edwin Weinstein, a neurologist and a close student of Wilson's personal and medical history, this was a pattern of change frequently seen in the victims of a stroke. Another characteristic is "selective amnesia," and Wilson may have suffered that. There can be no doubt that Wilson was a less balanced person emotionally after 1906 and therefore more susceptible to disagreements and conflicts.

To the ordinary observer, however, he had effected a complete recovery by the fall of 1906. His efforts at Princeton were generally interpreted as a courageous struggle for democracy and reform. Thus, over a period of several years, he enhanced his reputation nationally while losing a campus contest in the Ivy League.

From the president of Princeton to President of the United States, in two years, seems an impossible leap; but Woodrow Wilson had made a dazzling record as lecturer, writer, and academic statesman. He was a controversialist who seemed to be, with few exceptions, on the side of the angels. Some who heard him speak were completely carried away. Ellery

Sedgwick, for example, recalled that he became a "burning disciple" of Wilson's after one address and shouted to his wife when he arrived home, "I have been listening to a great man! I know it! Wilson will be famous." What happened, in essence, was fairly simple. Wilson was in trouble at Princeton and was ready to leave, while some of his friends and admirers began to push him, first, for the governorship of New Jersey and then, almost immediately, for the presidency. The Democratic leaders of New Jersey, and notably one James Smith, Jr., were receptive to the idea of a new face. They also thought that Wilson, if given the nomination and assisted into the governor's chair, would, in turn, take care of his political friends. But they did not know their man. Woodrow Wilson had some very different ideas.

Wilson could never have enjoyed the success he had in politics unless he had been changing in the direction of progressivism. Like other reformers, but later than most, he moved to the left, sensing the mood of the country and adopting new positions which he justified with eloquence. For the first time, in 1908, he warned that the corporations had become a threat to national life and must be brought to heel. Rather abruptly, he stopped talking about the dangers of governmental power and began to assert that the real dangers lay with the "power of capital." In his New Jersey campaign of 1910 he actively supported a platform calling for measures to control the corporations, for tax reform, and for a wide range of corrective actions, thus gaining the approval of progressives in both parties. When he won the election and then made good on his promises, he was, at once, a possibility for the presidential nomination in 1912.

It is most unlikely that Governor Wilson of New Jersey could have carried the day in Baltimore in June 1912 in the Democratic convention, except that his credentials as a progressive were well established. He benefited from the approval of William Jennings Bryan and, ultimately, from a long struggle in which Champ Clark, the front runner, could not win the necessary two-thirds majority. Finally, on the forty-sixth ballot, Woodrow Wilson was the winner. It was almost a miracle that this "amateur" from the college campus should emerge victorious over the professionals. He had taken a long step toward the presidency.

Governor Wilson made his enemies along the way, as he would continue to do in the White House. When forced to choose between his support of "principle" on the one hand and his loyalty to political friends on the other, he often chose principle. Someone said of Wilson about this time that he was "clean, strong, high-minded and cold-blooded." It should not be assumed, however, that he was innocent of politics or theoretically opposed to the idea of political bosses and their handiwork. As a matter of fact, he had written in his *Constitutional Government in the United States* (1908) that bosses were "indispensable" to the American system, for at least they gave "constant and professional attention" to the task of making the political machinery go. Only with difficulty could a better and more responsible system be attained. By 1912, however, Wilson certainly believed that very large and important improvements were likely under his kind of leadership.

He went on to wage a brilliant campaign, to formulate his New Freedom, and to make possible in a period of months a rehabilitation of the Democratic party. How he did all this is not a simple matter. The "New Freedom," a term which he first used in Indianapolis on October 3, 1912, implied a number of things. It implied that Americans had lost their economic freedom—without which other freedoms were also imperiled—in the preceding generation or so. This had been a period of Republican dominance and, through the Republican party, of big business control. The trusts had virtually taken over America. Primarily through the tariff duties, raising the cost of living for every American, they had made exorbitant profits and added still further to the monopoly power. Neither the Republican party nor the Progressive party, Wilson asserted, could be trusted to fight successfully against these great privileged interests. Taft, Roosevelt, and other Republicans had already had their chance and had failed.

Wilson could not accept TR's proposal for a new powerful government commission which would regulate business and, presumably, keep monopolies under control. To license the "juggernauts" and try to guide them did not strike Wilson as a practical idea. He was much influenced by Louis D. Brandeis, whom he first met in August 1912. After a long talk with Brandeis at Sea Girt, New Jersey, the Democratic nominee spoke with new confidence of the need to "regulate competition," to nourish and preserve it. "What has created these monopolies?" Wilson asked. And he replied: "Unregulated competition. It has permitted these men to do anything that they chose to do to squeeze their rivals out and to crush their rivals to the earth." So the nation must take appropriate action. Wilson's trust program was, in fact, still rather fuzzy. He did not intend to break up the trusts in any sweeping way, recognizing no doubt the great difficulty of doing so, and was in part simply offering a program to counteract that of Roosevelt.

Wilson's tone in the campaign was predominantly one of confidence and good humor. He even joked at himself occasionally, as in the following limerick, delivered to an audience in Minneapolis:

> For beauty I am not a star;
> There are others more handsome by far
> But my face, I don't mind it,
> Because I'm behind it;
> It's the people in front that I jar.

Once he referred to Theodore Roosevelt as a "very erratic comet now sweeping across our horizon," drawing a laugh from his audience. A characteristic of Wilson's style, however, was to avoid any personal attack on Roosevelt, Taft, the leaders of Wall Street, Republican stand-patters, or others. It was the "system" instead, the many inequities, that deeply concerned him. The Democratic party, he preached, could best represent the American people and carry on a fight against special privilege; it would restore opportunity and put into effect the reforms so long needed.

Some have argued that Wilson was a reactionary in 1912, with a sorely misguided faith in competition, small business, and the "old America." Others believe that the difference between Wilson's New Freedom and Roosevelt's New Nationalism was approximately the difference between "tweedle-dum" and "tweedle-dee"; that, in fact, Wilson was a man of action who would use national power to solve the nation's problems; that he had already been drifting to the left, changing many of his views drastically since 1908; that his general statements of humanitarianism and concern for social justice were strongly indicative of what he would eventually do in the White House.

At Allentown, Pennsylvania, for example, from the rear platform of a train, Wilson started with these remarks:

> A government is intended to serve the people that live under it. Now, there are a great many ways in which to serve the people that live under it, and our government has neglected some of those ways. We are only just now beginning to learn how to take care of our people, to prevent accidents, where accidents are obviously apt to occur in a great many employments, to prevent unreasonable hours of labor, to prevent women [from] being overworked, to prevent young children from being worked at all. There are a score of things which nowadays we regard as the function of the government, but government has been neglectful of these things because it has been taking care of the particular groups of people and not thinking of the life of the people as a whole.

When Wilson said in this passage, "We are only just now beginning to learn how to take care of our people," he seems to have made a revealing statement; he had a sense of his own limitations. Certainly he was learning and had not yet decided just how far he should go in the use of national power. His stress on tariff reduction, banking reform, and antitrust action clearly stamped him as a traditional liberal and a kind of Jeffersonian. Yet no less significant was the emphasis on change in many of his addresses. Wilson recognized very well that the nation had changed enormously since the days of Thomas Jefferson and, in fact, had been altered almost incredibly in the preceding twenty years. He noted on

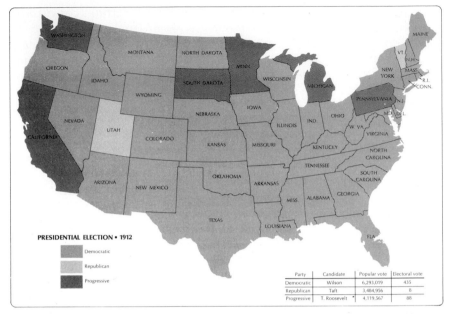

Party	Candidate	Popular vote	Electoral vote
Democratic	Wilson	6,293,019	435
Republican	Taft	3,484,956	8
Progressive	T. Roosevelt	4,119,567	88

Figure 11 The Election of 1912. (*From* A History of the American People, *by Norman A. Graebner, Gilbert C. Fite, and Philip L. White. Copyright © 1970 by McGraw-Hill, Inc.*)

the subject of the American Constitution and the need to reinterpret it that the Darwinian principle should be recognized, for the nation was "a living thing and not a machine."

On some points this candidate seemed a conservative; on others a progressive or a radical. But few could deny that he was a man of brains and ideals, with an erudition out of the ordinary; and that he was proposing to make himself a servant of the people, to the limit of his energy and ability. His skillful appeals to all sections of the country and to businessmen, farmers, the Irish, the Italians, and voters of all descriptions could leave no doubt on another point: He was a working politician.

Wilson carried the election easily against the divided opposition with 435 electoral votes to 88 for Roosevelt and 8 for Taft. Eugene V. Debs, the Socialist candidate, received nearly a million popular votes but none at all in the electoral college. The popular totals showed Wilson to be a plurality winner, as a majority of Americans had voted for Roosevelt, Taft, or Debs. Democrats also assumed control of Congress, carrying both houses, but, again, they had benefited from the Republican split.

The election over, the immediate future promised a most interesting time of testing for the scholar-politician from New Jersey. Every man elected to the presidency is, in some sense, an unknown quantity. In Woodrow Wilson's case there was added cause for interest and speculation. How well could this "man of words," this professor, actually conduct the office of President of the United States? He had written in a scholarly way, for example, on the problems of public administration and was a pioneering figure in that field; and he also had gained some administrative experience at Princeton and at the governor's desk in Trenton. But could he now demonstrate a practical ability to run the affairs of a great country with some 90 million citizens? Wilson was, of course, ready for the effort, and he seemed to have in his favor extraordinary resources of mind and spirit.

SUGGESTIONS FOR ADDITIONAL READING

This chapter has suggested the importance of Wilson's own writing and that of his correspondents. The best place to gain an acquaintance is in *The Papers of Woodrow Wilson,* Princeton Univ. Press, Princeton, N.J. (1966–   ), now numbering eighteen volumes in a projected total of forty. At present these volumes, edited by Arthur S. Link and staff, come to a stop at 1909; so students must continue to use *The Public Papers of Woodrow Wilson,* 6 vols., Ray Stannard Baker and William E. Dodd (eds.), Harper, New York, 1925–1927, along with other collections of letters, speeches, and documents. An outstanding example is John Wells Davidson (ed.), *A Crossroads of Freedom: The 1912 Campaign Speeches of Woodrow Wilson,* Yale, New Haven, Conn., 1956. This is a book of some 500 pages based on the shorthand notes of a stenographer who traveled with the Democratic nominee on the campaign trail. See also E. David Cronon (ed.), *The Political Thought of Woodrow Wilson,* Bobbs-Merrill, Indianapolis, 1965. Among Wilson's books, the best known is *Congressional Government: A Study in American Politics,* Houghton Mifflin, Boston, 1885, but *Constitutional Government in the United States,* Columbia, New York, 1908, is also important for what it reveals about an author soon to become a governor and President.

The leading authority on Wilson is Arthur S. Link, whose books and articles have been published steadily over the last thirty years. His monumental biography, *Wilson,* has now come down to 1917, in five volumes (Princeton Univ. Press, Princeton, N.J., 1947–1965). Other works by Link are *Woodrow Wilson and the Progressive Era, 1910–1917,* Harper, New York, 1954; *Wilson the Diplomatist,* Johns Hopkins, Baltimore, 1957; and *The Higher Realism of Woodrow Wilson and Other Essays,* Vanderbilt, Nashville, Tenn., 1971. In *Woodrow Wilson: A Profile,* Hill and Wang, New York, 1968, Link provides an editorial introduction that is extremely valuable for its assessment of the writing on Wilson to that time and for comments on the new evidence lately made available.

Among the short biographies, two of the best are H. C. F. Bell, *Woodrow Wilson and the People,* Doubleday, New York, 1945, and John A. Garraty, *Woodrow Wilson: A Great Life in Brief,* Knopf, New York, 1956. For the pre-Presidential years see especially George C. Osborn, *Woodrow Wilson: The*

Early Years, Louisiana State Univ. Press, Baton Rouge, 1968, and Henry W. Bragdon, *Woodrow Wilson: The Academic Years,* Harvard, Cambridge, Mass., 1967. Interesting and still valuable is Alexander L. George and Juliette L. George, *Woodrow Wilson and Colonel House: A Personality Study,* John Day, New York, 1956. But see also the article by Dr. Edwin A. Weinstein, "Woodrow Wilson's Neurological Illness," *Journal of American History,* September, 1970, pp. 324–351, and Link's comment in the introduction to *Woodrow Wilson: A Profile.*

An insightful book for the New Jersey period is James Kerney, *The Political Education of Woodrow Wilson,* Century, New York, 1926. On the religious theme see Henry F. May, *Protestant Churches and Industrial America,* noted previously, and Link's essay "Woodrow Wilson and His Presbyterian Inheritance" in *The Higher Realism;* also two excellent studies of William Jennings Bryan: Paul W. Glad, *The Trumpet Soundeth: William Jennings Bryan and His Democracy, 1896–1912,* Univ. of Nebraska Press, Lincoln, 1960, and Lawrence W. Levine, *Defender of the Faith: William Jennings Bryan: The Last Decade, 1915–1925,* Oxford Univ. Press, London, 1965.

Chapter 9

Wilson and the Nationalization of Reform

The country was eager for leadership in 1912, as Woodrow Wilson noted in a remark that was mildly critical of President Taft. Demands for reform were continuing and Wilson responded to this pressure, using the opportunity also to apply his own ideas. The net result was a "new public policy" in the form of pathbreaking economic legislation, with attention to the demands of different groups, and with the President acting as a "people's lobbyist," or trying to do so. Wilson also did much to drag the Democratic party into the twentieth century, to change its image as a collection of ne'er-do-wells and agrarian radicals. Its failings were serious, indeed, but the party gained a new respectability and began to emerge as a more liberal and a more responsible organization nationally than was the opposition.

In the choice of his Cabinet, during the fall and winter of 1912–1913, the President-elect gave a suggestion of how the times were changing. A Southern flavor in the new administration was quite noticeable, while conservative lawyer types were less conspicuous than they had been under Taft. Wilson's adviser in making the choices was Colonel Edward M. House of Texas, a shrewd judge of men who had achieved a close rapport with the Democratic leader. House had been prominent in Texas politics for many years, but was Eastern-educated and a well-traveled man of affairs. Half the Cabinet was either Southern or "Southern transplant," as was the President himself. William G. McAdoo, the Secretary of the Treasury, was an able and aggressive Georgian who had made his career in New York. Secretary of Agriculture David F. Houston, originally a North Carolinian, had become an economist and was in 1912 the president of Washington University at St. Louis. Josephus Daniels of North Carolina, the Secretary of the Navy, was editor of the *Raleigh News and Observer.* James C. McReynolds of Tennessee served only briefly as Attorney General before going on to the Supreme Court. The Postmaster General was Albert S. Burleson, a Congressman from Texas, who now became the chief patronage dispenser.

Adding greatly to the variety and political strength of the group were men from the West and North. William Jennings Bryan of Nebraska became the new Secretary of State. William B. Wilson, a Congressman from Pennsylvania and formerly an official of the United Mine Workers, assumed the Labor Department portfolio. Lindley Garrison, a judge from New Jersey, was the first Secretary of War in this Cabinet and an able administrator. Franklin K. Lane of California, formerly a newspaperman, and a Commissioner of the Interstate Commerce Commission, headed the Department of Interior. William C. Redfield of Brooklyn, New York, became the Secretary of Commerce.

The new President did not give appointments merely to the progressive members of his party. Reluctantly, Wilson concluded that to gain the necessary support in Congress, he had to work with city bosses of the North (including erstwhile enemies in New Jersey), with conservatives from the South, and others. It was a painful awakening—similar to that suffered by Taft before him. Yet Wilson had the great advantage over his predecessor that the Democrats had long been out of power and needed his support even more than he needed theirs. He was the leader to whom they gladly looked, provided only that he treat them decently and give the customary favors.

As Democrats gathered together in the spring of 1913, they had little thought of difficulties that might lie ahead. This was a glorious time of party control in both houses of Congress and in the executive branch, with positions to be filled from the highest diplomatic position to the lowest post office. A shift in the seat of power was now occurring, and no one could be certain how it would all turn out. Democrats came, in considerable numbers, from the North and West, but most of all from the South. One journalist wrote: "In Washington you feel it in the air, you

Figure 12 Inauguration Day. *(From the* Literary Digest, *March 15, 1913.)*

note it in the changed and changing ways of business; . . . you hear strange names of men to whom leadership and importance are attributed, and if you ask, you almost invariably learn that they are from the South." Actually, a new sectional coalition had come into existence, and—if the Democrats were to be successful—the needs of all sections had to be considered sympathetically.

Wilson's first inaugural of March 4, 1913, was one of the great addresses of American history, affording an example of his inspirational powers and his determination to lead the country. "The success of a party," he said, "means little except when the Nation is using that party for a large and definite purpose. No one can mistake the purpose for which the Nation now seeks to use the Democratic Party." Democrats were to be an instrument for progressive reform. In a typically eloquent statement, the President declared:

We have been proud of our industrial achievements, but we have not hitherto stopped thoughtfully enough to count the human cost, the cost of lives snuffed out, of energies overtaxed and broken, the fearful physical and spiritual cost to the men and women and children upon whom the dead weight and burden of it all has fallen pitilessly the years through. . . . There has been something crude and heartless and unfeeling in our haste to succeed and be great.

Speaking of the federal government and its failures he said: "The great Government we loved has too often been made use of for private and selfish purposes, and those who used it had forgotten the people." He was proposing now to use this government for better purposes; to restore old standards of integrity; to reform the tariff and banking system and the industrial system as well; to help the farmers and laborers; to save the nation's resources; to develop its water powers; and so on. In a striking statement, Wilson urged that means be found to put government "at the service of humanity, in safeguarding the health of the Nation, the health of its men and its women and its children, as well as their rights in the struggle for existence." He went on: "Society must see to it that it does not itself crush or weaken or damage its own constituent parts. The first duty of law is to keep sound the society it serves."

In a final burst of rhetoric the President declared:

> This is not a day of triumph; it is a day of dedication. Here muster, not the forces of party, but the forces of humanity. Men's hearts wait upon us; men's lives hang in the balance; men's hopes call upon us to say what we will do. Who shall live up to the great trust? Who dares fail to try? I summon all honest men, all patriotic, all forward-looking men, to my side. God helping me, I will not fail them, if they will but counsel and sustain me!

In this language one senses the glory and the tragedy of Woodrow Wilson. He wrote with the soul of a poet, but he could not know what a terrible and pitiless task lay ahead, especially in the period of World War I.

The new President called a special session of the Sixty-third Congress, which met on April 7. He came before the assembled senators and representatives to deliver a special message on tariff reform and, in doing so, broke a precedent of 100 years. All the Presidents since John Adams had delivered their messages to the Congress in writing. Wilson wanted action immediately to effect a drastic reduction of tariff duties. Banking reform and the trust problem were next on his agenda. This expert on party government was prepared to use all the techniques available to get his program through the Congress, to live up to party commitments, and to strengthen the Democrats for elections to come. Wilson conferred with party leaders in the White House, he went to Capitol Hill, and he approved the use of a caucus system by which rank-and-file members of the Democratic party would be bound (it was hoped) to support those measures discussed and decided upon in sessions of the caucus. The

President was also prepared to use his power of patronage to help those who helped him and to chastise those who did not, at least on the measures considered crucial. Obviously, he did not expect his supporters to agree on everything.

Through the spring and summer of 1913 the tariff fight raged. The difficulties were similar to those that had frustrated Taft in 1909. Democrats, like Republicans, faced the wrath of the protected interests, who would fight vigorously to retain their competitive advantages. Not a few in both parties were strong believers in protection and were prepared to do their best for that dubious cause. The Republican Senator from Utah, Reed Smoot, poured out his feelings on the subject, as follows: "I am a protectionist in every fiber of my soul. I believe in protection to every section of this country. I offer no apology for it. I believe just as surely as I believe that I am alive that it is for the best interest of this country."

The real battle came in the Senate. Previously, in the House, Oscar W. Underwood pushed to passage a bill that carried reductions of some 10 percent. It also contained an income tax provision that promised to become the first permanent tax of that nature in United States history. Highly controversial was a feature of the House bill, now brought under Senate consideration, to eliminate entirely the duties on wool and sugar.

An aggregation of senators from both parties, aided and abetted by lobbyists of many kinds, threatened to defeat the bill. At this point Woodrow Wilson did something unexpected. In a statement to the press on May 26, he criticized severely what was going on: "I think that the public ought to know the extraordinary exertions being made by the lobby in Washington to gain recognition for certain alterations of the Tariff bill. Washington has seldom seen so numerous, so industrious or so insidious a lobby. . . . Only public opinion can check and destroy it." On a suggestion of Senator La Follette the Senate decided to air the President's charge by investigating itself. All ninety-six members soon thereafter went before a lobby committee to give evidence concerning their own property holdings; did they, individually, stand to profit from the tariff positions they were taking? And were the lobbyists indeed active, as the President asserted? Wilson could hardly have hoped for better results. One senator, a member of the investigating committee, observed that Wilson had "bagged no end of game." He continued: "The probe has not only justified every stricture he made but has heaped discredit on the cause of those who oppose his ideas on free sugar. It has been demonstrated that the tariff has been maintained all these years only by the most reprehensible methods involving a lavish expenditure of money."

Wilson's case was virtually proven. By judicious pressure on a few members of his own party and with some help from progressive Republicans, he got the action he wanted. Almost incredibly, the duties were reduced still further below the level of the House bill to an average reduction of about 15 percent. This was an honest measure, with no tricks, providing for an ad valorem basis of calculation. More important, in the long run, was the income tax provision. Advocates of tax reform included Cordell Hull of Tennessee, who wrote the House provision, Senator James K. Vardaman of Mississippi (an extreme racist but a radical on economic matters), and La Follette of Wisconsin. These and other men insisted that the time had come for federal taxes to be based, to some extent, on the ability of a man to pay. The final result was a basic tax of 1 percent on incomes over $4,000 and a graduated surtax on high income, starting at $20,000. The basic tax of 1 percent was also assessed on corporate income. Inadequate though it was, here was the beginning of a modern tax policy, replacing the traditional reliance on tariff duties.

The banking fight came next. Long before Congress had completed the tariff legislation, Wilson appeared again to deliver a special message of importance, this time on banking and currency reform. This was another explosive issue. In one sense it was a highly technical matter that had little to do with progressive reform. In another it concerned the very essence of progressivism. No corporation or banking house, like J. P. Morgan's, should be permitted to exercise an extraordinary power in the economy, superior even to that of the national government. Rather, the government had a responsibility to exercise its leadership and provide supervisory functions. The old banking system, established in the Civil War years, was seriously lacking in this respect. Two committees of Congress had investigated the problem since the panic that occurred in 1907. The National Monetary Commission, headed by Nelson Aldrich, consisted of an equal number of senators and representatives, together with a staff of experts. They conducted extensive studies and finally recommended the establishment of a great new national bank, controlled by private capital, with the necessary branch banks around the country. But a second committee, in the House of Representatives, headed by Arsene Pujo of Louisiana, disagreed vigorously. It charged that a serious concentration of capital already existed and that the Aldrich plan for a national bank would aggravate the situation. Louis Brandeis offered a similar analysis. Wilson's own position was one of moderation, while searching for answers; he did not attempt to dictate specific provisions of this bill as he had in the case of the Simmons-Underwood tariff.

A compromise was the result. As Lester V. Chandler, an economist, stated several decades later: "The original Federal Reserve Act, which was Wilson's principal vehicle for monetary reform, certainly made many concessions to the existing financial system and to the whole complex of existing prejudices, vested interests, and pressure groups. But it was an important start toward monetary and banking reform, and from that start has gradually evolved the powerful Federal Reserve System that we know today." Almost everyone agreed in 1913 on two things: First, greater coordination was required in the banking system, so that when panic struck or depression impended the banks could give aid to each other; second, the issuance of money should be given a greater flexibility or "elasticity," permitting credit to be granted, and money to flow out, when credit was really needed.

At one extreme in the protracted struggle were men like Bryan and La Follette and the agrarian "radicals" who believed that the power of banking interests should be drastically curtailed. The money supply should be issued and controlled by the government. At the other were bankers or conservatives horrified at the thought of government interference. Respected leaders like Elihu Root evoked grim memories of "free silver" and 1896, predicting disaster if the Federal Reserve bill were passed. Paul M. Warburg, a key adviser to the National Monetary Commission and a relative moderate in his views, also gave a melancholy forecast.

In this difficult situation of conflicting views and dissension in his party ranks, Wilson gave another demonstration of leadership. At one point he declared that he would not let the American Bankers Association run the country. He also attacked certain Democratic rebels in the Banking Committee of the Senate. But he showed himself capable of conciliating and cajoling those who disagreed, and he won the support of Secretary Bryan on the one hand and of many businessmen on the other. Wilson personally made the suggestion that eventuated in the Federal Reserve Board, viewed as a "capstone" of the new system. Secretary of the Treasury McAdoo, Representative Carter Glass of Virginia, and Senator Robert L. Owen of Oklahoma were key figures in the final outcome. The Glass-Owen Act of December 1913 established a regional system of twelve banks presided over by the Reserve Board, which was appointed by the President. An "elastic" currency supply was now made possible as individuals could go to their local banks, seeking credit and with the necessary notes or "paper" as security. The local banks, in turn, would go to the Federal Reserve banks, from which Federal Reserve notes were now issued. By raising the rediscount (or interest) rate, the Board could discourage credit at any particular time and try to slow down the economy. In this and other respects the system encouraged coordination and the development of a new expertise, although much had to be learned. Also, the bankers remained very strong. In any case, the advantages of the Federal Reserve Act far outshone any disadvantages in the winter of 1913–1914.

Democrats were jubilant at the success they were having. One member of Congress noted in September 1913, with a tinge of regret, that the President wanted them to push on with their work; there should be no recess at this time. The country, he said, admired this quality in Wilson, and under him great things were indeed being accomplished. Another Democrat shouted out in Congress that this was a time for "rejoicing." He continued: "Labor is employed, wages are good, the earth has yielded abundantly, and the Democratic Party is in control, God reigns, and all is well with the Republic." William Howard Taft, now a professor of law at Yale University, was also impressed, although in quite a different way. Writing to Elihu Root, he noted Wilson's power to "coerce men to follow his lead." His "use of the press" and of "political instruments" aroused Taft's "very great admiration." It also proved that Theodore Roosevelt was not the "only pebble on the beach" in the exercise of such skills.

The next problem that demanded a solution, in Woodrow Wilson's judgment, was the trusts. In particular, further tendencies toward "trustification" must be averted, if at all possible. Appearing before Congress on January 20, 1914, the President discussed this difficult and sensitive question and called for action. Then, in the weeks to come, two different though related approaches were followed, resulting in two pieces of legislation, each to be famous in its own way. The first approach was to strengthen the Sherman law of 1890. Why not draft a measure specifically listing those actions in restraint of trade which were prohibited? Why not impart a new precision to the law, and enforce that law? The second approach was based on a belief that such specificity was impossible, that violators would always find a way, and that a far more logical method was to employ a commission having the power to grapple with cases as they arose. In other words, something similar to Roosevelt's proposal of 1912 might be adopted.

Strange though it seemed to some, Wilson moved toward the "Roosevelt plan"; yet he did not abandon the other idea of a revised antitrust law. The whole subject of regulatory commissions and their effectiveness had been long debated, and Wilson got into this discussion in 1914 from a new vantage point, earnestly seeking the best solution available. With his background in governmental studies, the problem was not a new one, but he seems to have been influenced rather strongly by Louis Brandeis and George Rublee, a New York lawyer. They helped to resolve his doubts and to bring about the creation of the Federal Trade Commission in September 1914. The FTC owed a great deal to the Old Bureau of Corporations under Roosevelt, although it did have the power to act more forcefully. Its function was, for one thing, to investigate business practices and to make reports; this could be a useful and revealing line of work. The major function of the commission, as Wilson envisioned it, was to stop the growth of trusts in the bud; to issue "cease and desist" orders, thus attempting to prevent businessmen from using methods that were either illegal or unethical. Wilson's plan was a moderate one. He hoped to establish a code of fair practice. He believed that the business community was essentially well intentioned and primarily in need of guidance. However, those failing to cooperate might be prosecuted, and the FTC would act in conjunction with the Department of Justice.

The Clayton Antitrust law of October 1914 helped to delineate those actions that were illegal and subject to prosecution. It seemed to do so, at least. But, in fact, it contained a very large loophole. As an example, for one corporation to hold stock in a rival corporation was a practice expressly banned. Yet the language of the act conveniently provided an "out." Did the matter in question *materially* lessen competition? This was the key point in the entire measure. Thus the Clayton Act was highly susceptible to interpretations of the Attorney General or government officials concerned, much as the Sherman law had been before it.

Wilson's antitrust policy was, at best, a mixed success. Yet the ambivalent course he followed, with a sincere belief in the virtues of competition, and some measures to stimulate it, along with a reluctance to attack "natural history" by breaking up the trusts, was something of a pattern for the future. One scholar declares: "The choices made by the Wilson administration have been, and still are, the basis of our industrial policy." Much depended upon appointments that were made—upon the men in high positions given responsibility for carrying out the law. Some of these under Wilson were of the "Brandeisian school," as was, for example, Thomas W. Gregory of Texas, who became Attorney General in 1914 and continued to 1919. No one could accuse him, justly, of being soft on big business. The Federal Trade Commission contained some members, also, who sought to carry out the apparent purposes of the antitrust law and the FTC. It was an endless battle, full of discouragement.

Organized labor and the farmers, as well, pressed for attention in the Wilson administration. They expected, at the least, a sympathetic hearing, which many felt they had not received from Republican leaders. Wilson's attitude was by no means one of firm support, and Arthur Link has argued that the President moved slowly and reluctantly toward the concept of positive intervention in the economy for the purpose of giving aid to the different economic groups. In any case, he did move, and it is difficult to see how he could have failed to do so. First of all, he was sympathetic toward the working people generally and appreciative of their difficulties. Second, the Democratic party drew much of its strength from the South and West, where farmers were principally located. It claimed, also, to be a party of the producing classes, by contrast with the Republicans; it wanted and it needed the labor vote. Finally, Wilson's ideas had swung to the left since 1908 and, not surprisingly, they swung a little more in that direction. This was especially understandable since he and his advisers were looking ahead to the next presidential election.

Samuel Gompers noted in his *Seventy Years of Life and Labor* that Wilson's inauguration, together with Democratic control in both houses of Congress, presented a situation "fraught with great possibilities." Many in the labor movement expected that Wilson "would inaugurate a national policy in which human welfare and social service would be the dominant purposes." There was reason to believe this, and, in any event, Gompers and others were prepared to do their utmost to obtain such results. The American Federation of Labor now had a membership of about 2 million. Notwithstanding some setbacks in the preceding ten or fifteen years, the gains made by labor were considerable. Slowly they added to their political capability; they could hardly be ignored. Gompers and the craft union members were seeking fair play, with a minimum of protective legislation, and they were eager to find friends in high places.

Unionists had noticed Wilson's speeches of a friendly type and especially his defense of their right to organize. At Fall River, Massachusetts, for example, he discussed lucidly the injustice of a legal situation in which owners could join together with other owners, forming powerful associations, while they refused to hire laborers because they were union members or might join a union. The thing was "absolutely one-sided," Wilson declared. He knew that government leaders and judges bore much of the responsibility for this perversion of justice: "The courts have held that union labor has not the right to boycott a concern because it is employing nonunion labor, and yet it says that the concern may boycott them because they are unionized." One could imagine, he said, how businessmen would "howl" if they were told that they could not organize.

Comments like this were exactly what laboring people wanted to hear. But they also wanted the necessary action to prevent their being prosecuted under the antitrust laws for forming combinations "in restraint of trade." They wanted relief, as well, from antilabor injunctions. Eight-hour laws, child-labor laws, protection of the rights of merchant seamen, and the restriction of immigration were other matters in which labor leaders and their friends showed a keen interest. It was soon apparent that Woodrow Wilson was the closest to being a prolabor president of any in American history up to that date. He maintained a cordial relationship with the laboring people and was able to satisfy them in the great majority of their demands. Quite important was the presence in his administration of people like William B. Wilson as Secretary of Labor and Louis Post as his assistant in the Department. Post, a single-taxer, a publicist, and something of a radical, had many friends in the labor movement and among the progressives.

Most urgent, it seemed to the labor leaders in 1913, was the problem of suits brought against them under the antitrust law. Members of Congress took a first step to correct the situation soon after they met in special session. They supported a measure which banned the use of federal funds to prosecute labor unions under the Sherman law. Then, as the Clayton bill moved toward passage in 1914, the AFL obtained what Gompers and some others hailed as a "magna charta" for labor. Section 6 stated: "Nothing contained in the anti-trust laws shall be construed to forbid the existence and operation of labor, agricultural, or horticultural organizations, instituted for the purposes of mutual help . . . nor shall such organizations, or the members thereof, be held or construed to be illegal combinations or conspiracies in restraint of trade, under the anti-trust laws." In the last section of the act an attempt was made to limit the use of injunctions in the federal courts and to guarantee employees basic rights of peaceful assembly and freedom of speech in the job situation.

This so-called magna charta in the Clayton Act fell considerably short of what it was supposed to do. Yet the labor movement received unprecedented attention in its fight of 1913–1914, and the justice of its cause was widely recognized. Unions were active as never before at the national level. Lobbyists of the AFL vied with those of the National Association of Manufacturers and the U.S. Chamber of Commerce. Though labor had not yet "arrived" as it did in the 1930s, it was on its way and was a force to be reckoned with.

The La Follette Seamen's Act, as it was named after its chief sponsor, brought the culmination of one long struggle for protective legislation. Andrew Furuseth, of the Seamen's Union, had lobbied in Washington since the 1890s and vividly impressed those who would listen to his stories of tyranny on the high seas and the need for federal legislation. After some doubts, especially because of international ramifications, the Democrats took up his cause in 1914–1915. Shipowners were among the few who opposed reform legislation. The Seamen's Act of March 1915 basically gave more freedom to the members of merchant crews. An increase in living space was required and a larger allotment of food. Safety precautions were increased and especially the requirement that enough lifeboats be provided for all. Seamen were now able to demand one-half of the wages they had earned and get off a ship. Imprisonment for desertion was abolished if the sailor had left his ship in a safe port. An effort to protect the seamen's wages was a blow at the "crimping system," which had often kept them in a state of virtual peonage. Much depended upon the interpretation of this act, but it proved generally successful.

As Wilson's first term neared an end, other measures to assist labor were passed by the Congress and received Presidential approval. The Keating-Owen child-labor bill, a workmen's compensation plan for federal employees, and the Adamson eight-hour bill for railroad workers all became law. It was difficult to resist the legitimate demands of labor in 1916 when Wilson was campaigning for reelection; and the threat of war, as well, encouraged the granting of concessions. These related issues of war and peace will be touched on later.

More than anything else, the Wilson administration was a gathering of "agrarians," with countless disciples of Jefferson and Jackson to be found. Most did not actually have farms, but they had drunk deeply of Democratic principles and traditions. They also knew, from a practical standpoint, that the South and West—their home regions in most instances—were still predominantly agrarian. If agriculture languished, then banking, retail sales, and other lines of endeavor would suffer as well. The farmer was something of an underdog, and Wilsonian Democrats were sincerely sympathetic. Farmers had not benefited from the protective tariff as industry had, nor from the banking system and tax policy. They deserved a friendly administration in Washington, although problems on the farm were partly of their own making and their own wishful thinking. They were victims to some degree of an "agrarian myth," as Richard Hofstadter and others have argued.

The Wilson administration outdid its predecessors in meeting the needs of farmers. In the Federal Reserve Act, credit was permitted on agricultural "paper," although a time limitation of six months proved highly displeasing to many. After much agitation and early opposition from the President, agricultural interests obtained in 1916 the Federal Farm Loan Act, which was a basic piece of legislation and widely helpful, providing only that the borrower had land and improvements to offer as security. To give some help to those who wanted loans on their crops, the Congress passed in 1916 a Federal Warehouse Act. Here was a direct forerunner of the commodity credit operations in later decades.

One of the most influential policies of this period was that of dollar matching. The theory was to aid the states and local governments in worthy causes having national significance. How better to do this than to match the local government, dollar for dollar? The Smith-Lever Act of 1914 provided for matching funds in aid of agricultural extension work. Wilson commented in a letter to Representative A. F. Lever of South Carolina, one of the sponsors: "This piece of legislation is one of the most significant and far-reaching measures for the education of adults ever adopted by any government. . . . It will permit the placing in each of the 2,850 rural counties of the Nation two farm demonstrators and specialists, who will assist the demonstrators in the more difficult problems confronting them." Another plan of this type was the Smith-Hughes Act of 1917 for federal aid to vocational education. Still another measure of interest to the farmers, but to others as well, was the Federal Highway Act of 1916, providing that state and federal funds would go into the construction of highways nationally important on a matching basis.

Another great question dominated the attention of many leaders in the Wilson administration. This was the conservation (or the preservation) of natural resources. Men from beyond the Mississippi River were freely charging in 1913 that the Roosevelt-Taft policy of withdrawing land had placed these public resources out of reach; had "hermetically" sealed them up and thereby sharply restricted opportunities for development in the Western states. Some members of Congress, therefore, had a handful of bills to introduce on water-power development, mineral lands, the national forests, the national parks, and other matters. Woodrow Wilson was interested in these things but tended to leave the decision making to his subordinates and especially to Secretary of the Interior Franklin K. Lane.

"Frank" Lane brought both strengths and weaknesses to his position. He was a dynamic man, brimming with ideas, and hopeful that controversies over the public lands could soon be settled amicably. But Lane was a Westerner and proud of it. He wanted the West developed, with "fuller and freer" use of resources, he said in an annual report. He wanted the needs of "his" people to be met, and their success would contribute to national success. This seemed to many a policy that favored the West and especially the business leaders of that region. Lane's reputation eventually suffered, much as Ballinger's had a few years earlier; yet most of his program went into effect by 1920.

For the national parks, this was the beginning of a great period, and Lane's contribution was substantial. The American people, for diverse reasons, moved to establish and then preserve the finest park system in the world. Even the exploiters of America, it often seemed, could recognize that the line must be drawn somewhere; that the parks were something special. One can speculate that this was a form of compensation for the greed they displayed, or condoned, in the rapid development or spoliation of resources generally. As one member of Congress commented dryly: "Human nature is very much the same everywhere. . . . The ordinary citizen feels that anything that he can divest his Government of and give to himself with color of honor he ought to do it." But Americans had a different attitude concerning the national park areas. They thought, sometimes, of the future and of their "better selves," with results that were fortunate.

A place with a strange-sounding name leaped into the headlines in

1913 and had a significant influence on the park movement. This was the Hetch-Hetchy Valley, located about 150 miles east of San Francisco in Yosemite National Park. The question at issue concerned the city's water supply. Allegedly the people of San Francisco needed water badly and it could be obtained only by building a dam in the Hetch-Hetchy Valley. An Act of Congress, however, would be required for the municipal authorities to proceed. During Roosevelt's administration, in the aftermath of the earthquake and fire that devastated San Francisco, this dispute began to evolve, with many complexities in it. Since the project proposed was a municipal one involving public power, progressives for the most part were won over. (If the Pacific Power and Electric Company had been the initiating party, responses would have been more hostile.)

To invade a national park—even for the best of purposes—was a troublesome matter. Roosevelt at first supported the project, then reversed himself. Gifford Pinchot, however, lent his support, as did Secretary Lane and many congressmen. The friends of the parks were outraged. Lyman Abbott of *Outlook* magazine, Robert U. Johnson of *Century* magazine, Horace McFarland of the American Civic Association, John Muir, the naturalist, and members of the Sierra Club, for example, were on the attack. Was nothing still sacred in America? The God-given beauty of Yosemite Park must be preserved. Ultimately the bill passed, and San Francisco got its dam and reservoir. Yet future incursions in the national parks were much more difficult. The issue had become a national one, and the conscience of Americans had been touched. Senator "Jim" Reed of Missouri expressed his amazement that a matter like this, simply a little matter of a dam, had stirred so much excitement.

In the wake of Hetch-Hetchy came the establishment in 1916 of the National Park Service, with Stephen Mather as its head. Supported by Secretary Lane, Mather laid down certain principles that became basic in the Park Service: First, trained personnel were indispensable, and the Service must be lifted out of the patronage politics that had been characteristic in previous years; second, the parks should be held and preserved for the enjoyment and spiritual enrichment of future generations. With such ideas and aggressive leadership as well, the modern era had now opened for America's national parks.

The Wilson administration was seldom lacking in a crisis or dispute of some kind, and one in 1916 had even more significance, perhaps, than the Hetch-Hetchy fight. This was the nomination of Louis D. Brandeis to be a Justice of the United States Supreme Court. Earlier, in 1913, Wilson had considered very seriously the possibility of making Brandeis his Attorney General. The opposition had been strong, however, and Wilson had yielded at that time. Three years later, when an opening occurred on the Court, the President was determined that his friend and adviser should receive the honor. If Brandeis were confirmed, he would be the first Jew ever to serve on the Supreme Court. Many who knew him believed that he had extraordinary ability and ought to be confirmed for that reason alone. If he was indeed a "radical," said a friend, perhaps it was a good idea and about time to provide a little variety on that very conservative court. In point of fact, Brandeis was not a radical but a believer in freedom and justice, with a strong sense of humanity. With his legal expertise and knowledge of economics the Boston lawyer had ably fought a succession of court battles and had made himself famous.

Louis Brandeis was a "maverick" lawyer of the sort then becoming fairly numerous. Clarence Darrow in Chicago and Francis Heney in California were other examples of this independent breed. They refused to be tied to a great corporation and often chose, instead, to oppose such interests. Brandeis was noted for his scientific brief in the case of *Muller v. Oregon* (1908). Refusing to be bound by precedent, he argued for "pragmatism of the law," for reinterpreting the law and the Constitution in the light of modern conditions. What were those conditions? They must be studied and brought into the courtroom, to aid in the decision. Precedents were often misleading. Such a philosophy might be considered as being intelligent conservatism, rather than radicalism, but the great majority of lawyers and judges did not see things that way in 1916.

The fight over Brandeis's confirmation was almost incredible. Wilson stood valiantly by his appointee, as did Attorney General Thomas Gregory, Robert M. La Follette in the Senate, and others. But the *New York Times* urged that he be defeated. The American Bar Association, including seven former presidents of that organization (Taft and Root among them) alleged that Brandeis was not fit to take a seat on the Supreme Court. Taft had asserted earlier that Brandeis was "a muckraker, an emotionalist for his own purposes, a socialist." A group of fifty-five Bostonians, in a petition, also threw their influence against Brandeis. Charles Francis Adams and the president of Harvard, A. Lawrence Lowell, were included in this number. Reacting to these and similar attacks, Senator La Follette showed his sense of outrage, referring to Bar Association presidents and university presidents as "sleek respectable crooks whose opinions have always been for sale." Brandeis himself was more generous to his opponents, many of whom, he said, had simply misunderstood him.

This fight turned into a party issue when the Republican leaders decided to oppose Brandeis. The action occurred primarily in the Judiciary Committee of the Senate. First, a subcommittee of the Judiciary Committee, consisting of three Democrats and two Republicans, held hearings for several weeks and proceeded to write their conflicting reports. Second, the full committee of about twenty members had to vote;

this was crucial. And at last the question reached the Senate floor for final settlement. As A. L. Todd has shown in a very readable book, it was Thomas J. Walsh, a liberal Senator from Montana, who argued the case for Brandeis most effectively and even brilliantly, beginning in the subcommittee, of which he was a Democratic member. In Walsh's judgment, the opposition to Brandeis came mostly from the fact that he was "an outsider," was successful, and was a Jew. Walsh declared: "The real crime of which this man is guilty is that he has exposed the iniquities of men in high places in our financial system. He has not stood in awe of the majesty of wealth. . . . He has written about and expressed views on 'social justice.' . . . They all contemplate that a man's a man and not a machine."

The vote in the subcommittee was 3 to 2 in favor of confirmation. In the full Judiciary Committee it was 10 to 8. But when the Senate itself voted on June 1, 1916, the margin had widened comfortably, and Brandeis gained his seat by a vote of 47 to 22. In some respects this decision was one of the greatest victories in Wilson's administration. Certainly it was satisfying to liberals, to Jews, and to many who believed simply in putting qualified men in high office.

In at least one instance the Wilson administration took a reactionary course concerning the nation's problems. The extreme racial views of some Southerners in Congress and in the Cabinet led them to exert pressure on the President, hoping to bring the Washington government into line with state policies in the South. This was a time of rampant racism, as described earlier, and no one could expect miracles of reform in the existing state of public opinion. But Wilson's election had been a welcome event to some who thought of him as a gentleman, a scholar, and a Christian who would work for racial justice. He had shown signs of his interest and of possible liberalism on this question. As a young man Wilson had set out deliberately to rid himself of a Southern accent, as his wife did too; but to slough off the distinctions of language was easier than to escape racial attitudes of the day. He remained a Southerner, loyal to most traditions of his region, and a believer in segregation. Every member of his Cabinet seems to have been a segregationist. It was the Southern members, however, and notably Burleson and McAdoo, who did much to initiate new policies of segregation in the federal departments and to downgrade blacks in the Civil Service system, firing some of them. The President acquiesced in what his subordinates were doing. He also went against the interest of blacks by failing to support the idea of a National Race Commission which, it was hoped, could study thoroughly the racial problem in America.

From a political standpoint, the President's attitude was hardly surprising at all. He needed Democratic votes to get his legislative

Figure 13 A Portrait by Robert Henri Printed in *Harper's Weekly* for February 21, 1914. This newsboy, a "full-blooded black," was seen by the editors as an illustration of the national race problem.

program through Congress. Southerners were numerous in that body, and they served as chairmen of virtually every committee. Wilson was not going to take chances on the race issue, which he considered a peripheral one, and thereby endanger his tariff bill, banking bill, and so on. He yielded to racists on the subject of appointments in the South and segregation in the executive departments in Washington, but he resisted some extreme demands and, occasionally, deplored the excesses of race feeling and intolerance.

It is possible to find a ray of light in the Wilson period on this subject, as the black historian Rayford Logan has done: The worst did not happen. Extreme bigots in the Congress saw an opportunity to pass federal laws comparable to those they had already passed in their own states; for example, laws banning interracial marriage. They kept trying but did not succeed. A few friends of the Afro-American spoke up in his defense, and such bills met their death in one house or the other. Then, as Logan notes, the Supreme Court began to hand down decisions that foreshadowed those of decades to come, barring certain types of discriminatory action. Most important really were the black organizations and their leaders who protested the course of national policy. William Monroe Trotter and W. E. B. Du Bois were two such leaders. Trotter once took his protest personally to Wilson's office and almost got thrown out for his trouble. Du Bois, editor of the *Crisis* for the National Association for the Advancement of Colored People, had a strong influence in the black community and was not to be silenced. Giving considerable aid, too, was a minority of white leaders, men and women, progressives and humanitarians, who would not permit the race problem to be casually dismissed or swept under a rug. They could agree with an old black leader who said, prophetically, that politicians might think they had solved this race problem—that segregation was the answer and that an "inferior" people who were not assimilable must be kept segregated. But such people had not even started to solve it or to understand the difficulties, and fifty years later their failure would be apparent.

Wilson's record as a reformer—the race question aside—was a good one. The legislative achievements from 1913 to 1916 were remarkable, even though some measures inevitably failed or had a mixed success. Farmers and laborers fared well on the whole in Wilson's first administration, while Catholics and Jews among the minority groups could note some tangible gains in their status. This President, like Taft before him, refused to support a literacy test for immigrants, thus adhering to the traditionally liberal policy. Most striking of all was the resurgence of the Democratic party, with its Southern, Northern, and Western wings. Whatever happened in the future, this party had gained a new basis of pride and integrity, and a new name could now be added to those of the Democratic chieftains Jefferson and Jackson.

SUGGESTIONS FOR ADDITIONAL READING

Arthur Link's *Woodrow Wilson and the Progressive Era,* mentioned previously, is focused on the same period as this chapter and on most of the same issues, but it should be supplemented with later works by the same author, such as *Wilson: The New Freedom* (1956) and *Wilson: Campaigns for Progressivism and Peace, 1916–1917* (1965); also with studies by others that cover the period from a different perspective. Particularly valuable are several books cited earlier: George E. Mowry, *Theodore Roosevelt and the Progressive Movement* (1947); Harold U. Faulkner, *The Decline of Laissez Faire* (1951); Eric F. Goldman, *Rendezvous with Destiny* (1956); and Robert H. Weibe, *Businessmen and Reform* (1962). An attempt at a new synthesis is Otis L. Graham, Jr., *The Great Campaigns: Reform and War in America, 1900–1928,* Prentice-Hall, Englewood Cliffs, N.J., 1971. Another work by Graham, *An Encore for Reform: The Old Progressives and the New Deal,* Oxford Univ. Press, New York, 1967, sheds light on the ideology of reform, as does Charles Forcey, *The Crossroads of Liberalism: Croly, Weyl, Lippmann, and the Progressive Era, 1900–1925,* Oxford Univ. Press, New York, 1961.

Books of a documentary or primary nature should be added to those noted in the previous chapter; for example, the following: Charles Seymour (ed.), *The Intimate Papers of Colonel House,* 4 vols., Houghton Mifflin, Boston, 1926–1928, and Ray Stannard Baker, *Woodrow Wilson: Life and Letters,* 8 vols., Doubleday, Garden City, N.Y., 1927–1939. Among the autobiographical accounts, the following are especially recommended: Cary T. Grayson, *Woodrow Wilson, An Intimate Memoir,* Holt, New York, 1960; Joseph P. Tumulty, *Woodrow Wilson As I Know Him,* Doubleday, Garden City, N.Y., 1921; David F. Houston, *Eight Years with Wilson's Cabinet, 1913 to 1920,* 2 vols., Doubleday, Page, Garden City, N.Y., 1926; and Jonathan Daniels, *The End of Innocence,* Lippincott, Philadelphia, 1954.

Special studies and biographical works are numerous indeed and only a few can be noted at this point. William Diamond, *The Economic Thought of Woodrow Wilson,* Johns Hopkins, Baltimore, 1943, is still useful. Earl Latham (ed.), *The Philosophy and Policies of Woodrow Wilson,* Univ. of Chicago Press, Chicago, 1958, offers evaluations by political scientists, economists, historians, and others. Successive volumes in the History of the South series contain chapters that are important: C. Vann Woodward, *Origins of the New South, 1877–1913,* Louisiana State Univ. Press, Baton Rouge, 1951, and George B. Tindall, *The Emergence of the New South, 1913–1945,* Louisiana State Univ. Press, Baton Rouge, 1967. See also Hugh C. Bailey, *Liberalism in the New South: Southern Social Reformers and the Progressive Movement,* Univ. of Miami Press, Coral Gables, Fla., 1969. Graham Adams, Jr., *Age of Industrial Violence, 1910–15,* Columbia, New York, 1966, is an interesting examination of the United States Commission on Industrial Relations and its inquiries. Hyman Weintraub, *Andrew Furuseth, Emancipator of the Seamen,* Univ. of California Press, Berkeley, 1959, is a good study that does not fail to criticize its subject. Two books on Brandeis are readable and informative: Alden L. Todd, *Justice on Trial: The Case of Louis D. Brandeis,* McGraw-Hill, New York, 1964, and Alpheus T. Mason, *Brandeis: A Free Man's Life,* Viking, New York, 1946. On the racial situation see books mentioned previously, along with August Meier, *Negro Thought in America, 1880–1915: Racial Ideologies in the Age of Booker T. Washington,* Univ. of Michigan Press, Ann Arbor, 1963; Stephen R. Fox, *The Guardian of Boston: William Monroe Trotter,* Atheneum, New York, 1971; Francis L. Broderick, *W. E. B. Du Bois: Negro Leader in a Time of Crisis,* Stanford Univ. Press, Stanford, California, 1959; and W. E. B. Du Bois, *Dusk of Dawn: An Essay toward an Autobiography of a Race Concept,* Harcourt, Brace, New York, 1940.

Chapter 10

Looking Outward: The 1890s to World War I

As the United States was altering its domestic relations in a manner profoundly significant, it also reached a point of departure in its foreign affairs. In 1898 and the years immediately following, the nation gained far-flung possessions and "protectorates" and could never go back to the relative isolation of the 1880s. This change may be attributed to the progressives and reformers and to their vigorous and optimistic cast of mind. William E. Leuchtenburg has argued that the ideological content of imperialism was much like that of progressivism and that the reformers of the early twentieth century "did not oppose imperialism, but with few exceptions, ardently supported the imperialist surge or, at the very least, proved agreeably acquiescent." In the activities of Theodore Roosevelt, Senator Albert J. Beveridge, and many others this statement can be amply supported. Nevertheless, it is conspicuously true that Henry Cabot Lodge, Elihu Root, Philander Knox, and other conservatives of the time were also ranged on the side of expansion and empire. The fact seems to be that few Americans had an alternative to the often-mentioned "destiny" that placed the United States among the great powers of the world by the early 1900s.

Long before 1900, a rising nationalism was apparent. Thus, one editor of a Western newspaper in June 1889 turned his thoughts to military affairs, writing in the best patriotic fashion: "West Point has just graduated 48 more warriors. Foreign nations with expensive standing armies please take notice." The "empire days" of the United States were presaged in the administration of Benjamin Harrison, some ten years before the great adventure of 1898 which catapulted the country into world affairs. Harrison, for example, was anxious to annex the Hawaiian Islands but could not manage this before leaving office in 1893. The Cleveland administration, in its turn, was not so inclined toward expansion, but it was bellicose and nationalistic. It even took the risk of war with Britain in a dispute of 1895 over the Venezuelan boundary.

Americans were increasingly aware that their nation, with a population of some 75 million, with its states and territories spanning the Continent from ocean to ocean—and even to the Bering Sea in Alaska— with its fabulous potential and its growing industrial might, must be considered among the great nations of the world. This was an age of imperialism, as the more highly developed nations, including England, France, Germany, Russia, and Japan, reached out to grab what they could, or to protect what they had already taken. Africa, China, the Pacific islands, and Latin America were promising areas for exploitation. It was all very exciting. The search for profits was a highly important consideration in the minds of many business leaders and others. If the American frontier had come to an end, as census takers and scholars were saying, then it was time to look outward for new markets and raw materials. The nation's growth must continue. Patriotic Americans could not imagine that their great country would be left behind.

This was an era of Darwinism, Anglo-Saxonism, the "white man's burden," and the "Yellow Peril." Such ideas were pervasive in the Western world, but Americans had their own special way of using them and of invoking them frequently to justify territorial expansion or military preparedness. In the words of Alfred Thayer Mahan, an admiral who was also a historian, it was a Darwinian world in which people found themselves, a world of incessant struggle; for struggle was the law of life itself: "Everywhere nation is arrayed against nation; our own no less than others." In similar language Theodore Roosevelt, a disciple of Mahan's, once declared:

> I preach to you, then, my countrymen, that our country calls not for the life of ease but for the life of strenuous endeavor. The twentieth century looms before us big with the fate of many nations. If we stand idly by, . . . if we

shrink from the hard contests where men must win at hazard of their lives and at the risk of all they hold dear, then the bolder and stronger peoples will pass us by, and will win for themselves the domination of the world. . . . It is only through strife, through hard and dangerous endeavor, that we shall ultimately win the goal of true national greatness.

It was common to argue in these years that the Anglo-Saxon peoples were the best of all people in their stock and ancestry (such terms were much in vogue). They would carry the burden of international leadership. The United States and England, notably, had proved their capacity to establish institutions in which democracy and liberty flourished, while Christianity had its finest opportunity. Anglo-Saxonism seemed especially attractive during 1898 and the years that followed, for Great Britain showed friendship toward the Americans during the Spanish-American War, while Europe generally did not, and the Germans gave evidence of real hostility. The Americans and British were moving, in fact, toward a resolution of their principal difficulties. This new cordiality was to be highly significant in the decades to come.

If the Americans, the British, and so-called Nordic types were the "superior" peoples, the "inferior" ones obviously belonged to the colored races and the swarthy breeds of mankind. It had to be recognized, however, that some of these, like the yellow people of China and Japan, were extremely hard-working and frugal and that, potentially, they posed a threat to people of the Occident. This racist pattern of thought played into the hands of Southern leaders and others who frankly advocated a caste system for the United States. The logic was hard to resist. When the "superior" race was to dominate in Africa or the Philippines, why should it be reluctant to do so in Georgia, Mississippi, or Illinois? Thus Henry W. Grady of the *Atlanta Constitution,* a spokesman for the "New South," declared as early as 1886 that the national policy of the United States had been, and must be, one of white supremacy. The Indians had been beaten and subjugated, the Chinese were being excluded, and the blacks could not escape their separate destiny. "What God hath separated," he said, "let no man join together." The Anglo-Saxons must prevail.

Ideas of a racialistic and nationalistic type seemed to be almost everywhere. Harry Thurston Peck, for example, was a professor at Columbia University who published a book in 1906 under the title *Twenty Years of the Republic, 1885–1905.* Its pages were laced with Darwinism and Anglo-Saxonism as he discussed the Spanish-American War and its results. The Spanish had behaved outrageously, according to his interpretation, and the United States was thoroughly justified in going to war against them. In the fighting that occurred in Cuba, the American boys were not exactly contemptuous of the Spanish, as sometimes alleged, but they did call them "dagoes" and refused to take them very seriously. Spain was, of course, a "dying" state, while countries like Great Britain and the United States were living nations. Discussing Commodore George Dewey, whose fleet steamed from the British port of Hong Kong to destroy the Spanish ships at Manila Bay, Professor Peck said that Dewey was "by birth a Vermonter, of the very best New England stock." His sailors were also of "the Anglo-Saxon type," and the British in Hong Kong had recognized them as "blood-brothers." Peck was indignant that the German sailors in Manila Bay had been unfriendly. It remained for them, he said, to give a final example of "stupid insolence." In some respects the Philippine leader Emilio Aguinaldo was to be admired as a man of intelligence and energy. But, concluded the author: "Aguinaldo was at bottom a shifty Oriental, with all an Oriental's vanity and with the treachery inherent in his Malay blood."

The typical thinking of Americans on these subjects was suffused with "destiny" and "Mission." Thus John Hay, Secretary of State from the autumn of 1898 to his death in 1905, referred to a "cosmic tendency" which Americans must accept. "No man," he wrote, "no party, can fight with any chance of final success against a cosmic tendency: no cleverness, no popularity avails against the spirit of the age." By no means did all Americans believe in the necessity of annexing the Philippines in the far Pacific, or of pursuing the "large policy" advocated by Theodore Roosevelt, John Hay, and others. But few were left completely unaffected by the new nationalism. At least the annexation of Hawaii was justified, as was the expulsion of Spain from its colonies in the Caribbean. The United States should proceed, obviously, as the dominant power in the American hemisphere. It had a duty, also, to advance the cause of democracy and Christianity in backward corners of the world.

The attitudes of Americans were diverse, but the trend was to an assertion of national rights and duties. Much depended upon current leaders and the commitments they were ready to make. One Roosevelt scholar, Howard K. Beale, reached the conclusion that strategically placed expansionists in the years 1897–1898 had an influence of extraordinary importance. Seldom have "so few done so much," Beale wrote, paraphrasing Winston Churchill in a later war. Each helped the others into key positions in government, and they corresponded frequently and worked together for the common objectives. Massachusetts Senator Henry Cabot Lodge, for example, did much to get Roosevelt appointed as Assistant Secretary of the Navy, in which position he was prepared to carry out the strategy of Admiral Mahan. It was Mahan, apparently, who first put Roosevelt and the expansionists to thinking of the Philippines and how, in the event of war with Spain over Cuba, the Pacific islands should also be attacked. Most important of all, in the final outcome, these men and others with such ideas helped to persuade William McKinley that the Philippine Islands should be annexed, even though, in 1898, little but Manila Bay in the great archipelago had come under American control. McKinley's decision was a momentous one.

The Treaty of Paris of 1898 called for the annexation of the Philippine Islands, the island of Guam, and Puerto Rico. Cuba was, of course, to gain its independence from Spain. The United States Senate proceeded early in 1899 to ratify this treaty, although the vote was close. A short time before, the Congress, by joint resolution, had annexed the Hawaiian Islands, for they were now seen by President McKinley and most members of Congress as an extremely valuable possession that would also serve as a way station to waters of the distant Pacific. While Hawaii had not belonged to Spain, its acquisition in 1898 was a direct result of the war with Spain. Another territory picked up in the course of the war was Wake Island in the North Pacific, about 2,000 miles west of Honolulu. The American empire gained another plum in 1899 when Great Britain, Germany, and the United States, which had been disputing over the Samoan Islands in the South Pacific, arrived at an agreement. The United States took as its share the island of Tutuila with its excellent port at Pago Pago.

The growth of imperialism and the decision to acquire the Philippines soon produced a countermovement that was remarkable for its vigor and heterogeneity. It included Grover Cleveland, William J. Bryan, Andrew Carnegie, Samuel Gompers, Jane Addams, Mark Twain, and a host of distinguished leaders. One scholar, Fred Harvey Harrington, has declared that the "most active and enthusiastic" of the group were reformers of one sort or another—old abolitionists, men from the Liberal Republican movement of 1872, civil service crusaders, municipal reformers, prohibitionists, social welfare workers, friends of the Indians, and so on. E. L. Godkin, Carl Schurz, Charles Francis Adams, Edward Atkinson, and Charles H. Parkhurst are examples. Yet the anti-imperialists were completely unable to unite behind any political leader. Bryan, for example, campaigned on the Democratic ticket in 1900 with Adlai E. Stevenson as his running mate and with anti-imperialism as the leading issue. But the anti-imperialist Republicans would not support Bryan, nor was he a hero in some quarters of the Democratic party. McKinley and Roosevelt easily carried the day in an election that many interpreted as a great victory for the cause of expansion.

Politically the anti-imperialists had little success. They exemplified, however, the doubts of many Americans concerning the new course of world involvement. They raised questions of profound significance that future generations could ignore only at their peril. They protested and gave warning, and in that sense they often showed a caution and foresight that was far more creditable than the effusions of empire builders. The psychologist and philosopher William James was profoundly shocked by the decision to take the Philippines. He deplored the making of such decisions on an abstract basis, heavily laden with moralism, and without a serious consideration of the possible consequences or the attitudes of the native people. The United States, he said, had treated the Philippines as a great corporation treated a small one. He hated such "bigness" and "greatness." The United States had turned the "stars and stripes" into a "lying rag." The businessman and publicist Edward Atkinson, a leading member of the Anti-Imperialist League, published a pamphlet in 1899 with the title *Criminal Aggression: By Whom Committed?* Thus the moral aspects of the new policy were important to him, and he also predicted, accurately, that the hopes of a great trade with the Far East were a delusion.

The long-time foe of imperialism Carl Schurz touched on most of the criticisms that filled the air in a speech of 1899. It was hypocrisy, he said, for the United States to fight for a time to *free* Cuba and then to fight to *subjugate* the Filipinos and Puerto Ricans. Colonization, moreover, went against the American traditions of democracy and self-rule and would relegate the colonized people into a status of "second-class" Americans. He predicted that the United States would be drawn into world affairs, into countless disputes, and would have to rely upon England to assist in protecting the new territories. Extremely important in the argument advanced by Schurz was his Anglo-Saxonism. The people of America, he claimed, could not be expected to live in the intemperate regions such as those of Puerto Rico and the Philippines, and therefore the nation would assume an impossible task in trying to "Americanize" the conquered islands.

Almost all these critics were racists or Darwinists of one kind or another, resembling Schurz. Thus it has been argued that their moral position was not better than that of the expansionists. One group wished to uplift and civilize the "little brown brother," while bringing him under American control; the other group wished to avoid contact almost entirely. The anti-imperialists were rightly concerned over recent happenings, but not necessarily for the right reasons. They saw the danger involved, but the alternatives they could offer were not very satisfactory. The fact seemed to be, as the philosopher George Santayana observed, that the United States was now behaving like a great power and very much as other countries had behaved for centuries. To expect it to behave with generosity, or a sensitive respect for other peoples and cultures, was highly unrealistic.

But America *was* different. It could never forget entirely its belief in itself as the "last best hope of earth," or the noble expressions of the

Declaration of Independence, or the proud boasts of its national songs and benedictions: the "land of the free," the land of opportunity, the land of equal justice under law, and so on. High-minded leaders, especially, were affected. Thus the United States did not establish a "colonial office" or use the word "empire" in any official sense. Quickly, also, a movement was initiated to give the Philippine Islands their independence. Some people, like William Jennings Bryan, insisted upon the protection of the weaker nations and peoples from economic exploitation by American interests. Nevertheless, under McKinley, Roosevelt, Taft, Wilson, and successive leaders the policy of imperialism continued.

All in all, the impact of the Spanish-American War can scarcely be exaggerated. It cannot be limited, of course, to the effects of each individual acquisition of territory or to the additional spheres of influence. Much that happened was intangible and almost imponderable; no one could tell what the ultimate consequences of expansionism might be. A new spirit was abroad after this war, a new pride in America's power and greatness, and a determination that the nation should acquit itself with efficiency and distinction among the great powers of the world. An emphasis on efficiency was enhanced by the knowledge that the American military effort in Cuba had been incredibly disorganized. Nothing so disgraceful should ever be permitted to happen again. In this respect the trends in foreign and domestic policy nicely converged, for progressivism, too, brought an emphasis on civil service reform, efficiency, and a high caliber of leadership.

American policy was affected most immediately and significantly in the Caribbean Sea and the Far East; yet the implications were worldwide. England and Germany had strong interests in these regions, too, while France, Russia, Japan, and Holland were notably involved as colonial powers on the mainland of China or in the Pacific areas. In other words, without participating directly in European affairs, America now stood as a potential barrier to the ambitions of Europe. Through its presence in the Philippines, the United States directly confronted Russia and Japan, the Asiatic powers. Soon, by building the Panama Canal and controlling access to it (which could be denied in time of war), the United States had gained a strategic influence affecting much of the world. All it required additionally to be a formidable power indeed was to increase the size of its naval forces and the merchant marine, while taking some steps, as well, to update the Army.

The builders of the new imperial system were men like Elihu Root and John Hay, serving respectively as Secretary of War and Secretary of State in the last years of McKinley's Presidency, then continuing under

Roosevelt. TR, with his friends and advisers in eight years of office, had an enormous impact. Taft, along with his Secretary of State, Philander Knox, and the Secretary of War, Henry L. Stimson, contributed significantly. The Democrats, during Wilson's Presidency, did little to upset the system, although a change of emphasis was often apparent. They tended to be less imperialistic as a party.

Little or nothing could be done if the United States Army was weak and inefficient. Elihu Root, newly appointed to the War Department in 1899, moved to rectify the situation. Root believed in civilian supremacy over the military but had a capacity as well to understand the generals and gain their confidence. He enlarged the Army to a minimum of 60,000 enlisted men, while also making the National Guard the organized militia, with new national supervision and financial support. He created an Army War College and a general staff system. Military leaders would now advise on all matters and plan continuously for the eventuality of war. According to some observers, this reorganization under Root was the greatest contribution ever made by any Secretary of War. In Taft's administration, Henry Stimson had further success in consolidating Army units and preparing for possible action.

As Secretary of War, Root had much to say about Cuba, Puerto Rico, and the Philippines; for American troops were already there when he assumed office, and they were not to be removed until order was restored and civilian leaders were prepared to assume power. Root eventually sent more troops to the Philippines to fight the Filipinos (about 100,000 men) than had been sent to Cuba in 1898 to fight the Spanish. It was a tragic and ironic turn of events. But American arms prevailed, and the War Department thus proved that it had indeed attained a new state of efficiency.

The colonial system was inaugurated in Puerto Rico, which had been occupied without resistance in 1898. Secretary Root favored a policy of leniency toward the Puerto Ricans from a cultural standpoint; traditional customs should be allowed where possible. Also, the safeguards of the Bill of Rights should be granted. But, in actuality, he was not very generous. The powers of government should reside in a governor and council appointed by the President of the United States—and not in the native peoples themselves.

These questions were considered by Congress, and the Foraker Act of April 1900 determined the relations between the United States and Puerto Rico for some years to come. Leaders of Congress decided that tariff duties should be levied against this island, even though it now was a part of United States territory. They granted more power politically than Root had recommended, making the decision that the lower house of the Puerto Rican assembly ought to be elective. The real power, however, resided in the Governor and Council, consisting of officials who were chosen in Washington. In 1900 the new civilian authorities took office and Secretary Root turned his attention elsewhere.

As the fighting continued in the Philippine Islands, a commission was appointed with a strong charge from Elihu Root to move toward the establishment of civilian government. Root's plan was a conservative one under which self-rule was slowly to be introduced, while the natives were taught the great principles derived essentially from the "Anglo-Saxon experience." Every effort should be made, said the Secretary, to conform to the "custom," the "habits," and even the "prejudices" of the Filipinos. A bill of rights was to be guaranteed the people, and local officials were to be chosen by popular vote. The commission had the difficult task of deciding upon a form for the central government and therefore upon the degree of native control. Another sticky question was the 400,000 acres of Friar lands controlled by the Catholic Church. Should they be broken up and distributed? William Howard Taft headed this commission and became, in 1901, Civil Governor of the Philippines.

Julius Pratt, in his study of the American colonial system, has praised the "useful reforms and achievements" in the Philippines, effected especially under McKinley, Roosevelt, and Taft. The Friar lands, for example, were purchased from the church and distributed, rather widely, to those who had formerly been tenants. Church and state were separated. Reforms in the judicial system, says Pratt, made it possible for the Filipinos "for the first time," and "without money or influence," to hope for justice under the law. Local government was democratized, and under the Organic Act of 1902, passed by the United States Congress, the Philippines obtained an elective lower house of the territorial legislature. The Democrats made a contribution in 1912 and after by calling for the granting of independence.

The Philippine islands did not, of course, realize their dream of home rule, not for decades yet to come. The Jones Act of 1916 declared that the "purpose of the people of the United States" was—and had been—to grant independence. This was to be done whenever the Filipinos seemed capable of conducting their own government. The return of a Republican administration in the 1920s and later the outbreak of war in the Pacific (1941) meant a delay until a proclamation of independence for the Philippines finally came on July 4, 1946.

There was room for cynicism about the American policy, however generous it seemed to be. Even the granting of independence might be for the wrong reasons, such as allaying the racist fears at home, or to reduce the dangers of economic competition. In every American possession the policies adopted were different. The key to what was done was obviously the pressure of interest groups in the United States, subject to some

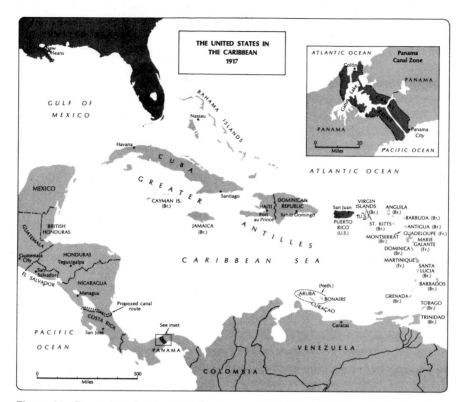

Figure 14   The United States in the Caribbean, 1917. (*From* A History of the American People, *2d ed., by Norman A. Graebner, Gilbert C. Fite, and Philip L. White. Copyright © 1970, 1975 by McGraw-Hill, Inc.*)

degree of executive persuasion and, at times, to decisions of the United States Supreme Court. The basic policy was laid down by Congress. Rights and interests of Americans, at *home,* were paramount. The Constitution, as the expression went, did *not* "follow the flag." Alaska eventually would come to statehood, and even Hawaii. But Guam was administered by naval officers, while Puerto Rico, with its Latin culture, moved ever so slowly toward the possibility of statehood.

Even more important in some respects than the places owned by the United States were the "protectorates," or other places heavily influenced by it. Ultimately this question of imperialism without ownership was to be the great one of the twentieth century. To what extent did the United States by its commercial relations, its investments abroad, and its far-flung ambitions play the role of an imperial power? This question has always been a difficult one to answer and obviously is bitterly controversial as well.

The island of Cuba was a case of special concern. When the fighting ended in 1898, a force of occupation remained; and Secretary Root maintained that the United States, while in Cuba, must clean up the island and modernize its governmental functions, helping to prepare it for effective self-rule. Cuba was too rich and important to permit its domination by a European power. Root placed General Leonard Wood, formerly of the Rough Riders, in charge of this effort. Wood and his army "for civilization" were to fight disease, improve sanitation, build roads and schools, and create a model regime. No one could doubt that this emerald of the Caribbean Sea was terribly backward in the educational level of its people, the number of its poor, and the exploitation of resources. It had suffered dreadfully, moreover, in four years of warfare. General Wood was highly successful, by the standards usually applied to armies of occupation. He and his men did, in fact, vastly improve the conditions of life in Cuba.

Yet Cuba did not receive its political independence, becoming, rather, a protectorate of the United States. Secretary Root recommended those policies embodied in the Platt Amendment of 1901. A convention of Cuban leaders had convened for the purpose of drawing up their new constitution, and Root insisted that the new government recognize the special relationship existing between Cuba and the United States. The island, in effect, must agree to supervisory action by its northern neighbor, while avoiding any impairment of sovereignty at the hands of another power. Cuba must provide the necessary lands for the United States to establish a naval station—which was soon arranged at Guantanamo Bay—and Cuban authorities were to expect periodic intervention by the United States, if necessary, to assure the protection of life, liberty, and property and to "maintain the independence of Cuba."

Roosevelt soon added the Republic of Panama and the Dominican Republic as protectorates, while Taft added Nicaragua, and the Wilson administration contributed Haiti. Roosevelt actually showed how to handle these small countries to the south, and he laid down principles which rationalized the many interventions that occurred. Some forty years later, after the rise of communism, the United States followed a policy worldwide resembling that inaugurated by McKinley and Roosevelt in the Caribbean Sea. To Americans, their country was and remained the great example of democracy and a protagonist of "liberal capitalism," to be distinguished from the old autocracies and the new, revolutionary tyrannies of a Hitler or Stalin.

In its policy toward Cuba, the United States assumed a policing power. The Roosevelt Corollary to the Monroe Doctrine, as it came to be called, explicitly asserted such a right—and duty—in the Caribbean region and the Americas. In his annual message to Congress of December 1904, Roosevelt declared:

> Any country whose people conduct themselves well can count upon our hearty friendship. If a nation shows that it knows how to act with reasonable efficiency and decency in social and political matters, if it keeps order and pays its obligations, it need fear no interference from the United States. Chronic wrongdoing, or an impotence which results in a general loosening of the ties of civilized society, may in America, as elsewhere, ultimately require intervention by some civilized nation, and in the Western Hemisphere, the adherence of the United States to the Monroe Doctrine may force the United States, however reluctantly, in flagrant cases of such wrongdoing or impotence, to the exercise of an international police power.

The self-righteousness of the United States has seldom, if ever, been demonstrated in a more transparent manner. Inevitably such assertions and the interventions that occurred left behind a legacy of distrust and hatred in Latin America.

Theodore Roosevelt was so influential in the development of a new foreign policy that he requires special attention and as much space as this account will permit. Much of his diplomacy is suggested by his personal characteristics, by his energy and restlessness. He was a man who loved action and the use of power. A widely traveled leader, he also maintained an extensive correspondence. He knew the Kaiser of Germany, for example, and leaders and diplomats from around the world. One of his favorites was Cecil Spring Rice of England, or "Springy," and another was Speck Von Sternberg of Germany, known to his friends as "Specky." Roosevelt loved to engage in personal diplomacy, although John Hay as his first Secretary of State and Elihu Root as his second can hardly be described as figureheads.

TR had ideas and a program. The United States, in his view, was a great country which had to play a role commensurate with its greatness. The people must be virtuous and patriotic, ever ready to serve and to fight—if necessary. Order must be maintained. And decency, too. Democracy must be furthered, if possible. Though Roosevelt had racist views of a sort, he did not stress the inferiority of a whole race or people on a biological basis. He viewed the Japanese, for example, with respect. In the building up of "civilization" they could do their part, much as did the people of a Western nation. Unfortunately, however, Roosevelt was so strong a nationalist that he saw other nations through jaundiced eyes. If they were weak and disorderly he showed contempt. If they seemed powerful and a threat to the United States he was wary and sought the means to weaken their influence through diplomacy or balance-of-power arrangements. A "realist" in most respects, he sensed correctly that the United States must prepare to be far more active in world affairs than it had been in the past. And he thought deeply on some aspects of the world situation.

With a foresight that was impressive TR wrote of the great nations of the world and the future that seemed to be marked out for them. His Anglo-Saxonism was apparent. To Cecil Spring Rice of England, he wrote in 1901 that he would be very glad for England to continue her guiding role in all of Africa, in Southern Asia, and parts of Eastern Asia. To an American correspondent he declared in the same year: "There is no danger [to us] from England now in any way. I think there never will be." In spite of certain worries concerning the rise of Germany, he believed the twentieth century would "still be the century of the men who speak English." He expected Germany to show herself as a "formidable rival," especially in military and industrial competition. She was the "great growing power," very aggressive and ambitious, and Roosevelt feared an eventual clash with her. She should be kept out of the Western hemisphere entirely, so far as this was possible.

The Russian bear did not concern him greatly, although with Spring Rice he believed that in the future the Russians would have "an enormous part to play, a great destiny." In the fashion of the day, and with much realism, Roosevelt thus thought of rising and declining nations, of conflict and potential conflict. His knowledge of history enabled him to allude to the Roman empire, to Holland, Sweden, France, and other countries, and to place them somewhere on the scale of national success or failure.

On one point Roosevelt was determined. The United States must be prepared militarily to protect its national interests. A war with another of the "civilized" powers, such as Germany, would be unfortunate; but to have such a conflict and lose it would be the "greatest of misfortunes." Having such views, Roosevelt almost exploded over the shortsightedness, or sentimentality, of those who opposed what he considered to be the necessary appropriations for national defense. Men such as Carl Schurz and E. L. Godkin, of the "Mugwump type," and Democrats such as William Jennings Bryan had no concern over the national honor, he charged, and were quite ready to see the United States humiliated. In one letter he referred to pacifistic publications, such as Godkin's *Nation,* as "accessories before the fact to murder." In another he spoke of "shrill eunuchs" who were opposing his policy in Panama.

How much Roosevelt was concerned with commercial and business expansion of the United States is not entirely clear. Certainly he did not ignore it, and he knew that an expanding economy demanded new markets, raw materials, and places for investment. He knew that the business system of America, a relatively free one, was worthy of export. Here, as in other matters, the United States could show the way. Yet the making of money, either at home or abroad, did not interest Roosevelt personally. He was far more concerned with strategic considerations of foreign policy and matters of honor and prestige.

When Roosevelt assumed the presidency, the United States was already launched upon a new course in the Far East, summed up in the somewhat vague term the "Open Door policy" for China. The ancient kingdom of China was in danger of disappearing in the 1890s as hungry powers gathered for the spoils. Germany, France, Russia, and Japan threatened to divide her. Russia was the principal aggressor, already holding Manchuria and apparently having the power to continue her dominance. Japan, which had defeated China in a war of 1894, was a rival to Russia. Great Britain, in these circumstances, was primarily interested in the trading possibilities. The United States, newly arrived on the scene because of the Philippine Islands and hopeful of trade with China, was led into cooperation informally with the British. Neither power was averse to some special rights in China, but most of all they wanted trading and business opportunities with the huge population of that country. Such business would not be possible if China were simply appropriated by France, Germany, and other nations. John Hay's bold tactic, initiated in 1899, was to issue a series of notes to the interested nations. He then assumed, without their actual agreement, that they would cooperate in this policy of maintaining an "Open Door."

Roosevelt thus inherited from McKinley and Hay a policy of doubtful wisdom. Why should the United States, 7,000 miles away, make itself a special protector for China, the "sick man" of Asia? Obviously the United States could not actually control the course of events on the Chinese mainland, nor, as many recognized, could it defend the Philippine Islands if a strong attack occurred. The trading possibilities with China were subject to much doubt. The future would show that any hopes of a greatly enlarged trade were illusory. Trade with the Japanese actually expanded far more importantly than that with the Chinese. Hopes that China would become a great Christian nation, with democratic institutions patterned after those of America, also were misguided. Yet the idea of an Open Door in Asia, much like that of the Monroe Doctrine in the Americas, captured the public imagination and that of American leaders. There was no easy escape from the legacy of 1898 or the rosy prospects portrayed under McKinley and Hay.

As early as 1901, TR suggested that a mistake might have been made in taking the Philippines. At least he thought it was "an intensely disagreeable and unfortunate task" that had fallen to the United States.

On the other hand, he reflected, the United States was doing its duty and might confer an immense "boon to humanity" by its work in those islands, much as Britain had done in her imperial efforts. The Russo-Japanese War of 1904–1905 helped to convince Roosevelt that the new American policy was dangerous indeed. Japan, surprisingly, won that war and gave further proof of her growing strength as a naval power. By 1907 Roosevelt had come to believe that the American presence in the Philippine Islands made the situation regarding the Japanese a dangerous one. Some "pretty clear avowal" of an intention not to keep the Philippines permanently would be a good idea, he thought. It was ironic indeed that a chief architect of the new, large policy for the United States should have changed his mind so quickly, deciding that the nation had overreached itself in the Spanish-American War and should retreat, if possible.

Theodore Roosevelt acted about as effectively as could be expected in the circumstances. He retreated slightly from the Open Door, recognizing that the interests of Asian powers in Asia were superior to those of the United States. TR, in fact, was drawn into an unofficial alliance with the British, who in 1902 had made an alliance with the Japanese. Britain was a key to much that was happening. She thought to isolate Germany in Europe and to weaken her in Asia. This was accomplished by the Entente Cordiale between France and England in 1904, ending a long and serious rivalry between those powers, and by a British-Russian Alliance in 1907. Concessions to the Japanese in Asia and new understandings with France, Russia, and the United States all contributed to a new sense of security on the part of Britain. Her policy for China was sacrificed, therefore, to the larger needs of the day.

Nevertheless, Roosevelt did not give up. On the one hand, he acknowledged the growth of Japanese power and her suzerainty over Korea, resulting from the war with Russia. The Taft-Katsura Agreement of 1905 signified the acceptance by Roosevelt and Secretary of War Taft of the new power balance in Manchuria. Three years later, when Elihu Root had become Secretary of State, the Root-Takahira Agreement was a similar understanding, of an executive nature. Unofficially and informally (without a treaty) the American government recognized the special Japanese interests in Manchuria. At the same time—and rather ambiguously—the Japanese government acknowledged the Open Door policy for China. The fact was that Roosevelt had come to think of Japan as a potential enemy, and a powerful one. He sought to limit her power and to restrain any truculence on her part. This could be done by attempts, alternately, to conciliate and appease the Nipponese and to let them know that the United States had strong and continuing interests in the Pacific Ocean. Thus, in 1908, he sent the American fleet on a round-the-world tour, during which it dropped anchor in Japanese ports, paying a friendly visit. The message was clear. So long as Roosevelt was President, the United States would stay in Asia. Yet it wanted no war. It was capable of conciliation.

An alarming aspect of U.S.-Japanese relations was the treatment of the Nipponese who had immigrated to California. One keen observer, Homer Lea, wrote that hostility to the Japanese permeated "the entire social and political fabric" of the Western states. California was the seat of difficulty. Organizations such as the Native Sons of the Golden West helped to stir up trouble, as did labor leaders and business groups, seeking to serve their own purposes by baiting the Japanese or even by dispossessing them. In a remarkable demonstration of leadership, Roosevelt did his utmost to prevent this situation from getting out of hand, and he was generally successful. At the same time, he used the threat of trouble in the Pacific as the way to agitate the Congress and to gain more appropriations for his naval program.

In brief, the continuing immigration of Japanese to the United States, either directly from their homeland or via Hawaii, after a temporary stay there, was a cause for much alarm. Californians, especially, began to demand exclusion of the "Japs," or severe restrictions on immigration. Yet many Americans, with Roosevelt himself included, regarded this outcry on the West Coast as totally unwarranted and even idiotic. The Japanese were an able people, whose rights must be respected. Gradually Roosevelt came to believe that the Californians were deadly serious, that the extremes of race feeling in the state were not to be ignored, and that the only solution was some type of limitation on the influx of Japanese laborers. Could this be accomplished, however, without causing a dangerous deterioration in relations between the two countries? The precipitating event was a decision of the San Francisco School Board in October 1906 that Chinese, Japanese, and Korean children must attend a special Oriental school in the city. Along with this discriminatory order there was a pattern of vicious attacks on Orientals. In response, a reaction occurred in Japan. Jingoes in that country were ready for war against the "poorly equipped army and navy" of the United States. The policy makers in Tokyo showed some restraint but were determined nevertheless that the insults to their people must be brought to a halt.

For the remaining years of his administration, Roosevelt was more or less engaged with this problem. In 1906–1907 it was his primary concern in the realm of foreign and domestic policy. What he did, in effect, was to negotiate both directly and indirectly with the jingoistic leaders of Japan and California. To the Japanese he regretted deeply what had occurred and he promised appropriate action. To the Californians he lent an understanding ear, although he denounced the extremes of their policy, and he wanted the school board's segregation order rescinded. He was able, at last, to effect a deal. If the school board did as he asked, he would win the Japanese to an agreement limiting the migration of laborers. Thus Roosevelt achieved his Gentlemen's Agreement with the Japanese in February 1907. According to a recent scholar, Raymond Esthus, no American President is so "admired and respected in Japan" as Theodore Roosevelt; and the episode just described amply illustrates why this is so.

Taft and Wilson did not escape the Japanese problem, nor did they handle it as skillfully as Roosevelt had. The United States was now committed to an Open Door policy for Asia, which meant both a sentimental interest in China and a desire for the expansion of trade and investment. President Taft was less cautious than his predecessor had been and adopted a policy of actively encouraging American investment in Manchuria. He did not succeed in this "dollar diplomacy" for Asia, except to offend both the Japanese and Russians. He did, however, continue with Roosevelt's program of naval construction. In the Wilson administration the Japanese question was a cause of serious concern, arising in part from the flareup, once again, of trouble in California. Also, the outbreak of war in Europe gave the Japanese an opportunity to improve their Far Eastern position and to increase the pressure on China. The tensions increased ominously, even though the Japanese were allied with the Americans in World War I.

Another question of the Taft-Wilson period had to be acted upon as it related to the world situation. This was the Mexican revolution, which started in 1910 with the overthrow of Porfirio Diaz. Leaders in the country fought for control, and, as the situation worsened, Woodrow Wilson tried to support the side of constitutional government. An incident in 1914 led him to send troops to Veracruz, and he came near to precipitating a full-blown war. This was a dangerous state of affairs, especially after war broke out in Europe a few months later. Wilson followed a tortuous course but had the good sense to stay out of actual war with Mexico and to avoid opposing the revolution as such. It was a popular revolution that changed the course of Mexican history.

Clearly discernible in the diplomatic events from McKinley to Wilson was a pattern of Anglo-Americanism that has been referred to previously. While relations with Germany and the Japanese were becoming more difficult, those with Great Britain were improving. This can be seen repeatedly under Roosevelt and in the Taft and Wilson administrations as well, leading on at last to the wartime alliance of 1917–1918. The causes for this new cordiality were many, but one of the most interesting was the frequent intermarriages that occurred. Charles S. Campbell has noted that by 1914 more than 130 American women had married into British titled families. The most famous, eventually, was the union between Lord Randolph Churchill and Jennie Jerome of New York, producing a future Prime Minister. But the Duke of Marlborough, George Curzon, and many others also found American wives.

Obviously the answer lay deeper than that. The self-interest of Americans and the British seemed to dictate a new era of cooperation and mutual benefit. The common boundary with Canada, the decline of old animosities, the prospects of accord in world trade, the suspicion of Germany—these and other things contributed to a better relationship. Difficulties remained. Yet one by one, most of these were solved.

SUGGESTIONS FOR ADDITIONAL READING

It may be apparent that there is not a little controversy over United States foreign policy and the motives allegedly behind it. The "marketplace" interpretation of United States imperialism has gained in prominence recently; that is, the search for markets is said to have been the chief influence leading to overseas involvement, war, and expansion. A classic statement of this interpretation may be found in William A. Williams, *The Roots of the Modern American Empire: A Study of the Growth and Shaping of Social Consciousness in a Marketplace Society,* Random House, New York, 1969. A second study with this general emphasis is Walter La Feber, *The New Empire: An Interpretation of American Expansion, 1860–1898,* Cornell, Ithaca, N.Y., 1963. Probably the majority of historians still prefer a more balanced interpretation. See, for example: Frederick Merk, *Manifest Destiny and Mission in American History* (1963), cited previously; Foster Rhea Dulles, *America's Rise to World Power, 1898–1954,* Harper, New York, 1954; Richard W. Leopold, *The Growth of American Foreign Policy; A History,* Knopf, New York, 1962; and H. Wayne Morgan, *America's Road to Empire: The War with Spain and Overseas Expansion,* Wiley, New York, 1965. Important for its criticism of legalism and moralism in American foreign policy is George F. Kennan, *American Diplomacy, 1900–1950,* Univ. of Chicago Press, Chicago, 1951.

Numerous works have centered on the Spanish-American War as the crucial event, especially for its momentous effects. Frank Freidel, *The Splendid Little War,* Little, Brown, Boston, 1958, is fair-minded in its synthesis and beautifully illustrated. An older account, also readable, is Walter Millis, *The Martial Spirit: A Study of Our War with Spain,* Houghton Mifflin, Boston, 1931. Important for its analysis of the 1890s, using foreign archives, is Ernest R. May, *Imperial Democracy: The Emergence of America as a Great Power,* Harcourt, Brace, New York, 1961. On the imperialists and anti-imperialists, see especially Julius Pratt, *Expansionists of 1898: The Acquisition of Hawaii and the Spanish Islands,* Johns Hopkins, Baltimore, 1936, and Robert L. Beisner, *Twelve against Empire: The Anti-Imperialists, 1898–1900,* McGraw-Hill, New York, 1968.

Some of the best studies are biographical in approach, for example, Howard K. Beale, *Theodore Roosevelt and the Rise of America to World Power* (1956), cited before, and Raymond A. Esthus, *Theodore Roosevelt and Japan*, Univ. of Washington Press, Seattle, 1966. Books on Roosevelt by George Mowry, William Harbaugh, John Blum, and Henry Pringle, all noted previously, will be valuable for their treatment of his foreign policy. For two of Roosevelt's fellow statesmen see Tyler Dennett, *John Hay: From Poetry to Politics*, Dodd, Mead, New York, 1933, and Richard W. Leopold, *Elihu Root and the Conservative Tradition* (1954), mentioned earlier.

Charles S. Campbell, *Anglo-American Understanding, 1898–1903*, Johns Hopkins, Baltimore, 1957, is one of the many special studies that are virtually indispensable. A few others that should be mentioned here are A. W. Griswold, *The Far Eastern Policy of the United States*, Harcourt, Brace, New York, 1938; William L. Neumann, *America Encounters Japan: From Perry to MacArthur*, Johns Hopkins, Baltimore, 1963; Roger Daniels, *The Politics of Prejudice: The Anti-Japanese Movement in California, and the Struggle for Japanese Exclusion*, Univ. of California Press, Berkeley, 1962; George T. Davis, *A Navy Second to None: The Development of Modern American Naval Policy*, Harcourt, Brace, New York, 1940; Julius Pratt, *America's Colonial Experiment: How the United States Gained, Governed, and in Part Gave Away a Colonial Empire*, Prentice-Hall, New York, 1951; Robert E. Quirk, *An Affair of Honor: Woodrow Wilson and the Occupation of Veracruz*, Univ. of Kentucky Press, Lexington, 1962; and Walter Scholes, *The Foreign Policies of the Taft Administration*, mentioned previously. For valuable perspectives on foreign policy and diplomatic history see the many essays in John Braeman et al. (eds.), *Twentieth-Century American Foreign Policy*, Ohio State Univ. Press, Columbus, 1971.

In the Maelstrom: 1914–1917

The American experience of progressivism at home and the apparent solution of many problems had enhanced a belief in human rationality and the improvability of mankind. This was a time of arbitration treaties under Taft and Wilson, of the Permanent Court of Arbitration at the Hague, of peace societies and peace arguments. Many in Europe were hopeful, too, of peace and progress. No one could win in a modern war, Norman Angell of England had argued in his *Great Illusion,* which appeared in 1910. But the Americans were notably naive, as suggested by an article that appeared in *Forum* magazine, some eighteen months before the outbreak of war in Europe. The author declared that a European war had been averted "for good" and that the world was "standing on the brink of universal peace." Such statements could be multiplied many times over. With an occasional exception, Americans were uninformed about world affairs, or they looked upon the international scene through rose-colored glasses.

The shock, then, of what happened in 1914 was truly profound. One congressman wrote to Walter Hines Page, the United States Ambassador

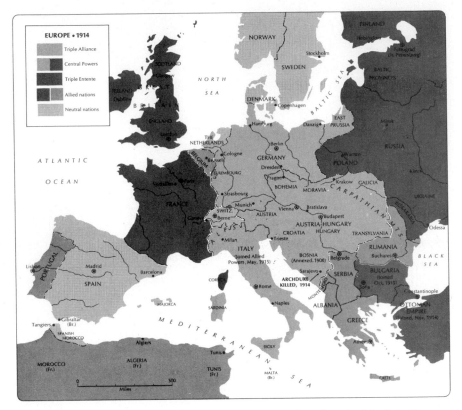

Figure 15   Europe in 1914. (*From* A History of the American People, *2d ed., by Norman A. Graebner, Gilbert C. Fite, and Philip L. White. Copyright © 1970, 1975 by McGraw-Hill, Inc.*)

in London: "This dreadful conflict of the nations came to most of us like lightning out of a clear sky. . . . Now the grim reality of it stuns you." Arthur S. Link has written that this period was like "an extended nightmare" for Woodrow Wilson. The tragedy in Europe was intensified by the tragedy in his household, for his beloved wife was dying of incurable disease.

Great "civilized" powers went to war against other "civilized" powers in 1914, contrary to the beliefs and predictions freely made by some optimists in the Darwinian tradition. An era of nationalism and imperialism, with its alliances and festering grievances, finally ended in a holocaust. Austria-Hungary, Germany's ally, sent an ultimatum to slavic Serbia, which was strongly supported by Russia. The latter, in turn, was allied to France and Great Britain. And the latter was allied to Japan.

Turkey associated itself with the Central Powers, while Italy, after some hesitation, decided to oppose its near neighbor and enemy, Austria. The countries of Scandinavia remained neutral, as did the United States for almost three years; but no country of any importance could remain untouched by this war. The belligerents, among them, controlled much of the world's production and the movement of goods on land and sea. The armies they mobilized were the largest and most formidable in the history of mankind.

In retrospect, the consequences of this war seem almost endless. The fate of great countries and political systems hung in the balance. The United States, which had entered world affairs significantly in 1898, now found itself truly embroiled. Beginning with human decisions and mistakes, the World War ended with death and destruction on a gargantuan scale. In four years of fighting about 9 million men were killed or fatally injured, while some 5 million were said to be missing in action and 7 million suffered disabling wounds. Casualties affecting the civilian popu-

Figure 16   Civilization Appalled by the Monster of War. (*From* Harper's Weekly, *May 29, 1915.*)

lation also ran very high. Early in the war there was little doubt about the brutal nature of the developing struggle, with huge armies mobilized and national economies behind them.

Europe was a long way off, and the fighting seemed a regrettable business that had little to do with Uncle Sam. President Wilson spoke eloquently for the nation when he said: "The effect of the war upon the United States will depend upon what American citizens say and do. Every man who really loves America will act and speak in the true spirit of neutrality, which is the spirit of impartiality and fairness and friendliness to all concerned." He warned, however, that Americans were "drawn from many nations," and chiefly from those now fighting each other. If the United States was to play the role of mediator and peacemaker that he wanted it to play, the tendency to take sides must be kept under restraint. "The United States," he declared, "must be neutral in fact as well as in name during these days that are to try men's souls."

Obviously Wilson did not succeed in these efforts. By April 1917, the United States was at war, and his decisions had helped to create the very situation he wished to avoid. On the other hand, his policies kept the country at peace for many months, and when peace no longer seemed possible the American people were fairly well united behind him.

Once the European leaders had made a decision for war (or actions that led to war), the United States was largely a victim of circumstances. It had little chance to stop the bloodshed, although Wilson tried to do so repeatedly with Colonel House as his emissary to Europe. Whatever the United States could do, the world was destined to be a vastly different place when this struggle ended.

But, according to one argument, the United States should have recognized that its interests lay on the side of Britain and France. President Wilson should have "educated" the American public, gradually leading the way in military preparedness and mobilization, with intervention coming by 1915 or 1916. The defeat of Germany and her allies a year earlier would have saved the lives of millions, while preventing also the further waste of money and resources. The argument fails to recognize sufficiently that Woodrow Wilson and the American people were not ready for war, although Theodore Roosevelt and a small minority were indeed calling for action.

What was the state of public opinion in the early months of the war? Obviously it was affected, as the President predicted, by the heterogeneous nature of the American population. In a total of some 92 million Americans, about 33 million were foreign-born or had at least one foreign parent. The census of 1910 showed that 11 million persons living in the United States had been born in Germany or Austria-Hungary or had a parent who was born there. For the Irish the figures approached 5 million.

These people, as a group, had no love for the British, and their sentiments could be understood by many others whose reasons were more complex, dating back, perhaps, to the American Revolution and the War of 1812. Yet the intellectuals and "opinion makers" were strongly pro-Ally as a group. The recent immigrants from England, the Italians, the French, and the Russians were inclined to support the interests of their homeland. Most Americans had a feeling that was predominantly pro-Ally, but this did not mean a readiness to go to war. Popular attitudes were affected inevitably by the actual course of events, with significant fluctuations occurring, even in the space of a few weeks.

Cedric C. Cummins has provided useful insights by studying the tides of public opinion in one of the most representative of all the states, Indiana. Hoosiers, he found, had an overly simplified view of the causes of the war. They attributed the breakdown of civilization in Europe to the failings of the monarchical system. In the United States, according to this view, such things could not happen. Of the warring powers, the Allies were viewed most favorably, while Austria and Germany, it seemed, by their lack of caution had really caused the war. Then too, the Allied side was the more democratic, in spite of czarist Russia. Even Russia could be defended on the basis that it had come to the assistance of tiny Serbia. The favorite country for Indianians was not England but France. Vice President Thomas Marshall, for example, testified to his "intense affection" for the French people and for Lafayette, whose aid had been so bravely given in the American Revolution.

Within a few weeks came what Professor Cummins refers to as the "stabilization of opinion." Anti-German feeling in the state diminished as many began to take a broader view of the war. Also, the German-Americans, the Irish, and the Hungarians began to speak up, making their presence known, with important results. Politicians became conscious again "of the 'German vote,' the 'Irish vote,' and the 'Hungarian vote.' What, after all, was a war in Europe when the election of county sheriff was but three months away?" The Allies were also hurt by the growing involvement of Japan, raising the bugaboo of a "Yellow Peril." England's traditional critics did not overlook the opportunity for striking out at the British and their record of imperialism.

Nevertheless, the tide began to swing back rather strongly toward the Allied side. Britain benefited now from the improved relations with the United States and from her support given over the years to American imperialism in the Caribbean and Far East. As the war continued, the news was focused on England, France, and especially Belgium, where the German Army had attacked, trying to reach France by the easiest route. The news from overseas was strongly colored by the fact that it came over English cables, for the cables from Germany had been cut. Most

Figure 17 An Image of German Militarism: Crown Prince Frederick William and His Aides. (*From* Harper's Weekly, *October 10, 1914.*)

important was the actual news. Germany undeniably had invaded its neighbor Belgium, and the destruction and suffering did not have to be imagined by newspaper writers. Both articles and pictures conveyed to America visions of shattered buildings and roads crowded with refugees. Belgium fought back bravely for a time, and its people were much admired.

Stories of harsh German tactics and even of atrocities did not help the German cause. The "Rape of Louvain" and similar accounts were much in the news. The sympathy for Belgium welled up in a highly organized campaign for relief, the success of which depended to a considerable extent on the portrayal of suffering and need—caused by German attack. Coupled with this evidence of military ruthlessness came a succession of articles and books on the German psychology, on attitudes of militarism and national superiority that lay behind the shocking events of recent days.

The image of Germany did not improve when it gained as an ally the "terrible Turk." According to the *Evansville* (Indiana) *Courier,* the Turks were religious fanatics with a well-deserved reputation for cruelty. They believed that "to kill a Christian in battle is a sure way to gain entrance to Heaven." The Turkish Ambassador to the United States tried to defend his country and had the "audacity" to bring up the subject of lynchings in the United States and torture tactics used by Americans in the Philippines. Soon thereafter the American government asked for his recall. This question of the Turks and their alleged persecution of Christian Armenians was a matter of much importance in Indiana. It was understandable that in the comic strips, when Mutt and Jeff joined the battle for freedom and democracy, they spent their time killing the Turks.

During 1914 and the early months of 1915, the United States established its principles of "neutral rights." It did this, for the most part, according to concepts derived from wars of the past. Decisions had to be made about the warfare now raging on the high seas (by 1915) with British ships patrolling the surface and the Germans threatening to destroy with their torpedoes any ship that ventured out of port. The United States wished to be neutral but also to continue with its commerce, legitimately conducted. What were its rights? Where could its ships and its people still go? In one scholar's phrase, neutrality was "knife-edged," and the United States could not really stay on that edge. It could not avoid or postpone a choice of policies that helped one side more than the other. What, then, would be the consequences?

To a later generation, acquainted with "total war," the "neutral rights" of 1914 are a little hard to understand. On the sea, at least, there was still a code of war with features of chivalry and romance that would soon disappear. A blockade in time of war against an enemy nation was considered legal, if conducted near the coast of the enemy. The United States, as a neutral, was not to be blockaded, nor were its ships to be stopped or seized (theoretically) unless they approached the coast of the combatants. Ships carrying contraband, or war material, might be seized or sunk. But the passengers and crew must be saved. This applied not only to a neutral ship but to the merchant and passenger vessels of nations at war. The people aboard were to be saved. By 1914 the most glaring weakness in such a code had become apparent. The submarine, a relatively new ship of war, simply did not have the capacity to stop merchant or passenger ships, conduct a search for contraband, and save the people aboard if sinking was considered necessary. A cruiser or a destroyer might do this, but a submarine had to depend upon the element of surprise, and merely by coming to the surface it made itself vulnerable to attack.

The code had other weaknesses, too, which had long been apparent. In time of peace nations might agree on the rights of neutrals, but when war actually began they disagreed; that is, the countries at war were determined to win and took advantage of the situation in virtually every way they could. The British in World War I had control of the seas and did not hesitate to use it. They adopted a category of "conditional contraband," which came to include almost anything that might help the enemy, and asserted their right to capture such materials, including those of the United States. They used also the doctrine of "continuous voyage." Cargoes bound, therefore, for Sweden or another neutral country could be captured on the argument that they were destined eventually for Germany. Finding that to stop ships and search them on the high seas was often dangerous, they assumed the right to take them into port and search at leisure. The mails were often ransacked in a search for secrets. They declared the whole North Sea a military zone and ordered ships to follow routes that were authorized. Firms in neutral countries that traded with the Central Powers were likely to be blacklisted, thus being denied profits from the Allied market. In other words, the British conducted an economic war, along with the actual fighting, and there was little that escaped their notice. They put Germany in a condition of siege.

German leaders were not to be outdone. The conditions of the war by 1915 were such that the submarine became their major weapon. Only in this way, it seemed, could they sink the British Navy, or damage it so badly that the avenues of commerce would be open. An argument raged inside the German government over the unrestricted use of submarines; for such action could lead to the death of many civilians, to a hostile world opinion, and to the probability of American intervention. German policy fluctuated for many months before the final decision.

In the fall of 1914 the submarine demonstrated its effectiveness in combat. Any doubts that remained on the matter were dispelled when a single U-boat, slipping through the cold waters of the North Sea, sent three British cruisers to the bottom. It then escaped undetected. Early in 1915 Germany announced that the waters around Great Britain were now a war zone in which ships of the enemy would be destroyed. Unavoidably, crews and passengers might be killed. The merchant ships of neutral nations should stay out of the zone, for accidents might occur.

American leaders found themselves in the position of responding to events, but with very little capacity to control them. Point by point, they established a policy. Not surprisingly, their interpretation of the rights of neutrals was one which favored the Allied side, although they protested generally against the violations of international law and probably were quite sincere in these attitudes. Thus they could agree with the *Springfield* (Mass.) *Republican* that neutral rights must be upheld, that precedents must be avoided which could "carry civilized warfare back to the vicious practices of the Middle Ages." Wilson and his State Department protested most vigorously against those practices which seemed particularly dangerous to "civilization," and that meant against the submarine and its use for sudden attack.

Within the administration, at times, there was serious disagreement. Secretary of State Bryan offered a suggestion that seemed logical and gained considerable support in Congress. American citizens, said Bryan, ought to be kept off the ships of nations at war, or at least they should be warned not to travel on belligerent ships except at their own risk. But Robert Lansing, counselor in the State Department, and more knowledge-able, it seemed, in these matters of international law, argued that no such surrender should be made. Even if ships of the merchant type or passenger liners had guns aboard, in his view, they were still "defensively" armed and could not be sunk without a warning. President Wilson was convinced by Lansing, and Americans continued to travel— and be killed—as Bryan feared they would be.

Another point, too, was crucial. Should there be an embargo on the shipment of munitions to the belligerent countries? According to interna-tional law, it seemed clear, this commerce in war materiel was perfectly legal, although the supplies could be intercepted and captured through a legal blockade. More than this, many argued as did the *Springfield Republican* that a ban on the shipment of war materiel to the Allies would be an unneutral act favoring the Central Powers, which were better prepared, and favoring in general any country that secretly prepared for war in advance. Under American policy, the flow of munitions continued. Still another question was the matter of loans, giving the belligerents the credit necessary to purchase munitions or other supplies. Obviously such credit, if permitted, would go mainly to the Allies. The administration, with Bryan's eventual agreement, decided that the loans of private individuals or groups were indeed permissible.

By the spring of 1915, the American government had established a type of neutrality slanted in favor of the Allies. Obviously important in this process were Robert Lansing, Colonel Edward House, and Walter Hines Page. All were Anglophiles who conveyed to the Allied leaders, at least in subtle ways, that the United States wanted them to win the war and would not, for its part, create too much of a fuss over interferences with American shipping. The President himself was more objective, strongly desiring to stay out of war and to avoid entanglement with either side. Yet he gave his approval to the program that has been described.

Cries of outrage filled the air for a time, as many Americans would not accept the idea that Great Britain had control of the seas, that American cargoes should move as Britain said they should. For practical purposes, the protests were futile. A good example may be found in the shipments of copper. In 1914 and early 1915 these cargoes were not moving, and the copper interests, along with their friends in government, were deeply concerned. They sought assistance from the State Department, and they denounced the British orders-in-council. Nevertheless, in a few months the "solution" had been found, as described by a senator from Montana, the leading state in copper production. "Not much is said about it in the newspapers," he wrote, "but the fact is that not a pound of copper leaves the port of New York except as Great Britain permits it. We may sell to Italy or Spain or Norway or any of the neutral countries when she says we may. . . ." In other words, the copper producers found a market abroad, but they did so under the regulations of a foreign power. The situation was not a happy one, but it did make possible the sale of copper at a good price. With business booming, a little pride could be swallowed, and it was.

The sinking of the *Lusitania* on May 7, 1915, was a momentous event and a turning point in the war, so far as American policy was concerned. This vessel was a British liner carrying some 2,000 passengers, en route from New York to Liverpool. Suddenly, near the coast of Ireland, it was hit by a torpedo. It listed sharply to starboard and sank in a few minutes. Most of those aboard went down with the ship, a total of nearly 1,200, including 124 Americans.

Cedric Cummins has described the impact of this tragedy upon the people of Indiana. The war came "home" to them for the first time. Stories of tragedy and heroism were almost too much to bear. The author Elbert Hubbard had perished, as did Alfred G. Vanderbilt, after giving up his life jacket to another passenger. The very old and the very young were not spared, including two children brought to shore "clasped in each other's arms." Angrily the state's editors commented on the situation, using words like "piratical," "sickening," and "hellish." Nothing so brutal had been seen since Attila the Hun, one editor implied. This atrocity on the sea was now associated in many minds with the previous German actions during the invasion of Belgium.

German-Americans in the state of Indiana, the most numerous of all minority groups, were placed on the defensive. Previously they had not hesitated to boast of German *Kultur,* to attack the slavic peoples as inferior, to denounce the British for actions on the high seas, and even to call upon American leaders to put into effect specific measures that would help Germany. Most notably, they asked or they demanded that the shipment of munitions to the Allies be stopped. After the *Lusitania* tragedy, recognizing a change in public opinion, they saw that the best to be hoped for was to keep the United States from entering the war on the Allied side.

In the Wilson administration a crisis developed. There was no doubt that a protest must be made to Germany over the *Lusitania,* but how vigorous or denunciatory should this be? The President took a middle course, so that he displeased the extreme advocates of peace on the one hand and the spokesmen for preparedness and war on the other. In a speech in Philadelphia, several days after the sinking, he made the comment, "There is such a thing as a man being too proud to fight." This could be construed as weakness, but a note to Germany that soon followed was nothing of the sort. The government of Germany would be held to "strict accountability" for its actions, said Wilson, and he used the occasion to assert strongly both the rights of Americans at sea and the illegality of submarine attacks. The reply from Berlin conceded very little, except that Germany would try to avoid attacks on neutral vessels and would be willing to pay damages for accidental injury. There was no promise to abandon the U-boat or to give warnings in cases like that of the *Lusitania.* The British, not the Germans, were responsible for the recent tragedy. The ship was carrying munitions which had exploded after the torpedo hit, and in other respects, too, claimed the Germans, the *Lusitania* had forfeited its right to be considered a mere passenger vessel. These contentions were not acceptable to Wilson, although he expressed gratification that the U-boats were under restraint, so far as the ships of neutrals were concerned. The crisis continued unabated.

At this point William Jennings Bryan had had enough. He was not disloyal to the President, nor critical of him personally, but he could no longer support the heavy emphasis on maritime rights at the risk of war with Germany. He resigned as Secretary of State, and was succeeded by Robert Lansing. This development gave a vivid demonstration that the American government had no intention of yielding and was now ready to think more seriously of the eventuality of war and the need to make some preparations. In the meantime, other sinkings occurred, notably that of the *Arabic,* another British liner.

The time had come for a fateful decision. The German Ambassador, Count Bernstorff, alarmed by the situation, gave a promise which was supported by his superiors. Passenger liners would not be sunk without a warning and efforts to save the passengers, provided they offered no resistance. Here was the key to German policy for the next year and a half. Under the *Sussex* pledge of 1916 they extended this restriction to merchant vessels. For the time being, the German U-boats were kept in check, and relations with the United States improved. Yet neither side really yielded on the principles involved. And in Germany the hotheads, the advocates of unrestricted submarine warfare to sweep the enemy from the seas, merely waited impatiently.

In public affairs, as in the affairs of an individual, one question leads to another. The submarine crisis notably was so disturbing to Americans that a "preparedness movement" now gained the necessary basis for support, including that of the President. The idea was basically that of defense, not attack. Yet "preparedness" itself was a fighting word in America, for many believed that the way to get into a war was to prepare for a war, and the way to stay out was to avoid all the apparatus of military things and of militarism, which—it could be argued—had really caused the war in Europe in the first place.

A study of preparedness, therefore, is a way to see the conflicting attitudes on the war. Prominent on one side were the interventionists, who were mostly Easterners, including Theodore Roosevelt, Elihu Root, George Harvey of the *North American Review*, Ogden Reid of the *New York Tribune*, and Lyman Abbott of the *Outlook*. Some of these people formed the American Rights Committee, calling for war preparation. The Navy League, the National Security League, and other organizations added their voices. By the summer of 1915 the submarine controversies and reports of German atrocities in Belgium had the effect of creating a genuine preparedness movement with thousands of members. This was allegedly a nonpartisan movement, but it was quite apparent that the leaders were mostly Republican and many were businessmen. Not a few showed their contempt for Woodrow Wilson, as did, for example, the poet Owen Wister, who classed the President with "public cowards, hypocrites, [and] poltroons." In Theodore Roosevelt's view, both Wilson and Bryan were "abject creatures," and would never go to war if they were not "kicked into it."

The state of Indiana had its branch of the National Security League and the Navy League and exemplified, in general, the national tendencies of 1915–1916. An editor of the *Lafayette Courier* in Indiana pointed to the advantages of military strength: "The best thing about a large army and a strong navy is that they make it so much easier to say just what we want to say in our diplomatic correspondence." Another editor commented, "A feller mightn't need a gun very often, but when he did need it, he needed it mighty bad." Some people of the state began to read books like *Defenseless America* (New York, 1915), by Hudson Maxim, and *The Invasion of America* (New York, 1916), by Julius W. Muller. Intellectuals, as a group, were among the strongest supporters of preparedness.

The opponents fought valiantly but without much success. For years the trend had been against them, as the United States followed its imperialistic course in Asia and Latin America. Colonies and protectorates, along with world trade, seemed to require—in the eyes of many leaders—a greatly enlarged military establishment that compared favorably with other Western powers. Why should America lag behind? In the emergency of 1914–1915, the United States still had a fourth-rate Army, at best, and a Navy far inferior to that of Great Britain. Could this condition

Figure 18 John Purroy Mitchel, Mayor of New York, a Preparedness Advocate, and a Private in the Training Camp at Plattsburg. (Mitchell fell from a plane in 1918 and was killed.) (*From* Harper's Weekly, *September 4, 1915.*)

be permitted to continue? Could the President of the United States and other responsible leaders in the government fail to take action?

Pacifists, progressives, enemies of Big Business, and others had an emphatic answer. The United States should stay out of war and tend to its own urgent problems at home. The American way was one of peace and progress, and even if the rest of the world had gone crazy the people of this favored land did not have to. Many of them believed passionately in the continuation of reform, which was possible only with the continuation of peace. The progressives usually emphasized economic causes of the problems that concerned them, both in domestic and foreign affairs. In large numbers they blamed the monopolists, the armor-plate manufacturers, the munitions makers, and assorted profiteers for the movement toward military preparedness and war. Leaders of this type included Robert M. La Follette, George Norris, Jane Addams, Claude Kitchin of North Carolina, Jeannette Rankin of Montana, and William Jennings Bryan. The last can illustrate some of the ideas and biases of this group.

Vigorously opposed to preparedness, Bryan mustered all the arguments and did not hesitate to attack by name those who were taking the other side on this question. Thus the ideas of Theodore Roosevelt, if adopted, "would provoke war instead of preventing it." No better proof was needed than to look at the conflict raging in Europe. "They spent twenty years preparing for it," Bryan declared. To him the use of force was abhorrent, the fighting of a war was barbaric, and even moderate measures of military preparation would lead down the very path to be avoided. He blamed the agitation for "defense" primarily upon selfish interests, and in large part such interests (he knew) were in the Republican party.

But the preparedness movement could not be stopped. By the fall of 1915 Wilson called upon Congress for major action to ready the nation's defenses. Secretary of War Lindley Garrison wanted a Continental Army, as he called it, a reserve force under federal control that would supersede the National Guard with greatly increased efficiency. Garrison was determined, but his plans hit a snag. The Military Affairs Committee in the House of Representatives did not support the Continental Army, and opposition in the Congress generally was strong enough to force a compromise. Secretary Garrison resigned. His replacement was Newton D. Baker of Cleveland, a leader in the progressive movement of Ohio and a moderate so far as preparedness was concerned.

With Garrison sacrificed, in effect, a number of agreements were soon possible. The National Guard was to be enlarged and brought more closely under federal control. Summer training camps, under direction of the War Department, were also authorized. The regular Army, meanwhile, was to be doubled up to a strength of about 200,000. In this new atmosphere the United States Navy was not to be left behind. A bill that passed Congress in August 1916 provided for the long-term construction of 156 ships, including 10 battleships, 16 cruisers, and 50 destroyers. Another measure of the same year provided for a Shipping Board with extensive powers to buy and build ships and otherwise to strengthen the merchant marine. Industrial mobilization had its beginning in 1916 with the creation of a Council of National Defense, whose duty it was to plan for the possibility of war.

The political situation helped, rather obviously, in the shaping of Woodrow Wilson's policies during 1915–1916. Any idea that the President was lacking in political ability might be dispelled by an examination of this campaign year. Certainly he was moving with public opinion and was leading it, to an extent, in the "right" direction for one who wanted fervently to have a second term in the White House. In a previous discussion of Wilsonian reforms, the point has been made that the President moved to the left from 1913 to 1916, accepting some ideas of federal involvement in the economy. Aid to labor was apparent in such measures as the La Follette Seamen's Act, the Keating-Owen child-labor law, and the Adamson eight-hour law—which passed during the summer of 1916. Aid to the farmer was notable in the Federal Farm Loan Act, whose principles of "class legislation" Wilson had earlier opposed.

The President had decided, in effect, that the government had a much larger function to perform than that of being an "umpire." When the national well-being was involved, government should act, and each case must be judged on its merits. In all probability this was an honest change on Wilson's part, but it also was an expedient one politically. It was intended, said one Republican, to "catch flies."

By no means was the President antibusiness in his point of view during these months. Even in 1914 but increasingly after that time he openly sought the support of the businessman. He did this partly because of his growing sophistication on the role of government and a desire to win favor among the different economic groups. But, also, by 1915 he had in mind the European war, the possibility of involvement, and the necessity of good relations with the business community. In 1916 Wilson accepted the idea of a tariff commission, which would determine by scientific means, its sponsors claimed, the level of duties to be fixed on various commodities. Business organizations had pushed very hard for the commission, and Wilson yielded. Another measure of the same sort gave an exemption, under the antitrust laws, to corporations that combined in the furtherance of overseas trade. American exporters, including the largest companies, did not have an enemy in Woodrow Wilson.

All in all, the year 1916 was among the most fascinating in American history. It brought a culmination of the progressive movement and an effort on the part of the leaders in both political parties to assess that movement, to react to it properly, and thereby to win the approval of the voters. The mood of certain "blocs" was a real concern to the political professionals in this campaign. Issues of domestic and foreign policy were entangled, as the Germans, for example, must be wooed by both parties in one way, the Irish in a somewhat different way, and the women voters in still another way. The farm vote, the business vote, the labor vote, the Catholic vote—these and other voting groups had to be considered. To win a solid bloc was most unlikely, but the right appeal delicately balanced between issues of "peace" and progressivism would give the margin of victory.

Each party enjoyed advantages. The Democrats, with control of the government and a record of achievement, had much to talk about. They might benefit as well from friendly officials in the Government Printing Office, in the Post Office, and in other federal agencies. The Republicans, at the same time, were still the majority party of the United States, and all they needed to do, it seemed, was to reunite the Taft supporters and "Bull Moosers" of 1912. Theodore Roosevelt was a crucial figure. By refusing a nomination from the Progressives, if offered to him, and by acting as harmonizer among factions of the GOP, he might assure a victory to that party. Thus he could compensate for the disastrous aftermath of his third-party movement in 1912.

Unfortunately for the Republicans, Roosevelt wanted the nomination for himself, and he felt so passionately on issues of the day that he simply was not able to pursue a course that contributed constructively to the GOP campaign. In the convention at Chicago he came nowhere near the strength necessary for his nomination. He toyed with the thought of a third-party nomination by the Progressives, but in truth he wanted to use this considerable backing to place himself on the Republican ticket. The Old Guard element did not want him, and the delegates generally were not impressed. Instead, they turned to Charles Evans Hughes, Associate Justice of the Supreme Court and formerly a progressive Governor of New York. As a reformer who had supported Taft in 1912 and who was acknowledged everywhere to be a man of ability and integrity, Hughes had an excellent chance, it seemed, to pull his party together and win the election. But the problem with the progressives of the party, including Roosevelt, was a most serious and continuing one. This was a stubborn and independent group, many of whom were not persuaded by any means that a ticket of "the two Charlies" (Hughes and Fairbanks), or the platform adopted, really had much meaning for the cause of progressivism. Also, one plank in that platform pledged the Republicans to an "honest neutrality," and it did not satisfy the interventionists like Roosevelt or the very strong peace group at the other extreme.

There was never any question that the Democratic delegates, meeting in St. Louis, would nominate the President for a second term. The convention came close to being a love feast. Speaker after speaker congratulated the party upon its great leader, Wilson, and its record of achievement that was unparalleled. Party leaders made a wise decision, with Wilson giving his approval, to include a woman suffrage plank in the platform. This would help in the Western states, and in a total of eleven states, where women already had won the vote. Most important in this convention was the wildly enthusiastic support given to Wilson's peace policies. There was no longer any doubt that the great majority of American Democrats—and probably other citizens as well—wanted to stay out of the European war. This realization had an impact on the campaign in months to follow.

It is apparent that the election of 1916 was a highly significant event. It determined that Woodrow Wilson and the Democrats would continue in control of the national government, that they would conduct the war in 1917–1918, and that they would be responsible for the postwar settlement, so far as the United States was concerned. The course of American history would have been quite different if Charles Evans Hughes and the Republicans had borne these responsibilities.

The Democrats did not win this contest easily, in spite of certain advantages already mentioned. The campaign in twenty-four Western states, directed from Chicago headquarters, shows the type of effort that was required. Serving as director was Senator Thomas J. Walsh of Montana, who was picked for his political acumen and knowledge of the West. Every effort was made to concentrate on the right issues in the right places and to throw the available support, financial and otherwise, to states where Democrats clearly had a chance to win. Illinois, for example, was not such a state. Neither Woodrow Wilson or other national leaders attempted to tell the Westerners what they should stress or what speakers they should send out, and, quite possibly, this willingness to delegate authority was the key to Democratic victory in the final outcome.

Most important of all the Democratic leaders, aside from the President himself, was William Jennings Bryan. The "Great Commoner" understood the West and perhaps the mood of the nation in 1916 as well as any public figure. He wrote, early in the campaign: "'He has kept us out of war' is our strongest slogan." Bryan's advice generally for conduct of the campaign was simple but sound: "Coach our speakers before they go out and be sure they know the facts and the arguments. We ought to win—we have earned it and the tide seems to be running our way, but we must not take any thing for granted. . . ." In report after report, the state Democratic leaders testified to Bryan's effectiveness on the platform and to a popular reception that surpassed anything they had ever seen.

But the Democrats had their problems too. In the Western headquarters, perhaps nothing caused more concern in the final weeks than the German-American vote and the threat of defections by the American Irish, often in key states. Senator Walsh and his staff made a many-faceted appeal to the Germans as good citizens, interested in the "magnificent achievements of the Wilson administration," not merely in foreign policy and alleged wrongs done to Germany. They also argued forcefully that Wilson had tried to be fair to Germany, while Republican leaders like Roosevelt and Senator Lodge had favored drastic action against the Fatherland. These "war hawks" in the GOP would gain greater influence if Hughes were elected President.

The Irish question was a much tougher one for the Democrats to handle and a painful business, all in all, since the Irish had been so identified with the Democratic party. The President became estranged from a good many when he failed to give support, as they thought he should, to the Easter Rebellion in Ireland (1916). He also denounced "hyphenism" and responded caustically to the criticisms of Jeremiah O'Leary, president of the American Truth Society. Wilson announced to O'Leary that he would be "mortified" to have anyone like him give support in the election and added that he might pass this word on to any of his disloyal friends. Obviously Wilson was hoping that most of the Irish were not in this category. But the *Irish World,* published in New York, attacked the President for his "know-nothingism" and denounced also the "Anglo-Saxon" fraud, or the idea that Americans should have a common type of patriotism. This was a nation of "many races," and differences should be recognized and tolerated.

Many of the Irish were just as agitated about Mexico and the treatment of Catholics there as they were about the war in Europe. They blamed Woodrow Wilson for not intervening forcefully and for the plight of priests and nuns under the lash of Mexican revolutionaries. Poor Wilson could hardly do anything right in this respect. He was castigated by extremists of the Protestant faith who pointed to his private secretary, "Joe" Tumulty, and to other Catholics in the administration as evidence that the President was dangerously involved with the forces of Rome. At the same time, extremists among the Catholics criticized him and his administration for his lack of sympathy and attention. Democratic "stars" like Bryan challenged the critics. They pointed to the fact that Wilson had stayed out of war with Mexico and, they argued, the President had succeeded generally in his policies south of the border. Of course, he had not done what the capitalist exploiters of Mexico would like him to do, nor had he interfered in the religious policy of that country.

While the Democrats were running an aggressive and highly effective campaign, for the most part, Charles Evans Hughes turned out to be a weak candidate. It is difficult to explain the blunders that he made, since his ability is unquestioned. Most notably, Hughes was unable to bridge the gap between the Old Guard and the progressives in his party. He failed dramatically as a harmonizer during a trip to California, seeming to align himself with conservative leaders of the state. George Mowry has observed: "It is possible that no presidential candidate ever managed to alienate so many voters in one region within so short a time." In spite of all, Hughes came near to winning and he did carry every state north of the Ohio and east of the Mississippi except for two, New Hampshire and Ohio. He also gained the support of Oregon, South Dakota, Iowa, and Minnesota.

Almost incredibly, while losing the East with its great population centers and a few other states, Woodrow Wilson won the South and most of the West and thereby the election. To win the South was customary, so that the states beyond the Mississippi were those which had changed and which seemed, in fact, to tell the story. California, for example, had gone to the Progressives four years earlier as its own Hiram Johnson ran on the

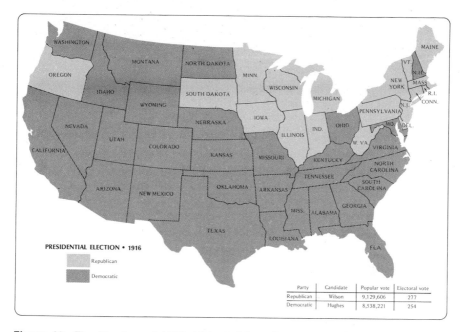

Party	Candidate	Popular vote	Electoral vote
Republican	Wilson	9,129,606	277
Democratic	Hughes	8,538,221	254

Figure 19 The Election of 1916. (*Adapted from* The United States: A History of a Democracy, *2d ed., edited by Wesley M. Gewehr, Donald C. Gordon, David S. Sparks, and Roland N. Stromberg. Copyright* © *1957, 1960 by McGraw-Hill, Inc.*)

ticket with Theodore Roosevelt. The campaign in 1916 was rightly seen as important, although California had a mere thirteen votes in the electoral college. By a margin of 4,000 the people of the state turned to Wilson. In the country as a whole the President had a plurality of 9,129,606 to 8,538,221; and the electoral margin was 277 to 254. This was, therefore, one of the closest elections in history and, as one Democratic leader wrote to another, the "greatest political event" of their lives.

To say categorically that California "won" this election would be foolish, since the tally from other states was also important, but the late returns from the Coast at least assured the victory, and it was strikingly apparent that if the thirteen votes of California were taken away from the President and given to Hughes, the Republicans would have assumed office in March 1917. From the standpoint of issues, also, the results from the West and from specific places like San Francisco gave an indication of what had determined the outcome nationally. The women of San Francisco voted strongly for Wilson, as did the labor groups, and the city went Democratic by a margin of 15,000. This bastion of strength offset the Republican vote in other areas of the state and was therefore decisive.

Progressives, laborers, women in the West, farmers in the South and West, friends of peace everywhere, and socialists—these were the groups primarily that gave Wilson his victory.

In a world of turmoil, the election of 1916 could give the illusion that men controlled events instead of being controlled by them. Surely the new recognition given to women, the strength of organized labor, and the triumph of peace sentiment were most encouraging signs. The progressivism of Woodrow Wilson had incorporated many elements of modern thought and of bureaucratic management, so that the public needs might be attended to more successfully than ever in the past. Threats of "hyphenism" or a campaign based heavily on religious prejudice had seemingly been averted. The Democratic party had solidified itself, becoming a truly national party, with the South, West, and East all strongly represented. Nor had the Republicans done badly. Taking the two parties together there seemed to be a new capacity for intelligent leadership and for progress.

In actual fact, the country was not in good shape. War was near, and much of the cement that held society together was coming loose. About the time the campaign got under way, Wilson had committed himself to break off relations with Germany if ships were sunk without a warning, according to his interpretation of the *Sussex* pledge. The President and his party were exceedingly lucky that the Germans adhered to this pledge—and that no accidents occurred—in the summer and fall of 1916. As Wilson himself commented to Josephus Daniels, "Any little German lieutenant can put us into the war at any time by some calculated outrage." In a less obvious sense, too, the forces of destructiveness and irrationality were loose in the world and in the thinking of many leaders.

The End of American Innocence, by Henry F. May, has tried to determine when it was that Americans lost much of their faith in progress, in conventional morality, and in a national culture devoted to the maintenance of traditional values. May concluded that these prewar years showed many of the signs often associated with the 1920s. The period of actual war only aggravated some of the doubts and tensions and the hatred, greed, and lust that often seemed to predominate over virtues long extolled. "Every idol" was falling, in the view of many whose idealism had been the purest. This pattern of thought must be explained in considerable part by the growing fascination with psychology, with getting to the actual sources of human behavior, however unlovely they might be. Did people really have the capacity to control themselves or their environment? Were they controlled by their emotions, as Sigmund Freud seemed to say? Was it necessary, perhaps, for an elite corps of experts to plan the course of any modern nation? Was government "of the people" and "by the people" actually possible in modern times?

As Woodrow Wilson went ahead with his duties after the exciting victory in November, he obviously did not think that democracy had failed. He knew very well, however, that it faced some extremely difficult tests. First on the agenda was still another attempt to end the fighting in Europe and thus, also, to guarantee that the United States would not have to get involved overseas except in keeping the peace. One of the curious and admirable features of Wilson's policy was an increasing stiffness toward the British in 1916 and early 1917. He was still trying to be neutral. He was indignant over the practice of blacklisting American firms and showed unhappiness with other aspects of British policy. The House-Grey memorandum, which seemed feasible for a time as a means to end the war, had failed. Colonel House, on another of his trips to Europe, had planned rather elaborately to bring about peace, if possible, through coercion: If the Allies agreed to make peace, while the Central Powers could not agree (as House expected), then the United States would feel compelled to enter the war on the Allied side. The President, however, did not share in House's enthusiasm, insisting that the word "probably" be inserted in any such pledge to the British. With the breakdown of this "peace" attempt that might have meant war, relations between the Atlantic powers took a turn for the worse.

Time was running out, so far as a negotiated peace was concerned. Yet Wilson made another effort, sending in December a circular to all the belligerent powers, inquiring as to what their aims were in the war and under what conditions they would stop the killing. This was a time at which the German high command was ready to have a negotiated settlement, for they were winning at the moment and were confident that the terms would be favorable. The Allies, by contrast, were disappointed and incensed that the President had addressed them as he had. Walter Hines Page reported from London that the President's remarks were interpreted by the British "as placing the Allies and the Central Powers on the same moral level." He should have known that this was a "holy and defensive war" with the aim of saving "free government in the world from a military tyranny." England and France were completely unwilling at the end of 1916 to accept a negotiated settlement.

Wilson refused to accept the rebuff. He could not end the war as he hoped; yet he did have the capacity, he believed, through his ideas and force of personality, to assume the moral leadership of the world. On January 22, 1917, addressing the Senate, he suggested there was little difference between the two sides, that both were fighting from motives difficult to justify. He called for a "peace without victory." The bitterness engendered by a victorious war, he said, would make a lasting settlement impossible, and what was needed, therefore, was a peace between equals. Trying to define a just peace, he used the language of soaring idealism: the "freedom of life," the "principles of mankind," the "equality of rights," the "equality of nations," the "freedom of the seas," the "guarantees of a universal covenant," and so on. "Right," he said, "must be based upon the common strength, not upon the individual strength, of the nations upon whose concert peace will depend." He was calling for disarmament, an end to entangling alliances, justice in world affairs, and a league of nations which would make peace secure "by the organized force of mankind."

About a week after this stirring message, Germany announced the resumption of unrestricted submarine warfare. All waters around the British Isles, France, and Italy were declared in a state of blockade; and vessels entering these waters, whatever their nationality, might be sunk on sight. The arguments in Germany had ended; the military high command finally had convinced the Chancellor, Bethmann-Hollweg, and the Kaiser that the war could be won quickly through an onslaught against Allied shipping. The United States would enter the war, they believed, but too late to be a decisive factor.

This threat, which had been hanging over the American people since the *Lusitania's* sinking, was now a reality. There was no way to avoid intervention, assuming that the German leaders adhered to their decision. Wilson went before the Congress again on February 3, 1917, and broke off diplomatic relations with the German Empire. He said he could not believe that the German authorities would "do in fact what they have warned us they will feel at liberty to do." The American people wished to stay at peace with the German people, and he still hoped fervently that this was possible. However, American honor and American interests must be defended.

Cedric Cummins, in assessing Indiana public opinion, has stated that, unquestionably, the "submarine dispute was of prime importance" in causing the Hoosiers to swing toward intervention. As American ships were sunk in March, with considerable loss of life, one newspaper wrote: "As sure as sun-up, as certain as nightfall, it is coming." Far away, in Massachusetts, came another strong reaction to the shift in German policy. The *Springfield Republican* asserted that unrestricted warfare, as announced, was "unwarranted aggression" and "impossible" to accept. It was a declaration of "guerilla warfare of ambuscade and murder," with neutrals to be treated as enemies.

Other influences worked toward war. In the country generally the news of a note from the German Foreign Secretary, Zimmermann, to the German minister in Mexico was shocking. Berlin authorities aimed to get the support of Mexico by promising her territories in the Southwest, formerly "stolen" by the United States, if Mexico would join the Central Powers in this war. Also, the Germans planned to approach Japanese leaders with the idea of effecting an agreement. No one knew what might happen next in a crazy world at war. From Russia came the exciting news of a revolution, which by toppling the czarist tyranny promised to give another great democracy to the nations of the world. Thinking of this event and of the "lovable, kindly Russians," Secretary of the Interior Franklin K. Lane rejoiced at the prospects ahead; his country might soon be fighting on the side of the Russians he so admired.

As war came closer, most Americans including the Germans, the Irish, and various of the peace groups tended to close ranks in patriotic fashion. There was a bandwagon effect. Some of those most subject to suspicion as disloyal Americans were under compulsion to prove their loyalty. The effect of economic involvement on the Allied side obviously cannot be discounted. At least in subtle ways, the loans to the Allies, the massive shipment of goods, and the boom resulting from war business contributed to a sense that Britain and France should not be permitted to lose this war.

Woodrow Wilson made the key decisions, as he had since 1914. Certain members of the Senate still sought to avert war by keeping American ships out of the war zone. The President, however, decided that he had the necessary authority to arm these merchant ships, giving them a chance at self-protection, and to send them out. Wilson agonized over the situation, believing that the war was almost intolerable, that it might do irreparable damage to American institutions. And yet he saw no way out. The only hope was that Germany would avoid sinking the ships of neutral powers and especially those of the United States. Wilson, in other words, was prepared to retreat from the *Sussex* pledge of 1916, so eager was he to avoid war. He did not adhere doggedly to an extreme interpretation of international law, as formerly believed.

Secretary Lane has given a vivid picture of the President's Cabinet meetings during the last weeks before a declaration of war. Writing to his brother in intimate detail, Lane was critical of Wilson for his "philosophic humanitarianism," or lack of "punch" at such a crucial time. The President seemed to be an "internationalist or a pacifist," and his patriotism was certainly not what it should have been. In the meeting of February 25, Lane posed an "innocent" question: Was it true, he asked, "that the wives of American Consuls on leaving Germany had been stripped naked, given an acid bath to detect writing on their flesh, and subjected to other indignities"? Secretary of State Lansing said, yes, the story was true. The President, however, accused some Cabinet members of trying to "work up a propaganda of hatred against Germany."

Thus Wilson continued to stand against the warmongers until finally he could do so no longer. His decision for intervention was made. As Secretary Lane wrote on April 1: "He [Wilson] is to be for recognizing war and taking hold of the situation in such a fashion as will eventually lead to an Allies' victory over Germany. But he goes unwillingly. The Cabinet is at last a unit. We can stand Germany's insolence and murderous policy no longer. Burleson, Gregory, Daniels, and Wilson were the last to come over."

The Wilson administration, it seems clear, was forced into war, primarily by German use of the submarine. Neither Wilson nor the American people wanted war. Large numbers, much like the President, hated the thought of it. If a mistake had been made, Wilson sweetened it by his sense of compassion and his well-known record of attempting to avoid the conflict. This was not to be a war against the German people, he said. Rather, it was an attempt to bring about a new world order. "The world must be made safe for democracy. Its peace must be planted upon the tested foundations of political liberty." Wilson was heavily influenced by his hope of attaining world leadership through participation in the war and gaining a seat at the peace table.

The study of history often suggests, as at this juncture, that the human capacity for rationalization has no limit. Woodrow Wilson and others who were being swept into the greatest struggle in history managed somehow to persuade themselves that they could now direct the course of events. What they could not control from the outside they could control from inside. What had been an unjust war would soon become, therefore, a just war and a means of preventing the occurrence—ever again—of such a holocaust.

SUGGESTIONS FOR ADDITIONAL READING

Several books published in the last fifteen or twenty years, based in part on foreign archives, have given new insights into the causes of American intervention. Karl E. Birnbaum, *Peace Moves and U-Boat Warfare: A Study of Imperial Germany's Policy towards the United States, April 18, 1916–January 9, 1917*, Almquist & Wiksell, Stockholm, 1958, accepts the seriousness of Wilson's desire for peace in 1916–1917 and his willingness to make concessions to Germany. He shows, however, that German leaders lacked faith in the American President while, simultaneously, the militarists of that country gained control of policy. Ernest R. May, *The World War and American Isolation, 1914–1917*, Harvard, Cambridge, Mass., 1959, also stresses the struggle inside Germany, leading to military control. He declares that close analysis of the policies followed by Wilson cannot "find the point at which he might have turned back or taken another road."

The works of Arthur S. Link provide the most comprehensive treatment. Particularly important are three volumes of his biography, *Wilson: The Struggle for Neutrality, 1914–1915* (1960); *Wilson: Confusions and Crises, 1915–1916*

(1964); and *Wilson: Campaigns for Progressivism and Peace, 1916–1917*(1965). In his preface to the last-mentioned volume, Professor Link gives a summary of his recent views, derived from continuing research. He concludes that "Wilson tried sincerely to pursue policies of rigid neutrality toward the Entente Allies"; that he was searching for a means of accommodation with Germany; and that peace was still possible in 1917 if the German leaders had willed it so. Charles Seymour, *American Neutrality, 1914–1917: Essays on the Causes of American Intervention in the World War,* Yale, New Haven, Conn., 1935, is an earlier work whose conclusions are, in many respects, like those given above. Two books on public opinion and the coming of war are Cedric C. Cummins, *Indiana Public Opinion and the World War, 1914–1917,* Indiana Historical Bureau, Indianapolis, 1945, and Kevin J. O'Keefe, *A Thousand Deadlines: The New York City Press and American Neutrality, 1914–1917,* Martinus Nijhoff, The Hague, 1972. An aspect of the preparedness movement is examined in John G. Clifford, *The Citizen Soldiers: The Plattsburg Training Camp Movement, 1913–1920,* Univ. of Kentucky Press, Lexington, 1972.

A number of works, both old and new, have been critical of American policy. The older ones, sometimes called "revisionist" because they departed from official interpretations of World War I, may be illustrated by the following: Walter Millis, *Road to War: America, 1914–1917,* Houghton Mifflin, Boston, 1935; C. C. Tansill, *America Goes to War,* Little, Brown, Boston, 1938; H. C. Peterson, *Propaganda for War: The Campaign against American Neutrality, 1914–1917,* Univ. of Oklahoma Press, Norman, 1939; and Edwin Borchard and William P. Lage, *Neutrality for the United States,* Yale, New Haven, Conn., 1937. Obviously these authors were influenced by the times in which they wrote and by threats of another holocaust. George F. Kennan is one of those who has argued, as in his *American Diplomacy, 1900–1950* (1951), that the United States should have entered World War I sooner, thus helping to bring to an end its terrible destructiveness. For conflicting interpretations, both of contemporaries and scholars, see Warren I. Cohen (ed.), *Intervention, 1917: Why America Fought,* Heath, Boston, 1966. A useful book of documents is Daniel M. Smith (ed.), *American Intervention, 1917: Sentiment, Self-Interest, or Ideals?* Houghton Mifflin, Boston, 1966. Close students of foreign policy and the changing interpretations should see again John Braeman et al. (eds.), *Twentieth-Century American Foreign Policy.*

A general study of the war period, which has been superseded only in part, is Frederic L. Paxson, *American Democracy and the World War,* 3 vols., Houghton Mifflin, Boston, 1936–1948. The first volume traces domestic and foreign policy from 1913 to 1917. Mark Sullivan's *Our Times* has a lively volume on the years 1914–1918. Daniel M. Smith, *The Great Departure: The United States and World War I, 1914–1920,* Wiley, New York, 1965, is brief and scholarly, as is Ross Gregory, *The Origins of American Intervention in the First World War,* Norton, New York, 1971. Two books of subtlety and originality are Edward H. Buehrig, *Woodrow Wilson and the Balance of Power,* Indiana Univ. Press, Bloomington, 1955, and N. Gordon Levin, Jr., *Woodrow Wilson and World Politics: America's Response to War and Revolution,* Oxford, London, 1968. Jack J. Roth (ed.), *World War I: A Turning Point in Modern History,* Knopf, New York, 1967, contains thoughtful essays relating both to Europe and America.

Ross Gregory, *Walter Hines Page: Ambassador to the Court of St. James's,* Univ. of Kentucky Press, Lexington, 1970, takes a new and sympathetic look at a notorious Anglophile. Other works on the diplomats are Charles Seymour (ed.), *The Intimate Papers of Colonel House,* and *Lawrence Levine, Defender of the Faith* (Bryan), both mentioned previously, and Daniel M. Smith, *Robert Lansing and American Neutrality, 1914–1917,* Univ. of California Press, Berkeley, 1958. Biographies of men in Congress opposed to war are Alex M. Arnett, *Claude Kitchin and the Wilson War Policies,* Little, Brown, Boston, 1937; Belle Case and Fola La Follette, *Robert M. La Follette,* 2 vols. (1953), cited previously, vol. 1; Richard Lowitt, *George W. Norris: The Persistence of a Progressive, 1913–1933,* Univ. of Illinois Press, Urbana, 1971; and William F. Holmes, *The White Chief: James Kimble Vardaman,* Louisiana State Univ. Press, Baton Rouge, 1970.

Many of the books referred to before have chapters or sections on the election of 1916. Link's *Campaigns for Progressivism and Peace* and Levine's *Defender of the Faith* are outstanding in this respect. See also Merlo J. Pusey, *Charles Evans Hughes,* 2 vols., Columbia, New York, 1963, vol. 1; Spencer C. Olin, Jr., *California's Prodigal Sons: Hiram Johnson and the Progressives, 1911–1917,* Univ. of California Press, Berkeley, 1968; and Anne W. Lane and Louise H. Wall, (eds.), *The Letters of Franklin K. Lane, Personal and Political,* Houghton Mifflin, Boston, 1922. For the German-Americans and the Irish-Americans in 1916 and the crucial months thereafter, one might start with the following: Clifton James Child, *The German-Americans in Politics, 1914–1917,* Univ. of Wisconsin Press, Madison, 1939; Niel M. Johnson, *George Sylvester Viereck: German-American Propagandist,* Univ. of Illinois Press, Urbana, 1972; and Carl Wittke, *The Irish in America,* Louisiana State Univ. Press, Baton Rouge, 1956.

Chapter 12

Fighting the War
on the Home Front

Life often seems a paradoxical affair and especially so during wartime, when the codes of behavior undergo a change, the pace of living intensifies, and death is imminent for many thousands. The first World War, by one criterion, was a great and successful effort in which a loyal citizenry, led by Woodrow Wilson, mobilized their diverse resources, produced the materials needed, trained and dispatched overseas their fighting men, and contributed decisively to the defeat of Germany. It was a war against the Hun, waged for the defense of freedom and democracy. The Germans were beaten, while the United States established itself as a world leader. At the same time, however, this war was a matter of faulted idealism at home, of self-seeking men and groups; of dominant forces and peoples calling for victory abroad while "keeping the lid on" in America. Numerous minorities were seen as a threat. German-Americans, notably, had a difficult time, both from official policy and from pressure exerted by the public. Blacks also were special targets. Matters of internal security and "forced harmony" were far more serious in 1917–1918 than they were in World War II after the continued assimilation and cultural progress of the 1920s and 1930s.

As the country went to war in 1917, life assumed a new urgency, and few were left untouched by the rush of events. Millions were willing to serve, and even to die, for what seemed a just cause. Leaders had to be found for the proliferating agencies; money had to be spent by the billions of dollars; decisions had to be made on countless matters, often at the expense of personal liberty. Inevitably, there were some who gained an advantage from the emergency. This did not mean necessarily any form of dishonesty or wrong conduct but, more likely, reflected a rationalization of the national interests that coincided conveniently with individual or group interests. A businessman could support the war and, at the same time, attempt to direct its course and to make absolutely certain that his own business was not affected adversely. In a similar way, farmers and laborers gave their support, while reformers tried to further their own programs in the climate of patriotism and nationalism. Human ambition was apparent in the sweat and striving of this war.

The spring and summer of 1917 was an exciting time. Secretary of the Interior Lane announced in one of his animated descriptions of the Washington scene that these were "great days." He was undisturbed by fears of what the war might bring, exhilarated by his meetings with Balfour of England, Joffre of France, railroad presidents, industrial magnates, and an endless stream of people. As a Cabinet member in the Council of National Defense, Lane saw the necessity for an unprecedented mobilization of people and resources. The strength of America in this crisis, he believed, could be found in the "adventuresome spirit and the exploiting energies" of people who had pushed into frontier country and taken up government lands. Yet this was not enough. The making of modern war demanded the utmost of the chemist, the geologist, the topographer, the utmost from the brains and civilization of America. Out of such an effort America should emerge "as the center of the world's thought" and of its morality.

Another official in Washington spoke of the "striving, energized, overcrowded population of the city." He went on: "A kind of madness seized the populace. . . . Nice discriminations were lost in the fever of production." Speaking to the coal operators of America in June, Secretary of the Navy Daniels made a statement that must have seemed like madness to some of those gentlemen. A draft of military manpower, he said, had become imperative; and a draft of other kinds of power was no less imperative. "No man owns an oil well or a coal mine except a[s] trustee. And if this war goes on long no man can say that he owns a gallon of oil or a ton of coal." The possibility of government control, or nationalization, was much on people's minds.

More than anything else, what brought the war home to Americans was conscription, or the draft. The administration sought authority to enlarge the military forces of the United States, temporarily, by a policy of conscription. Opposition in Congress was powerful, and continuous pressure from the administration, along with arguments from military men and preparedness advocates, was necessary for passage. The American people had always believed in the ability of citizen soldiers to defend the country. This tradition was not abandoned without a protest. Southerners and Westerners, especially, taking pride in their patriotism, argued that a volunteer system would produce far more manpower than required; compulsory service was an insult. Representative Champ Clark of Missouri expressed a widely held attitude when he burst out: "I protest with all my heart and mind and soul against having the slur of being a conscript placed upon the men of Missouri; in the estimation of Missourians there is precious little difference between a conscript and a convict." In like manner, there were protests that this was a plan to "Prussianize" America. Was the United States, in the name of democracy, about to adopt measures that would destroy it?

Some of those who opposed the bill did so by attacking the special interests behind it. This was a class measure, they said. "Go into any community in this land," exclaimed Edward Keating of Colorado, a prolabor Congressman, "and find the man who is most oppressive to labor and you will find that he is the man who is shouting the loudest for conscription." Big Business, to be sure, heavily favored the idea of a draft, and, rather obviously, so did the military leaders. Henry L. Stimson, formerly Secretary of War, could speak for many of them when he wrote in *Scribner's Magazine* (April 1917) praising military service, deploring the "decaying art of obedience" among the "undisciplined youth" of America, and suggesting that this was a time when a permanent system of conscription might be put into effect. The *Wall Street Journal* also saw social benefits to be derived from such a system. The Brotherhood of Locomotive Firemen saw the situation quite differently. Their journal declared: "Never in the history of any nation has there been a clearer demonstration of one class wanting another class to go and do the fighting while themselves staying at home safe and sound. These professional non-enlisting master class patriots are surely numerous at the present time in the United States."

Whatever the charges against the idea of conscription, Wilson and his advisers were not to be deterred. The very fact of opposition made the draft more desirable; for a failure to get volunteers in certain portions of the country, or in the industrial centers of the Northeast, might be interpreted as a negative referendum on the war. This could hardly be tolerated. The War Department had some excellent reasons for its insistence on the draft, not the least of which was the three years of slaughter on the battlegrounds of Europe, which had reduced somewhat the enthusiasm for combat duty. Another lesson and a grim one was the experience of Great Britain, which started the war in 1914 with a volunteer system and lost many of her best and bravest young men. A system of selective service might have permitted the assignment of these soldiers on a more rational basis of talent and training. It may be speculated that another reason for avoiding any system of extensive volunteering, or of volunteer units, was a rather personal one with President Wilson—to make absolutely sure that Theodore Roosevelt did not have the opportunity to organize his own army of Rough Riders, or some comparable group. Possibly he could become a hero, building his strength for another presidential run; and there was little doubt that Roosevelt would be difficult to control, once turned loose across the Atlantic.

Secretary of War Baker started his planning for the draft long before the bill actually passed. When the President called for its acceptance in his war message of April 2, the administration was ready to take all the steps necessary and to anticipate and prevent citizen opposition. If young men were forced into military service by soldiers from the regular army, there would be opposition and perhaps even violence. To avoid this, civilian "neighbors" might compose the draft boards and generally direct the proceedings. Men would go to register almost as if they were going to cast a vote. Then, later, their civilian neighbors and community leaders might call them into service. Almost incredibly a machinery of mammoth scope was set up quietly, ready for action when the measure went through. This was a cooperative effort involving the Government Printing Office, the Post Office, the War Department, locally appointed members of the draft boards, political leaders, and local law authorities.

Meanwhile, in April and May 1917, the bill encountered strenuous opposition in the Congress. Fiorello La Guardia, a Representative, later recalled how the Speaker of the House, the majority leader, and the chairman of the military affairs committee all opposed the draft bill. La Guardia believed that the draft would never have passed if congressmen had understood the military situation. Most of them had been persuaded that American boys would not be sent overseas to fight.

With the necessary pressure, the administration had its way. The bill passed, and plans quickly took shape for the young men to go and register. A proclamation by the President as he signed the bill helped to create the proper atmosphere. Mayors, business leaders, governors, and others did all they could to assist; and on June 5 the registration occurred. All men twenty-one to thirty (inclusive) had to go and sign up—or they were in trouble. Some 10 million were registered, while the War Department determined that from this number it wanted 700,000 soldiers almost immediately. By early 1918 more men were needed on the Western front, and a second registration was held for those boys who had reached the age of twenty-one since the year before. Then shortly the age limits were expanded to include men from eighteen through forty-five.

An occasion of real drama was the draft lottery, which determined who was to be "called" first. In no local district were there more than 10,500 men eligible for the draft. Therefore numbers from 1 to 10,500 were placed in a "fishbowl" in Washington, where dignitaries gathered and proceeded to withdraw the numbers. The first, drawn by Secretary of War Baker, was 258. Thus the "258s" in districts all over the country were eligible for immediate call. For those with the low numbers and for their families and friends the war quickly became a highly personal thing.

A number of men devoted their thoughts to avoiding the draft. Some valid ways were to be an alien without first citizenship papers, to be a minister or theological student, or to have dependents genuinely needing support. Conscientious objectors had a difficult time, and the only ones given consideration were members of religious denominations whose creeds forbade fighting. Even these men had to be willing to serve in the capacity of a noncombatant, under the direction of soldiers. Those who failed to obey orders and to cooperate fully were often subjected to brutal treatment or torture, as attempts were made to "break" them and force obedience. The most serious trouble came from nonreligious objectors, such as Germans who did not want to fight against their own country, humanitarians who wanted to kill no one, and radicals refusing to support a capitalistic war. Though accused of cowardice, such men were likely to have more courage than the usual draftee, who followed the path of least resistance and hoped that in his military service he would be lucky enough to escape the worst assignments. At the time, however, the draftee was a hero while the conscientious objector (CO) was widely regarded as a coward and a national disgrace.

During the summer of 1917 some organized resistance flared up against the draft. A near riot occurred in New York City on June 15 involving a large crowd of protestors and some soldier-patriots who found themselves badly outnumbered and completely unable to break up the demonstration. In August a group of marines and sailors in Philadelphia successfully prevented the holding of a similar protest meeting. Through the violent action of patriotic citizens or the procedures of law and order, opposition to conscription was crushed, with numbers of protestors going to jail.

On the whole, and considering the type of war to be fought, the draft was a success. It was far better than an attempt to rely solely upon volunteers. A total of some 24 million men took part in the several registrations; of these about 2,750,000 were drafted. With those who volunteered and others who already were in the service, some 5 million served in the armed forces, although far fewer than half actually went overseas. The total number of desertions throughout the war was estimated at 340,000.

It is at least possible that the Allies could have won in 1918 without American soldiers, but they could not have done so without American supplies or ships or money. Economic and industrial mobilization was of the utmost importance. This effort had started in a small way during 1916 with the provision for a planning agency, the Council of National Defense, consisting of six members of the Cabinet, with a director, a staff, and special planning committees such as one on munitions. It was apparent that if war actually started, this preliminary work must be largely superseded by specialized "control" agencies. Two years of experience in Great Britain and other countries had shown the necessity in a modern war of mobilizing the total resources of a nation, including scientific knowledge and every administrative skill. The will of the people also must be buoyed up by a campaign of persuasion and propaganda.

Most Americans did not require persuading. La Guardia, for example, in his autobiography gives a good sense of how the House of Representatives got caught up in the national effort. War measure after war measure came before the representatives, and some were blood-thirsty. La Guardia himself introduced a bill which prescribed the death penalty for the fraudulent sale of war materials. Louis Post of Chicago, another liberal, supported the war in much the same way. Total moral commitment was demanded in order to win, and guarantees of liberty in the American Constitution might have to be suspended. Carrying this thought still farther, a leading senator and constitutional authority delivered an address entitled "Who Is Afraid of a Dictator?" The war powers of Congress, he argued, gave ample power to prosecute the war as was being done under the President's direction. The basis for this power ultimately was the right of self-preservation, and he asserted that there was no reason to be afraid that Woodrow Wilson and the Congress would fail to surrender the new authority after "a triumphant democracy shall have assured a lasting peace to the world."

The President did, in fact, become a virtual dictator, although he preferred to delegate much of his power. Soon after war was declared it became apparent that Wilson needed an authorization to direct the production and control of foodstuffs and other necessary materials. As a result, Congress passed in August 1917 the Lever Act, named after Asbury F. Lever of South Carolina, chairman of the House Committee on Agriculture. The President gained authority to manage the production and allocation of food products, fertilizer, feeds, and the equipment that farmers required. Coal and petroleum were also brought under Presidential authority. Wilson and his agents could now stimulate production, not only by exhortation to patriotic endeavor but by economic controls and weapons that left very little to the imagination. They could fix prices, ban the production of items considered wasteful, such as alcoholic beverages, and even seize control of plants that were uncooperative. Many members of the Congress were dubious indeed about giving powers of this magnitude to the executive branch of government. A Democratic representative from Texas, for example, shouted out that this plan meant the dictatorial control and regimentation of the "little, humble farmer who is seeking to eke out an existence for himself and his hungry children." It was all to no avail, although the argument continued for many days.

In the spring of 1918 the Overman Act was passed, adding still further to Presidential power. What the administration sought and got from Congress was a freedom from statutory regulations and the conventional procedures, so that new agencies could be created and the function of others could be enlarged, reduced, or transferred—as the President thought necessary. One senator jokingly proposed an amendment that would read: "If any power, constitutional or not, has been inadvertently omitted from this bill, it is hereby granted in full."

Wilson gained another victory when the Congress failed to establish a watchdog committee on the conduct of the war, which many Republicans and Democrats advocated. This would have been a joint committee to investigate continuously the executive branch and its many agencies and to ascertain what mistakes they might be making, financial or otherwise. The failure to create such a committee left the President with what he had asked for, a full and untrammeled responsibility to lead the United States for the duration of the war. This did not mean, however, that he escaped criticism from inside or outside the halls of Congress; far from it.

To determine where the power lies in government and how it is being used is seldom easy, but in wartime such a determination seems almost impossible. Certainly there was much fuzziness about the agencies of 1917–1918, as changes rapidly occurred. Essentially the Council of National Defense continued with its work in 1917 until special agencies, such as the Food Administration, assumed the major duties with full-time administrators. Walter S. Gifford of the American Telephone and Telegraph Company served as director of the Council. An Advisory Commission included Daniel Willard, president of the Baltimore and Ohio Railroad Company; Samuel Gompers, president of the American Federation of Labor; Julius Rosenwald, president of Sears, Roebuck and Company; Bernard Baruch, a New York banker; and others. Hundreds of additional advisers came together in subcommittees, working part-time in

Washington. These were the famous dollar-a-year men, almost always business executives, organized to advise on problems of steel, lumber, coal, oil, shipping, munitions, and the like. Local councils of defense were also established, with a total of 184,000 branches on the state and local level. Thus the needs of the government were relayed from the national to local leaders, and their cooperation was elicited.

With so many businessmen gathered in Washington, the charge "conflict of interest" was often heard. One observer declared that these masters of capital sat in the morning as "foremost patriots," directing mobilization, while in the afternoon they conducted their own business with newly acquired inside information and often with government contracts. Obviously there was some truth to the charge. For example, the advisory committee for petroleum was headed by Alfred C. Bedford, president of the Standard Oil Company of New Jersey; and among the other eight members in July 1917 were the president of the Texas Company, the president of the Atlantic Refining Company, the president of the Gulf Refining Company, and E. L. Doheny of the Mexican Petroleum Company, along with Harry F. Sinclair of the Sinclair Oil and Refining Company. Independent oil companies and the industry at large, putting any doubts aside, gave their support to this advisory committee, hoping to avoid outright government control or stringent regulation.

To direct or guide the fuel companies, including those of both the coal and petroleum industries, was not an easy assignment. Even to learn the output of petroleum or the quantity in storage was difficult. Thus to determine a fair price was also difficult. Those in the mining business, those who had gained their wealth literally by ripping it from the earth, often seemed to think that God Almighty had bestowed his blessing on them and they should be responsible to no other authority. Time and again, the miners had behaved in a manner that provoked criticism, if not a public outcry. In the war years, their patriotism largely coincided with profits as the cry came for greater production. Some oilmen, however, took advantage of the situation rather flagrantly.

What happened, in essence, was a fight within the government over policies to be pursued, with some officials conciliatory and partial to the industry and others insistent on price fixing and close regulation. In some instances, there was "commandeering" of petroleum supplies at prices set by the United States Navy. But, in general, the voluntary cooperation of oilmen was solicited and apparently received. The point was not lost on some critics of the industry that oilmen drawn from California made up most of the staff of the Petroleum Division in the Fuel Administration. They had the power to make decisions enriching their own friends and corporations and consistently aimed in that direction; but at the same time, they argued the need for production and thus were helping mightily

Figure 20 "An Efficiency Expert at Work," Drawn by John T. McCutcheon, July 10, 1918. (*Rare Book Room, University of Illinois Library.*)

to win the war by providing the necessary fuel supplies. The profits were incidental.

Most important of those agencies trying to run the great production machine, and to do so equitably, was the War Industries Board, headed by Bernard Baruch. At first this was only a committee of the Council of National Defense. Its powers grew, and in 1918 the President turned over to Baruch an extraordinary authority. He was to try and manage the whole industrial system as one big factory, directing the flow of raw materials, controlling priorities, converting plants to war use, and seeing that the finished goods went to the Allies, to American armed forces, or elsewhere, as needed. Products were to be standardized for efficiency and every effort made toward the conservation of products and facilities. Baruch had the power to fix prices, and he did fix them on iron, steel, wool, lumber, and copper, for example. Mostly, however, he urged cooperation in the name of patriotism and obtained good results. Baruch was, when necessary, an economic dictator, subject only to Presidential overruling. The War Industries Board had to coordinate with the Food Administration, the Railway Administration, the Fuel Administration, the War Labor Board, the Shipping Board, the War Trade Board, and other agencies. Most important was the Food Administration, directed by Herbert Hoover, who, according to the *London Nation,* was the "biggest man" to emerge on the Allied side.

Real efforts were made to conduct this war democratically. Many of the old progressive groups were determined to carry their ideas forward, to protect the working people, to prevent profiteering, and to use governmental power in positive ways whenever possible. The fight over taxation is an excellent example. As usual in a war, it was possible to put the burden of payment on future generations by the government's borrowing through bond sales, with principal and interest coming due sometime later. The big difference in this war was the income tax, both on individuals and corporations, which along with other taxes, brought in billions of dollars. The basic income tax of 2 percent was raised in 1917 to 4 percent and then again in 1918 to 12 percent on all incomes over $4,000. The government also imposed an additional surtax on high incomes which went up, on a graduated basis, to 65 percent. Since the corporations paid regular taxes and also excess profits taxes, they did not escape lightly.

This wartime schedule was surprisingly democratic. Groups that had paid almost no taxes before 1913 were now paying heavily, and the real income of working-class people went up appreciably. The progressives in Congress, including members of both parties, were directly responsible for the changes that occurred. They were assisted both by the facts and stereotypes about Big Business and profiteering and by a determination that the rich should pay their fair share of the war expenses.

The working class of America enjoyed a success by 1918 that only wartime could bring; their labor was needed, it seemed, as never before, and concessions had to be made. At the same time, educated or enlightened officials in considerable numbers had become aware that labor unions and collective bargaining were thoroughly justified in the modern world. Friends of labor, often with a background of experience in the progressive movement, contributed to a policy that was logical and constructive, although, unfortunately, it had a short duration.

Indicative of labor's new status was the presence of Sam Gompers on the Advisory Commission to the Council of National Defense. He was thus in a key position to influence decisions from the start. Gompers believed that the war must be supported vigorously and that workers could be counted upon to do this, provided they were recognized as an integral part of the war effort and were treated justly. He called for a truce period in which neither capital or labor would attempt to gain advantage at the expense of the other. Secretary of Labor William B. Wilson also contributed to a developing policy in which many business leaders were persuaded to cooperate with labor as they had failed to do in prewar years. Actually, 1917 was a year of serious labor disturbances. Acting on the advice of Gompers and the Council of National Defense, the President appointed in September 1917 a Mediation Commission, with the assignment of looking into the causes of labor trouble. Secretary of Labor Wilson served as chairman, while the members were drawn from both labor and management; the secretary was Felix Frankfurter, a Harvard law professor and a future Justice of the Supreme Court.

The report issued by this group was remarkable for its humane understanding. Significantly, it coincided with a prolabor policy already developing in government circles and helped to justify its continuation. "Broadly speaking," said the Commission, "American industry lacks a healthy basis of relationship between management and men." The blame for this lay primarily with business leaders who had rejected the idea of labor unions and occasionally had perpetrated "acts of violence against workers." Violent tendencies also existed among the employees, as for instance in the Industrial Workers of the World; but such extremism had its strongest appeal when management had opposed all efforts at collective bargaining. The solution, then, was a recognition of mutual interdependence and of the need for understanding on both sides. Collective bargaining should be the national policy. This report also recognized the need for a national labor board to give overall direction to numerous committees and labor-controlling agencies which were then trying to handle employee problems in fragmentary and divergent ways.

What followed was the formation of the War Labor Conference Board, strongly supported by leaders of capital and labor. Former President Taft and a labor lawyer from Kansas City named Frank Walsh acted as cochairmen for the group, while Felix Frankfurter continued to have an important role. They laid down principles such as the following: No strikes or lockouts should occur in the war period; the right to organize, for both capital and labor, was recognized; workers should not be fired "for membership in trade-unions, nor for legitimate trade-union activities"; if women were employed in work ordinarily done by men, they must be allowed the same pay; and every worker had the right to a "living wage." Obviously the board believed that these and similar ideas, when put into practice, would do much to prevent labor controversies. The board also had power to mediate and conciliate in controversies that did arise.

Whatever the surface appearances, many in the labor movement did not get firmly behind the war effort or accept the leadership of Samuel Gompers. A socialist and pacifist group called the People's Council of America boldly expressed its criticism of domestic and foreign policy. The Industrial Workers of the World also followed their independent course. These were the "Wobblies," who "fought fire with fire" as they thought the occasion demanded in their struggle against employers. Government raids on the IWW, starting in September 1917, virtually destroyed this organization.

The IWWs and other radical dissenters had little chance. They faced the bitter opposition of government leaders, the American public, and leaders of the trade-union movement who identified themselves completely with the government's cause and were even subsidized from Washington. But when the war had ended, Gompers and the trade unionists had to suffer along with the radicals as a national reaction occurred against the labor movement generally.

In its efforts to organize public opinion and to shut off opposition to war policies, the Wilson administration made serious mistakes, not a few of which are remembered as horrendous examples of the violation of civil liberties and the mistreatment of minorities. The record of Washington officials could be explained in part by the presence of millions of aliens in America and a public concern over their loyalty; also by the strength of the pacifist movement, which had not been dissipated when the war began. In Wilson's view, and that of most leaders, the war must be justified, and the will of the people to serve and to fight must be stimulated. At the same time, measures had to be taken against enemy aliens, at least to determine which were dangerous. Spying and intelligence work and the punishment of certain "internal enemies" went along with the hard facts of war. Censorship of some kind was necessary.

Unfortunately, the public was not prepared for fine distinctions; nor was the Wilson administration. Those who dared to criticize, whether well-meaning or not, took a chance of bodily injury and of going to prison for long terms. Their danger was greatest in the state capitals and local communities, where the superpatriots had a field day.

Soon after war began, the President created the Committee on Public

Information, directed by George Creel, a newspaperman from Colorado. One function of this committee was censorship of news, but Creel stressed a second function, that of giving publicity to the war. He wanted "unparalleled openness" rather than a rigid censorship. This approach was one that appealed to the President, and he turned Creel loose with ample money at his disposal. Necessarily Creel had to work closely with other agencies of government and to use their resources.

The Committee on Public Information developed a far-flung pattern of operations. It had a Division of News through which official news about the Army, Navy, and war agencies was released every week. This went to more than 15,000 newspapers. Another division, stressing civic awareness and "educational" topics, issued pamphlets by the millions. The tone is suggested by one series, described as the "Red, White, and Blue Series." The Committee solicited aid from authors, such as Booth Tarkington, to write columns that were syndicated. They organized a woman's division; they enlisted public speakers by the thousands; they rallied all kinds of talent to the cause, including artists, psychologists, historians, movie producers, and so on. "All that was fine and ardent" in America, according to George Creel, came to their aid.

Most dramatic in its work was the Division of Four-Minute Men. This consisted of orators, some 75,000 in number according to one estimate, who performed mainly at movie houses, giving their short orations. Whenever a particular drive was needed, for example, to prepare the public for conscription or to sell liberty bonds, Four-Minute Men delivered the government's message and challenge to service. At other times they gave standardized talks to improve morale, to counteract detrimental rumors, and to sell the government's program. How much good or harm they worked with this great outpouring of words would be difficult to estimate.

So numerous were Creel's leaflets and broadsides that the Government Printing Office could not handle the work and Creel developed his own machinery for printing and circulation. He practically deluged the world with his propaganda, even getting it into the enemy countries. This, in fact, was one of the main ideas, to weaken the enemy at home and abroad by a war of words; to convince people everywhere that this was a struggle for freedom and democracy in which all mankind would be the victims should the Kaiser and his forces be permitted in some way to come out on top.

Creel's chief weapon and the example par excellence for all the Four-Minute Men was Woodrow Wilson. In speech after speech the President spun out the idealistic objectives of this war; he showed the way to the good peace; he castigated the despots in enemy nations, while sympathizing with the common people who were under the iron heel and yearning to be free. At the suggestion of George Creel and a subordinate, Wilson composed the Fourteen Points, essentially a boiled down version of what the President had been saying already. It would facilitate, however, the task of getting this message abroad. What the President called for in this plan for peace, which he delivered in a message to Congress (January 8, 1918), was the following: There should be new principles at work in international affairs, including "open covenants of peace, openly arrived at"; freedom of the seas; the lowering of barriers to trade; and the reduction of armaments. Colonial claims should be adjusted impartially. The new government in Russia should be given a chance, and its territory should be evacuated. Belgium should be "restored," as should the territories of France. Boundary questions must be settled for Italy, Austria-Hungary, Poland, and the Balkan states; the great principle to be followed, when possible, was the right of a people to "self-determination." Finally, Wilson called for a league of nations. He wanted even Germany to join this league and to assume a "place of equality among the peoples of the world."

Wilson and Creel thus aimed at the hearts and minds of people all over the world. Other agencies of the American government, less lofty in purpose, turned their energies to the task of censorship and repression. The Post Office Department, under Albert S. Burleson, conspicuously did this. Burleson assumed the power, under the Espionage Act of 1917 and the Trading with the Enemy Act of the same year, to ban from the mails what he considered treasonable material. Secretly he gave instructions to postmasters all over the country to check unsealed matter, such as newspapers, and to intercept anything that would "embarrass or hamper" the government's war effort. His language was considerably broader than that of the actual statute and opened the way for repressive action; the postmasters were diligent in their patriotic assignments. In a speech delivered soon after the war ended, Burleson gave a clue to his brand of leadership. He and his staff, he said, took it as their duty to read every American paper and to check foreign papers as well to "keep the minds of the American people from being poisoned by treacherous and seditious matter." To illustrate the lengths to which he would go, he once banned an issue of the *Public* (Chicago) because of its argument that the government ought to raise less money by bond drives and more by taxes. Such "radicalism" seemed dangerous to Burleson.

The Postmaster General was stubborn and determined. Moreover, his actions were sustained in the courts, even when they threatened to destroy some periodicals that had lost their mailing privileges. Occasionally the President registered a mild protest, but essentially he left this problem in the hands of his zealous subordinate. Burleson simply did what he wanted to do and got away with it. Soon after the armistice,

Wilson ordered the Postmaster General to cease his censorship. Apparently paying no attention, Burleson continued with his customary practices until the summer of 1919.

It was men in the Department of Justice who actually wrote the measures of repression, gave advice on matters of interpretation, and tried federal cases throughout the United States. Their influence was a pervasive one. The Attorney General, Thomas W. Gregory of Texas, was not so extreme as Burleson; yet the policy that developed under him was rather severe. The Espionage Act of June 1917 was framed on the basis of interference with the military effort of the United States. Anyone who *willfully* obstructed enlistment or *willfully* caused insubordination would be subject to a fine of not more than $10,000 or imprisonment for up to twenty years, or both. Some lawyers and judges read the language carefully and did not see any justification for widespread indictments. Others, however, were caught up in the war spirit and behaved much as Postmaster General Burleson did. To resolve the existing doubts about espionage and treason, a rephrasing of the act was proposed, and it passed in May 1918. This was the so-called Sedition Act, whose sweeping language made almost anyone who said anything critical of the government or of its leaders, its flag, or Constitution, or who said anything friendly toward the enemy, subject to severe penalties.

Lying behind this statute of 1918 was a rising spirit of intolerance, hatred, and hysteria. The order of the day was to lick the Kaiser, or, as he was sometimes called, the "Beast of Berlin" and the "werewolf of Potsdam." Louise M. Field, writing in *Forum* in September 1917, did her best to foment a hatred toward Germans in general, not just the Kaiser:

> We have, very many of us, taken our ideas of the German character and temperament from the tales of the Brothers Grimm and the poems of Heine . . . but we must disabuse our minds of such mistaken impressions . . . and look upon the German people as what they are: that people whose barbarity has earned them a nick-name, the name of greatest infamy that men have been able to remember or conceive—the Huns.

A few months later another writer in the same magazine directed his animus toward the German population of America, where, he believed, Kaiserism was spreading. Evidences of German thought and culture must be suppressed. Disloyalty and un-Americanism could not be tolerated. One justification for the Sedition Act, which passed about this time, was to put on paper, in plain English, the types of behavior that were considered punishable in the courts and to encourage legal proceedings, rather than letting private individuals take the law into their own hands, as happened often.

A significant policy in which the Justice Department took the lead was the surveillance and internment of "enemy aliens," which meant, primarily, Germans and German-Americans located in America when war began. Austrians and many others from the Austro-Hungarian Empire were included. Every country at war inherited this problem, but the United States, because of immigration, had more of these innocent victims to consider than did all the other warring nations put together. Most important in determining American policy on this subject was a lawyer in the Justice Department named Charles Warren, later noted for his study of the Supreme Court in three volumes, which won him a Pulitzer Prize. Warren did not trust the German population of America, nor did others who pointed to instances of sabotage and propaganda. Warren found an alien enemy statute dating back to 1798 and recommended that the United States apply its sweeping terms to the current situation. This was done, with the result that some half a million aliens of German origin were brought under summary control of the Wilson administration. For the most part, they were simply registered and warned not to be in possession of any weapons or signaling devices, and not to go near Navy yards, munitions factories, or other sensitive areas. Those aliens deemed to be dangerous could be arrested and taken away to a point of detention. Eventually 2,300 civilians were placed in internment camps, while others were bonded and kept under close watch. The result was a great deal of spying and probing into the alien population and much hardship for thousands of people. It was not so harsh a policy as that adopted in England and France, but was less justified in America, far from the actual fighting.

The truth seems to be that the American people or the great majority of them, and their leaders, virtually went crazy on the subject of internal security. They did not trust their neighbors, especially those of German origin, or those who seemed to lack enthusiasm for the war. They tended to equate radicalism and liberalism with something un-American. They feared the labor movement with its strange and turbulent elements. They feared the blacks, for whom mobilization in the war presented an opportunity to find new jobs and move out of the South, or even to go into the Army and to France, there to pick up ideas of racial amalgamation.

Security agencies multiplied. They included the Bureau of Investigation in the Department of Justice, an office of Naval intelligence, an office of Army intelligence, and the Bureau of Immigration. The Attorney General at one point actually invited American citizens to spy on their neighbors and report anyone who seemed suspicious, although later he seemed to regret what he had done. Responses came by the tens of thousands. Reckless accusations filled the air, and many who were not investigated by the government, or imprisoned, or deported, were

nevertheless hurt in their personal lives. The list of those who went to jail
is also a long one, including Eugene V. Debs, presidential candidate of the
Socialist party.

There were, of course, a few signs of light. The government refused
to endorse the recommendation of Senator George Chamberlain of
Oregon for a sedition law that would have been extremely harsh and
punitive. He proposed to consider as an outright spy anyone who, by
writing critically of the war effort, threatened the success of military
operations; he wanted to impose the death penalty for such activities. By
comparison the Justice Department, stern though it was, coupled its
actions with some warnings against excess; and in 1918 Charles Warren,
who had tried unsuccessfully to intensify the campaign of repression, left
the Department. The First Amendment was not quite a dead letter. A few
bold leaders continued to speak out, and a civil liberties group, later called
the American Civil Liberties Union, made a beginning. Sober second
thoughts, after the war ended, would add considerably to the American
concern for protection of individual rights.

For the first time, in the war period, many Northerners began to
realize that the question of race no longer could be ignored. Some 90
percent of 10 million blacks in the country still lived in Southern states,
but a mass movement in this period brought half a million to St. Louis,
Chicago, Pittsburgh, Washington, and to every Northern center where
opportunity seemed to beckon; large numbers were able to find jobs in the
war industries. Blacks also entered the Army and Navy in 1917 and 1918,
reaching a total enlistment of about 350,000. Many were ready for a
crusade for justice and democracy, as the President termed it, but they
could not forget the rights of their own group during that crusade. Black
organizations such as the National Association for the Advancement of
Colored People and the National Urban League gave a new leadership
and sense of direction.

The situation was really ominous. Whites were committed to a
segregationist way of life, and the racist rhetoric was often extreme.
Hubert Howe Bancroft, for example, a noted historian, wrote in 1912 that
the Afro-American was a "monstrosity" as a citizen. He was
"incompetent and unreliable for any use." When Bancroft and others,
highly educated, could speak in this vein, or treat the racial minority as
virtually a joke, it was no surprise that ordinary white citizens resented
the black man and even turned to violence to keep him "in his place." Not
unlike the enemy aliens, Afro-Americans lacked a political base by means
of which they could gain protection.

At East St. Louis on July 2, 1917, a race riot occurred in which thirty-nine blacks and nine whites were killed. This tragic affair, actually a series of disturbances, was precipitated by organized opposition in East St. Louis to the migration of Afro-Americans into that industrial area. Beatings and mob attacks led to retaliation by black men, and finally to shootings, the burning of homes belonging to blacks, and racial atrocities almost incredibly brutal. One surprising aspect was group resistance by many of the blacks. This pattern was to be repeated time and again during the war and in the bloody riots of 1919, as persecution and injustice brought a rising determination by blacks to trade blow for blow and bullet for bullet, to die like men if that was necessary. A kind of civil war was threatening, profoundly significant in its implications. White people were beginning to learn slowly that while they could keep the blacks down, much as in the past, a minimum level of decency and humanity was required, or the cost would be too high. Fear of those who fought back, and shot back, would become a major deterrent to racial persecution of the type that occurred in East St. Louis.

Worst of all, during the war period, was the treatment of blacks who wore the uniform of the United States. Discrimination was flagrant, and racial disturbances were the inevitable result. At Camp Greene, near Charlotte, North Carolina, for example, there were five recreational buildings run by the YMCA, available for the use of soldiers—but only if they were white. When black soldiers were abused and assaulted by civilians near the training camps, they did not receive protection from the Army but were treated as troublemakers and in one instance were sent overseas quickly to solve the problem. Blacks were not accepted at all in the Marine Corps, and they could serve only as messboys in the Navy. While the Army made some concessions, it did so reluctantly, as when it consented to establish an officer training school, on a segregated basis, after much pressure was exerted for the school.

There were occasional hints of progress. In the fall of 1917 the Secretary of War announced that Emmett J. Scott, long-time secretary to Booker T. Washington, had been appointed as Special Assistant in the War Department to advise on racial matters. This appointment and others to lesser positions helped to assuage some of the wounds of racial injustice. Opportunities did exist, and hopes were encouraged for the future. Luckily for America, the vast majority of blacks tried to do their part in winning the war and they served remarkably well—this at a time when such a group of citizens could conceivably have been a source of serious disruption.

This chapter has taken a look at minority problems in the Great War. The problems were serious—far more than Americans were able to understand at the time. They would flare up repeatedly, or slowly fester, and they would remain to haunt the "land of the free" from that time to the present.

Yet the urgent necessity in 1917–1918 was to win the war, to do one's job, to do one's "bit." Logic seemed to decree that citizens in wartime must support the President, the Congress, the "food czar" Herbert Hoover, the military leaders, and others. The demands of self-preservation virtually compelled such support, or the semblance of it. The people of America worked, organized, and produced; they shared in the excitement and, with their President, hoped for a new basis of peace and accomplishment. In the immediate results, at least, this great national effort was highly satisfying, notwithstanding the tragedy and the loss of American lives.

SUGGESTIONS FOR ADDITIONAL READING

A number of works mentioned earlier will be important for this chapter as well. For example, the second volume of Frederic Paxson, *American Democracy and the World War,* treats in considerable detail the period of actual conflict. Especially important for the development of military policy and the actual engagements on land and sea is Edward M. Coffman, *The War to End All Wars: The American Military Experience in World War I,* Oxford, New York, 1968. See also Frank Freidel, *Over There: The Story of America's First Great Overseas Crusade,* Little, Brown, Boston, 1964. For the nonmilitary side, Allen Churchill, *Over Here: An Informal Re-creation of the Home Front in World War I,* Dodd, Mead, New York, 1968, is readable and often perceptive in its judgments. David F. Trask (ed.), *World War I at Home: Readings on American Life, 1914–1920,* Wiley, New York, 1970, offers a good selection of contemporary writings.

Important for its economic analysis is George Soule, *Prosperity Decade: From War to Depression: 1917–1929,* Harper, New York, 1947. Robert D. Cuff, *The War Industries Board: Business-Government Relations during World War I,* Johns Hopkins, Baltimore, 1973, is recommended for its own merits and for its bibliography of works in economic history, both contemporary and recent. A contemporary overview that captures much of the wartime spirit is Grosvenor B. Clarkson, *Industrial America in the World War: The Strategy Behind the Line, 1917–1918,* Houghton Mifflin, Boston, 1923. How one state mobilized its resources can be seen in Marguerite E. Jenison (ed.), *Illinois in the World War: War Documents and Addresses,* Illinois State Historical Library, Springfield, 1923. Case studies of a later vintage are the following: K. Austin Kerr, *American Railroad Politics, 1914–1920: Rates, Wages, and Efficiency,* Univ. of Pittsburgh, Pittsburgh, 1968; Melvin I. Urofsky, *Big Steel and the Wilson Administration: A Study in Business-Government Relations,* Ohio State Univ. Press, Columbus, 1969; and J. Leonard Bates, *The Origins of Teapot Dome: Progressives, Parties, and Petroleum, 1909–1921,* Univ. of Illinois Press, Urbana, 1963.

Margaret L. Coit, *Mr. Baruch,* Houghton Mifflin, Boston, 1957, is a readable biography. A fine study of the Secretary of War is Daniel R. Beaver, *Newton D. Baker and the American War Effort, 1917–1919,* Univ. of Nebraska Press, Lincoln, 1966. Frank Freidel, *Franklin D. Roosevelt: The Apprenticeship,* Little, Brown, Boston, 1952, has a number of chapters on FDR as Assistant Secretary of the Navy. Two primary sources of importance are *The Letters of Franklin K. Lane* (1922), mentioned previously, and E. David Cronon (ed.), *The Cabinet Diaries of Josephus Daniels, 1913–1921,* Univ. of Nebraska Press, Lincoln, 1963. Emmett J. Scott put together the very informative *Official History of the American Negro in the World War,* Homewood Press, Chicago, 1919. His account is fairly candid about the segregation and discrimination affecting black soldiers, and it might be compared with a discussion of the blacks in Coffman, mentioned above.

The mobilization of public opinion has been a topic of keen interest to scholars. Two of the standard works are: James R. Mock and Cedric Larson, *Words That Won the War: The Story of the Committee on Public Information, 1917–1919,* Princeton Univ. Press, Princeton, N.J., 1939, and James R. Mock, *Censorship, 1917,* Princeton Univ. Press, Princeton, N.J., 1941. George Creel gives an account of his agency in *How We Advertised America: The First Telling of the Amazing Story of the Committee on Public Information That Carried the Gospel of Americanism to Every Corner of the Globe,* Harper, New York, 1920. George T. Blakey, *Historians on the Homefront: American Propagandists for the Great War,* Univ. of Kentucky Press, Lexington, 1970, thoughtfully assesses the problem implied by his title. A classic work on civil liberty is Zechariah Chafee, Jr., *Freedom of Speech,* Harcourt, Brace, and Howe, New York, 1920. Harry N. Scheiber, *The Wilson Administration and Civil Liberties, 1917–1921,* Cornell, Ithaca, New York, 1960, is hard on Woodrow Wilson. For other critics of government policies see: H. C. Peterson and Gilbert C. Fite, *Opponents of War, 1917–1918,* Univ. of Wisconsin Press, Madison, 1957; Randolph S. Bourne, *War and the Intellectuals: Essays, 1915–1919,* Carl Resek (ed.), Harper, New York, 1964; William Preston, Jr., *Aliens and Dissenters: Federal Suppression of Radicals, 1903–1933,* Harvard, Cambridge, Mass., 1963; Joan M. Jensen, *The Price of Vigilance,* Rand McNally, Chicago, 1968; and Donald O. Johnson, *The Challenge to American Freedoms, World War I and the Rise of the American Civil Liberties Union,* Univ. of Kentucky Press, Lexington, 1963.

The division among laborers is traced in Frank L. Grubbs, Jr., *The Struggle for Labor Loyalty: Gompers, the A.F. of L., and the Pacifists, 1917–1920,* Duke, Durham, North Carolina, 1968. For the pacifists there is C. Roland Marchand, *The American Peace Movement,* already mentioned, and Charles Chatfield, *For Peace and Justice: Pacifism in America, 1914–1941,* Univ. of Tennessee Press, Knoxville, 1971. For the IWW see Melvyn Dubofsky, *We Shall Be All: A History of the Industrial Workers of the World,* Quadrangle, New York, 1969, and Norman H. Clark, *Mill Town: A Social History of Everett, Washington, from Its Earliest Beginnings on the Shores of Puget Sound to the Tragic and Infamous Event Known as the Everett Massacre,* Univ. of Washington Press, Seattle, 1970. Elliott Rudwick, *Race Riot at East St. Louis, July 2, 1917,* Southern Illinois Univ. Press, Carbondale, 1964, is authoritative. For the German-Americans see Carl Wittke, *German-Americans and the World War (with Special Emphasis on Ohio's*

German-Language Press), Ohio State Archeological and Historical Society, Columbus, 1936; Carl Wittke, *The German-Language Press in America,* Univ. of Kentucky Press, Lexington, 1957; Frederick C. Luebke, *Bonds of Loyalty: German-Americans and World War I,* Northern Illinois University Press, De Kalb, 1974; and Niel Johnson, *George Sylvester Viereck* (1972), mentioned previously. Finally, an indispensable work for Congress in this period is Seward W. Livermore, *Woodrow Wilson and the War Congress, 1916–18,* Univ. of Washington Press, Seattle, 1966. Howard Zinn, *La Guardia in Congress,* Cornell, Ithaca, N.Y., 1958, should be added to the political biographies already mentioned.

Chapter 13

Victory and the Politics of Disorder: 1918–1920

The political and military phases of a war seem to be almost inseparable, since the politicians need victories off at the front, while armies need support from the people and leaders at home. No country illustrated this better in 1917–1918 than America's ally, Russia. Failures in leadership and a lack of support for the war led to revolution in early 1917 and the Bolshevik seizure of power later in the year. V. I. Lenin and his Communists proceeded to make peace with Germany and to create untold difficulties for the countries formerly allied with Russia. Highly alarming was the ideological factor, the threat of radical ideas, which knew no national boundaries and might sweep through Europe, Asia, and America. Political instability was increasingly apparent in Europe, and the United States did not escape this phenomenon. The immediate aim of the United States in 1918 was a military victory, but such a victory could be an empty one amid prejudices and hatreds spawned by war and with political leaders unwilling or unable to give leadership that the times demanded.

The first year of American military activity was largely devoted to training men, although the Navy with its ships already afloat was able to get into action quickly. Its work in convoying merchant vessels and in fighting the German submarines was crucial. Naval vessels of the United States also joined those of the British in 1918 to lay a mine field in the North Sea from Scotland to Norway, thus trying to bottle up the German ships.

Meanwhile, General John J. Pershing went to France in June 1917 to establish headquarters. An able man with organizational talent, Pershing was determined to lead a separate United States Army in France, but was willing temporarily to disperse soldiers among the Allied armies where they were badly needed. When the American expeditionary forces began to arrive in France, problems of transportation and supply were extremely difficult. Dock facilities were needed, as well as roads and railroads to carry all the supplies inland. The route for American military material went to Brest and St. Nazaire on the western coast of France to take the pressure off the Channel ports, where the British facilities were concentrated. This meant, then, a long route for the Americans across France to an area south of Paris where they built their camps and made last preparations for action. One urgent necessity was timber and lumber for the facilities that were required. A special regiment of engineers drew the assignment of getting the wood from carefully managed French forests. William B. Greeley, later head of the U.S. Forest Service, served as a lieutenant colonel with this group, using his diplomatic skills as well as his technical training to solve the problems that arose.

As the lines of travel would indicate, the United States position on the front was south and east of Paris. French troops had the central positions, while the British were northernmost, toward the English Channel. The situation was a perilous one for the Allies. In the spring and summer of 1918 came the final great crises. The Austrians, with German help, had beaten the Italians at Caporetto in late 1917. Then Russia collapsed and made peace with Germany at Brest-Litovsk in March 1918. The French and British were much discouraged, expecting new powerful offensives that might succeed before reinforcements could be readied. These attacks began on March 21, 1918, under cover of fog and after the firing of gas shells that forced Allied troops to struggle into their masks. In repeated attacks through March, April, and May, the Germans threatened a major breakthrough that would end the war. Yet in several respects they met discouragement. They found in advancing over Allied territory that the enemy positions were well stocked with food and other provisions, in contrast to deprivation existing on the German side. The Allied blockade had been taking its toll. Was it possible, many Germans began to ask, that they could defeat an enemy so richly provisioned? Also, they were startled to find themselves fighting American forces of the First, Second, and Third Divisions. At Cantigny, Belleau Woods, and Chateau-Thierry, the Americans proved that—while they lacked some skills of the seasoned soldier—they were brave and spirited. The Yankees had indeed arrived, and no one could doubt that they soon would be in action by the millions.

A military historian has recently commented: "The defensive and offensive actions of the Third and Second Divisions exerted an influence far out of proportion to their size. Coming at the end of a long French retreat and at a time when French morale was at its lowest, the entrance of fresh American forces into the battle had a tonic effect. Up to the time the Americans entered into the battle zone, there seemed to be no stopping the Germans." By July, in the Second Battle of the Marne, the Germans knew they were beaten. Chancellor Hertling said dramatically, "The history of the world was played out in three days."

Knowing they were defeated, the German generals looked for the best way out of their dilemma and seem to have found it. The peace that Germany obtained was not a soft or easy one, but it preserved the illusion of a powerful Teuton army that could have continued to fight. The civilian leaders in Berlin, according to German militarists in later years, were responsible for the armistice of November 11, 1918, and for an agreement that had undermined the heroic fighting men at the front. Certainly it was true that a new government, headed by Prince Max of Baden, an antimilitarist, had negotiated with the Allies, while the Kaiser fled to Holland. Many years later it is tempting to believe that the Allies made a mistake, that they should have insisted on dealing with the Kaiser's government and his generals and should have loaded them down with the blame for a disastrous defeat. General Pershing and many Americans in public life believed in such a course: The Germans should be utterly defeated and their surrender should be on terms that were unconditional.

To Woodrow Wilson, however, and most Allied leaders the victory was already conclusive. The German armies retreated to the right bank of the Rhine River, as Wilson declared they must before an armistice could be arranged. The American President insisted that the Fourteen Points should form the basis for postwar settlements, and he obtained general agreement on that matter. To be sure, the French were determined on huge indemnities for the damage done by German armies, while British leaders had no thought that they would give up their control of the high seas. The dismantling of Germany's war machine and her loss of some territory was a foregone conclusion. In other words, it seemed in the fall of 1918 that further fighting and bloodshed, after four years of murderous warfare, was simply unnecessary.

On November 11 the fighting came to a halt. This was a great day of celebration and rejoicing for the Allies. Guns boomed for the occasion; church bells rang; soldiers and civilians danced in the streets; some simply got drunk and, when sober, got drunk again. Incredibly, the Great War was over. But already there was bitterness and cynicism about the killing and suffering, the regimentation and injustice. What many had seen and experienced was much at odds with the noble speeches and proclamations on freedom, democracy, and the brighter world ahead. The mere fact that such a war could occur was enough to bring a weakening of faith in the great and civilized powers of the Western world, with their vaunted leaders, values, and institutions. Books that began to appear, such as *The Economic Consequences of the Peace,* by John Maynard Keynes; *Three Soldiers,* by John Dos Passos; *A Farewell to Arms,* by Ernest Hemingway; and *All Quiet on the Western Front,* by the former German soldier Erich Maria Remarque, brilliantly captured the feelings of disillusionment.

Europe was never to be the same, nor was the United States. By comparison with millions of European casualties in combat, those of the Americans were light indeed. Some 50,000 had been killed, while 240,000 were injured, and 60,000 died of disease and other causes. This human toll was only the beginning. Far-ranging effects of the war have already been mentioned, and they must be a recurrent theme in the pages ahead. The world had been practically "revolutionized," as Senator George Norris exclaimed. No one and no country could escape the consequences of this war.

Struggling governments found themselves trying to achieve "reconstruction," as the expression went; trying to cope with explosive problems of hunger and disease, inflation, unemployment, strikes, revolution, and threats of revolution. Much of the trouble was real and tangible, from the chaos of war. But also, there was a fear of these changing times and what they might bring; the fear itself was dangerous. It may be argued that the months following the armistice were no less destructive and tragic than those of the war itself. The road to "peace" was not a happy one.

The armistice of November 11 helped to bring the fighting to an end, with Germany acknowledging that she had lost the war. Yet still in doubt was the actual settlement, the disposition of German territories, the fate of Austria-Hungary and the Ottoman Empire, and the means by which perhaps another great war could be averted. In Russia the Bolshevik Revolution boiled on, with the possibility that communism might spread into Central Europe and to many areas then in a state of political unrest. Just as the war had been worldwide in its origins and prosecution, so, too, the termination of war was affected by trends around the world. The conference of Allied powers that convened in Paris early in 1919 cannot be understood apart from events that either preceded it or ran concurrently.

It may be true, in fact, that the peace conference was doomed to failure before it ever began, and particularly by something that happened in America. On November 5, 1918, voters went to the polls to cast their ballots in the offyear elections. The result was a defeat for the Democrats, while the Republicans won the right to organize the next Congress and choose its leaders. Thus Henry Cabot Lodge of Massachusetts, who was known to be hostile toward the President and his peace plans, went on to become the new chairman of the Senate Foreign Relations Committee, with ominous portents for the future of Wilson's influence in Congress. Here was a vivid example of how the politics of Illinois, Colorado, or the states at large may determine not only who sits in Congress but the outcome of world affairs. Without any doubt, Wilson's peace plans and the League of Nations had a much better chance with Democrats running the Senate.

Wilson and his supporters in Congress suffered this disaster for a number of reasons. Most important, it seemed to many contemporaries, was the President's "partisan appeal," issued on October 25. Wilson asked the American people for the election of a Democratic Congress, reasoning quite logically that his own party members would support him more loyally than the GOP. If you have approved of my leadership, he said in effect, cast your ballots for the Democrats, so that plans can continue for winning the peace. The trouble with his appeal was that, theoretically, politics had been "suspended" during the war, with every American patriotically doing his or her duty. To be sure, the theory was different from the fact; politics was much alive. The Republicans had set out energetically to win this election behind a new national chairman, Will Hays of Indiana. But the President had made a mistake in his appeal and was vulnerable to the charge that he was playing politics and setting a bad example. Wilson would have been wiser to do one of two things: to remain silent on the election, or to ask the voters to support any candidate of either party if he had demonstrated his belief in a just and lasting peace, such as the President was trying to achieve.

Another issue did even more damage to the Democrats than did the October appeal. This was the Republican charge of sectionalism—alleging that Woodrow Wilson was a biased Southerner, that the Democratic party was dominated by Southerners, and that the rest of the country could not obtain fair treatment until leaders from the North and West came back into power. To bring them back, a victory of the Republicans would be required. Unfortunately for the Democrats, these arguments contained not a little truth. There was enough to hurt badly when Republican leaders and newspapers pounded away on the sectional theme, day after day, week after week. It was well known that Southern men occupied the dominant positions in Congress; and the President had often looked southward when he made his appointments. Privately, in fact, some Democrats had complained bitterly about the number of officeholders from south of the Mason and Dixon line. Westerners of the party were especially dissatisfied when they measured what they had gotten from the administration against the services they had rendered. They recalled the election of 1916 when Western votes had done so much to assure the President of his second term in the White House. Had he given the Western states the rewards they truly deserved? Had he paid enough attention to the economic issues that so concerned that region?

The South was "in the saddle," went the Republican refrain. Moreover, said one newspaper, Woodrow Wilson was the "absolute master" of the Democratically controlled Congress, creating a dangerous and intolerable situation. Power should be restored to the Congress, and the only way to do so was to vote Republican.

The Wilson administration had adopted one policy that turned out to be a political disaster, whether it was justified economically or not. In 1917 and again in 1918 the price of wheat was fixed at $2.20 a bushel. The idea originally was to encourage the production of grain by guaranteeing a high price. But by the summer of 1918 wheat farmers of the plains were convinced that the government should either raise the price of wheat or let it seek its natural level, this at a time when grain was in great demand. Congress actually passed a bill raising the price to $2.40, but the President vetoed it. Taken alone, this action might have had no serious consequences politically. But at the same time the administration chose not to set prices at all on cotton, which was produced almost entirely in the South. From a price of 6 cents a pound in 1914, cotton soared to 30 cents in 1917 and then went even higher. The South had a defense, but the striking fact was that its cotton production seemed to receive preferential treatment.

"Southern Cotton Growing Interests Want War Profits of Two Hundred Per Cent"; thus read a headline in the *Montana Record-Herald* of October 15, 1918, and it became the theme of this paper and many others for the next three weeks. The attack being made was in some respects a vicious and distorted one. Allegedly the Southerners were "slackers" in the war; they had not really done their part. And yet, now, when it came to "seizing the fleshpots of office" they were quite energetic and were taking all they could get, with the help of the Wilson administration. Some Democrats who were old enough, or who knew their history, compared this sectional attack with "waving the bloody shirt" in the election contests after the Civil War.

This election occurred during the great influenza epidemic, when meetings were often cancelled; but through the mails, the newspapers, and by printed matter generally the campaign was vigorously conducted. Voters were not deterred from going to the polls, with the final results showing the stinging defeat that has been mentioned. The Democrats lost most heavily in the Western states. Of twenty-three seats in the House now surrendered to the Republicans, eleven were in the Old Northwest, ten were in the wheat belt beyond the Mississippi River, one was in Rhode Island, and one in Maryland. The Republicans gained new Senate seats in Illinois, Missouri, Kansas, Colorado, New Hampshire, and Delaware.

Obviously the Democrats were hurt by a number of things. This was an offyear election in which the party in power traditionally suffers a disadvantage. The voters in 1918 had their opportunity to express disapproval of much that had happened recently: of Wilson himself and the "dictatorship" he was conducting; of rule by the Democrats that had now continued for six years; of interference with laissez faire (many in business wanted to get back to normal); of a "soft" peace policy; and of the Wilsonian ideas of peace and justice, to be preserved through a league of nations, which in the cold light of returning peace often seemed a bit silly. All kinds of people ganged up on the administration Democrats, for reasons that were different: liberals, conservatives, nationalists, isolationists, and so on. But, to reiterate, the sectional attack seems to have been the most damaging of all.

While the Democratic defeat seems thoroughly explainable later, it was profoundly shocking at the time—just before the armistice, with Allied armies pushing the Germans back and with Woodrow Wilson seeming to be at the pinnacle of his success. The magazine *Independent,* for example, had suggested that Woodrow Wilson might become the presidential candidate of both political parties in 1920, if the world situation continued to be a dangerous one. The *New Republic* showed a sense of dismay at the outbreak of partisan rancor. At a high cost to personal freedom, the nation had maintained its unity during the war. "Yet just when the government of the United States is most in need of a united public support in order to pluck the political fruits of this great effort of the national will, a powerful faction consisting of people who proclaim themselves to be super-patriots deliberately agitate to divide the nation morally against itself. They confront and embarrass the President with embittered, unscrupulous and irreconcilable opposition."

The *New Republic* editors believed that Theodore Roosevelt and other Republicans, by "undermining the ability of the President to redeem his pledges" had also "undermined the structure of good faith among the different American classes, which is the condition of orderly democratic progress." The Republicans were taking a dangerous course.

Not only might the President be destroyed, but the "mutual helpfulness" and democratic ideals of wartime, in which so many had believed, might be destroyed as well.

The defeat at the polls was only the start of Wilson's trouble. As noted, the war had brought an instability in which communism and other harsh doctrines could flourish. Often the forces of the left were locked in battle with the forces of the right, while Wilson, notably, carried the banner of "liberal capitalism," as one scholar has described it. Certainly the American President was attempting to follow a course of moderation; to involve the United States constructively in world affairs; and to give the revolution in Russia a chance to accomplish its goals peaceably, but meanwhile, to resist despotism of any kind in Europe. He supported the legitimate claims of labor in the United States, as he saw them, and urged upon capital and labor the equitable solution of their difficulties. The task that Wilson assumed was well-nigh insuperable and his health broke under the strain. In approximately a year, from the fall of 1918 to the fall of 1919, his plans were destroyed.

George Kennan has noted that for the people of Russia the year 1917 set in motion momentous events. The war against Germany lost its importance, while the battle for domestic control of the revolution affected the future of every Russian, and the issue could not be delayed. Lenin, Trotsky, and Stalin seized control in November 1917 in Petrograd; then the Bolsheviks also took control in Moscow and other centers of population. Their program, as announced, was for peace with Germany, for suppression of internal enemies, and the promotion of world revolution. They put Nicholas II and his family to death. Thousands of the old nobility and others in opposition were also eliminated. The Communist party, as it evolved in Russia in 1918, deliberately aimed to break with the Socialists and to follow a militantly revolutionary course.

Almost immediately, Woodrow Wilson and many other Americans had to contend with the Bolshevik Revolution. The United States, in fact, became involved in counterrevolutionary movements, both in the North Russian province of Archangel and thousands of miles to the east at Vladivostok. A contingent of 1,400 men went to the latter place under the command of General W. S. Graves, and a force of some 5,000 Americans was committed to North Russia. Some of these soldiers remained until 1920. While the episode may seem a minor one in American history, it has always loomed large in the minds of the Communists and Marxist writers, who argue that from the very start the United States was hostile toward the Russian experiment and did what it could to overturn the Soviet regime. Increasingly, American historians, including William A. Williams,

George Kennan, and Betty Unterberger, have found significance in this interventionism, the first of its kind in American history.

What was the United States trying to do? Why did it make its decision to intervene? It is apparent that President Wilson "sweated blood" over the matter and finally decided to send troops under much pressure from the Allied leaders, who were terribly concerned over the collapse of Russia as a military ally and the movement of German forces from the Eastern front to France. The argument was made that even a small army in Russia might worry the Germans and weaken their attacks in the West. Also, some military supplies in Russia might be saved from falling into the hands of either the Germans or the Bolsheviks. The expedition to Vladivostok in the Far East was directed against Japan probably even more than it was against the Russians. As one of the Allied powers, Japan had volunteered its services along the Trans-Siberian Railway in Russian Siberia. American leaders were wary of Japanese friendship and decided, apparently, that she should not be permitted to engage in this unilateral occupation. The Americans and Japanese then engaged in an occupation and confrontation on Asian soil, suggesting the differences that would continue in the Paris Conference and in the decades yet to come. A future war might almost be foreseen from the bitterness of Japanese-American relations in 1918–1920.

The idea of fighting the Bolsheviks seems to have been a minor aspect of Wilson's thinking. Yet, inexorably, the American forces were drawn into the struggle between the Reds and counterrevolutionaries. The Reds, incidentally, were sometimes considered to be agents of the Germans, since they made peace with Germany, took Russia out of the war, and sowed the seeds of dissension with their radical philosophy.

A look at the expedition to North Russia will suggest the ominous implications for the future of Soviet-American relations. A few American troops joined the soldiers of other nations to hold the Murmansk railroad, running south from Murmansk, in June 1918; but the bulk of American troops did not arrive until September. From the first, there was a presentiment of evil, since an influenza epidemic afflicted hundreds of the arriving Americans, and many died. Also there was the feeling, comparable to that decades later in Vietnam, that the Americans had no good reason for being where they were. They were lost and forgotten in "Mother Russia." When winter struck, with its snows and fierce cold, the sense of desolation was almost overpowering, according to one soldier who was there through the long months in the "grisly plain of pitiless, white Russia."

Theoretically, the Allied soldiers would have a rendezvous with certain Czecho-Slovaks who had fought the Germans and fled from the Bolsheviks, and they would find recruits wherever they could, opening a second front against Germany. Attempts were made to establish a puppet government, headed by one Nicolai Chaikovsky, and to recruit Russian mercenaries. Nothing, however, worked out very well, Chaikovsky was a Socialist of a visionary type who bickered with other Russians, while the Soviets gradually consolidated their control.

The Communists waged a propaganda war, quite skillfully, as they would do elsewhere in the years to come. They circulated thousands of leaflets, pamphlets, circulars, proclamations, and the like. Allied soldiers were urged to desert and join the Soviets. "The Bolshevik Revolution marked the culmination of the world struggle to set us all free. Strike off your shackles, comrades, we are your friends not enemies, and the only reason we seek to stamp out the parasitical capitalists by force is because force is the only language they can understand. . . . Comrades, you know the meaning of 'scab,' well, that is the part you are acting in Russia."

This propaganda was particularly effective among the Russians, many of whom were gradually won over. Spies were thick in the streets of Archangel. They gathered information and spread the doctrines of communism. Not a few, it seems, turned on their allies and killed them in the night, much as happened fifty years later in Vietnam.

Through the fall of 1918 and the winter and spring of 1919 the stalemate continued; there was not much actual fighting. Then orders came for the Americans to leave. According to an American soldier named John Cudahy, who wrote a book about his experiences, he and his friends had been miserable while in Russia but felt even more miserable about pulling out ignominiously as they did, leaving the British and other allies to try and extricate themselves. "We merely wilted from Archangel and came away." No war against Russia had been declared; no peace was made. The expedition had been a strange affair from the start, and information about it was always hard to obtain.

One facetious comment about the intervention had much truth to it: "Some might have liked us more if we had intervened less. . . . Some might have disliked us less if we had intervened more," but by intervening "no more nor no less than we actually did, nobody had any use for us at all."

Back in the United States, meanwhile, there was a hue and cry that had some resemblance to the convulsions of revolutionary Russia. Newspapers and magazines which had lashed out at the "slackers" of wartime also attacked the Bolsheviks of Russia, the Industrial Workers of the World, the anarchists, and miscellaneous radicals who were alleged to be pro-Bolshevik. The Red Scare was underway. Outrageous exaggerations were a daily occurrence, and only a few of the better publications kept a sense of proportion on the subject of radicalism, both domestic and foreign. It was, of course, true that some thousands of radicals in the

United States were using the rhetoric of revolution, and that the union leaders often sounded radical whether they were or not. The left wing of America, by its militancy, was vulnerable to the charges and attacks of a powerful, determined right wing.

With unseemly haste, meanwhile, government war agencies suspended their work, thus contributing to a sense of fear and uncertainty. Returning soldiers were given little aid or guidance by the federal government. The high cost of living, or the "HCL," as it often appeared in the headlines, brought a rash of disturbances, as working people fought to maintain their standard of living. Great capitalists and the employers in this postwar period were generally determined to assert their control over labor and management. The lifting of government restraints gave them a fine opportunity.

This was a time of nationalism and chauvinism, of plans to "Americanize" the immigrants and to "Americanize" the system of labor-management relations by destroying labor unions. "Anglo-Saxon civilization," it was widely believed, must be defended, whether against radicals in the union movement, aliens from Europe and Asia, or the blacks of New York and Chicago. Tolerance was a doubtful virtue in a country now accustomed to fighting the Huns and jailing the Reds and wasting little time over the Bill of Rights. An example of this mentality was a series of newspaper cartoons featuring one "Everett True," each cartoon portraying the hero in some patriotic outburst or vigorous action. Superpatriotism was having its heyday.

In retrospect, it is clear that the workers, the immigrant groups, the blacks, and the less privileged classes generally were not asking very much. They sought to obtain some opportunity of the type so often found in America. But they lacked solidarity of class and race. They checked or opposed each other on many things, thus helping to weaken their own cause. Also, Woodrow Wilson did not exercise the leadership in domestic affairs that he had earlier demonstrated. If he had given a little more attention to the home scene and a little less to world diplomacy, the United States would have fared better. It is within the realm of credibility, for example, that his influence, along with that of a few business leaders, could have brought a wider acceptance of labor unions. Some liberalism and flexibility in this matter would have helped greatly to satisfy and win over the "dangerous" left wing, as eventually happened in the New Deal years and World War II.

The existence of radicalism in America was a fact. In the excited state of public opinion, radicals and alleged radicals contributed greatly to the "politics of disorder." They were acted upon, however, more than they acted. As described earlier, the Socialist party, dating from 1901, was the largest organization that might be considered radical. It functioned as

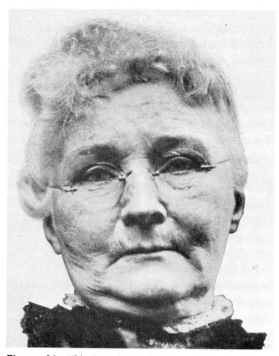

Figure 21 "Mother Jones," Labor Agitator. (*From* Harper's Weekly, *November 7, 1914.*)

a true political party and the great majority of its members did not believe in violent action. Yet they could be connected, at least loosely, with members of the IWW, with the Bolsheviks after 1917, with anarchists, and so on. That the Socialist party had expelled the IWW in 1912, that many Socialists gave support to the war effort, and that only a small percentage of the party ever joined the Communists was not enough to compensate for its general reputation. It continued, even in wartime, to oppose injustices of the capitalist system; and, in truth, the overwhelming majority of Socialists objected to American participation in the war. Eugene Debs, Kate Richards O'Hare, Rose Pastor Stokes, and others were tried and sentenced to jail, often for statements that seemed innocuous and quite possibly did not violate the law at all. Much depended upon the sitting judge and how emotional and prejudiced he was.

The case of Eugene Debs created a sensation. Here was a leader whose vote in the presidential election of 1912 had approached 1 million—now being tried and sent off to the federal penitentiary. About a

Figure 22 Radical Leaders "Big Bill" Haywood (right), Carlo Tresca, and Elizabeth Gurley Flynn. (*From* The Survey, *June 7, 1913.*)

year after his trial, he ran for the presidency again while confined to a cell in Atlanta (1920) and received over 900,000 votes.

Of the radical groups, the Industrial Workers of the World was handled most severely. The reasons seem apparent. This was not a political party but a syndicalist type of organization that believed in direct action and industrial unionism. Wobblies took to the streets in "free speech" campaigns, and when treated roughly by employer groups, sheriffs' deputies, vigilantes, and the like, they had the nerve to fight back. Given enough provocation, they would even shoot back and set off a few dynamite charges. They also made jokes about things that were considered sacred in America, such as the religious faith in a life hereafter, with its ultimate reward ("pie in the sky") and the love of flag and country. An anonymous Wobbly wrote in April 1917:

> I love my flag, I do, I do,
> Which floats upon the breeze
> I also love my arms and legs,
> And neck and nose and knees.
> One little shell might spoil them all
> Or give them such a twist
> They would be of no use to me
> I guess I won't enlist.

The Wobblies bragged of "One Big Union" and "Solidarity Forever." They promised workers to "dump the bosses off your back." Obviously they did not fit in very well with the conformity of wartime America, although leaders of the IWW chose not to oppose the war in an organized way. IWWs were interested primarily in the job situation and in getting their rights on the job.

If they hated their bosses, the latter reciprocated in full. Employers wanted the union destroyed and 101 leaders of the IWW were brought to trial in Chicago on various charges of obstructing the war effort. The government was determined to put these men behind bars. Kenesaw Mountain Landis, the judge, by his general attitude and his rulings, contributed to the government's case. The men were being tried not as individuals but as members of the IWW. All were found guilty, with the leading defendants, such as "Big Bill" Haywood, receiving twenty-year sentences and heavy fines. The total of fines for the entire group was more than $2 million. This, and other trials or arrests, which drained the IWW of its funds and locked up its leaders, virtually destroyed the organization.

Like the others, Haywood went to jail. Later, however, he got out on bail pending an appeal, skipped his bail, and went to Russia. As his ship passed the Statue of Liberty he looked up (according to his autobiography) and said to "the old hag": "Goodbye, you've had your back turned on me too long. I am now going to the land of freedom." Big Bill thus showed his naiveté about Russian communism. He was quite right, however, in believing that the IWWs had been denied a fair trial and that freedom in America had been overrated somewhat.

From 1918 to 1920 the Red Scare picked up in momentum. Strikes occurred by the hundreds, and these were alarming to the public. In February 1919, a general strike was called in Seattle. "The Revolution" had arrived, it seemed to many, including the mayor, Ole Hansen, who blamed the trouble on Bolsheviks and IWWs. In April came one of those shocking events that fed the public's anxiety and seemed to prove beyond a doubt that revolutionists were threatening to take over the American government. A number of bombs were sent off in the mails, addressed to A. Mitchell Palmer, the Attorney General, to former Senator Thomas Hardwick of Georgia, and others. One package came to Senator Hardwick's home in Washington and exploded, seriously injuring his maid. Other packages, held in the post office for insufficient postage, were intercepted without damage. The Attorney General and many other officials, along with thousands of citizens, were now determined to "get the Reds," although no one had proven that a Communist or any person in his right mind had mailed the packages.

The Great Steel Strike of 1919 was especially significant. In previous strikes of 1901 and 1909 a union of iron and steel workers had been broken and a policy of the open shop maintained. Conditions of work did not improve. About half the men worked a seven-day week and a twelve-hour day (eighty-four hours a week). During the war, however, the steel executives found themselves yielding to government policy and dealing with the workers according to the guidelines established. At the end of hostilities the situation immediately changed. Judge Elbert Gary of U.S. Steel and others of the steel men would not talk with employees or listen to government recommendations. Workers were fired for joining the union, even though some had been with the company for ten years or so. They were apparently punished to serve as examples. Spies among the workers helped to make things difficult. Nevertheless, the American Federation of Labor launched a vigorous organizing campaign. Steel workers, stirred by the "war to save democracy," called for liberation at home as well. John Fitzpatrick, of the Chicago Federation of Labor and one of the best of union men, assumed the management of this great union effort.

Yet, somehow, everything went wrong. Woodrow Wilson, about this time, issued a call for an industrial conference which would address itself to problems exemplified in the steel industry. He sought a delay in the steel strike until the delegates had an opportunity for discussion and perhaps for compromise on some form of union recognition. Enlightened leadership, it seemed, might find a way to continue the cooperative efforts of wartime. The President's request came too late. Union leaders, pressured impatiently by workers, already had called for the strike to begin.

In the struggle that ensued a determined management showed little mercy toward its workers, while the latter discovered that "the more things changed the more they remained the same." Some 350,000 wage earners went out on strike and violence threatened in dozens of communities, some of which were company towns completely controlled by mill owners and their allies. The Union leaders were portrayed as Communists. Mostly these charges were false, but investigators did find some concrete evidence. William Z. Foster, they learned, formerly had belonged to the IWW and had done some radical writing of a syndicalist type; he was a young man then and a product of the Philadelphia slums. Later he supported the war effort, becoming identified with conservative unionism. But, based on his previous record, he was charged with being a Communist and an outside agitator. The argument was effective; it gained even more effectiveness when workers, accused with Foster of being revolutionaries, replied defiantly, yes, they *were* aiming at a revolution and they would achieve it, too!

Some violence occurred, in which about twenty were killed, mostly workers. The strike was lost. Unionization in the steel industry was set back until 1937 when the political climate had become more favorable.

This was a period generally of victory for the open shop in steel, in the "big five" packing houses, in the building trades, and elsewhere. In the coal strike of 1919 the federal government played an important part, as A. Mitchell Palmer authorized an injunction that helped to force a settlement, although the miners, led by John L. Lewis, succeeded in making some gains.

Frequently, business groups smeared their opposition or put them on the defensive by crying "Red." A rising veterans' group, the American Legion, was adept at this practice. Its national commander once compared the Legion to Mussolini's forces in Italy: The Legion, too, if necessary, would take over the government to save it from the Bolsheviks.

In some communities vigilante groups took violent action, as they decided the situation demanded. The worst incident occurred in Centralia, Washington, where a lodge of the IWW had been forced to close down for a time in 1918, then came under new attacks when it reopened. Legionnaires broke into the place and beat up the men who happened to be there. Finally came the climax on Armistice Day, 1919. Another attack was expected in connection with the parade and festivities. The Wobblies were now prepared, some with guns. They opened fire and four of the attackers fell dead. Legionnaires advanced again and captured the hall. One Wobbly who fled the building and continued to resist met a fate worse than death before he finally was allowed to die. His captors beat him up, dragged him behind a car, castrated him, strung him up temporarily from a rope, hung him by the neck, and riddled him with bullets. The man was Wesley Everest, an American soldier, still wearing his uniform. In the aftermath his killers suffered no penalty, but eleven members of the IWW went to jail for long terms.

The Boston Police Strike was another fracas of 1919 which had the incidental effect of making Calvin Coolidge, the Governor of Massachusetts, into a national hero. Long hours and low pay in a time of rising prices led many of the Boston policemen to join an affiliate of the AFL. They were ordered not to join the union or strike but did so anyway. Obviously such a movement by policemen was a serious matter, especially in a large city. Governor Coolidge, sensing the public mood and the political opportunity, intervened in this affair with a ringing statement that was widely applauded: "There is no right to strike against the public safety by anybody, anywhere, any time." The forces of law and order (and of antiunionism) scored another victory in this Boston episode.

As far as government action was concerned, the thing that capped all this disorder, lawlessness, and intolerance was the Palmer Red Raids in 1919–1920. A. Mitchell Palmer was a former Congressman from Pennsylvania and a Democratic politician who served as the Alien Property Custodian during wartime. Early in 1919 he assumed the post of Attorney General. His attack on the Reds began not long after the bomb outrages in which he was an intended victim and the front of his home was wrecked. A certain anxiety on his part is understandable. Palmer formed a new "radical" division in his Department, headed by J. Edgar Hoover and staffed with eager young Red-hunters. The legal basis of this crusade was the immigration laws, which gave authority to deport aliens for their advocacy of force or violence. Actually the Labor Department had primary responsibility in this work and proceeded to round up some known Communists and anarchists who were also aliens. But the Justice Department was not to be outdone and launched raids of its own in November 1919. A few weeks later 249 hapless people were deported on the *Buford,* or the "Soviet ark," as many called it.

Impatient with halfway measures, Palmer and his assistants went ahead, refusing to collaborate as they should have with the Labor Department. On January 2, 1920, agents of the Justice Department, acting simultaneously in many parts of the country, swooped down on private homes, pool halls, and meeting places. They rounded up thousands of people without obtaining search warrants as required in United States laws and the Bill of Rights. Immediately there were protests against the wholesale seizures and violations of personal liberties. Francis Fisher Kane, for example, the United States Attorney in Philadelphia, resigned from the Justice Department and condemned its illegal practices. In May 1920, a brochure appeared under the auspices of the National Popular Government League entitled *To the American People: Report Upon the Illegal Practices of the Department of Justice.* Twelve outstanding lawyers stood behind this report. They included Felix Frankfurter, Roscoe Pound, Zechariah Chafee, Ernst Freund, and Frank Walsh. In the introduction they stated that they favored no radical doctrine but as lawyers with a duty to uphold the laws and the Constitution of the United States they believed they must bring to the attention of the American people "the utterly illegal acts which have been committed by those charged with the highest duty of enforcing the laws." Nineteen exhibits were offered as proof.

The Red hysteria subsided during the summer and fall of 1920. Highly important was the fact that the "Revolution" did not come, as Palmer had predicted; the Attorney General suffered other blows to his prestige. Inside the Wilson administration a struggle raged over the policies to be pursued and Palmer lost ground to William B. Wilson, Secretary of Labor, and Wilson's assistant, Louis F. Post. The latter, starting in March 1920, systematically examined the cases of many who had been seized in the raids of January, and he soon dismissed more than

1,500. He refused, for example, to accept the idea that merely belonging to a radical organization was enough to justify deportation. Palmer and J. Edgar Hoover were so incensed that they supported a movement to impeach this subversive official in the Labor Department. But they failed. Palmer also failed in his bid to win the Democratic nomination for President, which he had based chiefly on his work in saving the country from radicals and bomb throwers.

In American race relations, the year 1919 was a terrible time and a year of lost opportunities. A little more courage and charity on the part of even a few white leaders might have made a difference. Constance McLaughlin Green has shown, in her work on Washington, D.C., that the black people were asking little. They wanted a recognition of contributions to the war effort, a minimal acceptance in city affairs, and an avoidance of racial abuse in the city newspapers. Instead, the vast majority of whites, in Washington and throughout the country, expected the black to stay in "his place"—to do his work without causing any trouble and preferably without getting much attention or credit. The Afro-American, if discussed at all, was likely to be an object of humor and ridicule. The laziness, the stupidity, the lack of chastity, and other alleged qualities of blacks were stressed in most articles or cartoons concerning the race. Mrs. Green blames the *Washington Post* and other newspapers for making a bad situation worse with their kind of news coverage, which helped to cause the riots in July.

The summer of 1919, according to James Weldon Johnson, was the "red summer." He was referring not to the Bolsheviks but to racial conflict and to the blood that flowed in cities all over the country. Nine men died in the Washington riot and more than thirty suffered injuries that proved fatal. In Longview, Texas; Winston-Salem, North Carolina; Knoxville, Tennessee; Omaha, Nebraska; Elaine, Arkansas; and other cities racial disturbances flared up in an unparalleled way. The worst occurred in Chicago, where the rioting went on for almost two weeks. Thirty-eight died and over five hundred were injured. Whites suffered casualties almost as heavily as did the blacks, but property damage and burned-out homes were located mostly in the black neighborhoods.

How much the Ku Klux Klan was involved in these riots of 1919 is not clear. But the modern Klan had been organized in 1915 in Atlanta, Georgia, under the guidance of William J. Simmons, and it profited from a war atmosphere with the developing intolerance and hysteria. Klansmen helped to chase draft dodgers and in other respects tried to do "their duty" in wartime. By 1919 the organization had some 3,000 members. In 1920 Simmons concluded a deal for membership recruitment with Edward Y. Clarke and Mrs. Elizabeth Tyler, who were skilled publicists and organizers. The Klan was now ready for a great surge in growth which would spread its message of 100 percent Americanism of the Anglo-Saxon variety. Thus the Klan movement nicely converged with other movements for "Americanization" of immigrants, the restriction of further immigration, the exportation of alien radicals, and the suppression of labor organizers or others who seemed a threat to American civilization. Among those to be suppressed were the blacks, if they stepped out of their appointed "place."

In the politics of disorder, as outlined in this chapter, rational discussion and democratic government lost ground. The principal damage was, of course, in Europe, where the effects would be appreciated more fully after the Depression of 1929 and the start of a second world war. The war of 1914–1918 brought Communist Russia into being, and it prepared the way for fascism both in Italy and Germany. The results in the United States were less obvious. The progressive movement was weakened by 1920, though not destroyed. The forces of labor lost some of their wartime gains, while Big Business picked up strength. Civil liberties and human rights took a fearful beating. Political fortunes were made and lost inevitably amid the turmoil of social adjustment. After the defeats in November 1918, the Democratic party was in serious difficulty. Woodrow Wilson, for reasons not entirely clear, did not give strong leadership on the home front as the war came to an end. In part, he seems to have swung back toward his ideas of the New Freedom, but he was also obsessed with the world situation and with his desire to create a League of Nations. Then, too, he suffered a breakdown in health.

The world of 1918–1920 was a precarious place. It would not be kind to Woodrow Wilson or to the cause of internationalism with which he identified himself.

SUGGESTIONS FOR ADDITIONAL READING

For military strategy and Allied victory, Coffman, *The War to End All Wars,* is particularly recommended. See also George T. Davis, *A Navy Second to None,* noted earlier; Elting E. Morison, *Admiral Sims and the Modern American Navy,* Houghton Mifflin, Boston, 1942; Harvey A. DeWeerd, *President Wilson Fights His War: World War I and the American Intervention,* Macmillan, New York, 1968; and David F. Trask, *The United States in the Supreme War Council: American War Aims and Inter-Allied Strategy, 1917–1918,* Wesleyan Univ. Press, Middletown, Conn., 1961. The Chief of Staff to General Pershing, James G. Harbord, left a valuable account in *The American Army in France,* Little, Brown, Boston, 1936. Frederick Palmer, also attached to Pershing's staff, and a war correspondent, became one of the ablest and most prolific writers on the war experience. See, for example, *America in France,* Dodd, Mead, New York, 1918.

Burl Noggle, *Into the Twenties: The United States from Armistice to Normalcy,* Univ. of Illinois Press, Urbana, 1974, will be valuable both for its synthesis and the up-to-date bibliography. A dozen or more books cited in the previous chapter on economic and political questions, or civil liberties, are also relevant to the later period. See Paxson's third volume for a general coverage; Seward Livermore on Congress and the elections of 1918; and Cuff, Kerr, Urofsky, Bates, and Soule for matters more or less economic; also Chafee, Scheiber, Preston, and Johnson for problems related to civil liberties and radicalism.

The studies listed below are indispensable on labor disturbances and the Red Scare: Stanley Coben, *A. Mitchell Palmer: Politician,* Columbia, New York, 1963; Robert K. Murray, *Red Scare: A Study in National Hysteria, 1919–1920,* Univ. of Minnesota Press, Minneapolis, 1955; David Brody, *Labor in Crisis: The Steel Strike of 1919,* Lippincott, Philadelphia, 1965; and Robert L. Friedheim, *The Seattle General Strike,* Univ. of Washington Press, Seattle, 1964. Dubovsky, *We Shall Be All,* continues to be important for the postwar period, as do several books on socialism. See Shannon, mentioned previously, and James Weinstein, *The Decline of Socialism in America, 1912–1925,* Monthly Review, New York, 1967, for a reinterpretation. Ray Ginger, *The Bending Cross: A Biography of Eugene Victor Debs,* Rutgers, New Brunswick, N.J., 1949, is a readable account. A contemporary work by Louis F. Post, *The Deportations Delirium of Nineteen-Twenty: A Personal Narrative of an Historic Official Experience,* C. H. Kerr, Chicago, 1923, did much to further the author's reputation as a civil libertarian and an intrepid public servant. Also, a book on the Wobblies, still valuable, is Paul F. Brissenden, *The I.W.W.: A Study of American Syndicalism,* Columbia, New York, 1919.

Obviously the subject of United States–Russian relations is large and controversial. A good sense of the viewpoints and the problem generally may be obtained from Betty Miller Unterberger (ed.), *American Intervention in the Russian Civil War,* Heath, Lexington, Mass., 1969. Another book by the same author, *America's Siberian Expedition, 1918–1920: A Study of National Policy,* Duke, Durham, N.C., 1956, concerns the Vladivostok region chiefly, and argues that the American intervention had "positive" results and that it exercised a restraining influence on the Allies. For the North Russian expedition see Leonid I. Strakhovsky, *Intervention at Archangel: The Story of Allied Intervention and Russian Counter-Revolution in North Russia, 1918–1920,* Princeton Univ. Press, Princeton, N.J., 1944; George F. Kennan, *Russia and the West under Lenin and Stalin,* Little, Brown, Boston, 1961; also Kennan's *Soviet-American Relations, 1917–1920,* 2 vols., Princeton Univ. Press, Princeton, N.J., 1956, 1958. Most relevant to this chapter is the second volume, *The Decision to Intervene.* For the view that American intervention had an anti-Bolshevik purpose, William A. Williams, *American-Russian Relations, 1781–1947,* Rinehart, New York, 1952, is especially important. Gordon Levin, *Woodrow Wilson and World Politics,* has a similar interpretation. Two studies of public opinion are Peter G. Filene, *Americans and the Soviet Experiment, 1917–1933,* Harvard, Cambridge, Mass., 1967, and Christopher Lasch, *The American Liberals and the Russian Revolution,* Columbia, New York, 1962.

John Hope Franklin, *From Slavery to Freedom,* mentioned earlier, contains a good general treatment of the racial disturbances and an extensive bibliography.

William M. Tuttle, Jr., *Race Riot: Chicago in the Red Summer of 1919,* Atheneum, New York, 1970, is an excellent study; and see, on the same city, Allan H. Spear, *Black Chicago: The Making of a Negro Ghetto, 1890–1920,* Univ. of Chicago Press, Chicago, 1967, and Arvarh E. Strickland, *History of the Chicago Urban League,* Univ. of Illinois Press, Urbana, 1966. For Washington there is Constance McLaughlin Green, *The Secret City: A History of Race Relations in the Nation's Capital,* Princeton Univ. Press, Princeton, N.J., 1967; while a far-ranging appraisal is Arthur I. Waskow, *From Race Riot to Sit-In, 1919 and the 1960s: A Study in the Connections Between Conflict and Violence,* Doubleday, Garden City, N.Y., 1966. For the Ku Klux Klan, David M. Chalmers, *Hooded Americanism: The History of the Ku Klux Klan,* Doubleday, New York, 1965, is a broad and entertaining survey; while Kenneth T. Jackson, *The Ku Klux Klan in the City 1915–1930,* Oxford, New York, 1967, offers a new interpretation. An older work, still useful, is John M. Mecklin, *The Ku Klux Klan: A Study of the American Mind,* Harcourt, Brace, New York, 1924.

Chapter 14

Ideals and Self-Interest: The League Fight

In thinking of the Versailles Treaty with its League of Nations Covenant, one thinks immediately of Woodrow Wilson. His ideals were embedded in this treaty—which was to fail so tragically only fifteen years later as Europe advanced toward a second world war. But, of course, Wilson was not responsible for every part of the treaty, and his own country had refused to join the League. A separate peace had to be made after Wilson left the White House. Was he, then, merely ahead of his time in 1919? Was he vindicated when the world had its "second chance" in the period of World War II and proceeded to establish the United Nations? It is a noteworthy fact that the United States served as the geographic location and chief advocate for this new "league." To many of Wilson's admirers, the former President was a prophet and a martyr, although the critics were numerous as well.

One thing is certain. Woodrow Wilson had an enormous impact on his own and other countries and his career is crucial to any study of the League of Nations. If not a martyr, this President was at least a pioneering figure in a great cause. He saw the horror of war and the necessity of international cooperation; he worked himself to death, quite literally, in his quest. Moreover, he was a highly intelligent man who gave long and deliberate thought to world affairs (especially after 1915). Wilson made his mistakes, of course, and the evidence to date suggests that he was fundamentally wrong in his belief that a system of law and justice could be established throughout the world. Yet some Americans still cling to that idea half a century later.

Internationalism, as a movement and an ideal, promised for a time to give Wilson considerable support. For centuries there had been an effort to extend the sway of international law. Hugo Grotius was a notable writer on the subject. Efforts at arbitration and mediation and the establishment of the Hague Court were indicative of a widespread interest. Woodrow Wilson himself taught courses in international law and comparative government, and he was knowledgeable concerning the general problems. By 1918, however, he and others, deeply concerned to prevent future wars, took a step forward that could be considered radical. They wanted a positive program of "guarantees." Whether they could count upon a wide variety of "internationalists," more cautious in outlook, was to become a momentous question.

The idea of "collective security," to be achieved through the League of Nations, presented difficulties. As Roland Stromberg has said, it came mainly from an "emotional need, not from a strictly rational analysis." Allegedly the problem of nations and their rights and needs was similar to that of individuals and to the protection of their rights through the establishment of law and order in society. If the law of the jungle could be abolished for individuals, why not for nations as well, demanded the proponents of collective action? All nations, large and small, had rights, much as people did; and some nations were peace-loving, while others were aggressive and in need of restraint. What was required, therefore, was an association of nations with the authority to plan, to act, and to keep the peace. There were many in America who thought of their own country with its "allied" states as a pattern for the world to follow. The idea was appealing, but nations, in fact, were not like states of the United States, and they were not like individuals. No nation, including the United States, was willing to surrender its sovereignty in 1918—or even fifty years later, for that matter. There was the rub. Proponents of the League also did not take sufficiently into account the problem of imperialism.

The obstacles against Wilson were almost insuperable. He had to struggle against the national interests of other countries—when they seemed unreasonable and provocative; against the interests of groups at home, such as the Irish-Americans and Italian-Americans, when he believed that they were unreasonable; and against the Republican party as it began to oppose him with increasing effectiveness in 1918–1919. But he also was plagued by divided counsel among his friends and by the outright opposition of many who were fellow internationalists in their persuasion.

Insofar as Wilson failed, it may be asked, did he fail because of his ideas or because of his personality? Essentially in the League fight he was acting according to his basic beliefs and his theories of the Presidency. Arthur S. Link has supported this view with a quotation from the Blumenthal lectures, which Wilson delivered in 1907. The President's power in foreign affairs, Wilson declared, was "very absolute." And he went on:

> The President cannot conclude a treaty with a foreign power without the consent of the Senate, but he may guide every step of diplomacy, and to guide diplomacy is to determine what treaties must be made, if the faith and prestige of the government are to be maintained. He need disclose no step of negotiation until it is complete, and when in any critical matter it is completed the government is virtually committed. Whatever its disinclination, the Senate may feel itself committed also.

The evidence is strong that Wilson's failure was primarily one of theory. He was too convinced of his own ability, of his oratorical power, and of Presidential prerogatives. He made mistakes in his assessment of the Senate and of his own ability to guide and control that body.

The fight over the League began in earnest shortly after the November elections in 1918, when Wilson announced that he was going to Paris to conduct the negotiations personally. This was startling to many; nothing like it had happened in American history. Some critics argued, in fact, that such a trip was unconstitutional. A Republican Senator from Illinois, Lawrence Y. Sherman, offered some amusing comments that were meant to be serious. The intention of the founding fathers, he said, "was to guard the President against the insidious influences and flattery incident to the servile adulation and absurd pomp of the kings and council chambers of the Old World. . . . A courtier's smile and the bending knee of a sycophant have often in history entangled a nation in fatal alliances. A kiss of a sensuous woman has changed the course of empire. We ought not to put him [Wilson] in temptation." Far more serious were the remarks of another Republican, outside the Senate. The embittered Theodore Roosevelt told leaders of Europe that they need give no attention to Woodrow Wilson in forthcoming negotiations, for Wilson had been repudiated by his own countrymen in the recent elections!

This was a dubious interpretation, at best. The vast majority of Americans seemed to be in favor of an association of nations, and Wilson's prestige had not been impaired seriously by the congressional losses of his party. Wilson was still a hero and a spokesman for mankind, or so it seemed. Upon his arrival in Europe, he received ovations as he toured in England, France, and Italy. One woman wrote to him: "Wilson! Wilson! Glory to you, who like Jesus, have said: Peace on Earth and Good will to men." Reportedly, a few even placed his picture in the family shrine and worshipped him, along with Jesus Christ and the Virgin Mary.

In truth, however, Wilson was treading in dangerous waters. As his enemies were organizing against him at home, they also organized across the Atlantic. The leaders of France, for example, had no intention of letting Wilson dominate the peace conference, or of turning him loose in French crowds to make his idealistic appeals. They used their control of the newspapers to counteract Wilson's influence. The American President was by no means insensitive to critical opinion, at home or abroad, or to the need for some compromise. Nevertheless, he was too optimistic and too narrow in his approach. He could have done more to win support in America and especially to hold the loyalty of fellow internationalists who differed from him only in degree.

The makeup of Wilson's peace commission was a mistake. Since 1917, Colonel House had been arranging for a staff of experts, "The Inquiry," who would study every question of the postwar settlements and give the advice that was required. Brilliant journalists like Frank Cobb and Walter Lippmann added their skills to the academics like James T. Shotwell, a historian at Columbia University, Sidney B. Fay, a historian at Smith College, and I. M. Rubinow, a native of Russia and an economic statistician by profession. Dozens of specialists came on call or volunteered their services. Some, like David Hunter Miller, a New York lawyer, were distinguished men who would add greatly to their reputation in years to come. Far more important, in public opinion, were the major figures on the peace commission. Colonel House, Secretary of State Lansing, General Tasker Bliss, and Henry White were Wilson's choices. Only White was a Republican, and hardly a luminary in his party. All could be described as rubber stamps.

Surprisingly, the President did not take a single senator with him, even though he knew that a two-thirds majority must be obtained for the approval of any treaty that he made. Thus, some Democratic senators, who looked forward to a trip to Europe, were disappointed, and the Republican leaders had another example of Wilson's "disdain" or "insolence" that they could point to. Actually, Wilson's choice was a hard one. Should he have taken Henry Cabot Lodge with him, in spite of the fact that he and Lodge were personal and political enemies? If he did not take Lodge, the ranking Republican in foreign-policy matters, whom would he take? In all probability, Wilson should have attempted to disarm the adversary by inviting William Howard Taft, or possibly Elihu Root, formerly a Senator and a highly respected leader.

In the sessions at Paris, one thing was strikingly apparent. The American President asked less for his country than did the leaders of other victorious powers. Clemenceau of France, the "tiger," was dominated by a determination to protect the interests of France. He wanted security, with every guarantee that could be obtained, and he wanted compensation in full for the death and destruction caused by German arms. To a lesser degree, Lloyd George talked the same language for his British constituents, as did Orlando for Italy, and the representatives from Japan. Germany, of course, was not present. This was a peace conference for the victors only.

Wilson had to compromise. He could not control the leaders of other countries. He had to compromise even more after he went back to the United States in February, heard complaints that the Monroe Doctrine was being neglected, and agreed that, on his return, he would ask for its recognition. For the concessions made to him, he had to give some concessions in return. The Versailles Treaty, as completed, was a harsh and punitive treaty. It could have been harsher, without question, but Germany did lose substantially in her population and her control of resources. She also lost the colonies in Africa and the Pacific; and her leaders were forced to sign on the dotted line, accepting responsibility for the cause of World War I. To the Germans, to German-Americans, and to some students of the war, this was an unjust treaty and a settlement that violated the promises Wilson had made in his Fourteen Points.

As faithfully as he could, Wilson struggled for the "self-determination" of peoples. Thus the Poles must have their own country, the Austro-Hungarian Empire must be broken into its constituent parts, and the Ottoman Empire must be destroyed. Wilson needed all the advice he could get from his corps of experts, but he needed even more. He needed a device—which he did not have—to compel the Italians, the French, and the Japanese to restrain their national appetites. Perhaps also his policy was a mistake, that is, to help create new, small nations that were relatively weak. In Wilson's mind, such a course would be complemented by the League of Nations, with its provisions for enlightened self-interest and cooperative action.

The case of Italy will illustrate the problems that Wilson faced. Italy had joined the Allies in 1915 on the promise of territorial gains, to be made at the expense of Austria-Hungary. With the end of war, she insisted on acquiring not only the Austrian Trentino and the city of Trieste, but also the port of Fiume on the Dalmatian coast, to which Italy did not have a good claim. In an extremely bitter conflict, Wilson would not yield to the Italian demands. The issue remained unsettled in 1919, and the American President was no longer a hero in the eyes of Italians or Italian-Americans, a large and vocal group.

Wilson's best moments at the peace conference came early. The

League idea, now identified with him, was accepted in February 1919 by the delegates, and Wilson read the entire Covenant to a plenary session. He also largely had his way on the question of colonies. No longer, he argued, should the victorious powers in a war proceed to gobble up the enemy possessions. He wanted, rather, a system of "mandates," with the major powers administering former German colonies under the watchful eye of the League of Nations. Sometimes deprecated as a meaningless change, this reform actually helped to destroy the old-fashioned imperialistic system. World War II would virtually finish that job, preparing the way for a new system of "satellites."

The hope for international cooperation was much larger than Woodrow Wilson alone and much larger than the League of Nations. Even the "irreconcilables," the sixteen senators who opposed Wilson to the bitter end, included internationalists of a sort who showed not a little idealistic concern for all of mankind. Generally speaking, it was the "mild reservationists" and the "limited internationalists" who might have cooperated with Wilson, thus providing the necessary support for ratification. In both parties and among the particular groups, as alignments developed, idealism could be found. But politics "as usual" was also in evidence. The Republican party, led by Henry Cabot Lodge, was determined that, if this treaty went through the Senate, it would bear the trademark of the GOP; it no longer would be termed the "Wilson treaty." By amendment or reservation they could, conceivably, make it into an acceptable document.

It will be remembered that this was a time of domestic turmoil and of much unhappiness over the state of the nation. The Democratic party clearly was in trouble. Quite naturally, members of the United States Senate were alert to the signs. A senator from Massachusetts, New York, or Illinois, for example, hardly needed to be told that the German-Americans were dissatisfied, as were the Irish-Americans, the Italian-Americans, and others. In many states of the North and West, self-interest seemed to dictate to the politician that he think long and carefully before he gave his support to the Democratic leader in the White House. Some proof of independence might be the better part of valor. There were, as usual, a few who voted their conviction "without fear or caution." Many senators had a home base so secure that they could simply vote as they pleased without any fear of defeat. The Southern Democrats especially were in a position to back the President, if they wanted to.

The Republican party, led by the "lean and acid" Henry Cabot Lodge, determined the lines of battle. On March 4, 1919, Lodge presented in the Senate a round-robin resolution which had been signed by thirty-nine senators or senators-elect. By their signatures these men indicated that they would not support Wilson's peace program as it then stood. The President was warned, in effect, that he must be prepared to compromise on the League. About the same time, vital appropriations bills pending at the end of this Sixty-fifth Congress were defeated. Thus the Republicans forced Wilson to call a special session of the Sixty-sixth Congress, which met on May 19. The GOP now had control of the Congress, although their margin in the Senate was but two seats.

What the Republicans wanted was a sounding board. They proposed to use the Senate and its Foreign Relations Committee to discuss and attack the treaty. They also used delaying tactics, for public opinion, it seemed clear, was turning their way; and time was on their side. Lodge read aloud the entire treaty to his committee. Then he held hearings. Finally the committee reported to the Senate, with many proposals for amendments. These were discussed at length. They were defeated, but Lodge then substituted reservations, which also had to be discussed at length. Fourteen of these were accepted, one by one, and in the later debates of 1920 a fifteenth was added. If the treaty were accepted, with all of these reservations tacked on at the end and phrased strongly as they were, it would be a crushing defeat for Woodrow Wilson.

The Republican party, however, was not united. Wilson had a chance, especially in the summer of 1919, to effect a compromise with mild reservationists of the GOP. In that way he might have weakened any reservations while avoiding the anxiety and the physical exertions that led to his breakdown in September. Thomas A. Bailey has made the point that since these reservations were adopted by a simple majority vote, they would not have passed if a handful of Republicans had joined the Democratic opposition. Who were these Republicans with whom conceivably the President might have made an alliance? They numbered about twelve, including some of the fairest and ablest men in the Senate. For example, Porter McCumber of North Dakota was a genuine friend of the treaty who once pleaded with Democratic colleagues to accept some modifications so that they could bring their ship "into port," even if it was "battered somewhat." Frank Kellogg of Minnesota, a future Secretary of State, strongly favored ratification of the treaty and blamed the Democrats for failing to compromise in a reasonable way. Wilson recognized, of course, the importance of trying to win over every possible senator whose mind was not completely closed. He talked with many of them. Unfortunately, his own mind was too nearly closed. He would consider only the mildest of interpretive reservations.

Outside the United States Senate there was a broadly based and powerful desire for compromise, which approximated that of the senators like McCumber and Kellogg. What it seemed to mean was this: While the President had no right to compel the acceptance of his own views, neither did the irreconcilables or others have that right as they now tried to defeat the treaty in toto or to weaken it severely through reservations. This was, then, a positive sentiment to which Wilson might have appealed with all his eloquence and with personal blandishments. Many of his own advisers in international affairs, such as James T. Shotwell, Manley O. Hudson, and David Hunter Miller, believed in the advisability of compromise. They saw the necessity of congressional support and of cooperation with the people on Capitol Hill. Robert Lansing, Colonel House, William Jennings Bryan, Elihu Root, William Howard Taft, and a host of others were "compromisers" of one type or another who would not follow the President all the way with his precious Covenant of the League of Nations.

The "strong reservationists," led by Lodge, insisted upon the rights of the United States and of Congress, as against the President. To a considerable extent, they were reacting against Wilson personally. They laid down the conditions under which, possibly, the United States might join the League. Certainly it must not join if this meant surrendering control over domestic affairs; and the United States alone must be the judge of its right to withdraw from the League. Most important to Lodge, as to Wilson, was Article 10 of the Covenant, according to which members of the League would assure the territorial integrity of other members. This was the basic provision that would bring collective security and a new hope to the world, according to Wilson's thinking. But Lodge and his associates wrote a reservation which seemed especially strong at that time. The United States would act under this article, they said, only when the *Congress* decided it should do so; and they went on to declare that Congress had the sole power to declare war. Possibly Lodge, Warren G. Harding, and others of this group were trying to kill the treaty without admitting the fact. When the time came to vote, however, they did vote for the treaty—with reservations.

Most interesting of all were the irreconcilables. They always voted against the treaty, with or without reservations. Three times they said no on one day, November 19, 1919, and once again in the final showdown of March 19, 1920. But the motivation for this bitter and unyielding opposition varied greatly within the group, and herein lies much of the fascination. Some were opposed most vigorously to the treaty provisions as they applied to Germany or other countries. To others, these provisions were really all right and not too harsh, but the League idea was intolerable. Some were conservative and others progressive. Some were extreme isolationists, while a few were internationalists of a sort. In personality as well they ran the gamut, from the ebullient and idealistic William E. Borah, to the "cynical and morose" Frank Brandegee of Connecticut, who killed himself in 1924, the same year in which Wilson died.

In addition to Borah and Brandegee, the Republicans included Albert B. Fall of New Mexico, Joseph I. France of Maryland, Asle J. Gronna of North Dakota, Hiram W. Johnson of California, Philander C. Knox of Pennsylvania, Robert M. La Follette of Wisconsin, Joseph Medill McCormick of Illinois, George H. Moses of New Hampshire, George W. Norris of Nebraska, Miles Poindexter of Washington, and Lawrence Y. Sherman of Illinois. Illinois had the honor of supplying two irreconcilables, Lawrence Sherman and Medill McCormick.

As Ralph A. Stone has noted in his book *The Irreconcilables*, Senator Borah came to be something of a "spiritual leader of the group," and virtually no one "questioned his sincerity or the depth of his convictions." Hiram Johnson has been called the "noise" of this "battalion of death," since he led the oratorical forces. But he was passionate in his isolationism, and he lived on to oppose the United Nations at its inception twenty-five years later. Philander Knox was a different breed. Formerly an Attorney General under Roosevelt and Secretary of State under Taft, he was much respected for "his brains and experience." Knox maintained that the United States should play an active role internationally, but not through the League of Nations, which, to his mind, was foolish and impractical. All in all, this was a powerful and formidable group, although some members, such as Norris and La Follette, stayed in the background.

Two Democrats joined in with this extreme opposition to the President. James A. Reed of Missouri, formerly a prosecuting attorney in his home state, was independent and iconoclastic, "disdainful of party discipline." Increasingly by 1917, he had disapproved of Wilson's foreign policy, and he may have been influenced by disputes with the White House over patronage matters. Charles S. Thomas of Colorado had a history in his home state of nonconformity, and he continued to find his own way in the Senate. Though voting with the irreconcilables, he refused to attend their meetings and was skeptical of their motives. Once, when he talked with the President, he apparently shocked him with his deeply held convictions, so much at odds with Wilson's own. Thomas argued, in effect, that the treaty was impractical; that, while its policy on Germany could be justified, nevertheless the Germans would not accept it or abide by it, except at the point of a gun. He noted also the rise of nationalism, which Wilson's own program had helped to encourage, and which ran contrary to the hopes for a peaceful world of cooperative action.

Thomas was almost a prophet in some of these views, which help to explode the old idea that the irreconcilables were bitter and negative, playing politics or making trouble needlessly, while Woodrow Wilson and his loyal supporters were on the side of angels. In the long and grueling fight, to be sure, Wilson's opponents often made charges that were farfetched; they distorted some issues and occasionally maligned the

President most unfairly. But they also raised questions of great importance.

Democrats of the Senate gave battle as best they could. They were handicapped severely by their loss of organizational control after March 4, 1919, and by the fact that their ranking leader in the Foreign Relations Committee, Gilbert Hitchcock of Nebraska, was not a particularly able man. Most of all they suffered under the stigma of being subservient to the President's will. They were taunted by the opposition on this point, time and again. Democrats of the North and West, especially those running for reelection in 1920 or 1922, were forced to take heed and to avoid the label, if possible, of being on Woodrow Wilson's string. At the same time, most Democrats believed sincerely that the President ought to compromise, that he simply must compromise, if the treaty was to be passed. All one had to do was look around the Senate and see that most of the members were Republicans, and they would never vote for this treaty unless the President made concessions.

The Democratic party at this time could ill afford to suffer defections en bloc, but that is exactly what threatened to happen. The problem of the Irish is illustrative. A few members of the Senate, like David I. Walsh of Massachusetts and Thomas J. Walsh of Montana, had parents who were Irish and were influenced as well by vociferous sons of Erin back in their home states. Walsh of Massachusetts, particularly, seemed sensitive to the Irish and their denunciations of the British Empire and of the League as a creature of that empire. Many senators, with thousands of the Irish voting in their states, showed an interest that can be imagined.

Since the election of 1916 and the Easter Rebellion of that year in Ireland, the administration had been accused of taking the British side and of failing to show sympathy for the cause of Irish independence. Not too strangely, the friends of Ireland saw World War I as a new basis for independence. Would it not be hypocritical, in fact, for the American President to make speeches about self-determination, if he did not help the long-suffering Irish in their struggles against British control? In June 1918, the Senate passed a resolution expressing sympathy for the Irish and their hopes of independence. Each time that Wilson departed for Europe, he received appeals from Democratic senators to do what he could on this question. Undoubtedly the President was annoyed and he had some reason to be, since the peace conference largely concerned the terms of peace with the Central Powers, not the internal problems of victor nations.

Wilson was not particularly impressed with the politics of this Irish question, but his supporters in the Senate were. Walsh of Montana, for example, argued that Ireland would be helped by the League of Nations. For hundreds of years her people had tried to gain independence and had

Figure 23   "Ireland's New Champion," Drawn by John T. McCutcheon, June 7, 1919. (*Rare Book Room, University of Illinois Library.*)

failed. But Article 11 of the Covenant would permit this problem to be brought before the world organization for discussion and possible action. Republicans scoffed at the idea. As a matter of fact, they asserted, the opposite was more likely to occur. If Ireland rebelled, the United States could be forced under Article 10 to assist the British in defending her territorial integrity and thus in crushing the rebels. This and some similar statements bordered on the ridiculous. Still, it was a fact that the British had an empire and were trying to maintain it without giving freedom to Ireland. The Irish were angry. And in view of the President's attitude, he and his congressional friends were placed on the defensive.

When the first votes were taken in the Senate on November 19, 1919, the President had already suffered his stroke and the situation was a cheerless one for Democrats. The only hope was a compromise. Some Democrats loyal to the President had sought to win his approval. He rejected the idea, however, except on the basis of his own interpretive reservations. In November 1919, the Democrats were ready to carry out the President's wishes and, after meeting in caucus, they proceeded to vote—almost to a man—as he wanted them to.

Lodge was in command. First Lodge permitted a vote on the treaty with his fourteen reservations attached. The tally showed fifty-five who voted no to only thirty-nine in favor, as a strange combination of the irreconcilables at one extreme and Wilsonians at the other beat those in the middle. A second vote, also with the reservations attached, produced a similar result. Then Lodge permitted a vote on the treaty without reservations. He knew what the result would be, and this was a way of grinding salt in the wounds. The Wilsonians could muster only thirty-eight votes for the treaty in a "pure and undiluted" form. The irreconcilables opposed, as they always did, and were joined this time by the reservationists.

Congress now adjourned. Many thought that the whole affair had ended. But the public pressure for action proved to be irresistible, and the senators came back to Washington in December, went through the arguments again, and finally came to their last vote on March 19, 1920. The pressure for compromise was significantly stronger than in the fall and it gave promise of constructive results.

Senator Lodge decided he should appoint a bipartisan committee to explore the possibilities. Republican members were Lodge, H. S. New (Indiana), Kellogg of Minnesota, and Irvine L. Lenroot of Wisconsin. The Democrats were Furnifold Simmons of North Carolina, Kenneth D. McKellar of Tennessee, Robert L. Owen of Oklahoma, and Walsh of Montana. They met frequently in the last two weeks of January, and agreement seemed near. Then suddenly they broke up. Senator Walsh believed strongly that Lodge had really wanted to compromise but that the irreconcilables had exerted pressure on the Republican leader to prevent this. Borah and Hiram Johnson particularly were determined men who had the power to threaten a third-party movement in 1920, which might bring disaster to the GOP—if Lodge dared to compromise with that man in the White House.

No compromise occurred. Lodge, in fact, added a new reservation that gave support to Irish independence and to the admission of that country to the League. This could entice some additional Democrats to vote for the reservations but probably was not written for that purpose. Lodge was thinking more of the GOP and its enhanced popularity at the polls.

At last came the vote. A significant number of Democrats by this time had decided to break with the President (if necessary) and support the Lodge reservations. The argument for this course was a powerful one. One senator noted that if they did not vote for compromise, they were joining the irreconcilables to defeat the treaty. To join Senator Lodge was not easy either, and yet the treaty with reservations was better than no treaty at all. This was the last chance. Although the President now pinned his hope on the election in November, it was a vain hope. If the Democrats should win in the fall, even if they gained five Senate seats, they still would need fourteen votes from across the aisle in order to have the two-thirds majority needed. They had to compromise to win those Republican votes and now was the best time. Bipartisan support was indispensable if the treaty was to be ratified.

The Senate test of March 19 was a close one, with forty-nine in favor to thirty-five opposed. A shift of seven more votes would have brought approval. Independent Democrats made the difference, as they decided in considerable numbers that "half a loaf" was better than none at all and therefore deserted their own President to accept the Lodge reservations. Some other Democrats almost bolted but could not quite bring themselves to do so.

A regional pattern was apparent on the Democratic side. Twenty-one of that party voted for the treaty with reservations, and all but four of these came from the North and West. Twenty-two Democrats stood loyally with Wilson; all but two of these came from the South. This was a striking division of some importance, which is explained by Thomas A. Bailey in the following manner: The Southerners had voted out of blind loyalty to Wilson and the Democratic party: "At the polls, as well as on the floor of the Senate, decent southern Democrats voted 'the way their fathers shot.' As between bothersome world responsibility on the one hand, and loyalty to President, party, section, and race on the other, there was but one choice." Northern and Western Democrats, on the other hand, says Bailey, were voting intelligently and with the best interests of the country at heart.

It is probably true that the Southerners were mistaken and were guided too much by loyalty to Wilson and to the party. This did not mean, however, that senators from North of the Mason and Dixon line were courageous men unaffected by politics. Luckily for them and their reputations, the course they took was safest in a political sense and also "wise and statesmanlike," as they favored compromise and ratification. Mutual suspicion of political motivation may help considerably to explain the acrimony among the Democrats in their national convention of 1920 and in other gatherings of the party. Certainly the loyal Wilsonians were angry in the belief that they had been betrayed.

To put it mildly, the forces of internationalism were in disarray. Wilson, though beaten, still looked to the November election as a chance for vindication. He even hoped that he could run again and lead the fight. Certainly, too, he expected that the events of history would bring him vindication. The Democrats, in their convention at San Francisco, nominated James M. Cox of Ohio and Franklin D. Roosevelt; the platform gave support to the League of Nations, with only mild reserva-

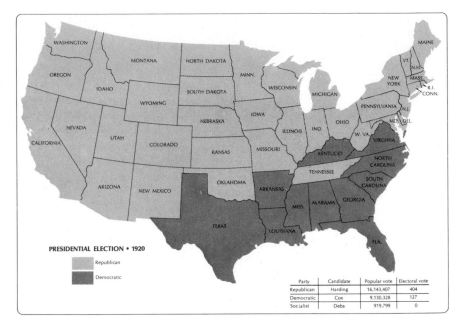

Figure 24   The Election of 1920. (*From* A History of the American People, *by Norman A. Graebner, Gilbert C. Fite, and Philip L. White. Copyright © 1970 by McGraw-Hill, Inc.*)

tions. During the campaign Wilson talked with Governor Cox, seeming to get him committed more strongly to the League.

The Republicans, in their Chicago convention, nominated Warren G. Harding and Calvin Coolidge. The platform was anti-Wilson and conservative, with strong notes of nationalism. It declared that the GOP was in favor of a league of nations but not the Wilson League. To confuse the issue further, as the campaign progressed, thirty-one distinguished Republicans, including men like Elihu Root, Charles Evans Hughes, and Herbert Hoover, said that they supported a league and the best way to achieve it was to elect Warren G. Harding. But another group of distinguished Republicans, led by Hiram Johnson, told how terrible a league would be and that the best way to avoid it was to elect Warren G. Harding.

The Republicans won in a landslide, and the League fight was over. For practical purposes it had ended back in March or much earlier, when the President refused to compromise. Possibly this entire question of the League has but little meaning, except historically. Possibly the organization would never have worked anyway, even with the United States as a steadfast member from 1920 to 1939. But, of course, it is intriguing to wonder what the consequences would have been if, through a bipartisan effort, the Americans had ratified the Versailles Treaty and participated fully in all the functions of the League of Nations.

Certainly it was true that thousands of Americans had begun to think of international problems and cooperative solutions. There was the League to Enforce Peace, the League of Free Nations Associations, the American Peace Society, the Carnegie Endowment for International Peace, the American Society of International Law, the American Association for International Conciliation, the Fellowship of Reconciliation, the Federal Council of the Churches of Christ, the Annual Conference on the Cause and Cure of War, and so on. The movement for a better and more peaceful world was far from over, and it has continued to this day. Doubtless the period of World War I can be viewed as a crucible in which ideas were tried and tested, and in which some halting progress was made.

SUGGESTIONS FOR FURTHER READING

A good place to begin is with a judiciously arranged volume of the "problem" type edited by Ralph A. Stone, *Wilson and the League of Nations*, Holt, New York, 1967. Another collection of high quality is Alexander DeConde (ed.), *Isolation and Security: Ideas and Interests in Twentieth-Century American Foreign Policy*, Duke, Durham, North Carolina, 1957. Two general works are Denna Frank Fleming, *The United States and the League of Nations, 1918–1920*, Russell & Russell, New York, 1932; and Thomas A. Bailey's volumes, *Woodrow Wilson and the Lost Peace*, Macmillan, New York, 1944, and *Woodrow Wilson and the Great Betrayal*, Macmillan, New York, 1945. Paul Birdsall, *Versailles Twenty Years After*, Reynal & Hitchcock, New York, 1941, is a strong defense of Wilson's policies. Two studies stressing the President's lack of "realism" are Roland Stromberg, *Collective Security and American Foreign Policy: From the League of Nations to NATO*, Praeger, New York, 1963; and Robert E. Osgood, *Ideals and Self-Interest in America's Foreign Relations: The Great Transformation of the Twentieth Century*, University of Chicago Press, Chicago, 1953. A broad survey of the internationalist movement is Warren F. Kuehl, *Seeking World Order: The United States and International Organization to 1920*, Vanderbilt, Nashville, Tenn., 1969; while Ruhl J. Bartlett, *The League to Enforce Peace*, Univ. of North Carolina Press, Chapel Hill, 1944, examines a major group in the movement.

A number of books cited previously on Wilson and his policies will be useful for the issues of this chapter. See, for example, Levin, *Woodrow Wilson and World Politics;* Kennan, *The Decision to Intervene;* Gerson, *The Hyphenate;* Wittke, *The Irish in America* and also his *German-Americans and the World War;* Seymour, *The Intimate Papers of Colonel House*, vol. 4; La Follette and La Follette, *Robert M. La Follette;* Zinn, *La Guardia in Congress;* and Link, *Wilson the Diplomatist;* also Link's important essays in *The Higher Realism of Woodrow Wilson.* One may study problems of the nationalities abroad mingled with politics at home through a number of works: Victor S. Mamatey, *The United States and*

East Central Europe, 1914–1919: A Study in Wilsonian Diplomacy and Propaganda, Princeton Univ. Press, Princeton, N.J., 1957; Louis L. Gerson, *Woodrow Wilson and the Rebirth of Poland, 1914–1920: A Study in the Influence on American Policy of Minority Groups of Foreign Origin,* Yale, New Haven, Conn., 1953; Joseph P. O'Grady (ed.), *The Immigrants' Influence on Wilson's Peace Policies,* Univ. of Kentucky Press, Lexington, 1967; Charles C. Tansill, *America and the Fight for Irish Freedom, 1866–1922: An Old Story Based upon New Data,* Devin-Adair, New York, 1957; Alexander DeConde, *Half Bitter, Half Sweet: An Excursion into Italian-American History,* Scribner, New York, 1971; and Rayford W. Logan, *The Senate and the Versailles Mandate System,* Minorities Publishers, Washington, D.C., 1945. The last shows a keen interest in Africa and questions of race and nationality. For an analysis of Wilson literature see Richard L. Watson, Jr., "Woodrow Wilson and His Interpreters, 1947–1957," *Mississippi Valley Historical Review,* vol. 44, pp. 207–236, September 1957.

Following is a variety of important studies, both general and specialized: Selig Adler, *The Isolationist Impulse: Its Twentieth Century Reaction,* Abelard-Schuman, New York, 1957; Julius W. Pratt, *Challenge and Rejection: The United States and World Leadership, 1900–1921,* Macmillan, New York, 1967; William A. Williams, *The Tragedy of American Diplomacy,* World Publishing, Cleveland, 1959; Carl P. Parrini, *Heir to Empire: United States Economic Diplomacy, 1916–1923,* Univ. of Pittsburgh Press, Pittsburgh, 1969; John M. Thompson, *Russia, Bolshevism, and the Versailles Peace,* Princeton Univ. Press, Princeton, N.J., 1966; Lawrence E. Gelfand, *The Inquiry: American Preparations for Peace, 1917–1919,* Yale, New Haven, Conn., 1963; Laurence W. Martin, *Peace Without Victory: Woodrow Wilson and the British Liberals,* Yale, New Haven, Conn., 1958; Ralph A. Stone, *The Irreconcilables: The Fight against the League of Nations,* Univ. of Illinois Press, Urbana, 1970; W. Stull Holt, *Treaties Defeated by the Senate: A Study of the Struggle between President and Senate over the Conduct of Foreign Relations,* Johns Hopkins, Baltimore, 1933; John Chalmers Vinson, *Referendum for Isolation: Defeat of Article Ten of the League of Nations Covenant,* Univ. of Georgia Press, Athens, 1961; John A. Garraty, *Henry Cabot Lodge: A Biography,* Knopf, New York, 1953; Claudius O. Johnson, *Borah of Idaho,* Univ. of Washington Press, Seattle, 1967, [1936]; and Wesley M. Bagby, *The Road to Normalcy: The Presidential Campaign and Election of 1920,* Johns Hopkins, Baltimore, 1962.

Chapter 15

The "Golden Twenties"

No one in his right senses can think that the 1920s was a splendid, golden era of American history. Too much was silly, negativistic, and socially misguided. At the decade's end came the Great Crash and a period of depression, the causes of which must be traced back through the twenties. Nevertheless, this decade stands between the greatest war in history to that date and the greatest depression; and it was in many ways a happy time for Americans. It was a time of creative thought and constructive achievement. Often the serious side has been slighted, while focusing on the "Jazz Age." In actuality most people of the 1920s were working hard and grappling with the modern world of cities, factories and assembly lines, mass education, consumerism, increased travel, and technological unemployment. Needless to say, many of the same problems have not been solved fifty years later, if indeed they ever can be.

Those who grew up in the twenties will remember, perhaps, small towns and cities where life could be fine indeed; with open spaces for baseball and other play; with houses being built one after another—

incomparable places for climbing, crawling, and jumping (in the long evenings when workmen had gone); with fields and woods to stir the imagination. There was skating and bicycling, Ping-Pong and tennis, and a hundred other amusements. There were exciting times of vaudeville, movies and radio, and automobile rides in the country. Heroes were in the news, too: Gene Tunney, Jack Dempsey, Charles Lindbergh, "Al" Smith, Herbert Hoover, and local stars at the ball park or the schools. There were books at home and in the Carnegie Library. There was the prospect of a broader life and achievement; of problems and discontents, invariably, but a chance to learn and even maybe to set a few things right. For many Americans the twenties was not a time of lost hope.

Bobby Short, in his *Black and White Baby,* tells how he grew up as a Negro in Danville, Illinois, and was not "trapped in an urban ghetto." He lived "on a pleasant street, in a pleasant neighborhood," and personally suffered very little from racial prejudice. As a talented child and a musician, Bobby Short had special advantages; but the road to achievement was not a closed one for him or many others of the disadvantaged minority. To be sure, in the "tribal twenties," with their Ku Klux Klan and immigration laws and other evidences of prejudice, the human condition was far from ideal. The Klan, however, proved a failure, a Catholic was nominated for President in 1928, and a watershed was reached in the realm of racial and ethnic thought. Gradually, and especially among the well-educated, the ideas of tolerance and of cultural pluralism were making gains.

Enough has been said to suggest how complicated these years were. In the judgment of Henry F. May, a perceptive scholar, "The twenties were a period in which common values and common beliefs were replaced by separate and conflicting loyalties." Values that America prized highly in 1912 had been destroyed, or at least showed a serious deterioration, while new values were emerging to take their place. Yet with few exceptions the old was not really gone, and the new had not really prevailed. In other words, the 1920s witnessed a kind of cultural battle. It occurred first "in the minds of men," in the books, articles, and movies; in the schools and universities. It erupted in the church and home and in the headlines of daily newspapers. It turned political conventions into scenes of sanguinary conflict. The whole nation at times seemed virtually in turmoil over one question alone, that of prohibition and its enforcement. Matters that normally were personal and private got dragged to the public arena. Obviously the war and its disruptive influence provide a large part of the explanation for powerful currents of change, set athwart other powerful forces of conservatism or tradition.

Interpretations of the twenties started in the decade itself, with writers of many types and schools. Almost all the disagreements, in later writing, had precedents in contemporary opinion. Spokesmen for the business world, historians, sociologists, economists, literary intellectuals, Marxists, humanists—these and others made their views known, providing a rich literature. Sometimes they later changed their own evaluation of the trends. Only as the decade approached an end was its reputation seriously impaired. From 1929 to 1939, this reputation went into a precipitous decline, and the causes are fairly apparent. In 1929 came the Great Crash, followed by ten long years of depression. The boasting of business, the paeans of growth and achievement, now were ended. Since the business community and its political spokesmen had taken credit for prosperity, it was only natural to debit them, as well, for the depression that arrived. Not too long after came the rise of Adolph Hitler and the German attack on Poland. The 1920s could be blamed for that too, since the United States had failed to join the League of Nations and to follow a true peacekeeping role.

The Depression and New Deal era led writers to look back critically, if not caustically. The twenties stood as a barren interlude between the progressive movement, with all of its splendid ideas and achievements, and the vigorous leadership of Franklin D. Roosevelt. This was partly a Democratic view of the Republican years that had preceded. It was also an intellectual assault on "business civilization." With the passage of time, it is not so easy to parcel out the blame or to be certain about the causes of the Great Depression or of World War II. The progressive record does not look so pristine as it once did; nor does the New Deal; and the 1920s can be seen as a lively and interesting time, a many-faceted decade.

Americans in the twenties seemed to retain their faith in opportunity and progress. Disillusionment could easily be found, and not a little desperation, but the majority view was one of optimism. Many proclaimed that a "new era" had arrived, that out of the great effort of World War I a new civilization would grow and the United States would be its center. The basis of this brighter world was science, efficiency, technology, high wages, and enlightened leadership. Luckily the United States had escaped serious damage in the war, emerging as the strongest nation on earth, and the richest. Its military men had been tested and proved on the field of battle, while at home the versatility of America and its productive capacity were amply demonstrated. If the physical frontier was gone, a new frontier had been found. It was the laboratory and the imaginative use of human intelligence. The burgeoning schools, colleges, and universities were—in themselves—a marvelous resource. Never had the world seen anything to equal the United States of America. With its physical resources and great human potential, along with the blessings of orderly government, there seemed to be no limit to its possible achievements.

This vista could be glimpsed most clearly from an executive suite or a country-club veranda, but it was not restricted to the business leaders. Historians, social scientists, and others in professional groups saw wonderful new possibilities, for example, through the use of techniques discovered during the war. The intelligence test seemed, at that time, to have had a successful record. Quantitative methods and the insights derived from new psychological studies might be applied in many fields, so the challenge from a research standpoint was truly exciting. Financial support would, of course, be needed and ought to be available for classroom and laboratory, since the benefits of specialized work were understood after the war as they had not been before.

How the government could help was apparent. As early as December 1918, President Wilson had commented on the fact that there never had been so many agencies with a specialized knowledge of industrial life, and he was putting this knowledge "at the disposal of the business men of the country." Government aid was quite acceptable. Regulation by the government was something else, although intelligent people recognized that in some spheres of life an expanded role for government simply could not be avoided. New responsibilities concerning automobile transportation, commercial aviation, and wireless communication were examples. The collaboration in wartime suggested strongly that business and government should be mutually helpful on a continuing basis, and the government in many instances should give its legitimate advice and services. That dangers were involved did not escape the keen observer.

The twenties did unfold, year by year, much as hoped for in the dream of a new era. An economic recession that struck in the fall of 1920, with serious effects, soon lifted for most of the country, and all the ingredients of prosperity seemed at hand. One catalyst was the rapidly increasing use of electricity, a highly efficient source of energy. Seventeen million homes had electric power by 1929; and, as factories also electrified, the productivity per capita was almost 60 percent higher than it had been in 1900. A second great catalyst was the automobile, or more broadly, the internal combustion motor. Ten years after the war had ended, with its many restrictions, some 25 million cars were on the highways, thus causing momentous changes both economically and culturally. No one could escape this pervasive influence. Transportation by water was also speeded up, and the vast potential of airplanes could be guessed. The zeppelin, too, had its day of glory but proved so difficult to maneuver in heavy winds that its practicality was seriously doubted.

The radio was a new product to the people of this decade, but by 1928 some 7,500,000 sets had been sold. The telephone was now coming into general usage, and the movies exercised an extraordinary appeal. In 1927 the "talkies" began and thus a new era in movie making and the heyday of

Hollywood stars. This was a time of rapid expansion in the chemical industries, with new products by the score. Increased production of petroleum, and experiments in the laboratory, were building a petrochemical industry whose importance would be increasingly recognized. A proud symbol of all this progress was the skyscraper. The Chrysler Building, with its 77 stories, and the Empire State Building, with 102 stories, firmly established New York as the city to emulate. The leaders and "boosters" in cities around the land did not hesitate to show what they could do. A "scraper" of 20 or 30 stories was only the promise of greater things to come.

Looking back from 1929, the federal Committee on Recent Economic Changes, staffed by social scientists, saw with considerable accuracy what had been happening in the decade. They also employed the language of the times and, inevitably, made some mistakes. "Intensified activity," from 1922 to 1929, impressed them most. The main characteristic was a "rising standard of living," the highest in national history: "Broad social advantages" spread through the land; and while there were regional differences, the growth and improvement, such as highway construction, were to be found in all parts of the United States. They noted that the nation now used more electrical energy than all the rest of the world combined. A significant new flexibility had come into existence. Factories no longer needed to "cluster about the sources of power," but rather could draw their energy from "huge reservoirs of power."

National prosperity and rising wages had brought a new cycle of production and consumption. In part, the phenomenon was accidental, but it also came from a recognition by business leaders that high wages would maintain purchasing power. These leaders "began consciously to propound the principle of high wages and low costs as a policy of enlightened industrial practice." Thus occurred a striking increase in the capacity both to produce and consume. Moreover, the consumption of leisure was now recognized as an economic fact, and this brought the necessity of new "service industries" that must attend to the needs of many people: travel, education, entertainment, cleaning, and communication were just a few categories requiring a vast increase of facilities to serve the public.

At times the committee seemed to swell with pride. "The population as a whole can enjoy the rising standard of living—the music which comes in over the radio, the press, the automobile and good roads, the schools, the colleges, parks, playgrounds, and the myriad other facilities for comfortable existence and cultural development." They saw correctly that Americans longed for the good things of life and that many millions still had not acquired them. Electric appliances, for example, could be sold in much greater numbers without reaching the saturation point. Less than one-third of the homes wired for electricity had been equipped with washing machines, while few more than that had vacuum cleaners. Only 5 percent had discarded the old icebox in favor of an electric refrigerator. Highly popular were the new "electric flatirons," and most women had bought them, if they were lucky enough to live where electricity was available. In other words, concluded the committee, expansion could be expected to continue: "We have a boundless field before us." They recognized some dangers in the economy but thought they were not very serious.

Obviously these students of society made a mistake. The Great Depression was about to hit in all its ferocity, leaving the country in shock, with conditions of economic collapse and stagnation. Nevertheless, the positive gains of the period 1920 to 1929 cannot be ignored. Newly built homes, automobiles, manufacturing plants, roads, hospitals, high schools, colleges, libraries—these and a thousand other achievements gave testimony to lives and careers that had an enduring value.

American colleges and universities were swept along in a tide of "progress" during the 1920s. A dean of liberal arts at the University of North Carolina commented soon after the war, "We are now living in North Carolina upon a wave of prosperity the like of which we have not seen in several generations, and for the first time in our history a large number of people are able to afford a liberal education." Prosperity, together with the need for skilled employees and a people hungry for education, brought an educational boom to the college campus. In some of the rich states especially, there was a determination to catch up with Harvard and Yale in as many respects as possible and to provide a wide range of services to the state or region. According to the president of the University of Michigan, they must "keep pace with the sane demands of a rapidly changing social and economic order."

The decade brought, then, an impressive growth, with a diversification and specialization never seen before. The Universities of Illinois, Michigan, Minnesota, and North Carolina all erected great libraries, accompanied by a "books race" to see which could acquire the most books in a few short years. These and other universities had the serious purpose of building up their graduate programs, stimulating research, and creating centers of learning that would be admired near and far. The university press, as for example at North Carolina, was sometimes high on the priority list. An expansion of medical schools, at Johns Hopkins and Chicago, for example, was a notable trend. The growth of special schools, or colleges, took many students and much of the old authority away from the college of liberal arts. The college of commerce, the college of agriculture, the college of education, the college of engineering, the college of business administration, the school of library science, and other divisions showed graphically the growth of specialization.

The University of Michigan established in 1927 a School of Forestry and Conservation, supplanting a former department in the college of liberal arts. The president's report declared that one important function of the new school was to teach the "philosophy of conservation as the fundamental basis for national prosperity." Samuel T. Dana, formerly of the U.S. Forest Service, on becoming dean, announced that he hoped for close cooperation with state agencies, private groups, and others interested in the great work of conservation. He referred proudly to the school's forestry library, with its own librarian, helping to make this a "unique and outstanding institution." Almost immediately, in fact, the school seemed to be thriving, and it cooperated in the development of a forestry program for Brazil.

In most of the universities a great enthusiasm developed for extension programs, correspondence courses, and special bureaus, "surveys," and like agencies sometimes associated with the state or federal government. The "extension service" included a variety of approaches: classes to be held in designated centers, single lectures, lectures in a series, correspondence courses with or without credit, programs of visual aid, library extension service, and aid to high schools. The University of Wisconsin was an acknowledged leader in this important field, but others did their best to catch up in the twenties. Some comparative figures for the state of Michigan will suggest the impact. In 1920–1921 about 94,000 persons were affected by the extension offerings, but the number in 1927–1928 had increased to well over half a million.

In the more traditional curricula, the social sciences made great gains. History, sociology, and political science did especially well, in part because of the growth of library collections providing the necessary materials for research. At Michigan, for example, the William L. Clements Library was a notable collection of manuscripts. At Chapel Hill President Harry Woodburn Chase laid his plans for a collection of Southern historical materials. Every self-respecting college or university now had a nucleus of reference works, newspapers, journals, publications of the United States Congress and of the League of Nations, and so on. Needless to say, momentous problems of modern life, highlighted by the Great War, acted as a stimulus to study and research.

Psychology, as a separate discipline, did not outpace the traditional subjects, but its ideas and insights were now penetrating literature and the social sciences. In the field of social work, for example, there was much greater concern with man's "insides" and a new sensitivity to problems of personality. Writing of his work with juveniles, Judge Ben Lindsey showed the heavy influence of psychological study. He compared himself with an artist of submarine landscapes. "My work is like that. It is delicate, it is an artistry, a *human artistry* wrought upon material inconceivably fine. . . . Here dwells in naked beauty the human spirit," stripped of masks and hypocrisies. He had learned, he said, "not to judge anybody any more for anything," and to call nothing uncommon or unclean. "The human spirit is beyond human judgment." He showed no great confidence about the solution to human problems, but the truth, he declared, was "curative."

There were regional overtones to many of these developments. While the East retained its supremacy in academic matters, the South and West were coming up. They saw the possibilities and found the leadership to make large improvements. In 1923, for example, President Chase of North Carolina had this comment:

> In the past (excluding from consideration Johns Hopkins) no considerable amount of graduate work has been done at southern institutions, and the South is immeasurably the poorer by that fact. Not only have the distance and expense of northern schools been a prohibitive barrier to many whose capacities fitted them for such expert training, but affiliations formed by many a southern youth at northern graduate schools have been a factor that helped to determine that the North, and not the South should profit from the training. . . . My point is . . . that development here of a strong graduate school will mean more to the state and the South than it is yet realized.

In the 1920s and 1930s Chase and others proceeded with these plans, helping to establish the University of North Carolina as a leader in its region and as a national leader in several fields, such as sociology.

Figures for the 1920s reveal that attendance in college—and even in the high schools—was still small. It was going up rapidly, however. In 1920 the college enrollment, not counting teachers colleges, was 341,082. By 1930 that figure had more than doubled, climbing to 753,827; and the number of female students was now over 40 percent of enrollment. At the University of Illinois, construction of the first residence hall for women symbolized this significant national trend.

If the colleges and universities exhibited progress, they also exhibited the tensions of American society. In the new, complex order of things, a liberal or classical education had to yield to a far more specialized curriculum. Clearly, also, it was a secularized and rationalized curriculum; the library and the laboratory were gaining, while the religious and moral purpose of education played a lesser role and sometimes none at all. The rise of big-time athletics, and of college spirit associated with it, did little to rejuvenate the moral impulse on campus.

Critics of the new ways and emphases, often located on the campus, argued with skill and determination; sometimes they succeeded, for the forces of conservatism and traditional discipline were still strong. Even at the big university, supposedly a center of free thought and free love, much of the old formality and conventionality still prevailed. Even to smoke a cigarette in public might bring a reprimand. Girls were kept under lock and key. The "revolution in manners and morals," described so vividly by Frederick Lewis Allen and others, was a fact of life; but a large majority probably behaved much as they had before. At least the changes were mild indeed by comparison with a similar "revolution in morals" that occurred some forty years later. The changes in actual curriculum, to meet new economic conditions and demands on the job market, were quite a different matter. They could not be resisted very successfully.

A powerful protest against modern "progress" came from scholars like Irving Babbitt at Harvard University and the "fugitives" at Vanderbilt University. Often called the New Humanists, Babbitt and others of this school believed that modern education was succumbing to the false gods of materialism, technology, and bureaucratic authority. An attempt to cater to the people in a "service university" had its basis in a miscomprehension of human nature and of true education. The goal, they insisted, was disciplined study and thought leading to the acquisition of wisdom. Obviously not everyone was capable of a truly intellectual program in college, and the New Humanists believed that many of those arriving on campus should not be there at all. The group at Vanderbilt extolled an agrarian way of life, in which values of character and intellect would be maintained as against the ambiguous legacy of the modern world. Most famous of the conservative rebels was T. S. Eliot, born in St. Louis and a graduate of Harvard, who moved to England some years before he published his *Waste Land* (1922).

The decade of the 1920s is one of the greatest in American history for its literary works. Merely to call the roll is to be reminded of these modern classics or near-classics, some of them written before the twenties but contributing to the mood of criticism and disillusionment that would reach its culmination later. Theodore Dreiser, for example, had been writing for some thirty years before he completed his most ambitious work, *The American Tragedy,* in 1925. Ellen Glasgow published perhaps her greatest book, *Barren Ground,* in the same year. Sherwood Anderson wrote *Winesburg, Ohio* in 1919 and followed with some of his most famous short stories. A galaxy of figures is associated in a special way with the war and postwar years. F. Scott Fitzgerald wrote *This Side of Paradise* (1920), *The Beautiful and the Damned* (1922), and *The Great Gatsby* (1925). Sinclair Lewis was even more prolific with *Main Street* (1920), *Babbitt* (1922),

Arrowsmith (1925), *Elmer Gantry* (1927), and *Dodsworth* (1929). Ernest Hemingway wrote *The Sun Also Rises* in 1926 and *A Farewell to Arms* in 1929. John Dos Passos made his start with *Three Soldiers* (1921) and *Manhattan Transfer* (1925). Also just starting was William Faulkner, who published *Soldiers' Pay* in 1926 and *The Sound and the Fury* in 1929. In the field of drama, Eugene O'Neill had served his apprenticeship and began a brilliant career with plays like *Beyond the Horizon* (1920), *Desire Under the Elms* (1924), and *Strange Interlude* (1928). Willa Cather, Ring Lardner, Edgar Lee Masters, and many others may be identified, predominantly or in part, with the twenties.

Literary critics such as Frederick Hoffman, Alfred Kazin, and Sherman Paul have given some fulsome praise to writing of the twenties. Paul once declared it the greatest since the transcendentalists. In seeking to explain, Kazin has noted that many European writers were killed in the Great War, or wounded psychologically; whereas a new vitality surged up in the Americans. They were "children of the boom," "exploiters of a new privilege." The last defenses of Victorianism were weakened by the war, and the creative impulse found its chance. The psychological theories of Freud and others, meanwhile, and the disturbing events of recent times, led thinkers to probe beneath the surface for hidden meanings. Perhaps there was no rational explanation for most of human behavior. Perhaps there was nothing to life but to live bravely and die. The vogue of science was still strong, however, and many wished to apply the test of scientific study to human institutions and to people who had failed or were the victims of failure. To explode myths, to satirize, and "debunk"—this was a strong impulse of the era. A loss of faith in democratic government, or in the capacity of people to have their own government, was not at all uncommon.

If judged artistically, as they probably should be, Fitzgerald, Hemingway, O'Neill, and others were highly creative and successful. But they sometimes are judged by other criteria. Vernon Louis Parrington, for example, and later Henry Steele Commager saw them as belonging to a "cult of irrationality," as making an attack on reason which "reduced man, in the end, to gibbering." Yet Commager noted, too, that they gave a demonstration of faith merely by the work they pursued, and they showed a social awareness. That argument can be made even more strongly. Critical-minded intellectuals, whether they were expatriates or others of the "lost generation," seemed to be calling for something better, for a lessening of materialism and a new sensitivity to human values. They did not have the answers, necessarily, but they did go well beyond their own time in sensing the need for improved standards and a deeper quest for knowledge and humanity.

At this same time the Harlem renaissance was in full flower. Harlem was the haven, the "Mecca," to which talented blacks came from all over the Southern states, from urban centers like Philadelphia, and from the West Indies. Small wonder that the air was a tonic and that the "New Negro," as he was dubbed, gave fervent expression to his faith and determination. For its own sake, art should be studied and created, but a long-suffering black people was ready to affirm as well its spiritual and artistic heritage, its integrity and worth. Older men, like Alain Locke and W. E. B. Du Bois, were leaders; but the new talent included names soon famous: Langston Hughes, Countee Cullen, Claude McKay, Jean Toomer, and many others. It hardly needs be said that Afro-Americans made a large contribution to music in this, the "Jazz Age."

The predominant mood of blacks seems to have been highly optimistic. To be sure, Marcus Garvey at this time was leading a "back to Africa" movement, based on the hardships of black Americans and widespread disillusionment. But leaders of the race generally scoffed at the idea of quitting the country, and they prepared for a better future. Many of them did show an interest in Africa or pay a visit there, but they were in quest of a heritage primarily and were gaining in their pride as black Americans. A book entitled *The New Negro*, edited by the philosopher at Howard University Alain Locke, gives a good idea of the Harlem renaissance and its buoyant spirit in 1925. The editor quotes with approval one of the new black poets:

We have tomorrow
Bright before us
Like a flame.

Yesterday, a night-gone thing
A sun-down name.

And dawn today
Broad arch above the road we came.
We march!

The road ahead was long and difficult for black Americans, but they knew, quite accurately, that times were getting a little better. There was also the possibility (for some) of making a splendid success.

Traditionally the political leaders of the 1920s have fared badly at the hands of historians and other writers. Just briefly, it may be suggested here that the record is a mixed one with many bright spots. Harding, Coolidge, and Hoover can be blamed for policies that contributed to economic instability and eventually to the Depression. Yet the fact seems to be that the Depression was inevitable, that Democrats could not have stopped it, and even the economists were unprepared and confused as to what the remedies ought to be. Only gradually did the country learn to cope with an economic disaster of such unprecedented severity. Much that happened has to be examined on its merits without any direct relationship to the Crash of 1929 and the years of depression that followed. Then, too, the states and local governments often were pushing ahead, with constructive work, in addition to the educational advances previously described.

Programs for the conservation of natural resources not only survived occasional threats in the decade but actually gained wider support and acceptance. Donald C. Swain, in a careful study of federal policy, has summed up the progress that was made:

> Sparked by a vigorous bureaucratic leadership, federal resource agencies formulated important new conservation policies and expanded many of the existing resource programs. The National Park Service, riding a wave of aesthetic sentiment, challenged the Forest Service for national conservation leadership. A nation-wide soil conservation program got under way. The concept of multiple-purpose river basin planning enjoyed a rebirth, and scientific research became the commonly accepted basis for resource-policy decisions.

Much more attention was given to natural beauty and its preservation and the protection of wildlife. All in all, federal officials who specialized in resource problems were able to anticipate and prepare the way for many aspects of a "second conservation movement," led by Franklin Roosevelt in 1933.

The cities and states were not left behind. A casual glance at magazines like *The American City, Playground,* and *Survey* will suggest the keen interest in urban life and a determined effort to solve some of the problems that were more or less urgent, while seizing as well the pleasurable opportunities of urban living. The movement for city and regional planning had now gained considerable strength. Almost a thousand communities had prepared zoning ordinances or city plans of some description, while hundreds of others were moving in that direction. Most leaders believed that the tenets of laissez faire had to be modified and that careful study of a community was required, with coordinated effort and attention to the needs of an entire population. Pioneer thinkers and planners such as Aldo Leopold, Benton MacKaye, Robert Park, Morris Cooke, and Howard Odum were at work, writing their books and articles, while a thousand others were concerned with parks, playgrounds, forest preserves, traffic congestion, pollution control, public health, garbage collection, and all the daily requirements of an improved existence.

George B. Tindall, in writing on Southern politics of this period, has described the growth of a "business progressivism" that was highly significant. Southern leaders were interested in business growth and efficiency and in measures to stimulate the economy. They built highways and schools, improved administration, increased taxation, and provided public service on a scale never known before. Public health programs were especially important in this region so noted for its malaria, pellagra, hookworm, tuberculosis, and other diseases. In eleven states of the Southeast the number of county health departments more than tripled from 1920 to 1930, giving that region 347 county departments. Many thousands of people thus had access, without a social stigma, to free examinations and medical aid. The South has never been noted for its willingness to put money into welfare work, but by 1927 every state of the region, save one, had organized a state department of public welfare; and the expenditures rose noticeably. Tindall points out that the huge debts, acquired especially in highway building and the expansion of schools, became a serious burden during the Depression. Retrenchment was necessary. Nevertheless, the basis was laid for a society in which progress could occur, much as it did in Northern states, and with a better chance to eliminate ancient evils of racial discrimination, disease, and ignorance.

There is no question, then, that the 1920s brought a great advance on many fronts. It also brought, or intensified, some problems. Through the automobile, the radio, the movies, the telephone, and other products of modern times, the daily routine was drastically altered. Life had never been so interesting and hopeful to many millions of people. Life was also more complex and confusing. The emphasis on money and the need for money was greater than ever. The growth of advertising meant an endless appeal to one's desire for durable goods, consumer goods, education, travel, and status. There was something approximating a "revolution of expectations." Robert S. Lynd and Helen Lynd, in their classic *Middletown* (1929), graphically stated the change in popular attitudes which they saw as occurring in the previous thirty years. In the 1890s, people had lived as if on a plateau, knowing that up on the higher plateaus some were living better; but they did not really see above and were not especially sensitive about an inferior status. By the 1920s, however, everyone lived as if on an incline, having a clear view of the favored ones above and privileges they enjoyed. The result was not, by any means, a revolutionary spirit, but rather, a restlessness and vague dissatisfaction. There was so much more now to do and to buy, and if money was lacking, credit could surely be found. Buying on credit was much encouraged in the new consumer society.

It was "the best of times and the worst of times." For Republicans running the country, after so many years of "that other party," it was a happy era indeed. For the bitter critics of Republican policy it was a time of selfish profiteering, of business rule, and of a defeat for the ideals of progressivism. For the custodians of American morals, there was much to worry about. This was an age of "barbaric dancing" to the rhythms of a saxophone, with "wild young people," speakeasies, and racketeers. For the thoughtful students of nationalism and trends of the machine age, more serious questions sometimes arose: Was the system out of control? Were the machines rushing us on? Could another war be prevented—a war far more destructive than the last?

Meanwhile, the average American went about his business, putting in a full day at the office, factory, or school; neither rich nor poor; neither corrupt nor saintly. As time would show, he was too optimistic. He trusted too much the leadership of his own town and of Washington, D.C. His own failings were quite human and are a little easier to understand, later, than those of business and political leaders who confidently asserted their views and their "permanent solutions" for problems of the nation and the world.

SUGGESTIONS FOR FURTHER READING

The subject of this chapter may bring to mind Frederick Lewis Allen, *Only Yesterday: An Informal History of the Nineteen Twenties,* Harper, New York, 1931, a highly readable book that still is useful on many topics; but William E. Leuchtenberg, *The Perils of Prosperity, 1914–32,* Univ. of Chicago Press, Chicago, 1958, is almost as lively and it examines the twenties with a better perspective historically. Other accounts of a general nature are John D. Hicks, *Republican Ascendancy, 1921–1933,* Harper, New York, 1960; George Soule, *Prosperity Decade: From War to Depression, 1917–1929,* Harper, New York, 1968 [1947]; George E. Mowry, *The Urban Nation, 1920–1960,* Hill and Wang, New York, 1965; Elizabeth Stevenson, *The American 1920s: Babbitts and Bohemians,* Collier Books, New York, 1970; and Paul A. Carter, *The Twenties in America,* Crowell, New York, 1968. Mark Sullivan, *Our Times: The Twenties,* the last volume of this series, published in 1935, is informative on the stories in the news and the life of the people. For excellent articles and bibliographical comments see especially the following: John Braeman et al. (eds.), *Change and Continuity in Twentieth-Century America: The 1920's,* Ohio State Univ. Press, Columbus, 1968; Burl Noggle, "The Twenties: A New Historiographical Frontier," *Journal of American History,* September, 1966, pp. 299–314; and Richard Lowitt, "Prosperity Decade, 1917–1928," in William H. Cartwright and Richard L. Watson, Jr. (eds.), *Interpreting and Teaching American History,* National Council for the Social Studies, Washington, D.C., 1961.

Highly important for social and economic trends are two studies completed by social scientists in the 1920s and 1930s; they provide a gold mine of information. See *Recent Economic Changes in the United States: Report of the Committee on Recent Economic Changes of the President's Conference on Unemployment,* 2 vols., McGraw-Hill, New York, 1929; and *Recent Social Trends in the United States: Report of the President's Research Committee on Social Trends,* McGraw-Hill, New York, 1933. Another classic by the social scientists is Robert S. Lynd and Helen M. Lynd, *Middletown: A Study in Contemporary American Culture,* Harcourt, New York, 1929. Quite a number of books, added to the above, will suggest that the 1920s was a transitional time and not an easy one for most Americans. See Irving Bernstein, *The Lean Years: A History of the American Worker, 1920–1933,* Houghton Mifflin, Boston, 1960; Sterling D. Spero and Abram L. Harris, *The Black Worker: The Negro and the Labor Movement,* Atheneum, New York, 1972 [1931]; E. David Cronon, *Black Moses: The Story of Marcus Garvey and the Universal Negro Improvement Association,* Univ. of Wisconsin Press, Madison, 1955; Clarke A. Chambers, *Seedtime of Reform: American Social Service and Social Action, 1918–1933,* Univ. of Minnesota Press, Minneapolis, 1963; Clarke A. Chambers, *Paul U. Kellogg and the Survey: Voices for Social Welfare and Social Justice,* Univ. of Minnesota Press, Minneapolis, 1971; William H. Chafe, *The American Woman: Her Changing Social, Economic, and Political Roles, 1920–1970,* Oxford, London, 1972; J. Stanley Lemons, *The Woman Citizen: Social Feminism in the 1920s,* Univ. of Illinois Press, Urbana, 1973; Charles Larsen, *The Good Fight: The Life and Times of Ben B. Lindsey,* Quadrangle, Chicago, 1972; and John Higham, *Strangers in the Land,* mentioned previously. A number of the works cited earlier will be relevant to this chapter.

For literature and cultural trends see Malcolm Cowley, *Exile's Return: A Literary Odyssey of the 1920s,* Viking, New York, 1951 [1934]; Oscar Cargill, *Intellectual America: Ideas on the March,* Macmillan, New York, 1941; Alfred Kazin, *On Native Grounds: An Interpretation of Modern American Prose Literature,* Harcourt, New York, 1942; Frederick Hoffman, *The Twenties: American Writing in the Postwar Decade,* Viking, New York, 1955; Twelve Southerners, *I'll Take My Stand: The South and the Agrarian Tradition,* Harper, New York, 1930; Alain Locke (ed.), *The New Negro,* Atheneum, New York, 1969 [1925]; Nathan I. Huggins, *Harlem Renaissance,* Oxford, London, 1971; Arna Bontemps (ed.), *The Harlem Renaissance Remembered,* Dodd, Mead, New York, 1972; Bobby Short, *Black and White Baby,* Curtis, New York, 1971; and Edward A. Purcell, Jr., *The Crisis of Democratic Theory: Scientific Naturalism & the Problem of Value,* Univ. of Kentucky Press, Lexington, 1973. Two books that will serve as an introduction to the educational scene, along with Purcell, are: Frederick Rudolph, *The American College and University: A History,* Knopf, New York, 1965; and Lawrence Cremin, *The Transformation of the School,* noted previously.

Robert M. Miller, *American Protestantism and Social Issues, 1919–1939,* Univ. of North Carolina Press, Chapel Hill, 1958, is excellent for its subject. See also Paul Carter, *The Decline and Revival of the Social Gospel: Social and Political Liberalism in American Protestant Churches, 1920–1940,* Cornell, Ithaca, N.Y., 1956; Norman F. Furniss, *The Fundamentalist Controversy, 1918–1931,* Yale, New Haven, Conn., 1954; Ray Ginger, *Six Days or Forever? Tennessee v. John Thomas Scopes,* Beacon, Boston, 1958; Kenneth K. Bailey, *Southern White*

Protestantism in the Twentieth Century, Harper, New York, 1964; and George Tindall, *The Emergence of the New South,* mentioned earlier.

For the subject of planning and the environment see Donald C. Swain, *Federal Conservation Policy, 1921–1933,* Univ. of California Press, Berkeley, 1963; Donald C. Swain, *Wilderness Defender: Horace M. Albright and Conservation,* Univ. of Chicago Press, Chicago, 1970; Roy Lubove, *Community Planning in the 1920's: the Contribution of the Regional Planning Association of America,* Univ. of Pittsburgh Press, Pittsburgh, 1963; and Preston J. Hubbard, *Origins of the TVA: The Muscle Shoals Controversy, 1920–1932,* Vanderbilt, Nashville, Tenn., 1961; also some of the books mentioned earlier, such as Roderick Nash, *Wilderness and the American Mind.*

Chapter 16

Harding, Coolidge, and the "Conservative Revolution"

While the twenties seemed to be bursting with energy and creativity, they also contained currents of conservative thought, strongly reflected at times in the decisions of politicians. Writing in 1930, James C. Malin of the University of Kansas referred to the twelve years preceding as an "economic age," with an interest that had focused on "things material." He described what he called "The Conservative Revolution." First, came an "exaggerated nationalism," resulting primarily from the war. It was almost impossible to comprehend problems of either domestic or foreign affairs except in relation to the powerful influence of nationalism. Second, leaders made an attempt to go back toward laissez faire in economics. Starting with Wilson, this effort was intensified under Harding and Coolidge. At the same time, some aid to business was considered necessary and advantageous for the entire country. Third, an idea took hold that the business leaders had demonstrated during the war a capacity for sound and enlightened leadership. "Self-government" of business, or "self-regulation," was now possible—although the difficulty of such a course was recognized even by a few in the business world. Finally, there was a trend to turn some matters back to the states for solution.

Malin's analysis was close to the mark. The United States had indeed moved in a conservative direction politically, and it might have moved much farther. For this was an era of declining faith in democracy. Psychological "experts" had examined soldiers in the war period and decided that the mental age of Americans was around twelve. H. L. Mencken inaugurated his attacks on the ordinary American, who was "hopelessly bourgeois, provincial, hypocritical, cowardly, and stupid." Actually he attacked almost every group at one time or another. Mencken was one of many expressing elitist ideas. The United States Congress came under withering fire from self-appointed critics and experts, while the business leader, so sure of his answers, gained virtual glorification in these years of growth and prosperity. One sign of the times was Bruce Barton's book *The Man Nobody Knows* (1925), with its portrayal of Jesus Christ as a successful, go-getting businessman. Malin observed, and it may be true, that the United States was fortunate at such a time not to have a "powerful" personality running the nation who might have exploited more fully the antidemocratic currents.

The leader who came to power after the ailing Wilson had surrendered his office was Warren G. Harding. By no stretch of the imagination could Harding be envisioned as another Lenin or Mussolini. It is true, however, that the administration of this twenty-eighth President was a notable one for some of its personnel, for the basic policies it established, and for some glaring weaknesses. Since Calvin Coolidge served as Vice President and Herbert Hoover as Secretary of Commerce, the administration contained from its first days the officials who would occupy the White House for the next twelve years. That fact alone gave the Harding period considerable distinction. Then too, William Howard Taft became the Chief Justice in late 1921 and served until 1930.

In the campaign of 1920 Senator Warren G. Harding had gained his presidential nomination and proceeded to win a smashing victory over Governor James M. Cox, also of Ohio, on the Democratic ticket. The election was in considerable part a protest against Woodrow Wilson and what he represented, a vote against war and in favor of a condition called "normalcy." It could be interpreted by Republicans generally—and was by many—as a green light to destroy what was left of the progressive movement. Frank Knox, newspaper editor and a progressive Republican, lamented: "The trouble is that some of our present leadership persist in interpreting the election of 1920 as a mandate to go back to the political methods and practices of 1896."

In the fall of 1920 and for many months thereafter a battle was waged for the mind of Warren G. Harding. It continued, indeed, until his death in

August 1923. His affability and his wish to be popular with everyone seemed to make him susceptible to the latest proposal. A variety of groups and organizations did their utmost to influence the new leader. This was apparent, for example, in the conservation movement, as it was led by Gifford Pinchot. The former U.S. Forester and "Bull Mooser" was resourceful in trying to carry forward his ideas. He and his allies knew that Harding would be a rather weak executive, and this gave them hope that he could be swayed to their side. They tried in 1920 and in 1921, and they kept trying.

Any doubts about the President-elect with regard to political philosophy and major policies should have been largely dispelled by March 4, 1921. Harding's appointments gave small satisfaction to the progressive faction of his own party and virtually none to the Democrats. He did rather well in his selections for judicial positions, showing the capacity to accept good advice. For his Cabinet he announced that he wanted the nation's "best brains," and he had some success in finding them. Few could oppose the choice of Charles Evans Hughes as Secretary of State, Herbert Hoover as Secretary of Commerce, and Henry C. Wallace as Secretary of Agriculture. After that, some men of sufficient ability were highly questionable on other grounds. Thus Andrew Mellon as Secretary of the Treasury was one of the richest conservatives in the country and could be expected, in his developing tax policy, to favor the rich and well-to-do. Albert B. Fall, the new Secretary of the Interior, had consistently favored the exploitation of natural resources, of which he now became the custodian and administrator. Edwin Denby of Michigan became the new Secretary of the Navy, although he lacked a national reputation and probably did not have the qualifications to run his office.

This was the pattern. Worst of all were the "Ohio Gang," represented in the Cabinet by Harry Daugherty, the Attorney General. This lawyer, lobbyist, and political operator from Washington Court House, Ohio, had managed Harding's campaign. Few who knew him believed he was qualified to be head of the Department of Justice. But he received his reward. Along with Harding and Daugherty came men such as Dr. Charles Sawyer of Marion, now made White House physician and a brigadier general. Ed Scobey, one of the President's drinking companions, became Director of the Mint. Daniel Crissinger, a banker in Marion, assumed new duties as Comptroller of the Currency of the United States. Others came in such number that there was widespread comment. An intimate of Daugherty's named Jess Smith soon gained notoriety as an influence peddler, occupying a desk in the Justice Department, although he had no official position, sharing living quarters with the Attorney General and also sharing a bank account.

One Republican observed that members of Congress were "very

bitter over the large number of appointments . . . made from Ohio." The
president of Ohio State University, William O. Thompson, an educator
of progressive views and of personal integrity, expressed his dismay:
"We are now under a sort of family party government. I found myself so
much out of sympathy with the reactionary forces that I feel somewhat
like a disinherited son." Frank Munsey, a highly successful publisher and
a conservative Republican, said that he despised the spoils system and
was not in sympathy with this aspect of the Harding administration. He
went on: "The man who checks out government jobs to pay his own
obligations is not checking from his own bank account." This situation—
which looked ominous enough in 1921—would soon become a threat to
the life of the GOP; that is, especially in the elections of 1922 and 1924.

Such possibilities and fears of wrongdoing lay almost entirely
beneath the surface in the spring of 1921, as Warren Harding came to the
Capitol for his inaugural ceremony. Republican enthusiasm ran high as
March 4 approached. After all, the Democratic party, which had lost
control of Congress in 1919, was about to surrender the Presidency as
well. The somber and emaciated Woodrow Wilson rode with Harding to
the Capitol; and there, at the east portico, Harding took his oath of office
and delivered his inaugural message.

Superficially, at least, the most striking thing about this address was
the new President's repeated allusions to the Great War and its repercussions two and a half years after the fighting had ended. Thus he began:
"My Countrymen: when one surveys the world about him after the great
storm, noting the marks of destruction and yet rejoicing in the ruggedness
of the things which withstood it, if he is an American he breathes the
clarified atmosphere with a strange mingling of regret and new hope. We
have seen a world passion spend its fury, but we contemplate our
Republic unshaken, and hold our civilization secure." He said that
perhaps the best the United States could do now was to prove how
successfully this republic could emerge from the "wreckage of war."
True, the country did not have devastated lands and cities as Europe did,
but it had experienced a "delirium of expenditure," an "unbalanced
industry," and "unspeakable waste and disturbed relationships." Further
references to the war and failures of American policy were aimed in part
at Woodrow Wilson and his advisers.

Harding seems to have understood that the world was a vastly
different place, and he gave lip service, at least, to ideas for change and
reform. The "world upheaval," he said, had "added heavily" to his tasks.
A new order had to be recognized with "the closer contacts which
progress has wrought." Through "ties of trade," nations were bound
together "in closest intimacy, and none may receive except as he gives."
His most reverent prayer for the United States was "industrial peace,

Figure 25   The Wall Street Financial District, Which Gained in Prominence during the "Dollar Decade." *(Photograph by Underwood & Underwood.)*

with its rewards, widely and generally distributed, amid the inspirations of equal opportunity." In such a country as the United States, there ought to be a way to guard against the "perils and penalties of unemployment."

In other statements, sometimes contradicting those above, Harding laid down the actual lines of policy for his administration. He rejected the idea of a Wilson league or "super government" and declared that we would not become "entangled" with affairs of the Old World. Yet he professed his hope for international cooperation to achieve disarmament and the establishment of a world court. Most of all, he paid deference to the business system of America in which flowed the "lifeblood of material existence." References to "inexorable laws of nature" and the "dangerous tendency to expect too much of government," helped to reveal his reactionary views. Expenditures must be reduced and taxes as well; the "forward course of the business cycle" must be aided. In a confused and contradictory paragraph, he called for high protective tariffs along with expanded international trade.

In essence, Harding was calling for the restoration of a business-man's economy and a businessman's government, which he claimed would be beneficial to the society at large. And he was frank enough to say that some people would suffer in the necessary postwar adjustments. There was "no instant step from disorder to order." "We must face," he said, "a condition of grim reality, charge off our losses, and start afresh. It is the oldest lesson of civilization." Obviously farmers, laborers, and small businessmen would pay the heaviest penalties in this process of natural adjustment and liquidation.

One of the most disturbing features of this address was the President's complacency and self-righteousness about the United States and its role in the world; about the greatness of its institutions and its hope that other nations could some day rise to the "same heights" that we had attained. Undoubtedly he reflected the superpatriotism of the American people.

Other Republicans in the administration—like Coolidge, Hoover, and Mellon—would have said some of this differently, but their fundamental outlook was similar. The "pilot" had set a course for Republican policy in the 1920s. He had done so in the aftermath of war and in the middle of a severe recession, whose problems were not unlike those that would strike the nation with great force $8\frac{1}{2}$ years later.

Five weeks after Harding's inaugural ceremonies the first session of the Sixty-seventh Congress met to hear another address by the President, and it then turned to the task of implementing or rejecting some ideas emanating from the White House. In the meantime, other members of the administration were assuming their new duties. The importance of certain Presidential aides and advisers can hardly be exaggerated.

One of the obvious large consequences of the year 1921 was the inclusion in the Harding administration of the man who would take his place in the White House two and a half years later. Calvin Coolidge had gained a reputation in his Massachusetts career for having phenomenal luck, as when he became president of the Massachusetts Senate by one stroke of fortune, and then lieutenant governor, going on to the top position in the state. The Boston police strike of 1919 soon gave him a chance to become a national figure when he made a ringing statement in favor of law and order. A rebellion of delegates in the Republican national convention of 1920 then presented him with the vice-presidential nomination—against the wishes of party leaders. This was an amazing occurrence. The man from Massachusetts went on into the campaign with the presidential nominee from Ohio, who had taken no part in selecting him. Coolidge's recent biographer (Donald R. McCoy) has described a curious incident in that campaign. Harding and his running mate held a press conference together in the course of which the Ohioan paused to search in the grass for a four-leaf clover. He found one and pinned it on Coolidge's lapel. As the author remarks, "Harding should have kept that lucky clover, in view of what the future brought." About this time it was widely asserted in Coolidge's hometown, Northampton, "I wouldn't give two cents for Warren Harding's life."

This reputation for a charmed life added to Coolidge's political power in his home state. He also had the backing of a potent political machine, inherited from Senator Winthrop Murray Crane of Massachusetts.

In Washington, D.C., by contrast, Coolidge seemed a virtual nonentity. Since his salary as Vice President was inadequate, he lived in the New Willard Hotel and kept largely to himself except for the banquets and ceremonial dinners he had to attend. He did not mind these so much, he said. He had to eat anyway.

His first performance of new duties came on March 4, when he took his oath of office in the Senate chamber and gave a short address before the assembled dignitaries. His effort was almost meaningless, except for one reactionary idea. He declared that the American system of government was intended to protect the rights of the *minority*. Anyone knowing something of Coolidge's political philosophy could be sure that he did not mean Afro-Americans, Indians, or radicals. It was men of property he had primarily in mind. He had a conservatism that was much more doctrinaire than Hardings's.

When presiding over the Senate, the Vice President seemed to be intimidated by all the noise, argument, and shouting in the chamber. There were too many prima donnas there. He made the necessary rulings and said virtually nothing. Not a few senators and people of ability held the Vice President in contempt. He and Harding were quite possibly the weakest combination ever elevated to the high positions they occupied. In 1924, when Coolidge was running for President in his own right, Harold L. Ickes almost exploded in his anger. Harding, he said, had run in 1920 "to get the country back to normalcy." Coolidge's campaign was to "bring about subnormalcy." Mediocrity had become king and it was "a virtue to be lacking in initiative, forcefulness, qualities of leadership or even average ability. That President [Coolidge] is the greatest in our history who can almost qualify as a deaf mute." Obviously Ickes, who deserved his reputation as a "curmudgeon," was a bit harsh in this blast.

One of Harding's appointees who had an influence little less than that of the President himself was William Howard Taft. The former President had been, since his forced retirement from office in 1913, a professor of law at Yale University. He had also given important service in the war period as a member of the War Labor Board in Washington. One of his biographers, Henry Pringle, has observed that Taft was fortunate to hear and discuss during these years both the right-wing ideas with which he was most sympathetic and the opposing philosophies of those like Frank

P. Walsh on the War Labor Board. He remained a conservative but did not, by any means, have a closed mind.

In all this time Taft thought wistfully of the shrine of American government, the Supreme Court, hoping almost pathetically that he might win an appointment as Chief Justice. When Harding was elected, his hopes rose. Finally the President-elect called him to Marion for a breakfast of waffles and creamed chipped beef, after which they had quite a long discussion. Then Harding got to the main question: Would Taft accept a position on the Supreme Court? Taft was flattered, but disappointed. He was not offered the post of Chief Justice because, in fact, that place was already occupied by Edward D. White, an old man whose health was holding up disappointingly well. Taft waited in vain through the first six months of 1921. The Chief Justice continued to live and show no signs of resigning, while Harding's intentions remained unclear. Then came the news. The Chief Justice had died, and shortly thereafter Taft received his appointment. At long last, he had the position he had wanted—even more than the presidency.

Taft, as Chief Justice, was an extremely influential man. He added respectability to an administration that needed it badly. He also helped to carry forward, even beyond his own lifetime, doctrines of economic conservatism. Essentially this meant opposition to labor unions and to the expansion of federal or state power with respect to social problems. He did this by the decisions he wrote, or helped to write, and also by the associate justices he helped to appoint. In making his judicial appointments, Harding turned for advice to the Chief Justice. What happened, then, is reminiscent of the charges made against Justice Abe Fortas in 1968—that he gave advice to President Lyndon Johnson, contrary to the spirit of the Constitution in its separation of powers. Regardless of any theory, Warren Harding leaned heavily on his new Chief Justice. Taft was, of course, pleased to give assistance. His recommendations carried much weight in the appointment of Pierce Butler in 1922 and Harlan F. Stone in 1925. These men, along with George Sutherland (one of Harding's friends from the Senate) and Justice Edward T. Sanford, helped to assure a "safe" attitude on the high court. Actually, Taft was bitterly disappointed to discover that Harlan Stone often sided with Justices Holmes and Brandeis in liberal dissents for which they became famous.

According to Robert M. La Follette, this Supreme Court, headed by Taft throughout the 1920s, was more powerful than either the Congress or the executive branch. Clearly it had an influence of great importance. In the judgment of Felix Frankfurter, writing at the end of the decade, the court, "had invalidated more legislation than in fifty years preceding" and had resurrected "views that were antiquated twenty-five years ago."

Also affected by changes in personnel was the Federal Trade Commission. What happened in this federal agency was strongly indicative of trends in other agencies now gradually filled with the Harding-Coolidge appointees. The FTC, since its creation in 1914, had never been a great success, but some of its members had taken quite seriously their apparent duty of investigating business practices and trying to foster competition. They were looked upon as allies by progressives in the Congress, while business groups resented periodic investigations and "exposures." According to the theory of "self-regulation," there was little need for the federal government to investigate, or regulate. Gradually, the Wilson appointees were replaced by conservative or reactionary members of the GOP. In 1922 a former lobbyist for the National Association of Manufacturers took a seat on the commission. In 1924 a conservative Republican from Iowa gained the place previously held by Victor Murdock, a noted progressive. Finally, Coolidge appointed William E. Humphrey of the state of Washington, a former Congressman and lobbyist who was a self-proclaimed friend of Big Business and a critic of reformers. The Commission now frankly avowed its intention to be friendly and helpful toward business. Not surprisingly, it received words of praise from the business world, while progressives lamented that the agency had been taken over by the very interests it was supposed to regulate. In truth, the FTC had gone through a "transformation," as one scholar has shown.

Thus the changes that occurred were more than a matter of rhetoric. Harding believed fervently that the country needed "less of government in business as well as more business in government," and proceeded to put that idea into effect as much as he could. Coolidge did likewise. They were assisted by numerous spokesmen for a like point of view, such as Andrew Mellon and Harry Daugherty in the Cabinet, Charles G. Dawes in the Budget Bureau (elected Vice President in 1924), and leaders in the House and Senate. There were practical limits, however, to the backward steps that could be taken and to the duties that a government might abdicate. There was not a consensus in the GOP by any means. James M. Beck, Solicitor General from 1921 to 1925, was an extreme conservative who sensed correctly, from his vantage point, that the power of government was still growing, that leaders in politics made pragmatic compromises, and that true conservatism was difficult, indeed, to maintain in these administrations in which he served.

Warren Harding was a compromiser rather than a die-hard conservative. Both in the language he used and in the record of his administration this can be seen. Judging by rhetoric, primarily, it is quite possible to think of Harding as a mild reformer and a humanitarian. On April 12, 1921, when he spoke to the Congress, now assembled in special session, the new President said a few things that did not sound at all conservative. He discussed at length the developments in transportation and communication and the new federal responsibilities. There should be federal action with reference to national highways, the licensing of radio stations, and the "regulation of air navigation." In a different vein, he called for a concerted governmental effort in behalf of those "disabled saviours of our civilization"—the veterans. There should be hospitalization for them, rehabilitation, and vocational training. This must be done in a "most thoughtful" way, for it would involve the expenditure of billions of dollars over the next fifty years. If good intentions were enough, Harding would have succeeded splendidly in his plans for the veterans.

Turning from this idea of helping the veterans, which got much applause, Harding made a related suggestion and received almost no applause at all. He proposed the establishment of a department of public welfare, which would bring together in one department various governmental functions relating to public health, education, child welfare, and the conditions of industrial labor. Having made this statement, the President seemed to undercut his own proposal when he added that they must resist a "growing demand on the Federal Treasury" for services that really ought to be controlled by the *states*. Now the assembled congressmen gave him a big hand.

Surprisingly, Harding devoted a paragraph to the race question. Congress, he said, "ought to wipe the stain of barbaric lynching from the banners of a free and orderly, representative democracy." Thus he gave support to proposals for an antilynching bill. Another tangible suggestion was the creation of a commission, to include members from both races, that would study and report on the entire subject of race relations. Very little of positive benefit came out of these statements, but Harding had shown once again that he meant well.

The main burden of this address could be readily anticipated. Harding called for economy, tax relief, and an "instant tariff enactment" for emergency purposes. He declared: "I believe in the protection of American industry, and it is our purpose to prosper America first." One proposal on which Congress quickly acted was his request for a planned federal budget. This had been recommended under Wilson, and it also accorded with Harding's emphasis on economy and business efficiency.

In vehement terms, the new President stated his opposition to the League of Nations. As it now existed, it was a "world-governing" organization with "super-powers," and the United States would have nothing to do with it. He was applauded enthusiastically (at least by the Republicans). Then five more times they applauded as he stated that this country would be interested in cooperation with other nations generally and in efforts to promote peace, but *not* through the existing League.

Since the United States still was at war, technically, with the Central Powers of Europe, he asked for a resolution to bring that conflict to an end. Three months later, in July, Congress took the inevitable action.

In the address just described, Harding's domestic and foreign policy can be glimpsed in its major outlines. About a month later, speaking briefly at Hoboken, New Jersey, he added a note that would continue throughout his administration and that of Calvin Coolidge. The occasion of his comments was the arrival of 5,212 American bodies being returned from France for burial. Eloquently, Harding captured the mood of his fellow countrymen as he declared that the tragedy of war must be prevented in the future. This feeling for peace, widely held and supported, led on to the Washington Disarmament Conference of 1921–1922 and to a variety of peace ideas and movements, including the Kellogg-Briand Pact of 1928 which attempted to outlaw war.

Harding and Coolidge, well-meaning though they were, lacked the ability or training to do a good job in the White House. Believing, as Coolidge phrased it, that the "business of America is business," they limited their circle of friends and advisers. Harding tried to rise to the challenge of the Presidency and worked dutifully, but his health soon broke down. Coolidge, by comparison, was short of energy from the start and did less work than any other President in the modern era. He went to bed early and needed his nap every afternoon.

Robert K. Murray, in a sympathetic treatment of the Harding labor policy, portrays the Ohioan's strengths and weaknesses. He was not an enemy of labor and, as a newspaper publisher, had enjoyed good relations with his employees. He sympathized with the millions of unemployed in the difficult winter of 1921–1922, and he strongly supported Herbert Hoover in the conduct of a conference on unemployment, held in Washington. Though denying that the federal government should spend money, he actually encouraged some spending for authorized projects to lessen the severity of depression. When labor strife developed, however, the President was not able to cope. He wanted to serve as conciliator in the coal strike of 1922 and the railway shopmen's strike. The problems were difficult, and he failed. In his frustration he turned to Harry Daugherty, who was well known for his rabidly antilabor views. The Attorney General then went to a federal judge in Chicago, obtained the most sweeping injunction in American labor history, and broke the shopmen's strike. Harding knew what he was doing; he had deliberately thrown his influence on the side of management, though perhaps without knowing all the implications of the federal injunction.

Such an action was foreshadowed by the appointments Harding had made and the company he kept, both in the government and socially. Thus his Secretary of Labor, James J. Davis, lacked ability and did not serve effectively in speaking for labor, as Secretary Wallace did for the farmers and as most Cabinet members did for business interests. In addition to Daugherty, others in the Cabinet showed strong antilabor predilections. John W. Weeks, Secretary of War, and Mellon in the Treasury Department are examples. There could be no doubt that Warren Harding, in a crisis, would find it almost impossible to take the part of labor unions.

The President showed more sympathy for problems of the farmers. These were very real, as prices dropped precipitously from the high levels of the war and postwar period. Secretary Wallace of Iowa was a vigorous spokesman for agriculture who declared in 1921 that products of the farm were now selling at "bankruptcy prices." He tried constantly to alleviate depression conditions and to win Presidential approval for his measures. In the Congress numerous senators and representatives from the farm states, men of both parties, were eager to do what they could. But the solutions were difficult to find, much as they would be in later decades. The recovery of Europe and increased production in many parts of the world had created a surplus in the major commodities, notably cotton and wheat. More efficient farming, with the use of fertilizer, tractors, and other machinery, greatly increased the American output. Changes in living habits, meanwhile, with lighter meals and less clothing, tended to restrict the markets, as did a decline in immigration and the rate of population increase.

What, then, could be done? Neither Harding or Wallace would accept a radical plan, but they willingly supported a series of acts that might help: the improvement of credit facilities, especially in the Intermediate Credits Act of 1923, the encouragement of farmer cooperatives for marketing purposes, and some supervision of market conditions, notably in the stockyards and the grain exchanges, trying to correct the malpractices there.

None of these efforts did much to solve the basic problem. The farmers did not have "parity." Certainly it was clear that no aid given to agriculture was comparable to that extended to manufacturing. The tariff is an excellent example of the disparity. Higher duties for industry in the emergency act of 1921 and the Fordney-McCumber Act of 1922 could only mean higher profits for the favored interests. Farmers, it was alleged, benefited as well from protective duties on their crops. This was a bogus argument. It did not take an expert's knowledge of economics to know that wheat, cotton, and tobacco, which were export crops, had to compete on the world market; and the price was not determined by an American tariff on imports from abroad.

In spite of its efforts, the Harding administration lost ground in the farming regions. Its aid came slowly, if at all, and the image it projected was not a friendly one. If the duty of modern government, following the lead of Theodore Roosevelt and Woodrow Wilson, was to try to serve the people—evenhandedly—the Harding leadership fell short. Some powerful figures in the administration, notably Mellon and Hoover, really favored industry or the city as against the claims of agriculture. A new insurgency seemed to threaten among the Republican farmers of Western states, and to many in the East these agrarians of the hinterland looked like demagogues, "sons of the wild jackass," later-day Populists. They were, in fact, an aggregation of interest groups, not at all easy to please. Nevertheless, they had real and continuing problems, and they often felt ignored. According to one argument, the farm bloc of 1921–1922 was primarily a Western and Republican phenomenon and would never have been necessary under Woodrow Wilson. His administration had genuinely represented the South and West and was friendly toward agriculture. The point had some validity, for Southerners and Westerners in the Wilson administration owed much to the agrarian tradition and often had acted accordingly.

Popular discontent led to fear in the GOP that a defeat was looming at the polls. They were right, but the actual results when the votes had been tallied in November 1922 were even worse than expected. Democrats picked up seventy-eight seats in the House of Representatives and came within twelve of gaining control. In the Senate races, they elected Burton K. Wheeler of Montana, whose affiliations lay primarily with labor and the Nonpartisan League, and the total Democratic gain was seven seats. Most shocking to the Old Guard were the returns from Minnesota, Wisconsin, Iowa, Nebraska, North Dakota, South Dakota, and Idaho. The Farmer-Labor party of Minnesota and the Nonpartisan League, with its farmer constituency, showed the nature of this political uprising. Lynn J. Frazier came to the Senate from North Dakota; Henrik Shipstead from Minnesota; and Smith W. Brookhart from Iowa. Robert M. La Follette gained his reelection by a whopping vote. This veteran progressive had all the encouragement needed to rally the discontented, looking on to the election of 1924.

The positive record that Harding made was largely nullified by these political setbacks and by revelations of scandal, which began in 1922 and lasted long after his death. Most reprehensible of all was the corruption in the Veterans Bureau. Harding had picked a personal friend and one of his poker companions to head this agency, Charles R. Forbes. Almost immediately, stories began to circulate that Forbes was arranging kickbacks from his contractors and was swindling the veterans in every way he could think of. Meanwhile, hospitals and medical supplies were badly needed in these years just after the war. According to one story, Harding had a meeting with Forbes and forced him to resign. It remained for the Senate, however, to investigate the matter and show the moral squalor in which Forbes and some confederates operated. One of his coworkers, the chief counsel of the Bureau, killed himself. Forbes himself finally went to jail for a term.

Meanwhile, Attorney General Daugherty was getting into trouble. As early as May 1922, the *New York Tribune,* a staunchly Republican paper, called for him to resign. One scandal involved Daugherty, his friend Jess Smith, and the Alien Property Custodian, Thomas W. Miller. In essence, Miller, the head of this office, was paid at least $50,000 to turn over control of a metal company, worth millions, to men who fraudulently claimed it. Jess Smith got a payoff, too, as did a Republican leader named John T. King. Had Attorney General Daugherty shared in the loot? It seemed that he had, but to get the evidence was not easy. Miller was convicted, however, and went to prison for his part in the affair.

Jess Smith suffered a worse fate. He became notorious as a cheap fixer for bootleggers, income tax evaders, and the like. The President sent him back to Ohio, but Smith refused to stay. He returned to Washington and killed himself in May 1923.

Most sensational of all was the Teapot Dome scandal. This involved the fraudulent leasing of public oil lands and could be related directly to the political philosophy of men in Harding's Cabinet. The central figure was Albert B. Fall of New Mexico, Secretary of the Interior. A Senate committee, led by Thomas J. Walsh of Montana, found that two oil reserves of the Navy, Teapot Dome in Wyoming and Elk Hills in California, had been leased to two powerful oilmen about the same time that Fall had received gifts and "loans" from the two totaling more than $400,000. In a sense, this affair was the old, old story of public officials who lacked the capacity or the integrity to hold their high offices. But it was a little more complicated than that.

These scandals went back to the election of 1920 and to the Harding landslide, which seemed to mean a "mandate" for the GOP. To cast a ballot for Harding, Coolidge, and the Republicans was to vote against the recent past and some of its liberal ideas and apparent failures. An opportunity existed, in the new atmosphere, for militant reactionaries to take decisive action. This, essentially, is what Albert B. Fall proceeded to do as the new Secretary of the Interior. Fall, a veteran of ideological battles over public-land policy, had maintained for years that the federal government had no right to supervise or control the development of timber land, mineral land, grazing land, water power, and other public resources in the Western states. The West ought to be developed as the East had been, free from bureaucratic interference. As soon as possible, in fact, the Department of the Interior ought to be abolished.

Fall was reacting strongly against the federal conservation programs that had developed under Roosevelt, Taft, and Wilson. The Secretary did not receive payoffs, apparently, with the important exception of the arrangements in Wyoming and California that became his undoing. He really believed in his policy and did not necessarily have to be paid.

Secretary Fall left the Cabinet long before his actions were explored. He was evasive and untruthful, and the facts finally had to be forced out through the Senate inquiry mentioned. (If anything is clear from Teapot Dome and similar scandals, it is that lying is not unusual among high-placed officials, when under fire and fighting for their reputations.) Fall had to serve a short prison term for his mistakes, although the oilmen who had paid him were not convicted on a charge of conspiracy.

Attorney General Daugherty continued in the Cabinet in 1923–1924, after Harding's death. Daugherty resembled Fall in having ideas that were militantly conservative. He was closely associated with business interests, and he blamed the talk about corruption mostly on Communists, congressional radicals, and others. He wrote in a conspiratorial vein to President Coolidge that he should not be afraid of the scavengers in Congress; he (Daugherty) would give him the necessary protection. A sensible man, Coolidge was not impressed. Daugherty also used his control of the Department of Justice to launch an investigation of the investigators. He and his subordinates actually opposed for a time those in the Senate trying to get at the truth. Some of this, of course, sounds very much like the later Watergate affair.

The Attorney General was indicted for his own activities, but he refused to testify, pleading a fear of self-incrimination. When the jury failed to agree, Daugherty escaped a prison sentence. Thus, narrowly, the Harding administration avoided having a second member of its Cabinet go to jail.

The man with the most to lose from all of this, in a political sense, was Calvin Coolidge. Instead, through his own skill and the force of circumstance, he brought the country into a new and decisive phase of the "conservative revolution." Neither the Democrats nor Senator La Follette, with his progressive forces, were able to make headway on the basis of scandal and corruption, monopoly, labor discontent, or hard times in the farming regions. For conservatives of the GOP, the election of 1924 became another great victory, comparable to that of 1920.

In the early months of 1924, each party was looking toward its national conventions, to be held in June and July. Coolidge was trying to get a firm control over the Republican party so that he would receive the nomination without a fight. The leading contender among the Democrats was William G. McAdoo, son-in-law of President Wilson and highly regarded as a powerful figure in his own right. Since his wartime service

Figure 26 "Gushing," Drawn by Daniel R. Fitzpatrick. *(From the* St. Louis Post-Dispatch, *February 5, 1924.)*

as director of railroads, he had gone to California to practice law and won a strong political following in all regions of the country.

Meanwhile, the Democrats were reaching for what seemed to be a winning issue. Some of them reveled in it. Senator Thaddeus Caraway of Arkansas compared the infamy of the former Secretary Fall with that of Benedict Arnold. Moreover, the crooks were safe, he warned; so long as Harry Daugherty was Attorney General they could even sell the White House. Cordell Hull, Tennessee Congressman and chairman of the Democratic National Committee, issued a statement charging that the Coolidge administration was dominated by a "crowd of ruthless reactionaries" and was riddled with fifteen or more scandals. This statement formally announced that the Democrats were making corruption their leading issue in the campaign.

Coolidge's policy, then, had to evolve under considerable pressure. At first he showed hostility toward the congressional inquiries. Like Chief Justice Taft and many other Republicans, he even suspected a Democratic plot to discredit his administration. Recognizing, finally, that a scandal actually existed, and having decided to run for another term in the White House, he saw the wisdom of action. Meanwhile he had his own men—in the Public Lands Committee, for example—sniping at Senator Walsh; and one extremely partisan Republican, a senator from Missouri, made personal attacks that were wholly unjustified.

Coolidge consulted with his Republican advisers and set out to nullify any advantage that the Democrats might have gained. The Senate had raised the question of special independent prosecutors, since the Department of Justice under Daugherty could not be trusted. Anticipating this demand, Coolidge proceeded to appoint his own prosecutors, though the first two were not confirmed. The final choices were adequate but hardly the best available. One was Atlee Pomerene, a former Democratic Senator from Ohio, and the other was Owen Roberts, a Philadelphia lawyer and Republican who went on later to become a Justice of the Supreme Court. Coolidge also accepted the resignation of Edwin Denby as Secretary of the Navy, and he forced Daugherty out of the Cabinet. Generally speaking, Coolidge's administration was moving to clean up the mess by the summer of 1924. The "Harding gang" was no longer in power. Enough had been done to withstand any sweeping attacks on the Republican party. Coolidge went on without difficulty to receive the coveted presidential nomination.

Meanwhile, the Democrats' trouble was just beginning. E. L. Doheny, the Democrat from California who had leased Elk Hills, succeeded in his testimony before the committee in smearing a number of men who had been prominent in the Wilson administration, including William G. McAdoo. The latter, for example, had not been directly implicated in any way in the question of Naval petroleum reserves. But he had served as Doheny's lawyer and had received large retainers. That was enough to injure him badly as a "clean government" candidate, although he continued to campaign for the presidential nomination. To the extent that McAdoo was hurt, his rivals in the party gained strength. This was especially true of Alfred E. Smith, Governor of New York. A stop-McAdoo movement, which was to culminate in virtual civil war within the Democratic party, had become a powerful reality.

The movement for a new Progressive party also picked up momentum. If McAdoo had been able to continue with strength unabated, he would have had powerful support in the South, the West, and elsewhere. He satisfied most demands for a Democratic candidate who was progressive but not too progressive and whose experience equipped him to lead the country. Then, suddenly, his "fall from the pinnacle" created much uncertainty as to whether he could get the nomination, or was even worthy of it. The railroad labor unions and other groups that had looked favorably on a McAdoo candidacy now had to reconsider their position.

Those who expected a fight in the Democratic party were not

disappointed. The country had never seen anything like it. Meeting at Madison Square Garden, the forces of McAdoo and Al Smith slugged it out. Behind McAdoo were delegates from the South and West primarily, including many members of the Ku Klux Klan. The Californian was not a member of that organization and declared on one occasion that he was opposed to "intolerance or bigotry in any form"; but he also expressed his belief that the Klan was not very important, and he did not conduct an open fight against it. William Jennings Bryan and other Democratic leaders, including some Catholics, also believed in keeping the issue out of public debate. Not so the forces of Al Smith. They called for a plank in the platform specifically condemning the Klan and similar groups that acted secretly and illegally. In the platform committee, it was decided to make a general statement of condemnation, without naming the Klan. The Smith minority refused to accept this decision, so the question was taken to the floor of the convention for a debate that was bitterly personal and emotional. By a margin of 1 vote in a total of more than 1,000, the Smith delegates lost; the plank stayed as it was.

The platform controversy had been a marathon. Now came another in the balloting for the nomination. McAdoo led in one roll call after another, but could not get the two-thirds majority required. For a week, the roll call continued, as neither McAdoo nor Smith would yield. Finally, as the delegates neared exhaustion, they turned on the 103d ballot to a compromise choice, John W. Davis of West Virginia. An able man, Davis had served with distinction in the Wilson administration, but also, unfortunately, he was a Wall Street lawyer. To try and mollify the progressives, the delegates nominated Governor Charles Bryan of Nebraska for second place on the ticket; he was W. J. Bryan's brother and editor of *The Commoner,* their family newspaper.

What the Democrats had done was to exhaust themselves, to aggravate their conflicts, and to dramatize the reasons for a third-party ticket. They made a victory for Coolidge virtually certain.

Writing on the progressive movement of 1924, Kenneth MacKay has commented that it was a "calculated, determined experiment in group resistance to the economic and social classes in control of political authority." The Harding-Coolidge policies brought forth a countermovement. It was not a small affair. Almost 5 million people, in voting for Robert M. La Follette and Burton K. Wheeler, showed their dissatisfaction with both the major parties and with "Coolidge prosperity." The Progressives of 1924 had a good claim to the name they adopted, since some of their leaders had been active also in the Progressive party of 1912 and later formed a derivative group called the Committee of Forty-Eight. This committee then took a leading part in the efforts of the twenties, along with the Nonpartisan League, the farmer-labor parties of several states, the labor unions, the socialists, and assorted intellectuals. In 1922 the various groups came together in the Conference for Progressive Political Action, which included a number of leaders from Congress. Other meetings followed, with La Follette as a key figure. Finally, in 1924, the leaders decided to form a third-party ticket, and a conference of the CPPA gathered for that purpose in Cleveland, using the same hall where the Republicans had met earlier.

The message now coming from Cleveland was plain and clear. This potpourri of progressives still believed in democracy. The people of America, they said, had been trying for 148 years "to establish a government for the service of all and to prevent the establishment of a government for the mastery of the few." Thinking of Coolidge, Mellon, and company, they said: "The reactionary continues to put his faith in mastery for the solution of all problems. He seeks to have what he calls the strong men and best minds rule and impose their decisions upon the masses of their weaker brethren." In actuality, the rights and liberties of all the people must be faithfully represented by public officials. Their obligation of service was a high one, and they must be held to it. The conference advanced a program of "public service," as against the system of monopoly and special privilege. Public development of water power, public control of the railroads, public control and "permanent conservation of all natural resources . . . in the interest of the people," and "public works in times of business depression"—these suggested a major emphasis that stopped well short of socialism. The statements on taxation were democratic, with a call for increases on the wealthy, as through the surtax, the excess profits tax, and inheritance taxes. Farmers and workers, they said, must be protected in their rights to organize and bargain collectively. They endorsed, without qualification, the "constitutional guarantees of freedom of speech, press, and assemblage." Finally, the conference rejected a materialistic conception of America: "The nation may grow rich in the vision of greed. The nation will grow great in the vision of service."

After his nomination, La Follette drew up his own platform, which contained some differences of emphasis. Even more strongly than the CPPA, he denounced the "control of government and industry by private monopoly." He also stressed heavily the influence of privilege in the federal courts and the assumption of legislative power by the courts, which he termed unconstitutional; he called for a constitutional amendment, giving Congress the power to override judicial "vetoes." The Wisconsin Senator made clear his faith in the people, as against property-minded officials in the executive or judicial branches of government. His faith, though admirable, was not well supported by events just past or those about to occur.

The Coolidge administration had a beautiful opportunity to solidify its hold on the country. Rising prosperity, even in the wheat regions, assured the GOP of a political victory. Leaders did not hesitate to take credit for business growth, for orderly progress and stability. A Coolidge myth developed, in which the President was portrayed as another "Abe" Lincoln, a plain man of the people, of few words but strong character. He could be trusted. One phrase to express this was "Coolidge or chaos"; another was "Keep cool with Coolidge." Here was an effective way to respond to charges of scandal from the Democrats and to radical ideas of the Progressives.

Coolidge did little campaigning, partly because of the tragic death of his son in July. The vice-presidential nominee, however, General Charles G. Dawes, a banker from Chicago, pounded away at La Follette. The Senator from Wisconsin was vulnerable, and Dawes knew that very well. Energetic and dynamic, with the nickname "Hell and Maria," Dawes attacked La Follette as a demagogue and a kind of subversive who was trying to destroy the American Constitution. Numerous other Republicans blasted the Wisconsinite as an "enemy of the country," a radical, a party wrecker. One line of argument used skillfully by the GOP was the danger of a divided vote among the three contenders, which would leave Coolidge and Dawes without a majority in the electoral college and thus throw the election into the House of Representatives. If that happened, La Follette might gain the Presidency! The only safe course, they asserted, was for moderates of the country to vote Republican.

The GOP won a smashing victory. With nearly 16 million votes, it almost doubled the vote of the Democrats, while La Follette picked up close to 5 million. Coolidge won every state outside the South except for Wisconsin, which went as expected to La Follette. The defeat was a bitter one for the old warrior, and already in poor health, he died the next year. The Democratic party, left in a badly weakened condition, had no hope for the immediate future, although it did show some signs of a comeback in the offyear elections of 1926.

Thus the Republicans found themselves firmly in control. They had a green light to go on with the economic policies already laid down by Harding, Coolidge, Mellon, Hoover, and others. Enterprising men and their corporate organizations must be encouraged, not hindered, by government agencies. The incentive to profit was recognized as necessary and honorable. Through the Mellon tax plan, in fact, business must be stimulated by a reduction of taxes with particular benefit to the well-to-do. And, of course, the stimulation of business, with the additional jobs provided, served as a boost to the entire nation's economy. Soon after the election the President reiterated his belief that the business of the country was business, and he expressed his hope that citizens would stop thinking of governmental matters and get back to their real concerns.

As noted before, the twenties was a time of significant progress, and the Harding-Coolidge leaders, high and low, could boast of many achievements. There is no doubt, however, that the top echelon adopted too easily the "trickle-down" theory of prosperity. They were infused, much too much, with the business point of view and with a concern preeminently to aid and mollify those interests. Organized labor and the consumer, by comparison, received scant consideration. The approach was a narrow and limited one that soon would become virtually indefensible in national politics. The ideals of a democratic progressivism, though smashed in the politics of 1924, proved to have an extraordinary resilience.

SUGGESTIONS FOR ADDITIONAL READING

Some of the reading for the preceding chapter will be just as relevant to the topics of this one. See especially Leuchtenburg, Hicks, Soule, Mowry, Bernstein, Tindall, and Braeman et al. (eds.), along with the historiographical article by Noggle. Various other books, mentioned throughout, will also be important; for example, Goldman, *Rendezvous with Destiny;* Hofstadter, *The Age of Reform;* Nye, *Midwestern Progressive Politics;* and Cochran and Miller, *The Age of Enterprise.* Link, *The Higher Realism,* contains the author's well-known essay, originally published in the *American Historical Review* (1959), "What Happened to the Progressive Movement in the 1920's?" An indispensable work for Harding and the Republican policies is Robert K. Murray, *The Harding Era: Warren G. Harding and His Administration,* Univ. of Minnesota Press, Minneapolis, 1969. Stressing the pre-Presidential period is Randolph C. Downes, *The Rise of Warren Gamaliel Harding, 1865–1920,* Ohio State Univ. Press, Columbus, 1970. Andrew Sinclair, *The Available Man: The Life Behind the Masks of Warren Gamaliel Harding,* Macmillan, New York, 1965, is an idea book and quite readable; while Samuel Hopkins Adams, *Incredible Era: The Life and Times of Warren Gamaliel Harding,* Houghton Mifflin, Boston, 1939, is the best example of a highly critical approach rather typical of its times. A balanced and readable biography is Donald R. McCoy, *Calvin Coolidge: The Quiet President,* Macmillan, New York, 1967. See also Howard H. Quint and Robert H. Ferrell (eds.), *The Talkative President: The Off-the-Record Press Conferences of Calvin Coolidge,* Univ. of Massachusetts Press, Amherst, 1964; Claude M. Fuess, *Calvin Coolidge: The Man from Vermont,* Little, Brown, Boston, 1940; and William Allen White, *A Puritan in Babylon: The Story of Calvin Coolidge,* Macmillan, New York, 1938.

Herbert Hoover is strongly identified with Republican economic policy throughout the decade. See his *American Individualism,* Doubleday, Garden City, N.Y., 1922, and volume 2 of his memoirs, *The Cabinet and the Presidency: 1920–1933,* Macmillan, New York, 1951. Following are a number of works relating to the Republican leaders and their policies: Morton Keller, *In Defense of Yesterday: James M. Beck and the Politics of Conservatism, 1861–1936,* Coward-McCann, New York, 1958; James W. Prothro, *The Dollar Decade: Business Ideas in the 1920's,* Louisiana State Univ. Press, Baton Rouge, 1954; Joan Hoff Wilson, *American Business & Foreign Policy, 1920–1933,* Univ. of Kentucky

Press, Lexington, 1971; Robert H. Zieger, *Republicans and Labor, 1919–1929,* Univ. of Kentucky Press, Lexington, 1969; James H. Shideler, *Farm Crisis, 1919–1923,* Univ. of California Press, Berkeley, 1957; Donald L. Winters, *Henry Cantwell Wallace as Secretary of Agriculture, 1921–1924,* Univ. of Illinois Press, Urbana, 1970; Alpheus T. Mason, *William Howard Taft, Chief Justice,* Simon and Schuster, New York, 1965; David J. Danelski, *A Supreme Court Justice Is Appointed,* Random House, New York, 1964; Burl Noggle, *Teapot Dome: Oil and Politics in the 1920's,* Louisiana State Univ. Press, Baton Rouge, 1962; Morris R. Werner, *Privileged Characters,* McBride, New York, 1935; and Alice Roosevelt Longworth, *Crowded Hours: Reminiscences of Alice Roosevelt Longworth,* Scribner, New York, 1933. The last is justly noted for its saucy comments on people and affairs.

One of the best works on political tendencies of the decade is David Burner, *The Politics of Provincialism: The Democratic Party in Transition, 1918–1932,* Knopf, New York, 1968. For farmer-labor movements and a variety of studies, see the following: Theodore Saloutos and John D. Hicks, *Agricultural Discontent in the Middle West, 1900–1939,* Univ. of Wisconsin Press, Madison, 1951; Robert L. Morlan, *Political Prairie Fire: The Nonpartisan League, 1915–1922,* Univ. of Minnesota Press, Minneapolis, 1955; Gilbert C. Fite, *George N. Peek and the Fight for Farm Parity,* Univ. of Oklahoma Press, Norman, 1954; Kenneth C. MacKay, *The Progressive Movement of 1924,* Columbia, New York, 1947; LeRoy Ashby, *The Spearless Leader: Senator Borah and the Progressive Movement in the 1920's,* Univ. of Illinois Press, Urbana, 1972; William H. Harbaugh, *Lawyer's Lawyer: The Life of John W. Davis,* Oxford, New York, 1973; J. Joseph Huthmacher, *Massachusetts People and Politics, 1919–1933,* Harvard, Cambridge, Mass., 1959; Frank Freidel, *Franklin D. Roosevelt: The Ordeal,* Little, Brown, Boston, 1954; Arthur M. Schlesinger, Jr., *The Age of Roosevelt: The Crisis of the Old Order, 1919–1933,* Houghton Mifflin, Boston, 1964 [1957]. See also Richard Lowitt, *George W. Norris, 1913–1933,* and La Follette and La Follette, *Robert M. La Follette,* both mentioned previously.

Chapter 17

Paths to Peace?

Writing on peace movements of the 1920s, a scholar has recently referred to the "curious sense of hopeful realism that gripped reformers"—thousands of men and women who dared to believe that peace could be made the normal condition of mankind. As one possibility, there was the League of Nations and its affiliated World Court. Many in the United States assumed that eventually the nation simply must join the League. In the modern world there was no way to escape an international organization and, for the time being at least, this was the only one available. The breakdown of the League that occurred during the 1930s did not seem inevitable to scholars, activists, political leaders, or others a decade earlier. There was "reason to hope"; there was reason to act and strive.

James C. Malin showed his approval of this tendency when he completed a book in 1930, a study of the United States since World War I. He began with a section entitled "The United States and the Establishment of International Government." Thus, the nation had helped to create the League and set it in motion. Whatever the shortcomings of this organiza-

tion, it "marked a positive change," an evolutionary step toward cooperation among nations.

In the same period, the political scientist Clarence A. Berdahl
commented, "Whether we like it or not, the League of Nations is clearly
the most important, the most vital factor in international relations today."
A noted journalist and foreign observer went farther. The League, he
declared, had become the "central point in European political life," and
"all the liberal and democratic elements" in the major countries had
"adopted the idea and the machinery of the League as the basis of foreign
policy." Unquestionably, the League was important to Americans in the
1920s. In considerable numbers, they either studied its work and growing
influence, often hoping their nation might join, or, on the contrary, hated
and feared the organization. To isolationists in the Senate, for example,
there was always a chance that the nation might slip into the League by
"the back door."

The world organization was, then, a point of reference in American
thought and policy. Officially, the United States tried to stay out of it, and
members of Congress like Hiram Johnson and William E. Borah exerted
all the pressure they could on the State Department to prevent any
dangerous "fraternization." Yet the League had aims such as disarmament, banning the international traffic in opium, and—above all—the
prevention of war with which it was difficult to disagree. The problem was
how to accomplish these laudable purposes, in or outside the agency.
Americans had the right to act in many ways, and they did so, while the
government followed a course that cannot be described strictly as
isolationist.

Among those agitating for a policy of internationalism were the
Protestant churches. They showed no less interest in the issues of war and
peace than they did in the sale of alcohol or the dispute over evolutionist
doctrines. Some of the ablest leaders in the church, moreover, established
a brilliant record as humane, concerned citizens. The explanation seems
to be in part that many had a guilt complex concerning World War I, for,
with few exceptions, church leaders had supported that conflict whole-
heartedly. Then, in the immediate postwar period American Protestantism enthusiastically called for membership in the League of Nations. The
Federal Council of Churches of Christ in America, the Church Peace
Union, and similar organizations threw their influence into the cause,
while 14,450 ministers signed their names to a petition which went to the
Senate, with arguments for ratification of the treaty. A poll conducted late
in 1919 disclosed that virtually all ministers—Protestant, Catholic, and
Jew—favored the League of Nations; the exceptions were mostly Irish
Catholic priests, who were opposed in considerable numbers. The Protes-
tants, through their denominational meetings, went on record as strongly

favoring the world organization; and noted figures in the Church, such as Harry Emerson Fosdick of the Union Theological Seminary and Shailer Mathews of the Divinity School at the University of Chicago made their views known.

When the fight for ratification seemed over, in 1920, the church people did not concede defeat. The Federal Council of Churches, with its 20 million associated members, continued to give support financially to the League throughout the twenties and to praise its achievements. Conferences of the Northern Methodists, meeting in 1924 and 1928, heartily endorsed the world organization and bluntly informed the United States Senate of this fact. In one way or another many churches and their affiliated organizations continued to show loyalty to the League. Even more strongly they supported the idea of adherence to the World Court. Robert M. Miller has described a great campaign the Protestants conducted to convince the Senate to do its duty and vote for American adherence. The Federal Council of Churches and other church groups worked cooperatively to plan for a World Court Sunday and a World Court Week, to mail quantities of pro-Court literature, to have testimony given before the Foreign Relations Committee, to buttonhole every member of the Senate, to hold mass meetings in sixty cities strategically important, and so on. Ultimately, their effort was in vain.

The cause of disarmament was another that excited the churches. According to one estimate, 6 million church members signed petitions seeking the Washington Conference of 1921–1922. Their position made more sense than that of many officials like Hiram Johnson of California, who proposed to disarm the country at the same time they insisted the United States should not enter the League of Nations or even associate itself with the World Court. The church leaders seemed aware of some relation between disarmament on the one hand and a steady, responsible participation in world affairs on the other.

If the League of Nations was one point of reference in the twenties, another was the Washington Conference. This meeting of the great powers, called by President Harding in the summer of 1921, did much to establish basic policies of the administration in foreign affairs. To be sure, these policies were prefigured by Harding's well-known opposition to the League and by the determination of leaders in Congress to avoid any alliance or commitment similar to those recently proposed by the Democrats. Secretary of State Charles Evans Hughes assumed direction of the conference on November 12, 1921, after the President had made a welcoming speech. In the next three months, meeting in the Pan-American Building not far from the White House, Hughes and the other delegates managed to fashion agreements having major importance.

The situation in the Far East demanded attention. Some problems had come out of the war, and others went back much farther. In 1921 the Japanese still had an alliance with the British according to which both powers assumed an obligation to give military assistance if their respective interests in the Far East were endangered by the aggressive acts of another power. Conceivably this provision could be invoked against the United States. The British were under pressure, from Canada and other dominions and from the United States, to terminate this alliance. Obviously the question was a sensitive one. The best hope promised to be a treaty or series of treaties among the interested powers which would give Japan something of a substitute for her former alliance with Great Britain.

In the Four-Power Treaty involving Britain, Japan, France, and the United States the Anglo-Japanese Alliance was terminated. The signatory powers agreed to respect each other's Far Eastern insular possessions and to confer together jointly over threats to the peace. This was, then, a nonaggression pact.

Less important was the Nine-Power Treaty, in which the Open Door policy for China was affirmed. Six nations of Europe together with the United States, China, and Japan were the signatories. Chinese delegates were anxious to have this treaty, with its recognition of their rights as a nation; and they wanted tangible agreements for aid. Japan not only signed the treaty, she made further concessions including a promise to get her forces out of Shantung province in North China. She lived up to the promise.

Finally, there was the Five-Power Treaty. This embodied the attempt at naval limitation for the capital ships of major powers. On the first day of the conference, Secretary Hughes startled the assembled delegates by calling for immediate disarmament. He stated how many ships the United States should "sink"; then did the same for Britain and Japan. In fifteen minutes, as the saying went, he sank sixty-six ships. This was an unprecedented event. From Hughes' proposal came a "holiday" in the building of capital ships and the famous 5:5:3 ratio in capital ships established for Britain, the United States and Japan. France and Italy had the lower ratio of 1.67:1.67. To reassure Japan, which had wanted parity, Secretary Hughes promised that the United States would not add to the fortifications in its island possessions, with the exception of Hawaii.

Whatever its failings, the Washington Conference had some constructive effects. Certainly it helped for a time to ease tensions in the Far East. Richard W. Leopold has observed that the problems were "enormously complex" and that the effort at naval limitation should not be dismissed "as a typical example of American idealism, naive in its reliance on paper promises." Rather, these diplomats of the 1920s were trying to make the best of a difficult situation. They made mistakes, but leaders of the future, including those of the 1950s and 1960s, would make mistakes too, one of which was to rely too heavily on military power; and they failed to achieve disarmament.

The gains that were made through the Washington Conference were not enough by themselves. Two years later, in the Immigration Act of 1924, Congress gratuitously insulted the Japanese, leading to a worsening of relations. Japanese were excluded as immigrants under the quota system established. They were singled out for discriminatory treatment, although Secretary Hughes did his best to prevent this and to have the Nipponese placed under the quota, as were the nationals of other countries. Congress was not to be stopped. Racial prejudice and xenophobia were strong in that body. Another influence of some importance was a belief that the Japanese were not really much of a military threat. They were not crazy enough to fight the United States. A war with Japan was about as likely as a war with the moon, declared one senator.

Movements for peace in the 1920s were laden with pitfalls. In many efforts of the decade there is the poignancy of a lost cause. The Committee on Militarism in Education (CME), for example, was a nonviolent, pacifist group which determined to resist those interests that might take the country into war. What they feared specifically was a growing campaign in the midtwenties to strengthen programs for a Reserve Officers' Training Corps (ROTC) on a compulsory basis and for a system of military training camps. The War Department and its allies among the veterans groups, the school administrators, and others persisted in this campaign. They argued the value of military training and in some schools favored the expulsion of students who resisted the curriculum. Periodically, from 1925 to 1940, bitter conflicts flared up, as the CME and its student supporters and others were often active. The CME received its money and organizational support from the Fellowship of Reconciliation, the Fellowship of Youth for Peace, the Church Peace Union, and the National Council for the Prevention of War. In particular disputes, the American Civil Liberties Union did what it could to help.

A key figure in the founding of the CME was John Nevin Sayre, a minister of the Protestant Episcopal Church, who received his advanced degrees at Princeton University and the Union Theological Seminary. Soon he became a leader of the Fellowship for Reconciliation. This famous group, which was international in its membership, aimed to bridge the gap between social classes and to foster understanding. The means to do so was through Christian love, but it was recognized that the members must be ready to work and to sacrifice; for just causes must excite opposition. The members were pacifistic for religious reasons. They dedicated themselves to the building of a world without war. In 1921

Sayre replaced Norman Thomas as editor of the group's magazine, *The World Tomorrow,* which had as a subtitle these words: "A Journal Looking Toward a Social Order Based on the Principles of Jesus." The emphasis was broad, with many articles relating to problems that were international. Harry Elmer Barnes, the social scientist; Lewis Mumford, the critic and social philosopher; and Stuart Chase, the economist—these were among the noted contributors for one year only, 1925.

In the same year Sayre and some of his liberal associates organized the Committee on Militarism in Education. It seemed clear to them that military training, especially on a compulsory basis in the colleges and high schools, was antidemocratic, tending to inhibit freedom of speech and thought and to encourage a mindless patriotism. Military training and the military type of mind helped to cause wars; therefore the CME must oppose and find all the help it could in the press, among the educators and politicians, and most of all in the Congress, where the funds would or would not be appropriated for federal programs. With some success, the CME battled on, year after year, in the twenties and thirties. It benefited from a wave of disillusionment over the results of World War I.

Was this organization a constructive and forward-looking influence in America? Or was it, on the contrary, a group that sapped the American will to fight and encouraged the rise of dictatorships abroad? The obvious fact is that pacifism eventually was engulfed by events both in Europe and Asia, and the United States had to ready itself for war as it never had before. Men like Sayre were hoping that another war would not occur, but their democratic-Christian program turned out to be less than adequate for the world of Adolph Hitler. In the perspective of history, these and other crusaders for peace will perhaps not suffer badly. Their message of cooperation and social justice was a powerful one that did not die. They contributed, at the least, to democratic gains on the home front.

Another movement slowly accumulated support in the country. This was an effort to preserve the peace by outlawing war. Perhaps in a decade when the manufacture and sale of alcohol was banned by law, it was not surprising that many also came to believe in "outlawry," where war was concerned. Actually, as an alternative to the League of Nations, the renunciation of war seemed at least a step in the right direction. It was sufficiently broad and well-meaning in the twenties that many groups, for their own reasons, could back the plan. In 1918 a Chicago lawyer named Salmon O. Levinson had published an article on "The Legal Status of War." He noted that war, under international law, was recognized and accepted when it occurred and that all powers had to adjust their policies to it. Why should this be? he asked. If, on the contrary, nations refused to sanction war and treated it as a crime, "the force of the world could be organized to deal with the criminal." The code of nations must now be modified to put war beyond the pale. This approach sounded somewhat like the collective security idea as it had developed in 1919, but Levinson reacted against it and vigorously opposed the League of Nations. Then, year after year, the Chicagoan worked for his own plan. He gained able allies, including Raymond Robins, John Dewey, James T. Shotwell, and Charles Clayton Morrison, editor of the *Christian Century.* He needed a voice in Congress and courted William E. Borah, even though the Senator was a nationalist who would never consent to the idea of collective force to be used against a "criminal nation." By 1927 a popular movement for outlawry had developed impressively, with the type of church support described earlier and that of women's groups, for example, some militantly calling for an end to war.

   None of this meant very much unless governments took appropriate action. Finally, spurred on by the intellectuals, came a compromise agreement that was far short of the original Levinson idea. Aristide Briand of France and Secretary of State Kellogg for the Coolidge administration assumed the lead as fifteen nations pledged themselves to renounce the use of war as an instrument of national policy. Clearly they were not giving up any right to defend themselves. Yet each nation promised in this Kellogg-Briand Pact that it would seek to solve all problems by peaceful means. The pact was an "international kiss," scoffed Senator Reed of Missouri; others were skeptical or contemptuous. It was obvious in any event that intelligent, high-minded people had worked long and hard to take some kind of formal action against the institution of war. The force of nationalism was so strong and the disagreements so serious—even among the American peace groups—that a more meaningful course of action did not seem possible.

   One continuing source of mischief in the decade was that of the Allied war debts and German reparations. President Wilson had maintained that the Allies ought to pay back what they had borrowed, whether Germany paid them or not. Harding and Coolidge also took this position. Coolidge is supposed to have said, "They hired the money, didn't they?" From the American standpoint, Britain and France, for example, ought to repay cheerfully the billions of dollars in loans that had helped so much to achieve the final victory. From the Allied standpoint, however, this money had won a common victory, and most of it had been spent in the United States anyway. Europeans talked of "Uncle Shylock" across the Atlantic. Quarreling over money, year after year, was a terrible mistake. The United States would have been wiser simply to cancel the debts, as some leaders at the time realized.

   Whatever the disappointments, there were those who pushed ahead hopefully. Most impressive of all the planners for peace during the twenties was James T. Shotwell, a Columbia University professor of history. Charles DeBenedetti, a close student of Shotwell, has traced the remarkable role he played in trying to bring the United States into closer cooperation with the League of Nations. This specialist in medieval history became also an expert in problems of the twentieth century and a fervent believer in rational planning and system building as the means to avert war. In 1917 Shotwell was a founding member of the Inquiry, Wilson's group of experts who were mobilized to study every problem of the warring world and to plan for the peace to come. At the conference in Paris (1919) Shotwell worked especially in helping to create the International Labor Organization, one of the League's subsidiary groups. He became also a member of the Carnegie Endowment for International Peace and the editor of its monumental project, an *Economic and Social History* of the great war, resulting in 152 volumes. This was a near-exhaustive effort by the best scholars to understand the war and assorted problems that came with it.

As the war ended and the League of Nations made its shaky start, Shotwell watched with growing concern. He feared the League might collapse without having a real chance. With it, then, might go the International Labor Organization and all the cooperative work centered at Geneva—all the bureaus and agencies giving their attention to disarmament, to the removal of economic inequities, to fostering the welfare of women and children, to narcotics control, and so on. The possibilities for the future seemed encouraging if, by gradual means, the structure for peace could be added to and improved.

Shotwell became the rallying point for a group of specialists like himself who talked and debated endlessly over precise plans by which the influence of Geneva could be increased. These plans had to be subtle enough to gain acceptance by the great powers while, at the same time, they slowly added vitality to agencies of cooperative action. In 1924 Shotwell called a conference of his friends and former associates, and they met in New York over a period of many weeks, threshing out the possibilities. Included were General Tasker Bliss, a veteran of planning sessions in 1917–1918 as the highest-ranking American officer; General James G. Harbord, who had been the ranking officer in army supply; David Hunter Miller, formerly the legal adviser to President Wilson; and a number of others drawn in part from the Inquiry's group of academic experts. These were men of credentials who gained a friendly ear in Geneva and, at times, in Washington. They could rely on strong support from the League of Nations Non-Partisan Association and other pressure groups at home.

Of basic importance, they believed, was the insecurity of nations. The United States contributed to this as a great and powerful country in its economic affairs and involvements while it persisted in a foreign policy that was unilateral; in the event of another war it could not be relied upon. England, France, and other members of the League were left in a state of uncertainty. Shotwell and his group decided that the United States should move toward a revision of the neutrality laws, for they had proven unworkable in the crisis of 1914–1917. Why not recognize that neutrality was impossible for the United States in a modern war and that it must be prepared to make a discrimination on the side of peace. The country to be favored, at least passively, was the victim of an attack rather than the attacker. Neutrality laws should be altered, they said, so that "aggressor nations" would suffer a penalty rather than having the traditional rights of nations at war. By changing its laws in advance of trouble, America would help to discourage aggression, reduce world tensions, and promote disarmament. To some extent, also, it could add influence to the League of Nations without actually joining that organization.

But how was it possible to identify an aggressor nation? The Shotwell group tried to pin down the troublesome term with an automatic test. According to their plan of 1924, the aggressor was a nation which, being charged with breaking the peace, did not come before the World Court in a designated time to explain satisfactorily what had happened.

These were hard questions, but Shotwell at least saw the dangers and tried to meet them. A few years later, with the Japanese invasion of Manchuria, the Italian attack on Ethiopia, and the rise of Adolph Hitler, the world had a clear demonstration of what it was that leaders like Shotwell were trying to prevent. In a real sense, his work was a failure, along with that of thousands of others who had given their time to the cause of peace; but Shotwell went on in a few years to become an adviser to a new, rising organization, the United Nations. There were many, in fact, from the various countries whose experiences of the interwar years now contributed richly to the United Nations. The world had another chance, and the trials and errors of the 1920s were not without value.

SUGGESTIONS FOR FURTHER READING

Two standard works are Clarence A. Berdahl, *The Policy of the United States with Respect to the League of Nations,* Librairie Kundig, Geneva, 1932 and Denna Frank Fleming, *The United States and World Organization, 1920–1933,* Columbia, New York, 1938. Robert Murray, *The Harding Era,* and Donald McCoy, *The Quiet President* (Coolidge), both mentioned previously, provide a brief synthesis of Republican policies. For the Secretaries of State, whose influence counted for much under Harding and Coolidge, see the second volume of Merlo J. Pusey, *Charles Evans Hughes,* which is sympathetic to Hughes, and Betty Glad, *Charles Evans Hughes and the Illusions of Innocence: A Study in American Diplomacy,* Univ. of Illinois Press, Urbana, 1966, which is critical; also L. Ethan Ellis, *Frank*

B. Kellogg and American Foreign Relations, 1925–1929, Rutgers, New Brunswick, N.J., 1961. For Far Eastern policy and selected area studies see the following: Gerald Wheeler, *Prelude to Pearl Harbor: The United States Navy and the Far East, 1921–1931,* Univ. of Missouri Press, Columbia, 1963; Dorothy Borg, *American Policy and the Chinese Revolution, 1925–1928,* Octagon, New York, 1968 [1947]; Akira Iriye, *After Imperialism: The Search for a New Order in the Far East, 1921–1931,* Harvard, Cambridge, Mass., 1965; Robert P. Browder, *The Origins of Soviet-American Diplomacy,* Princeton Univ. Press, Princeton, N.J., 1953; Bryce Wood, *The Making of the Good Neighbor Policy,* Columbia, New York, 1961; and Dana G. Munro, *The United States and the Caribbean Republics, 1921–1933,* Princeton Univ., Princeton, N.J., 1974.

Robert H. Ferrell, *Peace in Their Time: The Origins of the Kellogg-Briand Pact,* Yale, New Haven, Conn., 1952, is highly useful for its informed discussion of men and affairs, although the tone is occasionally condescending toward the "appallingly naive" people of the 1920s. Below is a variety of books, relating primarily to the quest for peace: Merze Tate, *The United States and Armaments,* Harvard, Cambridge, Mass., 1948; John C. Vinson, *The Parchment Peace: The United States Senate and the Washington Conference, 1921–1922,* Univ. of Georgia Press, Athens, 1955; John C. Vinson, *William E. Borah and the Outlawry of War,* Univ. of Georgia Press, Athens, 1957; Wayne S. Cole, *Senator Gerald P. Nye and American Foreign Relations,* Univ. of Minnesota Press, Minneapolis, 1962; John C. Farrell, *Beloved Lady: A History of Jane Addams' Ideas on Reform and Peace,* Johns Hopkins, Baltimore, 1967; James T. Shotwell, *Autobiography,* Bobbs-Merrill, Indianapolis, 1961; Merle Curti, *Peace or War: The American Struggle, 1636–1936,* Norton, New York, 1936; Donald B. Meyer, *The Protestant Search for Political Realism, 1919–1941,* Univ. of California Press, Berkeley, 1960. See also Robert Miller, *American Protestantism and Social Issues,* and Charles Chatfield, *For Peace and Justice,* both mentioned previously.

Chapter 18

Progress
and Its Tragic
Dimension: 1928

The year 1928 stands in the shadow of the Great Crash of 1929 and the Second World War that began ten years later. Looking back, many have blamed the 1920s for disasters that should have been averted and for problems that should have been solved, at least in part. *Only Yesterday,* by Frederick Lewis Allen, is an early example of the historical works that evinced disillusionment with the twenties. Such books eventually came in a flood.

Perhaps a look at 1928 will shed some light on this question. To what extent were leaders at that point seriously concerned with solving problems? How able were the leaders? How difficult were the problems? The presidential election of 1928, pitting Alfred E. Smith against Herbert Clark Hoover, has been generally recognized as an election that should be studied carefully. It has yielded important insights on the nature of American society at this time and the direction of social change. Both Smith and Hoover, incidentally, were talented men with a wide experience in public affairs and a host of admirers. That they were qualified, however, to be President in 1928 or 1929 is not at all clear.

The social activist Norman Thomas, writing in 1928 with an eye to the future, found cause for some optimism. His chief concern at the moment was the prevention of war, and he believed that progress had been made, that the level of understanding had risen significantly since the early 1900s. It seemed to him, nevertheless, that the chance of another war was serious because "the stream of events has rushed forward in a more tumultuous torrent." He used an example (which he admitted was a crude one) of men learning to use gunpowder safely but without much benefit if they suddenly were forced to handle TNT. In the realm of economic problems, a cultural lag also existed. Incredible growth and change had occurred since the 1890s, and few indeed had sensed the total dimensions of that change.

If one looks to the intellectuals for an indication of trends in 1928, the results are ambiguous since thinkers seldom agreed and often were poles apart. This much, however, can be said. Observers had to take into account momentous events of recent years; and probably a majority were disillusioned by the war and its aftermath and by what they saw daily in the evolving society of the 1920s. Articles and books show a tone of irreverence or "decadence" not possible in the "good old days" before World War I; witness magazine articles such as "Adolescent America," "Hell in the United States," "Flaming Youth," and "Nothing Shocks Me." Most revealing are the quantity and variety of writing that exhibits a spirit more or less free and unconventional. The verbal pyrotechnics of H. L. Mencken and his *American Mercury* gained a wide audience. Other journals joined in the comment. The *New Republic,* the *Nation, Current History, Survey, Harper's, World's Work, Forum,* and the *Saturday Review of Literature* are examples. Of course, the critical note crept into the professional publications as well. One scholar, reviewing Charles and Mary Beard's *Rise of American Civilization,* published in 1927, expressed his belief that the professional would "find pleasure" in the Beards' "sly thrusts at ruling classes, military and technical experts, lawyers, doctors of finance, diplomats, and other inescapable pests."

But a sense of restraint is often to be found along with an urge to get at the truth and to take the long view. When John Dewey was called upon in 1928 for a critique of American civilization, he responded cautiously: "Where are we going? toward what are we moving? The value of any changing thing lies in its consequences, and the consequences of the present conditions and forces are not here. To make an evaluation is to prophesy, and where is there the astronomer who can predict the future of our social system?" He went on, however, to make some flat statements about American society with which students of a later day can hardly quarrel: "If ever there was a house of civilization divided within itself and against itself, it is our own today." An observer could find almost anything he was looking for, Dewey said. He could then make gloomy or optimistic statements in accordance with his predilections.

The philosopher noted some basic contradictions in American life. There was a broad aspect he termed the "public and official," or the "externally organized," which gave him considerable discouragement; "a hardness, a tightness, . . . a regimentation and standardization, a devotion to efficiency and prosperity of a mechanical and quantitative sort." On the other hand, in various activities of individuals and of groups there was "a scene of immense vitality" that was "stimulating to the point of inspiration." He gave examples. The Ku Klux Klan was still alive, and the forces of bigotry were powerful. Nevertheless, it was possible that a countermovement might succeed and place Al Smith, a Catholic, in the presidency in this same year. Intolerance and the violation of civil liberties, so flagrant in recent times and so disgraceful, also brought to mind the "gallant fight for freedom" in which a number were engaged. In foreign affairs, the imperialistic ventures of the United States were continuing, notably in Nicaragua, and the United States still exhibited its narrow patriotism and the fear of foreign "isms." At the same time, Americans had acquired a new interest in foreign problems and many were intelligently concerned with preserving the peace. They might be fooled by "glittering generalities" or by propaganda, but it would not be easy.

As befitted a person of his training, Dewey raised the fundamental question. How should a civilization be judged? By the level of its masses? By the standard of living? By the scientific, literary, and other achievements of an elite? Dewey had no real answer; all were important. Though critical of the United States on many points, he found encouragement in certain lines of progress. He emphasized that in his view the "industrial and technological phase" of the society was "central and dominant." The march of science and industry made possible a diffusion of culture, and the process, he believed, could not really be stopped in America.

Dewey spoke with amazement of the "revolutionary" changes in secondary schools and in higher education. Comparative figures for 1900 and 1928 showed a sixfold increase in the number of students attending colleges and professional schools; this had occurred in less than thirty years. Even if the education was assumed to be of poor quality, Dewey said, his generation was "in the presence of one of the most remarkable social phenomena of history."

John Dewey was prescient in his analysis, as for example, in giving emphasis to the increase of knowledge and the new sophistication on the part of some Americans. Whether politicians and public officials were affected significantly or not, it was reasonable to assume that, with any luck at all, the wider diffusion of knowledge would have a growing and perhaps eventually powerful impact on public affairs.

One idea sometimes offered in interpreting the twentieth century is that it really "started" in the 1920s. Exaggerated though the point is, it can be appreciated by anyone with a knowledge of the times. Certainly the atmosphere by 1920 was vastly different from that of 1900 and bore a resemblance to later, crisis-ridden decades. Even the optimists of the 1920s occasionally sounded a note of pessimism. For example, the distinguished historian Charles A. Beard edited a book in 1928 with the title *Whither Mankind?* to which some twenty other scholars contributed. As Beard explained, "thinkers and searchers" all over the world were reflecting over the future of mankind. The "devastating war" just past was the principal reason. He named "anxious inquirers" in China, India, Japan, Italy, Germany, France, England, Russia, Spain, and Argentina— not to mention the United States. In Beard's opinion the anxiety went far beyond intellectuals to public officials and the people.

He noted the postwar restlessness and uncertainty. Fascists in Italy and Communists in Russia had repudiated democracy and democratic socialism. If the Communists succeeded, they would be a "standing menace" to governments otherwise constituted. Germany was writhing and turning, with the future undecided. France, too, was restless and troubled after the frightful cost of the Great War. England had her problems, including a business system that was outmoded and colonies seeking independence. As for the United States, it seemed to be all right, with the security of an ocean on each side. It had profited from the war and reached out vigorously for more, "huckstering and lending money, evidently hoping with childlike faith that sweet things will ever grow sweeter."

In point of fact, as Beard observed, America had problems. This new "Leviathan" of the postwar world was regarded by some nations as a threat to their economic interests and to world security. The wisdom of American leaders concerning international issues was open to question. Criticism of the United States abounded, both at home and abroad. Beard went on to declare: "The age of Victorian complacency has closed everywhere; those who are whistling to keep up their courage and to deceive their neighbors merely succeed in hoodwinking themselves."

Charles Beard notwithstanding, there were a number of ways to be an optimist in the 1920s. One was to be in business and successful, as so many were. It was not difficult, then, to agree with Calvin Coolidge and Herbert Hoover that the country had entered a "new era" and that prosperity would go on indefinitely; most business leaders were boosters by nature. The hopefulness of this group came primarily from looking *outward* and finding satisfaction in the economic rewards and prospects. Another way to be an optimist of sorts was to look *inward*, to live a life of the mind, and to have the pleasures of a professional career. Perhaps no example of this phenomenon is so striking as that of the psychologists, who seized upon their opportunities to explore the human mind and personality. This greatest of all resources, one scholar observed, could now be understood as never before. The prospect was vastly exciting.

Inevitably there were those who said, facetiously or not, that the whole world ought to be psychoanalyzed; and, if they lived in the United States, their own people seemed the logical starting place. How *did* the student of psychology look upon the prospects of mankind in 1928? We have a splendid example of such an interpretation in an article that appeared in *Survey* magazine on April 1, 1928, entitled "We Adults Reconsider Ourselves." The author was Harry A. Overstreet, a professor of philosophy and chairman of his department at the College of the City of New York. Overstreet had turned his emphasis to the study of psychology and published a book on the subject intended primarily for the general public. His article, appearing almost immediately, embodied many of the same ideas. It seems doubtful that anyone who examined the "state of the nation," or of the American people, produced a more penetrating analysis of this type.

What Overstreet did was to look back over the last fifty years with reference to gains and losses from the human and psychological standpoint. He found that a subtle revolution had occurred. Psychologists like Cesare Lombroso of Italy and Jean Martin Charcot of France, along with Sigmund Freud of Austria, were for many years hardly appreciated. But this was no longer true by the early twentieth century. In America, G. Stanley Hall and William James were most notable among those who had helped to establish the importance of psychological studies.

In the meantime, America had experienced a "fairly great period" in which the main aim was the liberalizing of institutions. The most important of all accomplishments derived from this progressive period, so far as Overstreet was concerned, was "the political equality of woman and her right of entry into higher education and into careers outside the home." Yet along with these reforms came the Great War, to which Overstreet referred with the lines:

For we have watched the very sunlight wane,
And watched our world go down in blood and tears.

ARE YOU GROWN UP?

BEHIND THE ADULT MASK

Figure 27 Cover Illustration of *The Survey* for April 1, 1928.

It was a sad time, he recalled, and things seemed to be left in a "bewildering mess." Even so, the aim of liberalizing institutions still remained, and hope had not been lost. The two main objectives, as Overstreet saw them, were to get rid of war and to put "more reasonableness and humanity into the work of the world." Obviously the understanding of human beings and their problems was more important now than it had been before and the means existed to enrich this understanding.

A new age had been asserting itself. In hundreds of laboratories throughout the world psychological work was continuing, and the labs were to be found particularly in America. The changes, as a result, were profoundly important, Overstreet believed. No "respected reader" would now think that all his bodily ills were caused by physical problems alone. Whole libraries could be furnished with books on particular problems such as crime and its causes. And the study of children, which had seemed so silly in the beginning, had been enormously productive. Overstreet concluded that "a far more joyous education and family life have begun to take shape."

The times were not, then, entirely in a state of decay. With help from all the sources of knowledge and experimentation, Overstreet said, "we begin to turn inward and examine the greatest of our natural resources. We take stock of *ourselves.*" Briefly he surveyed the gains that had been made and the possibilities so exciting to him. At the same time, he realized difficulties lay ahead: first, in the actual study and understanding of human behavior; and second, in the attempt to apply those discoveries and insights as they ought to be applied. To change American society in the direction considered ideal would be extremely difficult.

Overstreet's analysis can be useful for understanding the American people in 1928. He reveals in his own outlook a part of the problem. He represents the growth of scientific naturalism; the declining faith, among educated people, in the "old time religion"; and the new belief in intellectual freedom and the desirability of greater freedom in matters of morality, bringing sexual matters out into the open, thus escaping some of the "taboos" and "tyrannies" of the past. With his interest in politics, also, he typifies the hope that political institutions, like others, could be subjected to scientific scrutiny and rational improvement.

Overstreet had his vision of the ideal society, but millions of other Americans had quite a different vision. They were conservative and tradition-bound. They were loyal to church, family, and group. Whether they were country people or city people, Protestants or Catholics, they had beliefs and values that could not be changed by scholarly talk or even by the pleas of their own leaders. On the other hand, almost everyone was affected to some extent by the gains of science and rising intellectual standards. In the exaggerated phrase of H. L. Mencken, "Even the stupidest man of today rejects as absurd ideas that were entertained seriously by Socrates, and even the most pious nun hardly believes some of the nonsense preached by high ecclesiastical dignitaries in the 13th century."

The tensions of a society, it is said, are reflected in its politics. A graphic example can be found in the campaign of 1928, when passions and hatreds flared up involving religion, prohibition, Tammany Hall, and "prosperity." The radio added to the popular interest.

Calvin Coolidge was out of all of this. In 1927 he had said cryptically: "I do not choose to run in 1928." There is the possibility that he acted on the advice of his doctor after a mild heart attack; or, conceivably, he had a premonition concerning an economic collapse. In any event, Herbert Hoover launched a campaign for the Republican nomination and was able to win on the first ballot. His running mate was Charles Curtis of Kansas, a long-term Senator.

Without much of a fight, Governor Alfred E. Smith of New York was able to win the Democratic nomination at Houston. Smith's rival of 1924, William G. McAdoo, had suffered a decline in reputation, and some of those opposed to Smith probably decided he would lose the election anyway. In the vice-presidential spot was Senator Joseph Robinson of Arkansas, helping to show the party's attempt at a compromise between the North with its Catholics and heterogeneous peoples and the South with its predominantly Protestant population. Something of a compromise was also apparent in the platform, which contained a mildly "dry" plank. Smith, a "wet," made it clear that he favored repeal of the Eighteenth Amendment; meanwhile, he said, he would enforce the law. As he went ahead in the campaign, forthrightly stating his views, opposition mounted.

Both the candidates were able men. The Irish-American Smith came from the slums of New York. He had little formal education. A veteran of Tammany politics, he also had a fine career in the State Assembly and went on to serve four terms with great distinction as Governor of New York (1918–1920, 1922–1928). Smith was dynamic and colorful, widely praised by Republicans as well as Democrats. In the developing campaign, however, his judgment was open to question on several points and many doubted that he could serve effectively as a national leader.

Herbert Hoover has often been mentioned in this account. Born in 1874, he was the son of Quaker Republican parents. He moved west, studied engineering at Stanford University, and became a mining engineer whose work was largely in Australia, China, Russia, and other countries. He was a millionaire by the age of forty. Then, in the period of the Great War, Hoover enhanced his reputation as administrator of relief to the Belgians and food czar in the United States war effort. He went on into the postwar period with a virtually unassailable record and added to it as Secretary of Commerce.

Facing such a man and a GOP majority, the Democrats did not have bright prospects. Of all the issues in 1928 the one that hurt the Democrats the most seemed the dullest and least dramatic. This was prosperity, which, as the Republicans described it, had been produced in a very special way by the policies of their leaders and the confidence they instilled in the general public. Smith's party was, by contrast, the depression party. Republicans pointed back to the depression of the 1890s which occurred under Cleveland and the severe recession of 1920–1921—a part of Wilson's legacy to the American people.

Republicans used this theme for all it was worth, and they would regret later some of what they said. On a tour of Indiana, Senator Curtis urged his audiences to remember the "full dinner pail," to elect Herbert Hoover if they would "continue the prosperity of the administration of Calvin Coolidge." Miss Beatrice Vare, the daughter of William S. Vare of

Pennsylvania, a Senator-elect, delivered a radio address maintaining that prosperity was the main issue. The election of Democrats, she said, would cause the "return of industrial ruin, idleness and unrest, charity instead of opportunity, soup houses instead of busy factories, homeless families and children begging for bread." Herbert Hoover pounded away on the same subject: "When we assumed direction of the government in 1921 there were five to six millions unemployed upon our streets. Wages and salaries were falling and hours of labor increasing. Anxiety for daily bread haunted nearly one-quarter of our twenty-three million families. . . . Within a year we restored these five million workers to employment. But we did more, we produced a fundamental program which made this restored employment secure on foundations of prosperity."

Again, speaking in Madison Square Garden toward the end of the campaign, Hoover declared: "Prosperity is no idle expression. It is a job for every worker; it is the safety and the safeguard of every business and every home. A continuation of the policies of the Republican Party is fundamentally necessary to the further advancement of this progress and to the further building up of this prosperity." These statements do not sound quite so boastful or foolish when balanced against some of Hoover's specific recommendations and his awareness that "constant study and effort" would be necessary in order to maintain a condition of peace and prosperity.

The Democrats argued that this so-called prosperity was really a myth. Some 4 million workers had no jobs, while specific industries, such as the textile mills of New England, were in a serious plight and the farmers were in great difficulty. Republican promises of a chicken in every pot and a car in every backyard were simply ridiculous. Insofar as prosperity actually existed, said the Democrats, it came from natural resources, the people's hard work, and a variety of causes—not from the GOP. But the Democrats could not win this argument, at least not in 1928. The times were relatively prosperous, and the public knew that very well.

The issues of the campaign that aroused people the most were prohibition and religion, two elements in a continuing cultural conflict. Al Smith, an avowed "wet" and a Catholic, was at the center of this controversy. Hoover took the safer course in the campaign by supporting the "noble experiment" of prohibition, and he enjoyed the advantage of being a Protestant. There was no doubt in the circumstances that Smith would lose some votes in the regions that were heavily Protestant and "dry," notably in the South. But he might gain votes as well from those who liked his stand and who resented the bitter attacks that were made on him. To this day scholars have not been able to explain the Democratic defections. How much did Smith lose because he was a product of

Tammany Hall and the sidewalks of New York? How much because he was "wet"? How much because he was a Catholic? The question is almost insoluble since few voters were willing to admit that they opposed him primarily for reasons of religion, whatever their actual motivation might be.

In all likelihood, the prohibition issue had greater importance than religion. First of all, Smith rather flagrantly offended those who believed in prohibition, or who wanted to give it a further period of trial. He openly supported the idea of repeal, and his own state of New York passed a law that, in effect, repudiated the federal attempts at enforcement. In the second place, Smith's attitude put him at odds with a powerful movement long intended to achieve social and moral reform. The antiliquor crusade can be treated as something harshly repressive and illiberal, or as a matter of misguided people; but it is best understood as an idealistic movement that came out of the nineteenth century, gaining adherents all the while, until it even had the federal government on its side. It also had the support generallly of medical science in this period, as researchers decided that liquor was a depressant and a poison, not a stimulant. James H. Timberlake has shown rather convincingly that progressive-type reformers joined in the prohibition movement for reasons that seemed quite valid in their day. The liquor habit was not conducive to efficiency. It caused industrial accidents. It destroyed homes and wrecked careers. Also, there was the question of the "selfish and monopolistic people" who produced and sold the liquor. Often they had foreign names, too, adding to the suspicion of native Americans. Some of the prohibitionists were fanatics and all of them had too much faith in what they could accomplish by changing the law and the Constitution.

This group was not ready to give up the fight in 1928. Robert M. Miller, in his study of Protestantism and social issues, has stressed the sincerity and earnestness of these people, as demonstrated by their concern year after year. They continued their efforts even in the 1930s after the Eighteenth Amendment had been repealed. The evidence is "overwhelming," Miller concludes, "that to millions of Protestants, both ministers and laymen, the crusade to drive liquor from America was the greatest moral issue in their lives." Baptists and Methodists, North and South, were most determined to defeat Al Smith. A Baptist paper asserted: "We care nothing about the politics of Mr. Smith, but we care a great deal about the war he has declared on prohibition. Let the churches everywhere fight him because there is a great moral issue at stake and because he has deliberately and defiantly taken the wrong side." In some states there was virtually a mass movement against the New Yorker, inspired and largely led by the Protestant ministers and lay leaders of the churches. Nevertheless, the great majority of Democratic politicians, including those in the South, supported Smith.

In point of fact, Al Smith was himself embarked on a kind of crusade. Prohibition, he declared, was an interference with the liberties of the people, and it had been a failure. Illicit drinking, racketeering, and the allied evils were breeding contempt for the law. These facts had to be faced and appropriate action taken. Smith's attitude was typical of that to be found in large cities of the Northern states.

Obviously many of the Protestants were alarmed, not only over prohibition, but over the thought of Smith's religion. Ignorance, bigotry, and a long tradition of anti-Romanism had a good deal to do with the bitterness of this campaign. The philosopher William James once observed that there is a certain blindness about human beings, a difficulty of understanding those who are different. Thus the Protestants, while taking an active role in public affairs, were trying to prevent the Catholics from doing much the same. Franklin D. Roosevelt, a Protestant himself, pointed to this fact and registered his protest. To be sure, it was possible to raise some valid questions about Smith's candidacy, including the religious aspect of it. If the Democratic nominee had been a Catholic of a different type, well-educated, tactful, and free from the taint of Tammany Hall, would he have run a stronger race? Probably so. David Burner in his *Politics of Provincialism* has shown that Governor Smith did not handle the religious problem very well. He seemed stubborn and needlessly provocative, much as he had been on the prohibition issue. He did not behave as a broad-minded politician and harmonizer. Thus, says Burner, a "provincial Catholic urbanism" contended in the campaign with a "provincial Protestant ruralism."

Both Smith and Hoover were progressives of a type, with each owing much to the traditions of his own party. Certainly the Governor was a believer in "cultural pluralism," and he had made a good record as a civil libertarian. He was noted for his support of social and industrial reforms, but also for a broader program that included the conservation of natural resources, the development of water power under public control, and the generous financing of public education. By 1928, however, Smith was caught in something of a dilemma. In his opposition to national prohibition, he made himself a spokesman for states' rights. His lack of radicalism on economic questions was dramatized by the choice he made for chairman of the Democratic National Committee. John J. Raskob, of New York and Delaware, was a multimillionaire and a high executive with the Du Pont Company and General Motors. Smith selected him partly because he was a Catholic and a crusader for the repeal of the Eighteenth Amendment. Raskob, needless to say, proved a divisive influence in the Democratic campaign.

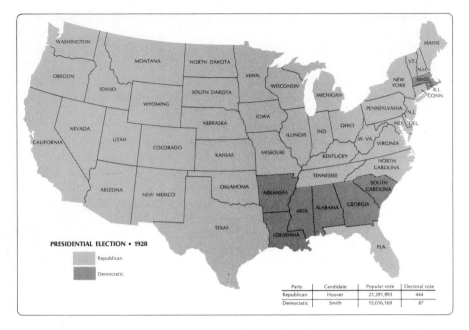

Figure 28 The Election of 1928. *(From* A History of the American People, *by Norman A. Graebner, Gilbert C. Fite, and Philip L. White. Copyright © by McGraw-Hill, Inc.)*

Herbert Hoover seemed, at times, more progressive than Smith. There was room to wonder, however, about some of his attitudes. Thus he liked to say that opportunities abounded in America and every boy and girl had a chance—presumably to rise to the heights as he had done. This, of course, was not true. He also tried to identify Smith and his program with socialism. Hoover's prestige was such that he had no need to make statements that were highly political or exaggerated, and yet he had a penchant for doing this. Even so, he placed himself in the progressive tradition, calling for the abolition of poverty, shorter working days, the acceptance of collective bargaining, an end to abuses in the use of the injunction, public aid to education, and extraordinary efforts to solve the farm problem. He indicated a readiness to expand the nation's public works if necessary to keep the economy going. In spite of all this, some observers identified Hoover with the business community in his general philosophy and approach; and they did so correctly.

When the votes were counted, Hoover had won an overwhelming victory: 444 electoral votes to 87 for Smith and 21 million popular votes to 15 million. The New York Governor lost his own state and carried only Massachusetts, Rhode Island, and six states of the South. He failed in five

Southern states where prohibition and religion hurt him badly—Virginia, North Carolina, Tennessee, Florida, and Texas.

Those states of the South which supported Smith most strongly were South Carolina and Mississippi. At first this seems surprising. But these were places where a Republican was mighty scarce and where the "solid South" was most solid. The sensitive question there was not drink and religion but race, the maintenance of white supremacy. Smith was no threat on this issue, for he firmly stated his belief in local control of local issues. With this attitude he did well in traditionally Democratic areas, especially in the rural regions. Hoover did best in the cities.

Scholars have had a field day with their analyses of the vote in 1928. It is no wonder, since the election had real significance as an indicator of social trends. The outstanding fact is that, while Smith was losing ground in the South, he made striking gains in Northern metropolitan areas. He carried 122 counties in the North that usually went to the Republicans. Also, because of dissatisfaction with the GOP on farm policy, the Democrats picked up strength in the agricultural states from Illinois to Montana. This was a bad sign for the Republicans in elections to come.

Some observers noticed during the campaign that the foreign-born in Northern cities were taking the trouble to register in large numbers and would probably cast the heaviest vote in history. They did vote and voted heavily Democratic. Samuel Lubell and others have explored this shift to the Democrats and its implications, which are important. In essence, the New Immigration, which had started in the 1880s, was now having its inevitable impact. As early as 1910 a government study disclosed that in thirty-seven leading cities the majority of schoolchildren had a father who was born abroad. In New York and Chicago more than two-thirds of the children had parents who were foreign-born. What had happened, then, by 1928 was rather simple. These boys and girls had grown up, and they were voting. Most of them were Catholic. Many were Jews.

What was occurring was a drastic alteration of social and economic patterns, with effects in politics. These people of recent foreign extraction had concentrated, as it happened, in states having the largest electoral votes. Life had not been easy for them, and they were forced to conform to Protestant, Anglo-Saxon institutions. They also resisted, and they achieved one success simply by having a high birthrate. The poor and underprivileged of the cities saw in Al Smith a friend, a kindred spirit who was attacked for his religion and cultural background much as they had been. To many of them, a political machine such as Tammany Hall, with which Smith had grown up, was a source of aid and comfort and did the things that the government often failed to do. They wanted a government that would help. Herbert Hoover, with his talk of "rugged individualism,"

Figure 29 Immigrant Children—Most of Whom Were Probably Voting by November 1928—on the Roof Garden at Ellis Island. *(Photograph by the Bureau of Immigration, published in* National Geographic Magazine *for May 1907.)*

seemed to come out of the agrarian past. Perhaps even more important, he was a WASP.

Of course, Hoover won the election in 1928. But the Democrats were getting stronger. They were moving toward a sectional coalition, somewhat like that fashioned by Wilson and his supporters in 1916. It would include, again, agrarians and small-town leaders of the South and West. The new and dynamic ingredient, becoming increasingly visible even before the New Deal, was ethnic leaders of the North, people who supported Al Smith and stayed with his party. Not unlike the nation itself, this party was acquiring a diversity and complexity formerly only hinted at, while the Republicans experienced a trend in the other direction, becoming a WASP organization for the most part. The GOP even started to lose the black vote, from which it had benefited since the Civil War period. A continuing migration of the blacks to Northern cities, where they became eventually a bulwark of the Democratic party, was a trend of enormous significance, comparable to that of the ethnic groups and their rise.

It would be easy to argue, as some have done, that the United States just before the Great Depression was a benighted place; that its energy was devoted mostly to the pursuit of wealth; that its leaders in economic affairs were selfish and obtuse; that religious prejudice was still very strong; that the Afro-Americans suffered under terrible discrimination in the job market, in educational opportunities and otherwise; that millions of people, particularly in the South, lived in poverty; and that the vaunted freedom and individualism of the country was severely circumscribed, both by custom and statute. Obviously, from the standpoint of national policy in 1928, there were troubles ahead of an unprecedented type. There was reason to worry about the economy and about the condition of world affairs.

Nevertheless, as described in the foregoing pages, the United States had made gains on many fronts. Most of all, it had become a different kind of country and was moving in the direction in which it would continue to move. It was now a modern state, with a complex economy that was enormously productive, with a heterogeneous people whose abilities were coming to be recognized, and with a new mobility provided by electric power and the internal combustion motor. Automobiles, trucks, buses, and tractors seemed to be everywhere. The economy was geared to production and consumption and more of the same, with a heavy reliance on credit. With the movies and radios and new possibilities of travel, the United States was hardly a place for calm, relaxed living. The machine age had truly arrived. Where the human being was left amid all this change had not become clear.

Even as early as 1928, more than a few Americans had developed strains of fatalism. Never had there been so much to learn and so much possible enjoyment in life. Never had there been such possibilities of human betterment from the accumulating knowledge and technology and from the medical work, for example, that already had gone far to eliminate the major diseases. Yet there was the human factor and the question of leadership. Was it really possible to use science constructively over a period of time? Was it possible to keep the machines under control? Ever since the events of 1914 to 1918 and the aftermath of that war, there was reason to be doubtful. In any case, as a contemporary observed, it was an exciting age in which to be alive, a new age of pioneering and discovery. One could only push ahead in this life, hoping for the best and ready to accept the consequences.

SUGGESTIONS FOR ADDITIONAL READING

For the politics of 1928, a number of works mentioned earlier will be important. See especially J. Joseph Huthmacher, *Massachusetts People and Politics;* David Burner, *The Politics of Provincialism;* Robert Miller, *American Protestantism and Social Issues;* and Kenneth Bailey, *Southern White Protestantism in the Twentieth Century.* To these should be added Edmund A. Moore, *A Catholic Runs for*

President: The Campaign of 1928, Peter Smith, Gloucester, Mass., 1968 [1956]; Ruth C. Silva, *Rum, Religion, and Votes: 1928 Re-examined,* Pennsylvania State Univ. Press, University Park, 1962; Virginius Dabney, *Dry Messiah: The Life of Bishop Cannon,* Knopf, New York, 1949; V. O. Key, *Southern Politics in State and Nation,* Knopf, New York, 1949; Oscar Handlin, *Al Smith and His America,* Little, Brown, Boston, 1958; Samuel Lubell, *The Future of American Politics,* Harper, New York, 1952; and John M. Allswang, *A House for All Peoples: Ethnic Politics in Chicago, 1890–1936,* Univ. of Kentucky Press, Lexington, 1971. Campaign speeches by Smith and Hoover are revealing. See *The New Day: Campaign Speeches of Herbert Hoover, 1928,* Stanford Univ. Press, Stanford, Calif., 1928; and *Campaign Addresses of Governor Alfred E. Smith: Democratic Candidate for President, 1928,* Democratic National Committee, Washington, D.C., 1929. Widely differing interpretations of the prohibition movement may be found in James H. Timberlake, *Prohibition and the Progressive Movement,* mentioned previously; Andrew Sinclair, *Era of Excess: A Social History of the Prohibition Movement,* Harper, New York, 1964; and Joseph R. Gusfield, *Symbolic Crusade: Status Politics and the American Temperance Movement,* Univ. of Illinois Press, Urbana, 1963.

Edward Purcell, Jr., *The Crisis of Democratic Theory,* and John Braeman et al. (ed.), *Change and Continuity: the 1920's,* both mentioned before, are concerned with some of the fundamental problems of the period. See, in addition, Kirby Page (ed.), *Recent Gains in American Civilization: By a Group of Distinguished Critics of Contemporary Life,* Harcourt, New York, 1928; Charles A. Beard (ed.), *Whither Mankind: A Panorama of Modern Civilization,* Longmans, Green, New York, 1928; Stuart Chase, *Prosperity: Fact or Myth,* Charles Boni, New York, 1929; H. A. Overstreet, *About Ourselves: Psychology for Normal People,* Norton, New York, 1927; John Chamberlain, *Farewell to Reform: The Rise, Life and Decay of the Progressive Mind in America,* John Day, New York, 1932; W. T. Couch (ed.), *Culture in the South,* Univ. of North Carolina Press, Chapel Hill, 1935; Richard Hofstadter, *Anti-Intellectualism in American Life,* Vintage Books, Knopf, New York, 1962; Morton and Lucia White, *The Intellectual versus the City,* Mentor Book, New York, 1964; Don S. Kirschner, *City and Country: Rural Responses to Urbanization in the 1920s,* Greenwood, Westport, Conn., 1970; Arnold Rose, *The Negro in America,* Harper, New York, 1948 (condensed from Gunnar Myrdal, *The American Dilemma*); John Higham, *Send These to Me: Jews and Other Immigrants in Urban America,* Atheneum, New York, 1975; and Thomas C. Cochran, *The American Business System: A Historical Perspective, 1900–1955,* Harvard University Press, Cambridge, Mass., 1957.

INDEX